LIBERAL DEMOCRACY:

ITS MERITS AND PROSPECTS

LIBERAL
DEMOCRACY:

ITS MERITS AND PROSPECTS

---

*J. Roland Pennock · Professor of Political
Science Swarthmore College*

RINEHART AND COMPANY, INC., NEW YORK

TO JOAN AND JUDITH

*FOR WHOSE GENERATION THE PROSPECTS
OF DEMOCRACY ARE ALL-IMPORTANT*

PREFACE

A great deal has happened and a great deal has been found
out since England and America committed themselves to
the ideals of liberal democracy and set about trying to put those
ideals into practice. Belief in the desirability and practicability
of democracy is widely associated with faith in the rationality of
man and also with an individualistic philosophy. But faith in
human rationality seems to have declined and the tide of individualism has certainly receded. These facts suggest the desirability of a reappraisal of the ethical case for democracy, of its
practicability, and of its prospects. The present volume is intended as a contribution to that task. It has been written on the
premise that political theorists should not confine themselves to
exposition and criticism of the ideas of others, and that they
should make as much use as possible of the innumerable sound
contributions to the subject already made.

To Professor Richard B. Brandt, Chairman of the Department of Philosophy of Swarthmore College, I owe a great debt.
If I have escaped even a few of the pitfalls that await the
philosophical layman who approaches the domain of ethics—as
one who ventures to appraise democracy (or anything else)
must—I owe that escape to him. My colleague Professor Bryce
Wood, and Professor Leslie Lipson, now at the University of
California (Berkeley), have each read several chapters of the
manuscript and made numerous suggestions for its improvement.
A similar service was performed by Professor Thomas I. Cook,

· *vii*

of The Johns Hopkins University. Finally, a friend and one-time student of mine, Barbara Schinnerer Tovey, has put me permanently in her debt by performing innumerable services, ranging from the laborious task of checking the footnotes to important suggestions as to content. Needless to say, the responsibility for errors and inadequacies is entirely my own.

Swarthmore College   J. R. P.
Swarthmore, Pa.

TABLE OF CONTENTS

Contents

Contents

PART ONE

INTRODUCTION

INTRODUCTION

"My dear, we live in an age of transition." With these words, some wag has remarked, Adam doubtless comforted Eve when they were expelled from the Garden. Institutions and "systems" are always changing, and the point in time selected by historians as representing the end of one set of institutions, or as representative of one way of life, is likely to be quite arbitrary. Nevertheless it is true that history does not march with even pace. Marx was right in observing that there are periods of gradualness and periods of cataclysmic change. No one can doubt that we live in one of the latter.

It has become a cliché to refer to World War II as a revolution, or—perhaps more properly—as the symptom of a revolution. One enthusiastic writer has gone so far as to identify it with five distinct, contemporaneous revolutions! [1] There is a widespread feeling abroad that we are witnessing the end of an era, if not indeed the beginning of the end of a civilization. Oswald Spengler, writing at the outbreak of World War I, led a procession of prophets of doom.[2] Like most philosophers of history, he worked on such a grand scale that historians had little difficulty revealing serious errors of fact and introducing important doubts about his interpretations. Nevertheless, his prediction of a coming age of Caesarism is one to give his critics pause—the more so since it was made when democracy appeared to be still expanding. Many searchers after the key to history—often men with quite different backgrounds and points of view—share with Spengler the conviction that our civilization has turned against

[1] Alfred M. Bingham, *The Practice of Idealism* (New York: Duell, Sloan and Pearce, 1944), Chap. 2. Bingham lists the Revolt of the Common Man, the Technical Revolution, the Political Revolution, the Failure of Nationalism, and the Crisis in Belief.

[2] Oswald Spengler, *The Decline of the West* (New York: Alfred A. Knopf, Inc., 1939).

man and against itself.[3] The crisis, that is to say, is by no means merely political. "It is difficult to escape the conclusion," as Professor Charles Morris has written, "that momentous days lie ahead, and that the middle-class cultural synthesis of the West has become a forlorn thing in rags and tatters, its social life disordered, its economic life in chaos, its art feeble, its vision unclear, its philosophy inarticulate." [4]

If the crisis is of these proportions, what point is there in studying a single sector of it? Or, even more devastating question, if liberal institutions are doomed, why waste time examining their death throes? Professor Morris, in the passage just cited, gives a partial answer. "Whether American democracy is only a disguised form of middle-class ideology or whether it contains as its essence the moral ideal of a classless functional society," he

[3] See Pitirim Sorokin, *Social and Cultural Dynamics* (4 vols.; New York: American Book Company, 1937–1941) and *The Crisis of Our Age* (New York: E. P. Dutton & Co., 1941). In the latter volume (Chap. 7), Sorokin enumerates and discusses the symptoms of decline of our "sensate" civilization. Nicholas Berdyaev sounds a similar note. He declares, ". . . the crisis in humanism . . . inevitably develops into anti-humanism and . . . its final stage is a denial of man."—*The Fate of Man in the Modern World*, trans. Donald A. Lowrie (London: Student Christian Movement Press, 1935), pp. 25–26. See also his *The End of Our Time*, trans. Donald Attwater (London: Sheed & Ward, 1933) and *The Meaning of History*, trans. George Reavey (London: Geoffrey Bles, 1936). Nor are such views confined to writers with European backgrounds. Lewis Mumford, for example, writes as follows: ". . . the fact is that before the war there was spiritually little health in us. Our elaborate mechanical organization of life had resulted in an increasingly purposeless society, in which some of the parts were neatly articulated and ordered, while the whole made little sense in terms of life-satisfactions and life-fulfillments. . . . We can no longer live, with the illusions of success, in a world given over to devitalized mechanisms, desocialized organisms, and depersonalized societies; a world that had lost its sense of the ultimate dignity of the person almost as completely as the Roman Empire did at the height of its military greatness and technical facility. All that the Nazis have done has been to bring to a more rapid climax a process that was more slowly, more insidiously, undermining our whole civilization."—*The Condition of Man* (New York: Harcourt, Brace and Company, 1944), pp. 395–396. By permission of Harcourt, Brace and Company, publishers.

[4] Charles W. Morris, *Pragmatism and the Crisis of Democracy*, "Public Policy Pamphlets," No. 12 (Chicago: University of Chicago Press, 1934), p. 7.

4 ·

writes, "is the basic issue which the decades will decide." [5] There are ideals and even specific institutions which in the past have survived drastic cultural reorganizations. Perhaps we can discover what is fundamental and what is not in our political culture-pattern. Possibly even, if enough people aid in sharpening this line, it will help prevent the good from going down along with the bad. An even more optimistic view would be to assume that the harbingers of disaster may have overdrawn the picture. The fate of liberal democracy may indeed be partly controlled by over-all trends affecting the whole structure of our culture, but on the other hand a sound analysis of these trends must depend upon the proper appraisal of developments in each of the several parts of the culture-pattern. There are then good reasons for attempting a study of the contemporary crisis affecting political ideas and institutions, even though it is but part of a much larger picture.

Forms of government may be subject to a law of inevitable change and succession. This notion is by no means new. Plato, Aristotle, Polybius, and Machiavelli are but a few of the most illustrious among political philosophers who have maintained that there are fixed cycles of political development. Although it is true that there was not complete agreement among the various writers as to the order of change, there was a disturbing amount of agreement to the effect that democracy tends to degenerate into despotism. The passion for equality eventually destroys freedom, majority rule becomes majority tyranny. This is the first step. The majority, whether because of divisions within its ranks or because of some other grave crisis in its affairs (such as war), becomes unable to handle the task of government itself and hands over its power to an elected dictator. This is plebiscitary democracy. The dictator, in turn, soon manages to free himself from popular control and sets himself up as a despotic ruler. These are the final stages of the cycle.

Nor are these but the idle speculations of arm chair philoso-

[5] *Ibid.*

phers. It was typical of the history of Greek city-states, as it was of
Rome, to pass from monarchical institutions through more or less
democratic forms into Caesarism. It is true that what we today in
America call democracy would have been called a mixed government by the ancients; and theorists from the time of Aristotle
and Polybius have agreed in denominating the mixed form as the
most stable. Yet even as Polybius apotheosized the Roman Constitution, degeneration had already set in.

We have every reason to believe that our own society is not
exempt from forces of cyclical change which may yet prove disastrous for democratic government. Modern democracy arose out of
an atmosphere of individualism. In the sphere of religion this took
the form of Protestantism; in the sphere of general philosophy it
was rationalistic; in economics it was capitalistic. Today Western
civilization is becoming more and more secular and less convinced of the efficacy of reason. Here, too, there may be a cycle.
As one writer has put it, "rationalism, scepticism, pessimism,
blind submission is a cycle too familiar." [6] Economic individualism is similarly on the decline. Laissez faire has gone and capitalism may soon follow it into oblivion. In the field of politics itself,
the retreat of liberal democracy before advancing authoritarianism is, if anything, an even more familiar phenomenon. No
thoughtful person fails to realize that even fascism reflects certain universal trends, indeed, certain responses to universal needs.
The same is even truer of totalitarian communism. That liberal
democracy faces a crisis needs no demonstration.

It will be well, however, to point out one further indication
of democracy's present straits, inasmuch as it provides one reason
for writing such a book as this. I refer to the divisions among the
defenders of democracy. Most well-developed institutional frame-
works which have been in existence for a substantial period of
time will call forth a variety of explanations and justifications.
Seldom, however, are they quite so mutually contradictory as in
this case. As to the philosophic basis, many writers are convinced

[6] Frank Fritts, *The Concept of Equality in Its Relations to a Principle
of Political Obligation* (Princeton: Princeton University Press, 1915), p. 10.

that democracy can have no sound foundation other than a firm conviction that there is an objective and absolute right and that this right flows from God and is represented by the principles of Christianity, which must be accepted on faith. Catholic defenders of democracy are uniformly in this group, but so also are many non-Catholics.[7] Other are equally insistent that relativism and skepticism provide the natural intellectual milieu for democracy and are its only safe foundation. Followers of John Dewey are prominent among those who align themselves on this side of the controversy.[8] Unfortunately, but not unnaturally, members of each group are inclined to believe that the others are doing great damage to the cause of democracy.

A similiar rift appears if we turn to the socio-economic basis of democracy. On one side are those who believe that there is an indissoluble link between democracy and capitalism. From the innumerable names which might be mentioned in this connection, that of Professor von Hayek may be singled out on account of the popularity attained by his recent defense of this thesis.[9] Equally vigorous and voluble are those who contend that only when it has freed itself of the incubus of capitalism can democracy hope to approximate its goals of liberty, equality, and fraternity. At the risk of being invidious, we may select from the

[7] See, for example, Patrick J. Roche, *Democracy in the Light of Four Current Educational Philosophies* (Washington, D. C.: The Catholic University of America Press, 1942); and John H. Hallowell, *The Decline of Liberalism as an Ideology* (Berkeley and Los Angeles: University of California Press, 1943) and the same author's "The Decline of Liberalism," *Ethics*, LII (Apr., 1942), 323–349; and also Lewis Mumford, who refers with scorn to the "shallow, desiccated pragmatism" that has failed to give adequate support to democracy. (See his *Faith for Living* [New York: Harcourt, Brace and Company, 1940], p. 196.)

[8] One of the most careful statements of this position is Marie Collins Swabey's *Theory of the Democratic State* (Cambridge, Mass.; Harvard University Press, 1937). See also Jacques Barzun, *Of Human Freedom* (Boston: Little Brown & Company, 1939), and Karl Pribram, *Conflicting Patterns of Thought* (Washington, D.C.: Public Affairs Press, 1949).

[9] Friedrich A. von Hayek, *The Road to Serfdom* (Chicago: The University of Chicago Press, 1944). See also, among recent books, William Aylott Orton, *The Liberal Tradition—A Study of the Social Conditions of Freedom* (New Haven: Yale University Press, 1945).

ranks of democratic Socialists Professor Finer, because he has written a direct reply to Professor von Hayek, and Mr. E. F. M. Durbin, because his volume is remarkable for its combination of breadth of scope with fair and careful judgments.[10] Before I am through I shall give my own answers to these contradictory interpretations. For the moment I am concerned only to point them out as symptoms of the crisis I propose to discuss.

The next chapter will attempt to delineate in highly schematic fashion, the essential concepts of "liberalism," "political liberalism," and "liberal democracy," with which we shall be dealing, and to give some slight indication of the background of ideas, conditions, and events out of which they arose. Part II, after a survey of challenges to democratic theory, will attempt to reappraise the social and political ideal of democracy. Part III will examine various developments, both in the realm of ideas and in that of events, which affect the operation of democracy and which might cast doubt upon its continued workability. Finally, Part IV, will consider the practicability of democracy under present conditions and its future prospects, with particular reference to the situation in the United States, and in Great Britain.

[10] Herman Finer, *Road to Reaction* (Boston: Little, Brown & Company, 1945); E. F. M. Durbin, *The Politics of Democratic Socialism* (London: Routledge and Kegan Paul, Ltd., 1940). See also the works of Harold J. Laski; for instance, his *Reflections on the Revolution of Our Time* (New York: The Viking Press, 1943).

CHAPTER I

LIBERALISM, POLITICAL LIBERALISM, AND LIBERAL DEMOCRACY

This book is about liberal democracy. Liberal democracy
is the form which democracy has come to take wherever
there was a liberal tradition, and especially in the English-
speaking countries. Moreover, as we shall see, there is a sound
logical reason why it should take this form. It is also a form of
political liberalism; and here again the development is implicit in
the original idea, liberalism.

1. Liberalism

To attempt to describe that great movement of thought and
recasting of institutions which took place in Europe roughly during the sixteenth, seventeenth, and eighteenth centuries in a few
paragraphs must be somewhat of a tour de force. It will be
treated here largely in analytical rather than genetic terms, although such a treatment involves a great oversimplification.
Also, it will be depicted as a revolt, or a series of revolts. This
approach should not be permitted to give the impression that the
movement was purely negative. Revolts are revolts *for* as well as
revolts *against*. People sought freedom *from* feudal ties in order
to have freedom *to* sell their services on the open market, and so
on.[1]

---

[1] From among the vast array of literature on this subject, a few items
may be selected for reference. Especially notable is Guido de Ruggiero's
The History of European Liberalism, trans. R. G. Collingwood (London:
Oxford University Press, 1927). An older but scarcely less valuable work,
dealing especially with the intellectual roots of the movement, is W. E. H.
Lecky's *History of the Rise and Influence of Rationalism in Europe* (rev.

Liberalism was a revolt against dogma and against the authority of the church as the great custodian of dogmatic beliefs. In many quarters this ultimately extended to a revolt against all belief in supernaturalism. That is to say, it began with an assertion of the right of the individual to use his reason to question "received beliefs." It ended by asserting the faith that reason can explain everything—or at least that nothing should be accepted as true which cannot be substantiated by reference to natural laws as found out by reason, using the methods of science.[2] More particularly, the assertion of the right of every individual to use his powers of reasoning to test prevailing doctrines came to be supplemented by argument to the effect that the freest possible interplay of opinions should be allowed in order to facilitate the discovery of truth by reason. The equalitarian implications of this position, at least as far as concerns the right to speak and write, are obvious. All men possess reason in some measure. Insofar as their opinions are the product of right reason they will contribute to the discovery of truth. Insofar as they are not they can be shown to be false by the rational powers of others, and so are not to be feared. The doctrines of toleration and of freedom of expression generally were logical products of the revolt against

ed., 2 vols.; New York: Appleton-Century-Crofts, Inc., 1890). Harold J. Laski's *The Rise of European Liberalism* (London: George Allen & Unwin, Ltd., 1936) emphasizes especially the relationship between liberalism and capitalism. Carl L. Becker's *Heavenly City of the Eighteenth-Century Philosophers* provides a subtle study of the changing climate of opinion in the "age of reason" as reflected in the assumptions of the leading thinkers (New Haven: Yale University Press, 1932). A useful popular survey is to be found in Irwin Edman's *Fountainheads of Freedom—The Growth of the Democratic Idea* (New York: Harcourt, Brace and Company, 1941). Finally, reference should be made to two invaluable special studies by J. B. Bury: *A History of Freedom of Thought* (New York: Henry Holt and Company, 1913) and *The Idea of Progress* (London: Macmillan & Co., 1924).

[2] Cf. Whitehead's remark that just as the Middle Ages was an "age of faith, based upon reason," so the modern age has been an "age of reason, based upon faith."—*Science and the Modern World* (New York: The Macmillan Company, 1925), p. 83, quoted by John H. Hallowell, *The Decline of Liberalism as an Ideology—with Particular Reference to German Politico-Legal Thought* (Berkeley and Los Angeles: University of California Press, 1943), p. 4.

the authoritarian control of belief by the church—this in spite of the fact that the first revolters (Luther and Calvin) and their immediate followers were no more believers in toleration than was the church against which they were rebelling. Even John Locke, whose *Letters on Toleration* are the classical statement of that case, was not consistent enough to carry the doctrine to its logical conclusion.

The same rationalism which undermined beliefs in the supernatural had as its counterpart a new emphasis on nature and especially on man. Men who had ceased to be so concerned about life in the hereafter paid more attention to human happiness in the present. Rationalism, humanism, and humanitarianism are all of a piece. Jefferson's use of the word "happiness" among the fundamental rights in the Declaration of Independence was no mere euphemistic substitution for "property," as has sometimes been suggested. The primacy of human happiness was one of the cornerstones of the emerging communal psychology.

On the side of economic and social arrangements, liberalism was a revolt against that vast network of economic restrictions and privileges which comprised feudalism. Whether capitalism was the cause of Protestantism, or Protestantism the cause of capitalism, or whether both were the common product of other factors is a problem which need not concern us here. Individual freedom was again the watchword—freedom to trade, to move about, and to dispose of one's services on the basis of individual bargaining, freedom of contract, and freedom of enterprise. The old monopolistic privileges were largely swept aside and, to a far greater degree than in the past, men were turned loose upon their own resources to gain a livelihood in proportion to their bargaining power (based upon their industry, thrift, ability, and good fortune). It goes without saying that, the institution of inheritance having been retained, there was from the start a vast source of inequalities which prevented the "career open to the talents" from ever approximating that state of equal freedom for all which was at once its ideal and its justification.

Politically, the revolt was against despotism and the reigning system of political privileges. What started as a demand for moderate reforms ended in the overthrow of governments not responsible to the people. Natural rights, the inalienable and imprescriptible rights of man, became the foundation of political philosophy. No government which was not based upon the consent of the governed was legitimate, and such governments existed for the sole purpose of protecting and maintaining natural rights.

The body of ideas which we call liberalism cannot be entirely set forth in terms of revolts, however. An exceedingly important part of it, possibly even a factor conditioning the revolts, was the idea of progress. Never before had the mass of mankind been accustomed to thinking that life was getting better and would continue to get better. Belief in the indefinite perfectibility of society gave a buoyancy and optimism to the spirits of men which went far toward making the idea a reality. Distinct though it was, this idea was logically related to the rest of the pattern of thought. Trust in the revealing and integrating power of reason and in man's inherent reasonability led naturally to faith in material, moral, and social progress.

Finally, two elements which were by no means new were taken up by the emerging pattern of ideas and made vital parts of it. One was the idea of natural law. Ever since the days of the Stoics this notion had played a dominant role in European thought. Varying in application from age to age, it always involved the basic belief that in matters of right and wrong, especially as they apply to the social order, there is an objective, universal truth, discoverable by reason. In general terms, its greatest contribution to liberalism was to supply a basis for universality, for general agreement, to an age which had cut itself loose from the authorities of church dogma and of custom. More specifically, it provided the corpus from which was carved the natural, inherent rights of individuals, which became the counterpart of the old natural law doctrine for the age of individualism.

The second of the old elements can also be traced back to the Stoics, although it received its great impetus from Christian thought. It is the idea and the ideal of equality—of the moral equality of all men. It may be expressed in terms of the absolute value of the individual or of his sacredness, or it may be put in terms of the Kantian imperative that each person ought to be treated not as a means but as an end-in-himself. Individualism in the sense of self-reliance may be thought of as new to the modern world with the Renaissance, but what we may call ethical individualism was indeed no new phenomenon, although it found its fullest flowering in the period ushered in by that great movement.

To recapitulate, the essential elements of the liberal *Weltanschauung* were the appeal to reason, the belief in happiness as the end, belief in liberty of opinion and conduct, toleration, natural rights, equality and faith in progress. Faith in the liberated reason of each individual is the key to it all—the individual being thought of as autonomous and largely self-sufficient. The potentially skeptical and anarchistic implications of this foundation were kept in check by the belief that the universe—human as well as inorganic—was governed by reason, that is by natural law. Just give men liberty—to learn, to think, and to act—and they would be led by the laws of the universe to the formation of a perfect society.

2. *Political Liberalism*

The basic elements of that aspect of the liberal complex in which we are primarily interested, political liberalism, have already been mentioned. They are the belief in liberty, in natural rights, and in government by consent.[3] Since natural rights were

---

[3] See John Locke, *Of Civil Government—Two Treatises,* Everyman's Library (New York: E. P. Dutton & Co., 1936), and Tom Paine, *Rights of Man,* Everyman's Library (New York: E. P. Dutton & Co., 1915). Among useful secondary references are the following: Carl L. Becker, *The Declaration of Independence: A Study in the History of Political Ideas* (New York: Alfred A. Knopf, Inc., 1942); Carl L. Becker, *Freedom and Responsibility in the American Way of Life* (New York: Alfred A. Knopf, Inc., 1945); George H. Sabine, "The Historical Position of Liberalism," *The American Scholar,* X (Winter, 1940–1941), 49–58; and Leonard Woolf, *After the Deluge* (2 vols.; New York: Harcourt, Brace and Company, 1931, 1939).

but the specific form given to the claim to liberty, the first two will be treated as one. These beliefs were thought to be the self-evident corollaries of the ultimate value of the individual. Together they may be thought of as the doctrine of limited government. Man's natural rights being inadequately protected in the state of nature, governments were instituted to aid in their enforcement. Any government which failed to perform this office or which itself transgressed against natural rights ceased to be legitimate, and revolt was justified. Men had given up to the government their individual police powers only on condition that it would enforce and respect their rights. If the condition was violated, the grant (contract) became void, or at least voidable. Not all the writers who helped establish the pattern of political liberal thought took the narrowest view of the legitimate sphere of government. Locke himself stressed the right of the government to protect the general welfare and made the majority the judge of the proper interpretation of natural rights.[4] But the development of laissez-faire economic theory in the late eighteenth and the nineteenth century, was accompanied by political theories calling for a minimum of governmental interference. Adam Smith's contemporary, Tom Paine, was typical of those who held the view that government at best was a necessary evil.

The specific liberties, or natural rights, that were insisted upon are to be found in the numerous bills of rights—English American, and French—which were proclaimed, and frequently cast in constitutional form, during the seventeenth and eighteenth centuries. First, there were limitations as to the sphere of government. Chief among these were the right to freedom of religious belief and observance; the right to freedom of speech and of the press and freedom of assembly; the right to petition for the redress of grievances; and the right to own property and to be protected in its use and disposal. A second group of limitations had to do with the methods of governmental control. Most

---

[4] See Willmoore Kendall, *John Locke and the Doctrine of Majority-Rule* (Urbana: The University of Illinois Press, 1941).

vital of these limitations—although perhaps it is more of a broad principle than a specific liberty—was the rule of law. In its most general significance, this is simply the principle that governments shall regulate the conduct of their subjects only through laws of general application, known to all, applied impartially and not retroactively. The principle was supported by numerous specific guarantees (directed against some of the most notorious violations), such as the right to a speedy and fair trial (and even more specifically the writ of habeas corpus), trial by jury, and the prohibition of ex post facto legislation. A somewhat more general guarantee of fair procedure to apply to cases involving property as well as life and liberty of the person was expressed in the American Constitution (Fifth Amendment) in terms of the famous "due process of law" clause. Criminals convicted in accordance with the rule of law were given further protection by a proscription of "cruel and unusual" punishments.

In addition to the specific substantive and procedural limitations placed upon the actions of government, another general principle was evolved as a check on the abuse of political power. This was the doctrine of the separation of powers. The emphasis given to, and the application of, this principle varied from country to country; but, with varying twists, in England, France, and the United States, during the period we are discussing, the doctrine prevailed that governmental power was of three kinds— legislative, executive, and judicial—and that to guard against its abuse each kind should be committed to a separate group of individuals, independent of each of the others and on a plane of equality with them.

It was the general belief of the exponents of political liberalism that these various devices for limiting political authority should be cast in the form of a written constitution. Although the idea had its birth in England during the Commonwealth period, there alone it failed to gain permanent foothold. But the difference, at least as between France and England, is more apparent than real, consisting largely in whether or not the various elements of the constitution are assembled together in a single document. Only in the United States did the document achieve the status of a body of higher law enforced by the courts against the other branches of government.

The second major constituent of political liberalism, the principle of government by consent, developed more gradually. In Locke's doctrine it was a theory of revolution. Consent was presumed to have been tacitly given; but if the government should violate the conditions of that consent (also presumed), the people would be entitled to rebel. Gradually, more orderly sanctions for the principle of consent were developed in the form of the institutions of representative government. The right of the parliament to be the sole lawmaking and tax-levying body was successfully asserted. The right of revolution was supplemented by faith in gradual, peaceful change through constitutional procedures. It remained for the democratic movement to carry the principle of representation to its logical conclusion.

3. *Liberal Democracy*

Although liberal-democratic government is a logical and one might almost say an inevitable development of the principles of political liberalism along the channels we have just been examining, it is well to pass under view the broader background of social democracy; for democracy, like political liberalism, is far more than a theory of government—it is a way of life.[5] It repre-

---

[5] In addition to volumes cited previously in this chapter, a few other works may be singled out for special mention. Among books dealing with the development of social democratic ideals out of the religious revolt, reference should be made to George P. Gooch and Harold J. Laski's *English Democratic Ideas in the Seventeenth Century* (2d ed.; Cambridge: Cambridge University Press, 1927); to A. D. Lindsay's *The Modern Democratic State* (London: Oxford University Press, 1943), Vol. I; and to Ralph Barton Perry's *Puritanism and Democracy* (New York: The Vanguard Press, 1934). An excellent account of the relationship between political and social democracy is to be found in George S. Counts's *The Prospects of American Democracy* (New York: The John Day Company, 1938). A useful historical sketch is supplied by Alan F. Hattersley, *A Short History of Democracy* (Cambridge: Cambridge University Press, 1930). The development of the theory of political democracy in its liberal form can nowhere better be observed than in the writings of James and John Stuart Mill. See especially James Mill, "Essay on Government" in Philip Wheelwright (ed.),

sents the full development of the Stoic-Christian concept of the essential moral equality of men. As long as the church itself was a vast, authoritarian hierarchy, representing also a privileged order, the realization of this ideal was not a practical possibility. But once the shackles of ecclesiastical authority had been cast off in favor of the liberty of the individual, where was the line to be drawn short of extending the liberty equally to all? By no means all of the Protestants accepted the position of the Colonel Rainboro who told Ireton that "the poorest he that is in England hath a life to live as the richest he." [6] But such was the unavoidable logic of their position. There were varying interpretations of the equality of men among the early democrats, and some were willing to go much further than others. But all were agreed on the basic proposition that all men have an equal right to liberty and happiness, and secondarily to equality before the law. [7]

But how should men be guaranteed this equality of treatment which was their right? The mere assertion of civil liberties as natural rights was not enough. Men soon seized on the idea that God helps those who help themselves, or, in other words, that each man is the best protector of his own liberty if only he is armed with the weapon of equal political power. Political equality was called into being to guarantee liberty to all, on equal terms.

The Utilitarians, and especially James Mill, attempted to give this theory scientific form in a way that dispensed with the doctrine of natural rights. It is the purpose of government, wrote Mill, to maximize the happiness of each individual. Men always act in their own interests as far as they know them, and getting them to know their interests is simply a matter of education, [8] so

---

Essays on Government, Jurisprudence, Liberty of the Press, and Law of Nations (New York: Doubleday & Company, 1935) and John Stuart Mill, *Utilitarianism, Liberty and Representative Government* (New York: E. P. Dutton & Co., 1910), all three essays. See also Leslie Stephen, *The English Utilitarians* (3 vols.; New York: G. P. Putnam's Sons, 1930).

[6] Quoted in Lindsay, *op. cit.*, I, 118.
[7] Woolf, *op. cit.*, I, 189–190.
[8] James Mill, "Essay on Government," *op. cit.*, pp. 203 ff.

the best assurance of good government is to give each man an equal share of political power, through the device of representative government. Although in this doctrine the belief in natural rights was explicitly abandoned, the essence of it remained implicit in the assumption that the happiness of each should count the same as that of every other. Moreover, the faith in the rational order of the universe persisted in the form of the belief that the combination of individual, self-seeking interests would produce a harmonious pattern of social well-being.

Finally, there was one other strand woven into the doctrines supporting liberal democracy of which we must take note. The difference is more one of emphasis than of kind. John Stuart Mill, becoming aware of the weakness of his father's great faith in man's proclivity to behave in accordance with his rational self-interest, and perhaps also sensing somewhat the questionability of the assumption of a rational harmony of interests, added the notion of benevolence. The powerful sentiment of sympathy, or the "social feelings of mankind," provided, he believed, the ultimate foundation for the democratic ideal.[9]

This pattern of ideas, with its attendant institutions, might be designated the classical pattern of liberal democracy.[10] It

[9] For a fuller treatment of Utilitarian theories as well as for later developments, see my "Reason, Value Theory, and the Theory of Democracy," *American Political Science Review*, XXXVIII (1944), 855–875.

No attempt to give a formal definition of either social or political democracy was made above for it is believed that the meaning emerges clearly from what has been said. The following statement by George S. Counts, however, is worth quoting. It clearly demonstrates the way in which social democracy is implied by political liberalism and political democracy by social democracy: ". . . it may be said that democracy asserts the worth and dignity of the individual human being and the fundamental moral equality of all men; that it proclaims a faith in mind and reason, in the capabilities of ordinary people, and in the indefinite perfectibility of human society. Also democracy believes in material security and independence for all, equality of opportunity for personal growth, reasonable equality of economic condition, general participation in the processes of government, safety of life and liberty of person, access to the sources of relevant knowledge, unfettered exchange of ideas and opinions, freedom of thought and conscience, and rule by majority decision."—George S. Counts, *The Prospects of American Democracy*, p. 319. By permission of The John Day Company, publishers.

[10] No reference is made here to Rousseau's concept of the General Will

forms one of those great complexes which stamp themselves on the face of an age. It has been widely copied and has proved remarkably tough. Under its aegis the world has witnessed by far the most remarkable advances in science and productivity ever known.

4. Weaknesses of the "Classical Pattern"

It is not to be expected that this pattern will remain unchanged. Indeed, the very concept of a "classical pattern" involves an oversimplification, because the pattern has been a constantly evolving one. At any given time it holds within itself inconsistencies and other elements of weakness. These weaknesses but point the direction of future development. It is well that we should call attention here to the weak points in the structure, both logical and strategic.

As has been seen, liberal democracy found support from two related but still quite different philosophies—those of natural rights and Utilitarianism.[11] Each has had its characteristic weaknesses. The natural rights philosophy relies heavily upon self-evidence or revelation. Especially is this true of the basic doctrines of equality and of the absolute value of the individual. They are therefore peculiarly susceptible to the corrosive influence of skepticism, the outcome of the appeal to reason. Utilitarianism, while it tried to hide the fact, made these same assumptions. Furthermore, in attempting a fuller justification of political democracy, it added two more questionable assumptions: that men always act in accordance with their own interest, and that the interests of all men are harmonious. Finally, Utilitarianism's

because it never really became part of the Anglo-American theory of liberal democracy. The contributions to democratic theory of T. H. Green and later writers are omitted here because they were not a part of the body of that "classical pattern" of liberal-democratic thought against which the reaction discussed in the next chapter came.

[11] Utilitarianism became the dominant philosophy in England in the nineteenth century but seems never to have been wholly adopted in the United States, where pragmatic and idealistic theories gradually merged with or supplanted the natural rights doctrines that even yet exercise a notable influence. See Paul A. Palmer, "Benthamism in England and America," *American Political Science Review*, XXXV (Oct., 1941), 855–871.

emphasis on pleasure as the final good tended to involve the case for democracy with an ethical system that was psychologically unsound.

Classical liberal-democratic theory tends to be atomistic. That is to say, it overemphasizes rights at the expense of duties, the individual at the expense of society, and competition at the expense of cooperation. The ultimate, practical consequences of these theoretical mistakes are a lack of cohesive force and of common purpose, and a certain feeling of emptiness on the part of the individual, resulting from the starvation of his social self.

Liberal or constitutional democracy also involved a dependence upon self-discipline, for two reasons. In the first place, a social order can stand a maximum of individual liberty only if its members use their liberty with some consideration for their obligations to society. Second, the rule of law and also the more specific constitutional restraints require a willingness to act in accordance with principle despite the fact that such action may occasionally involve a conflict with interest and even with justice, in a particular case. These kinds of self-discipline, as Professor Perry has shown,[12] were marked characteristics of Puritanism. With the waning of the Puritanical mores, constitutionalism loses a powerful support.

Finally, liberal democracy came into being along with a particular set of social and economic conditions: an expanding capitalism, accompanied by the rise to power of the *bourgeoisie* and a great restriction of the sphere of government. Inevitably its particular forms were adjusted to that situation. Conceivably they were limited to it. Could it survive conditions demanding of its citizens more complicated decisions and of its governments a far larger sphere of activity?

In succeeding chapters (II, VII, VIII, and IX) we shall sketch in very broad outlines the ways in which the development of ideas and the movement of events have exploited these weaknesses.

[12] Perry, *op. cit.*, pp. 178–197, and Chap. 15.

PART TWO

THE IDEAL CHALLENGED
AND APPRAISED

CHAPTER II

THE CHALLENGE
OF SKEPTICS
AND ROMANTICS

Nothing less than a detailed history of political philosophy during the last three centuries could do full justice to the subject of this chapter. For the purpose of this volume, however, it is enough to show the nature of the attacks that have been made upon the basic doctrines of political liberalism. The stages by which they developed are to us of only passing importance and will be dealt with but sketchily. Questions as to the mutual interactions between these ideas and the evolving democratic philosophy will be almost completely neglected. We shall be concerned with expounding, and dealing very briefly with, the development of criticisms of rationalism, individualism, and the belief in moral equality, and with the specific application of these ideas to the field of political theory.[1]

The term "rationalism," as used here, stands for several related but distinct concepts, all relevant to our concern, all part of democracy's heritage from the Enlightenment. First, there is the faith in the power of reason to discover eternal truths by direct insight, or "self-evidence." Second is the belief in a universal natural order or harmony, which includes a harmony among human wills. The third point is the confidence that man possesses a fac-

[1] There are three distinct lines of thought all of which are relevant to the desirability and prospects of liberal democracy. The first consists of ideas involving some logical criticism of the liberal-democratic ideal; the second includes facts and theories that tend to bring into question the workability of liberal-democratic institutions; and the third comprises intellectual movements and general shifts in the intellectual climate that tend to weaken popular support for these institutions. It is the first of these only with which the present chapter will be concerned. The other two will be discussed in Part III.

ulty, the practical reason, by means of which he can weigh various values and decide which is the greatest and which combination will give the greatest sum total of value. Finally, there is the assurance that men generally have a proclivity to use their rational powers and to act accordingly.

Serious doubts have been raised about all four of these propositions; the fourth, however, is primarily pertinent to a consideration of the workability of democracy rather than to the case for it as an ideal. For that reason, an exposition of the attacks upon rationalism in the last sense will be reserved for Chapter VII. Our primary concern here will be with attacks upon rationalism in the first sense enumerated; but as some forms of the case for democracy rely upon the second and third meanings, they, too, will come in for attention.

1. The Attack upon Rationalism

Faith in the power of reason to apprehend fundamental truth comprised the backbone of the natural law doctrine which was so basic to political liberalism. Locke is typical in this respect. The highest reason, he maintained, is that by which we ascertain true and clear principles. This is done by comparing two ideas directly and seeing whether or not they agree, as when we perceive immediately that the arc of a circle must be less than the whole.[2]

Furthermore, not only is reason capable of the direct apprehension of truth in this fashion, but by this process it is possible, though difficult, to attain to exact knowledge in the field of

[2] *The Works of John Locke* (12th ed.; London: 1824), II, 240–242, 257–259; or *Essay concerning Human Understanding,* Bk. IV, Chap. 17. In the same essay he writes: "It is on this intuition that depends all the certainty and evidence of all our knowledge; which certainty everyone finds to be so great, that he can not imagine, and therefore not require a greater: for a man can not conceive himself capable of a greater certainty, than to know that any idea in his mind is such as he perceives it to be; and that two ideas wherein he perceives a difference, are different and not precisely the same. He that demands a greater certainty than this, demands he knows not what, and shows only that he has a mind to be a sceptick, without being able to do so."—*Ibid.,* p. 70, *Essay Concerning Human Understanding,* Bk. IV, Chap. 2.

ethics. It is here that Locke is most susceptible to attack. Men are by nature equal, he maintains. This is the very cornerstone of his political philosophy. And yet he offers no proof beyond citing the authority of "the judicious Hooker" and proclaiming it as self-evident that "creatures of the same species and rank, promiscuously born to all the same advantages of Nature, and the use of the same faculties, should also be equal one amongst another. . . ." [3] There is no discussion, for example, of the significance of the fact that men's faculties vary greatly in quality. Clearly the proposition is not in the same class with that about the arc and the circle.

Even before Locke, Thomas Hobbes had taken a narrower view of human reason,[4] but it remained for David Hume, half a century later, to spell out in greater detail the consequences of such a view. It may be said that Hume turned reason against itself, meaning by that that he used logic to attack the notion that reason can apprehend a priori truths. The law of nature, as the law of reason, so fundamental to a great part of eighteenth-century political philosophy, is rejected. Particularly, reason is of no avail in matters of ultimate right and wrong.[5] Morals are derived from our passions, not from reason: "It is not contrary to reason to prefer the destruction of the whole world to the scratching of my finger." [6]

The implications of this position are far reaching. The whole ground of argument is shifted—from deductive to inductive logic,

[3] John Locke, *Of Civil Government*, "Everyman's Library" (New York: E. P. Dutton & Co., 1936), p. 118.

[4] "When a man *Reasoneth*, hee does nothing else but conceive a summe totall, from *Addition* of parcels; or conceive a Remainder, from *Subtraction* of one summe from another. . . ."—Thomas Hobbes, *Leviathan*, "Everyman's Library" (New York: E. P. Dutton & Co., 1928), p. 18.

[5] In the sentence above, stress must be placed on the word "ultimate." Reason is used in the calculation of consequences, which Hume recognized as an important part of the process of ethical evaluation. In the technical language of philosophers, it was only "synthetic" a priori truths whose existence Hume denied. Allegedly self-evident principles of right and wrong would fall in this category. (He believed that reason could apprehend "analytic" a priori truths, such as the laws of logic.)

[6] David Hume, *A Treatise of Human Nature*, "Everyman's Library" (New York: E. P. Dutton & Co., 1911), II, 128.

from rationalism to empiricism. Hume's own skepticism was limited. Hume retained the notions of right and wrong: he merely asserted that it was something which might be called the moral sense, rather than reason, that presents us with these notions and gives them their content. But this view immediately raises the question as to whether the moral sense is the same for all men. It had not been seriously questioned that reason was universal. No one doubted that any man who understood the terms would say that the part must be less than the whole or that the proposition that the sum of the angles of a triangle must equal two right angles could be demonstrated to anyone with normal intelligence. But a moral sense is another matter. Perhaps there is a moral sense and perhaps it is the same in all mankind; and perhaps not. These propositions are open to question and investigation.[7] Thus Hume made ethics an empirical science; he also opened the door to moral skepticism without limit—all the way down to the nihilist (fascist or otherwise) who asserts that the only values are his own changing purposes, which may run completely contrary to the purposes of others.

The full impact of this attack upon rational self-evidence as the foundation of ethics did not make itself felt until long after the time of Hume. As has been said, Hume himself merely transferred the locus of what might be called the ethical faculty from reason to feeling. The moral sentiment, he thought, was universal and everywhere the same. Other moral philosophers came to this same comforting conclusion. In particular, the Utilitarians, who dominated English thought for close to a century, found no difficulty in believing that the "greatest happiness principle" provided a solid foundation for a universal ethic, and, more specifically, for a belief in democracy, although not in natural rights. Abandoning belief in rational self-evidence and in moral sense, they achieved the same result (as far as concerns our purposes)

---

[7] Hume himself did not question them, declaring, in fact, that the chief use of history is "to discover the constant and universal principles of human nature," but that is beside the point. (The quotation is taken from Carl L. Becker, *The Heavenly City of the Eighteenth-Century Philosophers* [New Haven: Yale University Press, 1932], p. 71.)

by defining "good" in terms of interest and asserting a universal harmony of interests. They were rationalistic, that is to say, in the second but not in the first of the senses enumerated above.[8]

Certain later philosophers who continue, like the Utilitarians, to derive the Good from interest, no longer maintain that all interests can be rationally integrated. Professor R. B. Perry falls in this category. Good is defined directly in terms of the satisfaction of interest, without attempting to measure it by any standard outside the individual.[9] Insofar as there are constancy and universality about the nature of human desires, or interests, to that extent values are constant and universal. Reason does not always produce harmony and so provide a foundation for a universal good, but it is a tool which may be used to discover new ways of satisfying the maximum of desires harmoniously.[10] The fact remains, however, that, in Perry's view, there may be irresolvable conflicts between individual interests. In such circumstances, he holds, there is no ethical solution.[11] It is entirely compatible with this view to hold that in fact the area of agreement is large enough to support a case for liberal democracy. (Perry himself holds this position.) [12] Nevertheless, the door which Hume pointed out is here opened a small crack, suggesting the possibility of still further developments tending to undermine the foundation for universal value judgments.

Other writers have taken a less sanguine view of human nature than does Perry, thus tending to open the door wider. Two men whom we shall discuss in this connection are Nietzsche and Freud.[13] Nietzsche (who represents only the most extreme ver-

---

[8] Above, p. 23.

[9] Ralph Barton Perry, *General Theory of Value* (New York: Longmans, Green and Co., 1926), p. 115.

[10] *Ibid.*, p. 88.

[11] *Ibid.*, p. 655.

[12] See, generally, Ralph Barton Perry, *Shall Not Perish from the Earth* (New York: The Vanguard Press, 1940).

[13] These men are singled out for attention here because their particular attacks upon rationalism go to the heart of the ethical basis for liberal democracy. More generally, arguments to the effect that human beings are irrational are pertinent to a consideration of the workability of democracy. They will be discussed in later chapters (VII, XI, and XII).

sion of a line of thought that stems from his compatriot Schopenhauer) asserted that will, and more specifically the will-to-power, rather than reason is supreme. Life consists in, and finds its value in, struggle and the survival of the fittest. The individual can realize the good life only at the expense of other individuals. If this view were to be coupled with Perry's value theory, it is clear that the ethical basis of liberalism would be destroyed.[14]

From our present point of view, the significance of the great psychologist of the subconscious, Sigmund Freud, is similar to that of Nietzsche in that Freud, too, finds disharmony and conflict at the very roots of human motivation. He presents man as a creature whose behavior is determined by powerful driving forces welling up from the subconscious, beside which the restraints of "reason" are virtually helpless. Reason provides the justifications for actions whose true motives lie hidden even from ourselves in the subconscious. We are the less able to control them because we are not aware of what is motivating us. These drives can be, and often are, repressed; but then they come out in other and often socially less desirable forms. Here is the crux of the matter. Man's nature is bound to bring him into conflict both with himself and with others. He cannot find peace and contentment in society, nor yet out of society. He craves authority, yet rebels against it. He desires to be loved, yet will behave in an aggressive fashion which repels love. "The tendency to aggression," Freud wrote, "is an innate, independent, instinctual disposition in man. . . ."[15]

The full impact of Freud's theory on the ethical case for democracy which might be based upon Perry's value theory is apparent if we observe that it amounts to a denial of the efficacy of the practical reason to accomplish its function of weighing competing values and directing conduct in such a fashion as to achieve a maximum of value for the individual.

[14] That Nietzsche's own ethical theory was, if anything, even more directly opposed to liberal-democratic principles will appear below, pp. 33–34.

[15] Sigmund Freud, *Civilization and Its Discontents*, trans. Joan Riviere (3d ed.; New York: Jonathan Cape & Harrison Smith, 1930), p. 102.

Another line of attack is to be found in the works of such ethical relativists as Edward Westermarck.[16] Abandoning the identification of "good" with interests, he returned to a position more like that of Hume, relating moral values to emotions. His thesis, buttressed by a vast array of anthropological evidence, comprises three propositions of particular interest to us. First, he denies that moral values possess objectivity in the sense of real existence apart from any reference to a human mind. Second, he denies that moral principles or values are grounded on reason, asserting, on the contrary, that they are entirely relative to (certain) human emotions. Moral judgments, he declares, are not "absolute," but "relative to the emotions they express." [17] So far his position, though by no means identical with Hume's, from our point of view goes no further. The question is still left open whether or not the emotions which govern our value judgments are so uniform among all men as to provide a basis for morals just as universal as though it pertained to reason. But not for long. This possibility, which Hume left open, Westermarck definitely denies. After making all allowances for differing understandings of the facts, or judgments as to the probable consequences of certain actions, for inadequate reflection, and the like, Westermarck insists that there are fundamental disagreements on matters of morals even among philosophers. No amount of reflection and clarification as to just what is involved in a given situation will serve, he claims, to bring about agreement in moral valuations. The emotions upon which our judgments in the last analysis depend vary from individual to individual. In particular, our altruistic sentiments, which are fundamental to our moral judgments, vary greatly. For such reasons, he concludes, our moral judgments could not possibly possess "that universality which is characteristic of truth." [18] For example, he maintains that

[16] See Edward Westermarck, *The Origin and Development of the Moral Ideas* (2 vols.; New York: The Macmillan Company, 1906 and 1908), and the final statement of his position in *Ethical Relativity* (New York: Harcourt, Brace and Company, 1932).

[17] Westermarck, *Ethical Relativity*, p. 289.

[18] *Ibid.*, p. 218. And see generally pp. 197–219.

the principle of "rational benevolence" ("that each one is morally bound to regard the good of any other individual as much as his own, except in so far as he judges it to be less, when impartially viewed, or less certainly knowable or attainable by him") is not generally accepted by common sense or by all moralists.[19]

With less emphasis on the findings of anthropology and more on their own insistence upon operational definitions, the ethical positivists have come to much the same conclusions. They call attention to the vagueness of our usage of ethical terms and deny that there is or could be any proof of the validity of asserted values. Consequently they conclude that such terms have no cognitive meaning. Bertrand Russell, for instance (who at least in this connection may be considered as a positivist), declares that "ethics . . . contains no statements, whether true or false, but consists of desires of a certain general kind, namely, such as are concerned with the desires of mankind in general. . . ." [20] "The chief ground for adopting this view," he continues, "is the complete impossibility of finding any arguments to prove that this or that has intrinsic value. . . . Since no way can be even imagined for deciding a difference as to values, the conclusion is forced upon us that the difference is one of tastes, not one as to any objective truth." [21] An even more typical statement of the positivistic point of view is supplied by Professor Abraham Kaplan, who writes: "The expressions which constitute moral systems, and value-terms and expressions in general, in their characteristic use make no assertions but rather perform certain pragmatical functions, of which some of the more important are to express the speaker's emotions, to commit him to certain courses of action, and to urge others to share his attitude and commitments." [22]

[19] *Ibid.*, pp. 9 ff.

[20] Bertrand Russell, *Religion and Science* (New York: Henry Holt and Company, 1935), p. 249.

[21] *Ibid.*, p. 250.

[22] Abraham Kaplan, "Are Moral Judgments Assertions?" *Philosophical Review*, LI (May, 1942), 302–303. For a much fuller exposition of ethical positivism, see Charles L. Stevenson, *Ethics and Language* (New Haven:

It is clear that one of the important doctrinal supports of democratic theory in the past—natural law—is completely undermined to the extent that the theories just discussed gain acceptance. There certainly can be no rational, immutable, and universal principles of right if there are no universally valid human ends. This is not the place to trace out the history of the decline in the belief in natural law and natural rights which has in fact taken place. The main line of juristic thought has long since given up the attempt even to deal with the problem of natural law. Confining itself to the safer field of positive law, it has consigned all consideration of the justification of law to the nebulous field of "metajurisprudence." [23] And with natural law has gone its democratic counterpart, "natural rights." True, the word "rights" is still widely used in the ethical sense. We are inclined to believe that while there are no "rights" which are "natural"— meaning absolute, immutable, and universal—there are rights (claims for certain immunities or for certain powers) which under a given set of circumstances are valid. But it is easy to see that a theory of democracy in which even the right to self-government itself must rest on such a tentative foundation is greatly reduced in stature as compared with the notion of earlier days. It is also obvious that even this concept is threatened by the more extreme version of ethical relativism discussed above. We grow increasingly self-conscious in using the word "rights" at all, and while we continue to evaluate laws and to express our value judgments, we have increasing difficulty in justifying our evaluations in terms of any generally accepted norms. Mr. Justice Holmes was merely giving forceful expression to this direction of thought when he declared, as he was fond of doing, that right is just "the majority vote of that nation that can lick all the others."

Moreover, quite apart from the belief in natural rights, it

Yale University Press, 1944). See also Alfred J. Ayer, *Language, Truth and Logic* (New York: Oxford University Press, 1936), Chap. 6.

[23] Cf. Hans Kelsen, *General Theory of Law and State*, trans. Anders Wedberg (Cambridge, Mass.: Harvard University Press, 1945), pp. xiv–xv; and Hans Kelsen, *Der Sociologische und der Juristische Staatsbegriff* (Tübingen: 1928), p. 95.

would appear that the position of the positivists leaves no basis for asserting that democracy is superior to other social orders, except as an expression of personal preference.

2. The Attack upon Individualism

Other aspects of the liberal democratic complex than its rationalism have been subjected to the winds of erosive doctrines. Particularly is this true of its individualism. Individualism, like rationalism, is a very broad term. In a general way, we may say that it stands both for the principle of self-reliance and for the proposition that the individual is the center of value, that his welfare should be our primary aim. Both of these phases of individualism are intimately related, historically, to liberal democracy, but it is the second phase that is logically essential to the ethical foundation of liberalism. It is accordingly with the attacks upon the primacy of the individual that we shall be concerned in this chapter.

The whole stream—perhaps we should say torrent—of socialistic thought (both Utopian and "scientific") is, of course, opposed to individualism in the first sense. It has remained for the radicals of the right to push the opposition to individualism to its logical extreme. Doubtless it was such liberals as Mazzini whose nationalism began the process of elevating the collectivity above its members. Others—by no stretch of terminology to be denominated liberals—have extended the cult of the group to the point where the individual becomes secondary.

It may be said at the outset that it is difficult to set forth the reasoning by which many Romanticists have glorified the group to the extent of making it, rather than the individual, the center of value, because so little reasoning is involved. In large part it represents an emotional reaction rather than a rational argument. In some measure, too, it consists of a disagreement with ideas or values associated with, but not essentially related to, individualism as here defined. (As will be noted later, in another connection, this is largely because of a confusion between the two distinct meanings of individualism pointed out above.)

In connection with assaults upon individualism, it is pertinent to mention also attacks on the ideal of happiness as the goal of the individual. Although liberal democracy does not need (logically) to rely on this Utilitarian doctrine, and has not always done so, many of its supporters have made it basic to their reasoning. Furthermore, it is a fact that attacks upon happiness as the goal often merge, indistinguishably, into attacks on the primacy of the individual. Carlyle and Nietzsche are nineteenth-century representatives of this brand of thought. With them, duties were more important than rights, and discipline was superior to liberty. The truly free man, said Nietzsche, "treads under foot the contemptible species of well-being dreamt of by shopkeepers, Christians, cows, women, Englishmen, and other democrats!" [24] At least for Nietzsche, it followed that a mystic commitment to a higher authority was far better than self-government.

We need no reminder of the lengths to which these doctrines of belittlement of individual rights and glorification of duties to the state have been taken in our day by the fascists. Mussolini's statement that "Fascism conceives of the State as an absolute, in comparison with which all individuals or groups are relative, only to be conceived of in their relation to the State" [25] is typical. In the same essay he condemned the goal of happiness, which he identified with liberalism. The fascists, however, did not provide a logical attack upon the liberal-democratic ideal, although they denied its validity. As the Italian apologist for fascism, Gentile, himself declared, "Fascism is not a philosophy. . . . It is not even a political theory which can be stated in a series of formulae." [26] Insofar as they give any reasoned argument for their position, it deals with alleged evil consequences of liberalism.

[24] Friedrich Nietzsche, "Twilight of the Idols," in *Works*, trans. Thomas Common, ed. Alexander Tille (New York: The Macmillan Company, 1896), XI, 199.

[25] Benito Mussolini, "The Political and Social Doctrine of Fascism," trans. Jane Soames, *Political Quarterly*, IV (July–Sept., 1933), 352.

[26] Giovanni Gentile, "The Philosophic Basis of Fascism," *Foreign Affairs*, VI (Jan., 1928), 290–304, at 299–300.

These contentions will be set forth and considered in subsequent chapters.

3. *The Attack upon Moral Equality*

Finally, we must deal with the third major prop of liberal political thought, the principle of moral equality. Much of what has already been covered has a direct bearing on this, which will enable us to treat it briefly. Insofar as reason was thought to give grounds for belief in equality of rights, the case that has been made against reason as a source of ethical truths has direct application. Moreover, attacks on all ideas of objective or universal good include, of course, the principle of moral equality within their sweep.

A more specific attack on the equality doctrine is to be found in the writings of Nietzsche. To him the whole idea of human equality was anathema. The demand for equality, he declared, was nothing but a rationalization of the "most secret tyrant-longings" [27] of the weak.

Perhaps one of the greatest shocks to ethical equalitarianism was supplied by Darwin, whose painstaking elaboration of the theory of natural selection through survival of the fittest was taken up by a host of "social Darwinian" thinkers and writers. It should be made clear, however, that no specific political or social theory followed inevitably from Darwin's work. What Darwin did was to provide a framework on which it was easy to hang various social theories. In general, these theories were conservative and inegalitarian. At first, seizing upon the supposed beneficent effects of struggle, they tended to enthrone competition at the expense of equality.

The American sociologist William Graham Sumner typified this trend. In his view, the theory of evolution left no room either for equality or for the theory of natural rights. Democracy,

[27] Friedrich Nietzsche, *Thus Spake Zarathustra*, trans. Thomas Common (New York: Boni and Liveright, Inc., 1917), p. 112, quoted in George Catlin, *The Story of Political Philosophers* (New York: McGraw-Hill Book Company, 1939), p. 530.

"the pet superstition of the age," was a transient phenomenon, doomed to decline with the passing of the frontier. Later, as individualism gave way to solidarism, competition was transposed from the individual level to that of groups, especially races. In this fashion doctrines of Anglo-Saxon or Aryan superiority, although antedating Darwin in their earliest manifestations, were able to ride on the coattails of Darwin's popularity. Meanwhile, Mendel's studies of heredity and Galton's application of the laws of heredity to eugenics provided further support for the opponents of democracy. Not only were human beings vastly unequal in mental as well as in physical characteristics, but these differences tend to be inherited. When these facts are combined with democratic equality of opportunity, the result is a tendency toward the development of a pyramid of socio-economic classes corresponding to levels of ability.[28] Although such a structure theoretically might be combined with democratic government, the general trend of those who developed this line of reasoning was to be skeptical of democracy because its equalitarian ideal seemed to them so far removed from scientific truth.

It has been the aim of this chapter to give some idea of the most funamdental criticisms which have been directed against the liberal-democratic ideal and which will have to be considered in attempting to reappraise that ideal. The next four chapters will be devoted to such a reappraisal. It should be added that it has seemed more convenient to omit certain criticisms here and to consider them during the course of the positive argument of the following chapters. Especially is this true of the attacks upon the ideal of liberty.[29]

---

[28] See, for instance, N. J. Lennes, *Whither Democracy? Does Equalizing Opportunity Create Hereditary Classes? A Speculative Study* (New York: Harper & Brothers, 1927).

[29] It is not because liberty is a less fundamental part of liberal democracy than equality that specific attacks upon the latter and not the former are included here. Rather it is because the attacks on the primacy of the individual, which are included in this chapter, themselves comprise the most fundamental attack on the ideal of liberty.

CHAPTER III

BASES FOR
ETHICAL APPRAISAL

The house of liberalism has been severely shaken by the winds of doctrine. A child of the Age of Reason, it is now seeking to perpetuate itself in the Age of Relativism, or possibly even the Age of Unreason. A product of an age which had supreme faith in the power of reason to know the right and to assure progress, it now finds itself in an age when skepticism has seriously undermined this faith. For today, as Max Lerner has remarked, "the rational, right-thinking man has as surely ceased to be considered the center of our intellectual system as the earth has ceased to be considered the center of our planetary system." [1] Natural rights are no longer deemed self-evident. Indeed, if there is thought to be anything self-evident about them it is that they are self-evidently false; for do we not deny the validity of the natural right to life every time we conscript a soldier or sentence a criminal to death? [2]

It is time we turned our attention to a reappraisal of the liberal scheme of things. As a prelude to evaluating democratic government, we shall consider whether what was described in Chapter I as social democracy or the democratic way of life is a valid ideal, whether it is *the* way of life which we all should seek for ourselves and for the societies in which we live, as far as conditions permit. But this procedure presupposes an agreement on ethical standards, a matter about which, as we have seen, there is much dispute. Our first task then, the one to which the pres-

---

[1] Max Lerner, "Revolution in Ideas," *Nation,* CXLIX (Oct. 21, 1939), 435.
[2] Of course the asserted right cannot be so easily disposed of. The point intended is merely that the subject is a difficult one requiring careful thought and probably not to be settled by any simple, absolute formula.

ent Chapter will be devoted, is to see whether we can discover a basis for value judgments, and in particular for value judgments that support liberal democracy, which can hold its own against the criticisms discussed in the preceding chapter.

The trend toward skepticism regarding democratic values, especially toward the belittlement of rights and liberty, appears to have reached its apex in the thirties. For obvious reasons, the war has brought a countertrend toward the reassertion of the democratic ideals. Whether this will long outlast the occasion which brought it about remains to be seen. So far, at least, this reassertion has generally taken the form of a dogmatism which is no improvement either over that of its fascist opponents or over that which characterized the classical pattern of democratic thought.[3] It may well be doubted whether skepticism can be effectively pushed aside for long by a mere unsupported assertion of faith.

We are today acutely conscious of limitations to human reason of which the eighteenth century was unaware. But, in the absence of rational proof, blind faith is not the only alternative to complete skepticism. Reason may reveal grounds for plausible belief where final proof eludes us. In the everyday world most of our actions are based upon assumptions for which we have no more than probabilistic grounds for belief. But this is very different from saying that they have no basis at all. We make a distinction between the shiftless individual who neglects to provide for his family, having faith that "something will turn up" or that the Lord will provide, and the thrifty man who invests in insurance on the faith that the insurance company will pay up when the time comes. It has become fashionable to proclaim that we must always start from certain assumptions.[4]

[3] See, for example, Lewis Mumford's *Faith for Living* (New York: Harcourt, Brace and Company, 1940) and the very interesting sketch of Carl Becker's intellectual development by Professor Sabine in Carl L. Becker, *Freedom and Responsibility in the American Way of Life* (New York: Alfred A. Knopf, Inc., 1945), pp. vii–xlii, especially pp. xxxvi–xli.
[4] Cf. Willmoore Kendall, "The Majority Principle and the Scientific Elite," *Southern Review*, IV (Summer, 1938—Spring, 1939), 466. Similarly, Professor Hallowell asserts that the premises of men's reasoning can

This is true enough, but we must not allow it to obscure the fact that the important question is whether or not our initial assumptions are well grounded. Too often it seems to be implied that what assumption we start with is a purely arbitrary matter; but this is certainly not the case. My belief that the sun will rise tomorrow morning is an assumption. I cannot prove it, but at least in a pragmatic sense it is well grounded. The assumption it involves underlies all science. To assume that the sun will not rise tomorrow would be foolish, although no one could *prove* me wrong until after the event. In choosing which way to go at a fork in the road, I may have to assume either that the signpost is correct or that it is turned the wrong way. Under most circumstances there will be no question as to which assumption I should make.

In short, then, where reason cannot reveal final truth—which is most of the time—it may at least lead us to plausible conclusions. This is all we can hope for, and generally it is enough. We must make assumptions, certainly; but also we must examine them to determine their plausibility. The weakness of Locke and of the political rationalists generally was not their failure to prove the existence of the natural rights of liberty and equality but the fact that they made virtually no effort to support them, relying solely on their alleged self-evidence.

1. Essay at an Ethical Foundation

This capacity of reason to demonstrate degrees of probability suggests the possibility that the attacks on rationalism outlined in the preceding chapter may not have undermined the case for liberal democracy, although they did tend to refute the arguments on which, in large measure, it had hitherto been defended.

---

never be empirically demonstrated but must be accepted on faith (which indeed is true if we go back to *ultimate* premises). He further maintains that belief in the inherent equality of individuals is essential to democracy and that it is an ultimate premise. Both of these statements are open to question.—John Hallowell, "The Decline of Liberalism," *Ethics*, LII (Apr., 1942), 342, and n. 23.

I believe this to be the case, and accordingly in this chapter I shall seek to show that there is a foundation on which the case for liberal democracy can be built, considering the philosophical doctrines set forth in Chapter II only to appraise their bearing on the positive argument of the present chapter.

APPARENTLY DISCOURAGING FACTORS LESS SERIOUS THAN THEY APPEAR. Two factors today may tend to discourage those who would seek a plausible foundation for democratic values. One is the fact that moral philosophers are hopelessly at odds with one another regarding ethical theory, and the other is that much attention of late has been given to the variety of ethical practices and beliefs which the examination of cultures other than our own has disclosed. Neither of these facts is as serious for our purpose as may at first appear. The disagreements among moral philosophers relate far more to the method for determining true values than to what such values are.[5] A hedonist and a self-realizationist will be flatly at odds as to what constitutes the essence of goodness, yet they may agree almost to the letter as to what things are good and which better than others. Those who think that the good is a function of sentiment may agree precisely in practical matters with those who make reason rather than feeling the test.

Likewise the variations in ethical standards among different cultures have received disproportionate attention. They are far exceeded by areas of agreement. Honesty, at least in general and as among friends and neighbors, appears to be universally considered a good thing. Similarly, if there are those who would deny that friendship is on balance good, they have had a remarkable success in escaping notice. Undeserved pain is felt to be bad —and to inflict it wrong—with apparent universality. Murder, the deliberate and wanton taking of life—at the very least when it is

---

[5] This, of course, does not mean that there are no disagreements which are more fundamental. The contrary was indicated in Chap. II. With those who deny that there are such things as interpersonal values, we shall deal later. (See below, pp. 50–52.)

within the family group—is judged a crime in every known society.

The difficulties and differences in belief and practice have appeared particularly in the area of moral values and most especially when the attempt was made to discover a universal standard for *"the* good." It is suggested, therefore, that at the outset we avoid this problem. It might be that there is no such thing as *"the* good" and yet that we can pronounce a particular form of society as "good." If this seems paradoxical, consider for a moment the following situation. Suppose we were to define "good" merely as that of which I approve. And suppose further that you and I approve of different things. Clearly under these circumstances it would be impossible to speak of "the good," at least in the usual sense of that term. Yet it might be that we and everyone else would all approve of a particular society or would all find it essential for the attainment of things we individually approved. In either case, following customary usage, we would call it "good." This is not the position to be defended here but is set forth as a simple illustration of the proposition that the concept "good" need not be dependent upon that of "the good." [6]

MEANINGS OF "VALUE" AND "GOOD". We may begin our analysis with the term "value." We all have things which we value— which we desire, strive for, or set store by. I value my life, and I value the opportunity to play tennis, or to study and think about the nature of democracy. These things I value in and of themselves, that is to say, as ends. (At the same time they may be means to other ends, and I may value them as such.) These happen to be self-regarding ends, but of course some of my values relate to ends which are not purely or not at all self-regarding. The enjoyment of family life is perhaps both a self- and other-regarding end; my desire to alleviate the suffering of persecuted

[6] The analysis that follows owes a great deal to W. D. Lamont, *The Principles of Moral Judgment* (Oxford: The Clarendon Press, 1946). It is believed, however, that the argument of this chapter is not dependent upon acceptance of Mr. Lamont's ethical theory. As we shall attempt to demonstrate presently, it is compatible with a number of different moral theories.

and oppressed Jews would seem to be wholly other-regarding. Things which I value I call "good." [7]

Some things I value not in themselves but because they serve as *means* to things I value for their own sakes, as means to my ends. A law may be good because it improves my business or because it helps to raise the general level of public morality, which is a matter of interest (value) to me. Also I may think that a tax cut is good because it leaves me with more money to spend, but it may actually be bad because it may have other effects (such as promoting inflation) that interfere with my attaining my ends.

We have spoken of two aspects of making value judgments: the one by which we desire a certain end, and so judge it valuable, and that by which we calculate that X will contribute toward our realization of something we have judged valuable and therefore judge X valuable or good. There is yet another. We are continually discovering that we cannot have all the things we value; and more specifically that if we have some we shall have to forgo others. In other words, our ends conflict. Possibly we cannot enjoy both after-dinner coffee and a good night's sleep. Perhaps the mother of the family must decide whether she would rather have a new coat for herself or piano lessons for her daughter. The faculty by which we compare the conflicting values in such situations and arrive at a judgment of preference is often called the "practical reason". We are all engaged in this kind of activity a great deal of the time. We are constantly trying to select and especially to order our ends in such a way that they fit together with a minimum of conflict. After we have begun to build up a harmonious pattern of ends, we tend to evaluate new claimants for admission in terms of how well they fit into the pattern. At one time, let us assume, it might not have

---

[7] There are, of course, other senses of the word "good": for instance, the sense in which we say, "That is a good knife," or the sense in which we say, "He is a good [meaning morally good] man." The problem of distinguishing moral values from others is a difficult one we need not attempt to solve. Moral values constitute one of the kinds of value we are discussing throughout this chapter.

been very difficult for someone to have persuaded me to study law or medicine; but now, quite apart from practical considerations, I have developed a pattern of values which would lead me to rule out vocations, such as these, which would not give me time for scholarly activity or throw me into almost continuous contact with other people possessing predominantly intellectual rather than practical interests. Thus, when I call a particular end (such as comfort, friendship, or intellectual activity) good, what I tend to mean is not only that I prize it for its own sake but also that it fits with my other ends into a harmonious pattern or system of ends.[8] Furthermore, the successful pursuit of this pattern of ends tends to produce a state of total satisfaction or happiness.[9]

This account of the process by which we select our ends should be sufficient refutation of the objection (which might be advanced on the basis of Freudian psychology) that human de-

---

[8] It should be observed that it is not contended that we always do judge in this fashion, but only that we *tend* to do so. Furthermore, I may call something "good" in spite of the fact that it does not fit in with my other ends, but I should call it "better" if it did fit in with those ends; and, if I could find something else which (considered in itself) gave me the same satisfaction and also fitted in with my other ends, I should prefer it.

[9] It is important to note that happiness is not to be confused with pleasure or even with a sum of pleasures. It is a state of fulfillment that requires giving up certain pleasures for its attainment. It has been defined as "satisfaction with one's existence as a whole—with the past and the future as well as with the immediate present."—Hastings Rashdall, *The Theory of Good and Evil* (2d. ed., 2 vols.; London: Oxford University Press, 1924), II, 57. McDougall declares that happiness "arises from the harmonious operation of all the sentiments of a well organized and unified personality, one in which the principal sentiments support one another in a succession of actions all of which tend towards the same or closely allied ends."—William McDougall, *An Introduction to Social Psychology* (2d ed., Boston: John W. Luce Company, 1926), p. 161. See also Erich Fromm, *Man for Himself—An Inquiry into the Psychology of Ethics* (New York: Rinehart & Company, 1947), pp. 172–197.

It may also be true, as Professor Stace argues, that happiness is more than a sum of satisfactions, that some satisfactions tend to promote happiness more than others. (See W. T. Stace, *The Concept of Morals* [New York: The Macmillan Company, 1937], Chap. 6.) In our terminology this means that some satisfactions are *ultimately* more satisfying than others that produce as much *immediate* satisfaction. In making value judgments we tend to take both factors into account.

sires are inherently so irreconcilable that reason is impotent to conform conduct to a pattern which will yield a maximum of satisfaction.[10] It is important to note that for the present we are not concerned to argue whether human beings, especially when they engage in group activity, are sufficiently rational to enable democratic governments to operate effectively. We shall deal with this problem in a subsequent chapter.[11] We are now seeking a basis for ethical appraisal. In doing so we observe that people do in fact work out more or less harmonious patterns of ends, although of course unresolved conflicts frequently remain. We note further that people make judgments as to the desirability of acting on a given impulse in terms of the presumed effect of such action on their pattern of ends. One man, feeling that he cannot afford a Buick, may yet buy one at the expense of other, less conspicuous, accoutrements because he feels it essential to the maintenance of the general way of life he has established as his norm that he should drive a car in the Buick price class. Another man, even though he could afford a Buick and might in certain ways enjoy owning one, might stick to a Ford because he felt it more in keeping with the general scale of values he had adopted. He realizes, perhaps, that he would feel uncomfortable for not contributing the difference to some charitable work, and for this reason denies what might have been his more immediate and apparently urgent desire. All we are concerned to maintain

[10] In part we might attempt to answer the pessimistic conclusions of Freud and of some of the social psychologists by pointing to the works of other and generally more recent psychologists. The trend today is toward the conclusion that there is a deeper rationality within the subconscious itself. See for example the work of the English psychiatrist, Dr. Ranyard West. He writes: ". . . the best life may be defined as one in which *each of the natural instincts of man is allowed to make the contribution required of it for his life to be one of happy association with his fellows.* It is in pursuit of this ideal that the social instinct of normal man urges him to associate himself with others in attaining a permanent security against the disruptive tendencies of his own aggressive instinct . . . . I hold it established that such security is the major instinctive aim and interest of normal man . . . ."—Ranyard West, *Conscience and Society: A Study of the Psychological Prerequisites of Law and Order* (New York: Emerson Books, Inc., 1945), p. 174.

[11] See below, Chap. XI.

here is that people do, at least sometimes, behave in this fashion and that it is at least partly out of such situations that the notion of "good" arises.[12]

It should be noted that the kind of rationality we have been discussing cannot be discredited by rational analysis. We have not been dealing with the alleged power of reason to apprehend a priori truth; and the question of the extent to which men obey the dictates of reason does not concern us here. We have been dealing with reason as the power of inference and deduction and with the practical reason. To ask why we should be rational in this sense is a foolish question, for in the very act of doing so we are using and depending upon reason. Our act is self-defeating. Rationality is inescapable; we cannot question it without doubting the very process by which we raise the question.

It may be argued that we are here playing on two different senses of "reason"; that in using the power of logic to question the "practical reason," the power of making valuations, we are not arguing in a circle. But this is a mistake, for the two are not independent but different aspects of the same thing. The power of abstract thought is that unique human faculty by virtue of which man is able to comprehend the idea of himself as an entity and to seek the greatest possible attainment of his ends as a whole, rather than the satisfaction of particular, momentary desires and impulses. Furthermore, as Professor Lewis points out, the practical reason is basic.[13] Consistency is the very essence of

---

[12] It will be observed that the explanation above leaves plenty of room for that element of conflict which is characteristic of judgments of "oughtness." I would like to play bridge this evening but I feel that I ought to work at my book because my reason tells me that in the long run that will satisfy more permanent desires. Even if some element of my subconscious wells up within me and leads me to select what we have presumed to be my lesser good and to rationalize my conduct in terms of my need for recreation, I may regret the decision tomorrow and declare that I ought to have resisted the temptation, or that it would have been a good thing if I had done so.

For further consideration of why we "ought" to seek what is judged "good," see below, pp. 45–46.

[13] Clarence Irving Lewis, *An Analysis of Knowledge and Valuation* (La Salle, Ill.: The Open Court Publishing Company, 1946), pp. 480–482.

reason, "and consistency is, at bottom, nothing more than the adherence throughout to what we have accepted; or to put it in the opposite manner, the non-acceptance now of what we shall later be unwilling to adhere to." [14] The characteristic of man by which he judges now that he will be more content in the long run to forgo the chocolate before dinner and abides by that judgment is the very essence of reason. This *is* the categorical imperative. To quote Professor Lewis again, ". . . it requires no reason; being itself the expression of that which is the root of all reason; that in the absence of which there could be no reason of any sort or for anything." [15] In short, the practical reason is as much bound by the principle of rational consistency as is any other aspect of reason.

We may anticipate another objection at this point. Why, it may be asked, should we seek, by the aid of our practical reason and in pursuance of its rules, to maximize our satisfactions? In other words, why pursue our ends? Perhaps other ends are better? Or, to put the same thing in another way, perhaps we "ought" to pursue other ends? Of course if this means merely that a set of ends different from those we have adopted would give us fuller satisfaction, the objection does not touch us. If the situation is as supposed, then we have been acting irrationally and ought to mend our ways. But if it is asserted that something more than this is intended, the principal weakness of the position is the difficulty of explaining what is meant, and the principal embarrassment in criticizing it is in discovering what we should be attacking. Desires, objects of will, reason—these things are known to us by direct experience of them. Our use of such terms as "good," "better," "best," "ought," and "justice" can be explained in terms of those data of experience, in the fashion roughly outlined in the preceding pages. It would appear that the burden of proof rests on anyone who suggests a different explanation.

In fact, the only other approach is to assert that things can be known intuitively, or by direct ("rational") apprehension of

[14] *Ibid.*, p. 480.
[15] *Ibid.*, p. 481.

truth, to be good; or, alternatively, to assert that what we ought to do (rights and duties) can be similarly known. It is inherent in the nature of such claims that they can be neither proved nor disproved. If other explanations of experience do justice to the moral consciousness, there would appear (in accordance with the scientific principle of the simplest hypothesis) to be no reason for making the assumption.[16]

THE PROBLEM OF CONFLICTS BETWEEN SELF AND OTHERS. So far we have been approaching the problem of value judgments from the point of view of the individual seeking the fullest possible attainment of a system of ends. He will, of course, be forced to take into account the ends of others, for at least two reasons: first because he will need to enlist their cooperation and avoid their opposition in order to attain his own goals; and, second, because almost certainly the happiness of others (others in general and also certain individuals in particular) will find a place among his own ends. But what of the case where his own system of ends comes into direct conflict with some other system of ends? He must choose between ignoring the demands of others as far as he can and modifying his own demands in their favor. The ethical egoist sees no reason for pursuing the latter course.

With reference to the position of the egoist, we may first of all remark that there may prove to be less conflict between the

---

[16] It should be emphasized that the proponents of the view referred to in the paragraph above would be far from denying that satisfaction is normally "good." They would, however, deny that it is the sole source of value. A brief but penetrating criticism of the views of the leading exponent of the theory of intrinsic value, G. E. Moore, is to be found in Appendix I of Lamont, *op. cit.* It may also be observed that, far from representing the attack upon reason, the critic we have just been discussing is a representative of rationalism at its height. He is a believer in self-evident truth. Incidentally, it is more than likely that a catalogue of his self-evident truths would look very liberal democratic indeed. Cf. A. C. Ewing, *The Individual, the State, and World Government* (New York: The Macmillan Company, 1947), esp. Chap. 2; also the same author's *The Definition of Good* (New York: The Macmillan Company, 1947). Ewing's whole system rests on certain obligations whose validity is intuitively perceived. From these obligations are derived prima-facie rights; and his list of prima-facie rights might well form the bill of rights of any democratic constitution.

good of any individual and that of society than is generally supposed. Insofar as the conditions of my fullest satisfaction are consilient with the conditions for the satisfaction of others, even the egoist will find himself supporting the social ideal. We shall argue in Chapter V that this will be true to a very remarkable degree. Furthermore, as was suggested previously, there may be ultimate conflicts of interest on certain matters and yet unity of the interests of all in support of a democratic society.

Within the area of real conflict of interests, however, the proposition that individuals as subjects-of-ends, apart from relevant differences,[17] should count equally (the principle of equality of consideration), and that I am under obligation to recognize this equality as between you and me, seems to be part of the universal (at least as among civilized peoples) content of the moral consciousness. Nor does it appear to be denied by any philosophers who have given reasoned consideration to the subject, although their methods of explaining or justifying this imperative are numerous and various.[18]

We may note further that the acknowledgment of some rightful claim of others upon me is implicit in the very concept of obligation with which we raise the question: "What form of government and of social life ought we to seek to bring about?" The position of the egoist is in direct opposition to the very idea of a moral order and to common standards of right and good. It would reduce the common presuppositions of much of our discourse to nonsense.[19]

Although it is implied in what has just been said, I should

[17] For a discussion of what constitutes a relevant difference, see below, pp. 82–86.

[18] This is not a treatise on moral philosophy, so it is not incumbent upon us to solve the problem of justifying the principle. We are concerned, among other things, with appraising the validity of liberal-democratic ideals. Insofar as they rest on concepts of "good" about which there is a wide difference of opinion, we must examine these differences and attempt to resolve them; but where they rest upon principles that have gained such universal acceptance as that of equality of consideration we may rest content.

[19] See Frank Chapman Sharp, *Ethics* (New York: Appleton-Century-Crofts, Inc., 1928), Chaps. 7, 8.

point out that the egoistic position is not one that can be used to support the rule of some over others; it is useful only as an argument for each to rule over all others. It is no more destructive of democratic ideals than of any other ideals.[20]

SUMMARY. We may conclude that that form of social organization is best which gives fullest and most enduring satisfaction to all persons within its jurisdiction, subject to the principle of equality of consideration. The principle of liberty, which derives primarily from the value of satisfaction, will be further elucidated in Chapter IV, while the problem of interpreting and applying the equality principle, as far as is necessary for our purposes, will be dealt with in Chapter V.

2. *Consideration of Opposing Theories*

If the position just set forth and defended is sound, that fact itself is sufficient answer to rival views. Nevertheless, inasmuch as no specific reference has been made here to some of the ideas which were pointed to in Chapter II as being critical of liberal democracy or as having critical implications for it, they should be considered at this point.

THEORY OF THE GROUP AS END-IN-ITSELF. We may begin with the fascist. He challenges our basic assumption that the individual is the center of value and that it is to him that we must make our appeal. In this mood, the fascist contends that to talk about the good in terms of the individual or even of the sum of in-

---

[20] Readers interested in the problem presented by the egoist, and more generally in the relationship of reason to moral imperatives such as the principle of equality of consideration, will find it profitable to consult Lamont, *op. cit.*, especially Chap. 7. Briefly, his argument is to this effect: Reason may be defined as "the faculty of apprehending universal laws and of determining oneself to act in accordance with them."—*Ibid.*, p. 186. When I check my desire to eat a chocolate before dinner because reason tells me that it will spoil my appetite, it is reason, as defined above, that has determined my action. It is no more difficult to understand how reason can determine one to action than to see how desire can do the same. In the example given, reason was acting in a way that was instrumental to my ends; but in the case where I am confronted with a conflict with another person, reason prescribes the rule, "that each is to regard as appropriate to all what he regards as appropriate to himself."—*Ibid.*, p. 189.

dividuals misses the point. Rather, such a person will say, the state (or perhaps the race) must be considered as an end-in-itself, as the absolute to which the individual must, if necessary, be sacrificed.[21] What are we to say to such a doctrine? In the first place, if what is meant is that the state is literally a person, a human organism, as Mussolini himself declared,[22] we need do little but enter a categorical denial, challenge the opposition to offer one shred of evidence for such a position, and point out that the mere fact that the state possesses *some* characteristics of an organism is not enough to make it one. A state comes into being, it grows; after it passes through a period of growth and vigor, it may lose vitality and eventually cease to exist; and so on. But that this is a mere analogy is obvious. A moment's reflection will also serve to indicate that the analogy breaks down at an early point. Where is the state that can see and feel and think? Where is the self-conscious entity that corresponds to the very heart and soul of human personality? Until this has been identified we have at most the husk without the kernel.

So obvious is this that even the most fanatical adherents of the doctrine cannot maintain it consistently. Hitler himself, in belittling the creative powers of the masses, opposed to them not the race, as might be expected, but the individual.[23] Furthermore, in a curiously revealing passage, Hitler based his apotheosization of race itself on the individual, declaring that what he called the folkish view of life "not only recognizes the value of the race, but by this also the importance of the person and therefore makes the individual the pillar of its entire edifice." [24] What it boils down to is this: not even under the spell of Hitlerian mysticism could people be brought to think the ultimate end of human existence has nothing to do with human be-

[21] Benito Mussolini, "The Political and Social Doctrine of Fascism," trans. Jane Soames, *Political Quarterly*, IV (July–Sept., 1933), 352.

[22] ". . . the Fascist State is itself conscious, and has itself a will and a personality."—*Ibid.*

[23] See Adolf Hitler, *Mein Kampf* (Boston: Houghton Mifflin Company, 1939), p. 664, where he declares: "Not the masses invent and not the majority organizes or thinks, but all in all only the individual, the person."

[24] *Ibid.*, p. 668.

ings! That some should be sacrificed for others is an understandable concept. That all should be sacrificed for a nonhuman, abstract entity transcends the first principles from which all our reasoning about human ends of necessity begins. And yet it is only such a proposition which demands the concept of the absolute state or the absolute race for its support. This is not to say that liberalism is opposed to self-sacrifice. On the contrary, it is entirely compatible with liberal principles to argue that under certain circumstances individuals should sacrifice their individual good for that of the whole, meaning by that the whole body of individuals. This remains true when we include in the whole individuals as yet unborn. To believe that the living have obligations to future generations requires no belief in the sacrifice of human values for something that is less than human.

To pursue this last point a little further, it may well be that the individual cannot attain his own greatest good unless in fact he loses sight of his own "selfish" interests and commits himself to some ideal goal—even one for which he is willing to risk his life. The unsatisfactoriness of the life of an individual whose prime concern is for his own personal well-being, and the fulfilling effect of broadened interests, are facts so generally observed as to need no proving. What is maintained here is that such broadened interests must be human interests. Commitment to humanity, or to a humane God, yes. But there is no evidence in support of the value of commitment to any other abstract entity. The fact that the individual cannot secure for himself the fullest satisfaction or happiness without adopting a goal that takes him beyond himself cannot be a basis for concluding that ultimate value lies outside and is independent of individuals. No logical basis for reaching such a conclusion has been offered.

ETHICAL NIHILISM. With typical inconsistency, the fascist is likely to abandon the position of ethical absolutist, which we have just considered, and assume the pose of ethical nihilism. Making value completely an individual and unstable affair, he leaves no basis for discussion of values. It becomes meaningless to say that a certain form of government or way of life is better than another.

Such a view appears to be entertained by the American fascist Lawrence Dennis, when he declares: "The fascist scheme of things is an expression of human will which creates its own truths and values from day to day to suit its changing purposes." [25] If this is to be taken literally, it is hardly an ethical theory at all but a mere assertion of moral and intellectual irresponsibility. It is doubtful whether anyone consistently maintains such a position. In fact, it amounts to a denial of the claim for consistency, which, as we have shown, is self-defeating.

NIETZSCHE. Because of its influence on Fascism special mention should be made of the moral philosophy of Nietzsche.[26] In part his position appears to have been substantially that just dealt with. Resting his case more on vehement assertion than on reasoned argument, he leaves his critic little to attack. It should be pointed out, however, that in insisting upon the primacy of the claims of will (especially the will-to-power) over reason, he is simply ignoring the facts of human psychology, as described above. The will is not naturally a single, insistent, unitary demand; it is created by the operation of reason (reflection, calculation, evaluation) on our manifold demands, present and anticipated. Reason cannot be opposed to will: it is part of it. Moreover, in maintaining that the content of human will can be reduced to the will-to-power, he is exaggerating a part into the whole.[27]

---

[25] Lawrence Dennis, *The Coming American Fascism* (New York: Harper & Brothers, 1936), p. 105. It is typical of the intellectual irresponsibility of fascists that their position generally combines an attack on all rational values with an assertion of the absolute value of the state, or a particular nation or race.

[26] For a good brief criticism of Nietzschean ethics which I have found helpful, see W. T. Stace, *The Destiny of Western Man* (New York: Harcourt, Brace and Company, 1942), Chap. 12.

[27] For a (democratic) political philosophy based on the idea of the will-to-power (but not power for its own sake) as basic, see William Ernest Hocking, *Man and the State* (New Haven: Yale University Press, 1926). Apart from the doctrine of the primacy of the will-to-power, and apart from mere romantic and unsupported glorification of force for its own sake, Nietzsche attacked the democratic ideal of equality. This portion of his theory will be criticized in the chapter on equality (below, pp. 93–94).

ETHICAL POSITIVISM. A philosophically more sophisticated position than that of either Nietzsche or the fascists is that of the ethical positivists.[28] They deny that ethical judgments have any cognitive meaning whatever. They are not propositions; they are merely exclamations. To quote one of the clearest and most extreme supporters of this view, if I say " 'Stealing money is wrong,' I produce a sentence which has no factual meaning—that is, expresses no proposition which can be either true or false. It is as if I had written 'Stealing money!!' " [29] Such a view may seem surely to be incompatible with liberal-democratic ideals. As Professor Perry has said, "The canker at the heart of modern liberalism is the suspicion that its hallowed morality is only one prejudice among others." [30] But on closer inspection it does not appear that the positivistic position really undermines democratic ideals at all. First, positivism, like the other positions we have been considering, does nothing to democratic ideals that it does not do equally to all ideals. It gives no basis for preferring anything else to liberal democracy. In fact, it almost reduces itself to ethical nihilism. Positivists would deprive much of our discourse of any ("cognitive" or "factual") meaning. They are to be distinguished from ethical nihilists, if at all, by their assertion that ethical terms carry an "emotive" meaning. Such terms are exclamatory, generally indicative of approval or disapproval, and persuasive.[31] For our purposes it is sufficient to comment on

[28] See above, p. 30. It has been suggested that a more accurate appellation for the philosophers in question would be "interjectionists."

[29] Alfred J. Ayer, *Language, Truth and Logic* (New York: Oxford University Press, 1936), pp. 158–159. See Chap. 6 generally.

[30] Ralph Barton Perry, *Shall Not Perish from the Earth*, (New York: The Vanguard Press, 1940), p. 21. And see John H. Hallowell, *The Decline of Liberalism as an Ideology* (Berkeley and Los Angeles: University of California Press, 1943), pp. 10 ff. It may be remarked parenthetically that I do not believe that the positivists have substantiated their position against the general conviction that when we make value judgments we are stating propositions. It would appear that the positivists have laid too much emphasis upon the admittedly large area of disagreement in ethical matters, overlooking the significance to be attributed to the fact that there is a surprisingly large area of agreement. But this is not the place to pursue this argument.

[31] See Charles L. Stevenson, *Ethics and Language* (New Haven: Yale University Press, 1944), esp. Chap. 3.

this position as follows. Insofar as positivists seek to avoid the criticisms made against nihilism by making an attitude of approval a part of the meaning of ethical judgments, they put themselves in the category of the personal subjectivists, whom we shall consider in a moment. Otherwise it is not clear that they show any substantial distinction. Furthermore, we shall be concerned in the succeeding chapters to argue that the democratic way of life in fact maximizes the realization of individual ends within the framework imposed by the rule of reason (which is to say by part of that which is the nature of man). If we succeed in this attempt, and if the positive argument advanced in the first part of this chapter is accepted, it would follow that normal people who are fully aware of what is involved would make the judgment "Democracy is good." In our view, this would express the inescapable imperative of the practical reason.[32] In the positivist, or interjectionist view, it would be all that could be said on the subject, and all that would need to be said.[33]

---

[32] See above, pp 44–45. As Professor Lewis says, to quote him once more: "To act, to live, in human terms, is necessarily to be subject to imperatives; to recognize norms. Because to be subject to an imperative means simply the finding of a constraint of action in some concern for that which is not immediate; is not a present enjoyment or a present suffering. To repudiate normative significances and imperatives in general, would be to dissolve away all seriousness of action and intent, leaving only an undirected floating down the stream of time; and as a consequence to dissolve all significance of thought and discourse into universal blah. Those who would be serious and circumspect and cogent in what they think, and yet tell us that there are no valid norms or binding imperatives, are hopelessly confused, and inconsistent with their own attitude of assertion."—Lewis, *op. cit.*, p. 481.

[33] It must be kept clearly in mind that the ethical positivist does not say, "There is an objective 'good' but we cannot prove what it is." What he does say is that the statement "Democracy is good" is meaningless because the whole question at issue is meaningless. Even if this were true it would by no means follow that the statement in the text, viz., ". . . normal people who are fully aware of what is involved would make the judgment 'Democracy is good,'" would be meaningless. On the contrary, it could be both meaningful and very important.

Anyone who is interested in analysis of the position of the ethical positivists would find it useful to consult John Dewey, "Theory of Valuation," in *International Encyclopedia of Unified Science* (Chicago: The University of Chicago Press, 1939), Vol. II, No. 4, esp. Sec. II, "Value-

WESTERMARCK. Finally, we must consider the position of the personal subjectivist, as typified by Westermarck.[34] He concludes that moral judgments are simply judgments of personal approval (emotionally conditioned) and that in fact they lack "that universality which is characteristic of truth." [35] The arguments advanced above against the egoist are equally applicable to the personal subjectivist except insofar as he admits the claims of others to the extent that they find support in my emotion of approval. That admission greatly narrows the gulf between him and the position herein defended. There may be important differences among emotions of approval and yet there may be unanimity on the objective of a society which furnishes the conditions for a maximum of satisfaction. Other things being equal, it is hard to imagine that normal human beings would not prefer, and experience emotions of approval toward, a society in which human needs and desires were fulfilled in satisfying harmony to one where this was not the case. In other words, whatever may be the effect of Westermarck's theory on ethics generally, it does not seem to be inconsistent with the standard of evaluation which has been developed in this chapter.

Although the variety of ethical theories is almost without limit, it is believed that we have now canvassed the principal sources of attack upon the standard which we have advanced for evaluating forms of society and of government.[36]

Expression as Ejaculatory." A counterargument to Dewey appears in Stevenson, *op. cit.*, pp. 253–264.

[34] See the brief treatment of Westermarck's ideas above, pp. 29–30.

[35] Edward Westermarck, *Ethical Relativity* (New York: Harcourt, Brace and Company, 1932), p. 218.

[36] Hedonists fit easily within the present framework. They are concerned to assert something about the nature of man's ends (that they all boil down to the pursuit of pleasure). This is not a matter we are called upon either to affirm or to deny. The various kinds of self-realizationists are also talking about the nature of human ends and asserting that they are ultimately harmonious; and this is even more obviously true of those who define the good in terms of some sort of harmony. Again there is no conflict with the position herein defended. The same is true of those, like R. B. Perry, who define the good in terms of the objects of human desire or interest. (See Ralph Barton Perry, *General Theory of Value* [New York: Longmans, Green and Co., 1926], pp. 652–687; also his *Shall Not Perish*

3. Concluding Remarks

It is well to observe that, although the general formula for evaluating social systems herein defended is not absolutistic or dependent upon a belief in the supernatural, it is not incompatible with some such belief. Nor does it give any support to those relativists who sometimes assert that anyone who believes in absolute good and bad, right and wrong, necessarily seeks to impose his ideas on others, and that such a person will in the long run by unwilling to accept majority rule and to allow that measure of liberty which democratic ideals involve.[37] Whether or not there is a tendency for absolutists to behave in this fashion we need not inquire, for certainly there is no logical reason why they should. It is entirely possible for one to believe that the good is objective, that it is absolute, and that it is founded upon the will of God; and at the same time to believe that human beings are fallible, that the final truth is given to no one, and that that truth can be most nearly approached by giving the freest possible play to the human reason. One who is anxious that the good of a particular class must prevail must indeed be chary about giving liberty and political power to members of

---

from the Earth, pp. 20–26; and *Puritanism and Democracy* [New York: The Vanguard Press, 1934], pp. 48–50. For a fuller discussion of these theories as they apply to the theory of democracy, see J. Roland Pennock, "Reason, Value Theory, and the Theory of Democracy," *American Political Science Review*, XXXVIII [Oct., 1944], 855–875.)

Finally, we may mention the Ideal Utilitarians, typified by Hastings Rashdall. (See Rashdall, *op. cit.*) This theory combines a utilitarian definition of good in terms of a maximization of welfare achieved by the practical reason with an assertion that the constituents of that welfare—proper human ends, in other words—are known intuitively. This part of the theory is, for our purposes, identical with that of G. E. Moore and others who insist on the "intrinsic" nature of goodness. We have dealt with this already. We might add, however, that Ideal Utilitarians, in common with other Utilitarians, have accepted the principle of equality of consideration, and the same is true of G. E. Moore and other representatives of the absolutist school.

[37] See, for example, Hans Kelsen, *Vom Wesen und Wert der Demokratie* (Tübingen: J. C. B. Mohr, 1929), Chap. 10; and by the same author, "Absolutism and Relativism in Politics," *American Political Science Review*, XLII (Oct., 1948), 906–914.

other classes; but one who is committed to searching for the will of God will do well to allow the maximum of freedom to all His human instruments; and the seeker after absolute truth may well give fullest possible scope to human reason in both thought and action.

On the other hand, there are those in increasing numbers today who assert that theories which abandon a transcendental basis for democracy leave it without any firm foundation, that all relativism is destructive of the foundations of liberalism, and that democracy must be founded on faith in the inherent equality of individuals—a faith which is not susceptible to empirical proof, nor, apparently even to demonstrated plausibility.[38] Surely to assert the validity of the Christian ethics, for example, should be the end point of ethical reasoning rather than its beginning. To start with the assumption that human satisfaction is good, for instance, is hardly less plausible than to posit a belief in human equality at the outset; and to attempt to show reasons why the recognition of some sort of equality of rights is a good thing cannot be thought to weaken the case for democracy. The truth of the matter is that the proponents of "faith" as a basis for democracy are performing a poor service for their cause in being critical of those who seek to find plausible grounds for such faith. To move from that of which we have direct experience (human happiness and satisfaction) to realms which are at best more remote from our immediate perceptions is a legitimate path for rational analysis; but to begin with such a shift and to demand that the former should be tested by the latter would be to attempt to ground reason on faith rather than to support faith by rational considerations. Such a procedure flies in the face of the assumption which necessarily underlies all attempts at proof and all rational discourse—the assumption that reason is the avenue to truth.

Those who argue in the fashion just outlined may return to

---

[38] See, for example, Hallowell, *The Decline of Liberalism as an Ideology*, pp. 10 ff. and 108 ff.; and, by the same author, "The Decline of Liberalism," *Ethics*, LII (Apr., 1942), 342 and n. 23.

the fray on the pragmatic level, and contend that ideals are more effective in molding human conduct if they are believed to be "transcendental facts," having their basis outside the human realm. Whether or not this is true, it must be remembered that the present discussion is directed at those who wish to know the *grounds* for democratic faith—especially at those who are questioning those grounds. For such persons to appeal once more to faith would simply beg the question.

CHAPTER IV

THE IDEAL OF
SOCIAL DEMOCRACY:
I. LIBERTY

The problem of this and the succeeding chapter is to appraise the system of values that political democracy is supposed to maintain. That is, before considering democracy as a form of government we shall inquire whether democracy in the social realm is the best way of life.[1] If it is, the democrat is justified in the conviction that he is striving for a valid ideal of social justice, for the best as well as the expedient. In this respect he need feel at no disadvantage as compared, for example, with the communist. The one or the other may be correct in depicting the ideal or in determining how best to attain it, but they are equally concerned with the good life; the democrat has not resigned himself in advance to being satisfied with the lesser evil.

1. Definition of Liberty

Liberty will be the first of the elements of the liberal-democratic way of life to be examined. Exactly how to define this concept has long been a source of perplexity. Probably a more slippery term is not to be found in the realm of political philosophy. We must be brief and somewhat dogmatic in stating the sense in which the term will be used in this volume.[2] The es-

[1] Cf. Aristotle: "He who would duly enquire about the best form of a state ought first to determine which is the most eligible life; while this remains uncertain the best form of the state must also be uncertain."—
Aristotle's Politics, trans. Benjamin Jowett (Oxford: Clarendon Press, 1923), Bk. VII, c. 1, § 1.

[2] For extended treatments of the subject, see Dorothy Fosdick, *What Is Liberty?—A Study in Political Theory* (New York: Harper & Brothers, 1939); Ruth Nanda Anshen (ed.), *Freedom—Its Meaning* (New York: Harcourt, Brace and Company, 1940); Horace M. Kallen (ed.), *Freedom*

sence of democratic liberty is the opportunity for deliberate individual self-direction in the formation and accomplishment of one's purposes. The free act must be an act of uncoerced will.[3] But to be free in the fullest sense it must also be an act of will and not of mere impulse. It must have reference to the settled purposes (hence the use of the word "deliberate," above) of the doer rather than to a passing whim. Erich Fromm states the ideal well when he declares that "freedom consists in the spontaneous activity of the total integrated personality."[4] It needs to be added that the individual who is enabled to accomplish his purposes is to that extent freer than one who is not. Furthermore, an individual may be free even when subject to restrictions (and compulsions), if those restrictions facilitate the achievement of his purposes, and provided that he willingly accepts these restrictions, in principle.

This definition, or description, of freedom requires further explanation in various particulars. A moment's reflection will serve to show that life in society imposes on us certain restraints which in fact increases our powers of self-direction. For instance, a young man may decide that he can most completely fulfill his purpose in life by obtaining a college education. In making this choice, he will realize that certain restrictions and compulsions are implied. He accepts them in principle. Doubtless there will be many occasions when they seem to interfere with the student's "freedom." (Most of us would like to have our cake and eat it too.) But if the regulations are essential to the achievement of his purposes and if the student willingly continues the pursuit of his degree it cannot be said that his freedom is being curtailed. Indeed, the rules which prevent him from neglecting his studies

---

in the Modern World (New York: Coward-McCann, Inc., 1928); and Bronislaw Malinowski, *Freedom and Civilization* (New York: Roy Publishers, 1944).

[3] This means that it must not be in response to a motive (such as fear) by which one would not choose to be governed. See J. P. Plamenatz, *Consent, Freedom, and Political Obligation* (London: Oxford University Press, 1938), Chap. 5.

[4] Erich Fromm, *Escape from Freedom* (New York: Rinehart & Company, 1941), p. 258.

may properly be said to increase his true freedom.[5] This example illustrates both the point about restrictions being compatible with freedom and the distinction between whims or relatively fleeting desires and settled purposes, and shows the relationship between the two; for restrictions may promote liberty precisely by preventing the former from interfering with the latter. The two provisos implied above are important: the restrictions must be essential to the accomplishment of the purpose, and they must be willingly accepted in general even though they are felt as limitations on liberty in moments of rebellion.

Much more than this is implied in our definition. An individual who through education is able to exercise his powers more effectively than he otherwise could is thereby given greater true freedom. And one who, by learning to observe the rules of good manners, is better able to secure the cooperation of others in the accomplishment of his purposes has also enlarged his freedom. Further, if he has freely adopted purposes which are consonant with those of others about him and which therefore he can secure their aid in attaining, once more his liberty has been expanded. Similarly, one who has not the material means with which to gratify his desires is, other things being equal, less free than one who has.[6] But we must remember that the means to

[5] Ranyard West gives a psychoanalytical twist to this argument by suggesting that law represents a social instinctual desire to check our own instinctual aggressiveness.—Ranyard West, *Conscience and Society* (New York: Emerson Books, Inc., 1945), pp. 165 ff. However, West does not argue that law makes us free, although it does, as he says, "externally guide and internally oblige us towards a just proportioning of our instinctual satisfactions"—*Ibid.*, p. 172. It would be extending the definition of liberty further than we have gone, and probably further than is desirable, to make it include a case where those who are restrained are not aware of the fact that the restraint is aiding them in the accomplishment of their purposes.

[6] Logically, further extensions of the concept are possible. For instance, it might be said that the more able person was freer than one who had been less favored at birth. But I shall draw the line, somewhat arbitrarily, at this point, as going beyond general usage. It could have been drawn at an earlier point. The original meaning of absence of restraint (see below, n. 8) is surrounded by extensions of meaning in a series of concentric circles. Usage varies as to how many of these are to be incorporated in the present meaning of the word. A restriction one willingly accepts as a means

fulfill one's purposes may not be substituted for freedom in forming purposes. Furthermore, one who becomes concerned chiefly
with material things as sources of comfort rather than as means
to the full development of his powers may find that he has lost
that "total, integrated personality" whose spontaneous exercise
was the original goal of freedom. Hungry men cannot be fully
free; but they may be far freer than well-fed men who lack
other, more vital elements of freedom. President Wriston of
Brown University put this point well in the following words:

If a balanced diet is the indispensable preamble to liberty, the Pilgrims
must have been wrong after all, for they fled from plenty to scarcity in
order to secure freedom. Sentimental materialism makes mockery of all
the heroes whose lives have shown the falsity of its assumption. It
neglects utterly the contemporary heroism of the Chinese who would
rather abandon home and trek to Western China, enduring terrible
hardships, than be fed and submissive in Japan's shoddy "co-prosperity
sphere." [7]

One who uses this definition of liberty cannot insist too
much, however, that it must not be confused with the view that
freedom consists in doing what is right or rational, regardless of
the amount of constraint. The central core remains self-

---

to the accomplishment of his purpose is perhaps in an inner circle, most
easily assimilated to the original meaning. This is particularly so if the
function of the restriction is simply to prevent one of a person's impulses
from directly interfering with other desires. It may be said to be one stage
further removed if, like many rules of communal living, its function is to
promote cooperation. Some people would decline to go beyond this point,
refusing to acknowledge that such matters as wealth and income enter into
the picture. Obviously, the person who is impoverished is less able to accomplish his purposes, other things being equal, than one who is reasonably
well off; but to speak of this as liberty, it may be said, involves serious
danger of confusion. Yet we do persistently resort to saying that a person
cannot be *really* free when he lacks the means to exercise his powers. The
ease with which poverty may, under certain conditions, lead into peonage
certainly shows that there is substance in this usage. So long as we insist
that the possession of a sufficient income is not itself freedom, but only
one aspect of it we are on safe ground. The next circle, before which we
draw the line, is the possession or lack of natural abilities. Training and
education we accept, along with material well-being—all things somewhat
subject to human control; natural endowment, no.

[7] Henry Wriston, *Challenge to Freedom* (New York: Harper & Brothers,
1943), pp. 146–147.

determination. Without that there is no liberty. As Guido de Ruggiero insists (although he is one of those who refuses to define liberty as mere absence of restraint), "that which is free is simply that which is one's own, the fruit of one's own activity or the object of one's own choice, in contradistinction to that which one owes to the authority of dogma or the passivity of tradition." [8] Its fruition can be described only in terms of an integrated per-

---

[8] Guido de Ruggiero, *The History of European Liberalism,* trans. C. G. Collingwood (London: Oxford University Press, 1927), p. 23.

So-called "realistic" political theorists have generally insisted upon defining liberty as nothing but the absence of restraint, or of man-made restraint, upon one's ability to do as one likes. This definition has the advantage of being more clear-cut than the one adopted in the text. It might also be contended that it corresponds more nearly to what was meant by the great leaders of political liberalism and that therefore a consideration of the validity of this ideal of liberal democracy should define it as it was defined by them. I have nevertheless chosen the course followed in the text, for three reasons. In the first place, it is doubtful whether it can properly be said that the classical liberals did define liberty strictly in the "realistic" sense. They were fighting against restrictions, so this was naturally their emphasis. The positive side of freedom had to wait for the abolition of restraints, especially governmental restraints. But Mill, for instance, declared that "that man seems to me to act with freedom who yields to the impulse of the *highest motive* which demands his obedience, or which presents itself to his consciousness, at the moment of determination."—John Stuart Mill, *On Social Freedom* (New York: Columbia University Press, 1941), p. 56.

Furthermore, all the liberals were insistent upon the importance of education to enable men to attain that enlargement of their capacities which was their ideal. This leads to the second point: there is no reason why liberal democracy today cannot expand, or otherwise modify, the concept of freedom held by its founders. This is especially true when the expansion is simply, as in this case, by way of bringing within the concept of liberty elements of well-being that earlier liberals had recognized as desirable even when they did not include them under the heading "liberty." De Ruggiero's comment is again pertinent. He declares: "The absence of external compulsion is the merely outward aspect of . . . freedom; its inner value lies in the concentrated strength of the personality which dominates and controls all the factors and elements of its spiritual life."— De Ruggiero, *op. cit.,* p. 351. This notion of the free individual corresponds perfectly with the point of view of the early (as well as of modern) liberals. Third, the definition adopted here seems to correspond more nearly to general usage, and so to be less likely to lead to misunderstanding, than the "realistic" definition. This is indicated by the frequent contrast in general speech and writing between liberty as mere absence of restraint upon impulse and the *real* liberty that considers the nature of the impulse and its relation to the whole self as well as the restraint.

sonality in an integrated society; but its elements are the traditional items of freedom of expression; freedom of worship; freedom to choose a mate and to choose one's occupation and the place where we live and work; freedom to determine how we shall spend the money we earn, what clothes we shall wear, what books we shall read and what motion pictures we shall see; freedom from unlawful injury; and freedom from government by those over whom we have no control.

2. *Evaluation of Liberty*

Turning from definition to evaluation, we must now inquire what values are inherent in liberty. Why is it good? The short answer is that, as we have defined liberty, it is almost identical with one of the major elements of good as we defined that term in the preceding chapter. Things are good as they contribute to the attainment of our ends. But our ends must be selected and modified in such a way as to fit together in a consistent pattern. This each person must do for himself. Only he can know when this personal harmony has been attained. He must be left free to experiment and to judge.

Before this important point can be taken as proved, however, it will have to be elaborated and certain objections to it answered. Although the distinction is artificial, it will be useful for purposes of analysis to consider the question first from the point of view of the individual and then from that of society. Another way to express it would be to say that we shall first examine the values realized by the individual directly, and then those realized indirectly, through society.

DIRECT VALUES. First of all, then, liberty is good because we like it; because in exercising initiative, in spontaneous action, in making choices and acting upon them we get an incomparable feeling of positive satisfaction, of fulfillment of mission and of being alive and performing the distinctive function of human beings. It is true that not all our free acts are accompanied by such feelings. Too often we do not appreciate our freedom until we have lost it. This is one of the great tragedies of life. The free man takes his freedom for granted, as he does the air he breathes. But this does not detract from the value of the freedom any more than it does from that of the air. Each will be held cheaply only so long as it is in plentiful supply. Who does not feel frustration and resentment when his liberty is curtailed? The enjoyment of liberty is to be measured as much by the pain caused by its restriction as by the pleasure derived from the power to act freely. Happy slaves no doubt there have been; but the history of slavery attests to the fact that in general slaves have chafed at their restrictions and sought freedom until they obtained it. Nor do the facts support the contention that they knew not what they were doing, for from the constant stream of those who obtained their freedom history records hardly a case of one who, having tried both ways of life, sought to return to the former.[9]

We value freedom, however, for more than the immediate satisfaction attending its exercise. We value it chiefly because it makes possible the development of our capacities, the selection of which of our potentialities we wish to realize most fully, and the attainment of the balance of activities which best suits us. Without it, the attainment of that happy and harmonious fulfillment which we all seek is not conceivable. To reach this goal, we need freedom because we can appraise our potentialities only if we are free to experiment; we need it because the evidence as to what is the most harmonious and so most satisfying balance of our conflicting desires is subjective, capable of being finally appraised by ourselves alone; we need it because the very making of the decisions concerning the organization of our lives is itself a vital element in a satisfying life.

This last point needs elaboration. In weighing the competing claims of rival interests, in deciding whether to work longer

---

[9] The case of a democracy voting away its freedom to a dictator is not in point, for there freedom is but one element of the situation being abandoned, and lack of freedom but one part of the new situation. People in crisis give up freedom out of desperation.

hours to increase our income or to work less and have more leisure, whether to spend our spare time at a motion picture, watch-
ing a television show, reading, or supporting some group activity
for social improvement, whether to string along with the leader of
our union or the head of our company whom we believe to be following a socially undesirable course or to speak out against him
at some personal risk—in making decisions such as these we are
exercising that faculty of practical reason which more than anything else distinguishes us from beasts and marks us as men. As
Mill says, "He who chooses his plan for himself, employs all his
faculties. He must use observation to see, reasoning and judgment to foresee, activity to gather materials for decision, discrimination to decide, and when he has decided, firmness and self-
control to hold to his deliberate decision." [10]

Among the examples of personal decisions referred to in the
preceding paragraph, the last involved an element which goes
beyond the point there at issue. The man who decides to support a moral principle even at some cost in terms of his own immediate interest is doing more than developing his capacities for
observing, thinking, and reaching a judgment. He is exercising
his moral responsibility. In other words, liberty is valuable not
just because of the absence of frustration and of the positive sense
of spontaneity it entails, nor just because of the development of
the capacities generally which it makes possible, but especially
because of its contribution to the development of that particular
capacity whose nature it is to produce the maximum of harmonious satisfaction—the capacity of moral responsibility. The latter
concept involves a combination of a sense of obligation and the
faculty of self-control. Only when freedom is accompanied by
this appreciation of the total consequences of conduct and a compelling desire to produce the maximum happiness for others as
well as for ourselves do we get that harmonious satisfaction
which we have established as the end. But a maximum of individ-

[10] John Stuart Mill, "On Liberty," in *Utilitarianism, Liberty, and Representative Government* ("Everyman's Library"; New York: E. P. Dutton
& Co., 1910), p. 117.

ual freedom is a *sine qua non* for such an attainment, because a feeling of responsibility for society cannot develop where there is no choice, no freedom to decide whether or not to act for the benefit of society. If society takes this matter into its own hands, either by accepting the responsibility itself or by compelling the individual to act in a certain way, it effectively limits the development of individual moral responsibility.

The last statement requires both qualification and explanation. Freedom is essential to the development of responsibility, but so is discipline, within limits. This point is clearest in the case of children. There are, of course, great differences of opinion among educators as to the extent to which authority should be used to develop self-discipline. Few, however, would go so far as to confine the use of authority to cases where it is necessary for the well-being of others or to prevent children from doing physical injury to themselves. Even where the outright prohibition would be avoided, use would be made of all manner of social pressure to channel conduct along the lines that experience indicates are best. Gradually, in many cases, the child not only adopts these norms as his own but comes to understand the reasons for them and to appreciate their value. In this respect as in others, the line between immaturity and maturity is not a sharp one. Doubtless the existence of social pressure, through such mechanisms as approval and disapproval, helps to develop the sense of responsibility in adults. But it will be noted that we are speaking here of restraints that are short of prohibitions. This is another and important dimension of liberty to which we had not previously referred. Frequently, a pressure which exercises some restraint on freedom to do as one pleases and yet leaves a real opportunity for choice will be most effective in developing moral responsibility and in securing true freedom. In large part these social pressures, in a free society, will be pressures to live in accordance with rules that have been found generally useful, and useful particularly in contributing to the expansion of faculties and achievement of individual purposes—the latter because adherence to such rules is likely to facilitate that cooperation and

social intercourse without which the individual is well-nigh helpless.

There is, then, a very important distinction between those
limitations on conduct which are imposed by government and
those which are social but not political in origin.[11] The former
are likely to leave no freedom of choice (save the meretricious
freedom to choose between obeying and going to jail), while the
latter do. There is the further important point that social controls, insofar as they are controls exercised by groups and associations, leave open the opportunity of withdrawing from the
group in question. Quite apart from the matter of absolute prohibition, there is all the difference in the world between controls
imposed by a monopolistic authority and those imposed by voluntary groups in a situation where the individual is free to
choose his social alliances.

This brief discussion of the relative roles of liberty and co-
ercion in the development of moral responsibility sets the stage
for a consideration of one of the most powerful attacks upon the
whole position of those who give primacy to liberty as a means
to the individual's highest good. The critic who takes this position, be he fascist or other antiliberal, challenges liberty in the
name of discipline, rights in the name of duty, pleasure in the
name of work, and satisfaction in the name of sacrifice. More
specifically, he may assert that in fact people do not get the net
satisfaction from liberty which we have listed as part of its value.
Rather, he will contend, they do not want it badly enough to
bear the burden of responsibility it entails. This is the point made
by Dostoyevsky's Inquisitor in an oft-quoted passage:

I tell Thee [declared the Inquisitor] that man is tormented by no
greater anxiety than to find some one quickly to whom he can hand
over that gift of freedom with which the ill-fated creature is born. . . .
Too, too well they know the value of complete submission! And until
men know that, they will be unhappy.[12]

---

[11] This distinction was clearly recognized, for instance, by Mill. See his
essay, "On Liberty," *op. cit.,* p. 68.

[12] Fyodor Dostoyevsky, *The Brothers Karamazov,* trans. Constance
Garnett (New York: The Modern Library, 1929), pp. 302, 307.

Here, as so frequently, the critic of liberalism seeks to make capital of a half-truth. We may get satisfaction from temporary and voluntary submission to discipline in the knowledge that it is for a purpose we share. We may welcome authority if it offers us release from fear. And we may, of course, sacrifice the present enjoyment of liberty for a reward which we have reason to think will be forthcoming later if we accept authority today. Circumstances may convince people that they will have so much more security or prosperity under a regime of discipline that they will gladly give up their liberty. They may even come to condemn liberty itself because they have identified it with its exercise under circumstances where it was self-defeating. But these facts do not touch the fundamental desirability of liberty, *if it is practicable.* They are questions for consideration in connection with the practical operation of liberal institutions.[13] The fundamental fact is that normal human beings get satisfaction from being free to develop and realize their own purposes, in cooperation with others, and are unhappy when they are not able to do this. This is a matter of such common experience that it seems hardly possible to question it when the issue is thus clarified.[14] The man who craves to be told what to do and to be made to do it is either seeking an ultimate satisfaction for which he is willing to forgo a present pleasure, or seeking release from the frustration which

[13] See especially Chap. XII.

[14] It may be noted, however, that there is experimental evidence in support of it. Professor Kurt Lewin and co-workers carried out some very interesting experiments with children's play groups organized under autocratic, democratic, and laissez-faire leadership. In the democratic groups, the children decided in accordance with democratic procedures what projects they would undertake and how they would go about them. The leader gave suggestions but did not dictate. The leader of the laissez-faire group did no more than maintain a semblance of order, allowing the children to do much as they pleased. (Each leader took charge of each group, in rotation, so as to eliminate the factor of the leaders' personalities.) It developed that 19 out of 20 boys liked their democratic leader better than their autocratic leader, and 7 out of 10 liked the laissez-faire leader better than the autocratic one—Kurt Lewin, Ronald Lippitt, and Ralph K. White, "Patterns of Aggressive Behavior in Experimentally Created 'Social Climates,'" *Journal of Social Psychology,* X (May, 1939), 284–285.

has attended his failure to attain his ends by means of his own devising.

It is true, of course, that we all crave and need the guidance and support of society—of habits, of traditions, and of social compulsions.[15] But, as has been seen above, the conception of liberty that is here defended takes account of, and indeed relies upon, all this. That inner dynamic of the human animal which is ever striving for expression and expansion[16] needs to be channeled and controlled as well as allowed freedom. Self-control is the ultimate goal, but a certain degree of external control is a prerequisite for achieving it. What we are contending is that the ideal is freedom; authority is valuable and necessary as a means to this end and for other purposes insofar as the goal of disciplined self-direction is not fully attained.

We have been speaking of the claim for discipline as opposed to liberty and have concluded that although both are essential, the latter (as we have defined it) is more fundamental, more nearly an end-in-itself. We have yet to deal with the argument that duties should be accented rather than rights. Primarily this is a matter to be dealt with in Chapter VI, where we shall be speaking of rights. It should be remarked at this point, however, that it is of the essence of duty that it be done voluntarily. The fascist or pseudo fascist who takes the high line of appealing to moral principles completely defeats his professed purpose by resorting to authority and compulsion, not to develop liberty but

---

[15] Professor Mayo properly takes to task those who overlook this fact. He writes: "There are many of us who tend to think of the alleged 'new freedom' in act and thought, possessed by an individual in a modern society, as clear gain. Such thinking is heedless of two facts: these are, first, that a diminished social control demands an accession of intelligent self-control and, second, that any movement in the direction of this so-called freedom withdraws from the individual a measure of social understanding and support which he is usually unable to do without."—Elton Mayo, *The Human Problems of an Industrial Civilization* (New York: The Macmillan Company, 1933), pp. 128–129. Reprinted by Division of Research, Harvard Business School, Boston, 1946. This quotation is by permission of the Division of Research.

[16] See Fromm, *op. cit.*, pp. 287–289.

to replace it. Even those who, like Rousseau, define liberty as freedom to act rationally, insist that the rule of reason should be self-imposed.[17] We can even agree with Matthew Arnold when he announces that. . . . "what we seek is the Philistine's perfection, the development of his best self, not the mere liberty for his ordinary self"; [18] and with his further contention that renouncement is as much the law of life as liberty.[19] The liberal merely adds—but it is a vital addition—that the development of the Philistine's best self requires that he have freedom to make his own choices as to what he should become and how he should seek to attain his end. The liberal might also point out that, while renouncement also is an act of individual freedom, no one can sell or give himself into slavery and remain free.[20]

[17] Jean Jacques Rousseau, *Social Contract,* trans. G. D. H. Cole (Everyman's Library; New York: E. P. Dutton & Co., 1923), Bk. I, Chap. 8.

Cf. also Plutarch, who declared: "Those persons only who live in obedience to reason are worthy to be counted free: they alone live as they will, who have learned what they ought to will."—Plutarch, "Agis," quoted in Norman Cousins (ed.), *A Treasury of Democracy* (New York: Coward-McCann, Inc., 1942), p. 19.

[18] Matthew Arnold, "Our Liberal Practioners," in *Culture and Anarchy* (New York: The Macmillan Company, 1883), p. 173.

[19] *Ibid.*

[20] It is a difficulty of the definition of liberty we have adopted that its limits are vague. Differences between liberty and not-liberty tend to be matters of degree. A man who makes a contract to secure the aid of others in the accomplishment of his and their purposes may well increase his freedom even though he is not at liberty to revoke it the next day. A cattle-rustler protective association in a frontier community may well add more to the liberty of its members than it takes away. Does a man increase or decrease his liberty when he incurs the obligation of debt in order to educate his children? Or when he marries? These difficulties are inherent in the fact that human purposes tend to conflict with each other. The test is always the maximum of self-directed fulfillment and harmony. Clearly one who gives himself wholly and irrevocably into the power of another has lost both self-direction and (considering the nature of man) the possibility of full development.

At this point it may be well to state that the critic of "formal liberalism" on grounds of mystical religion is not really attacking the ideal herein set forth, except to say that it is not enough. True freedom can be known only by him who chooses the Truth. But he must *choose* it. There is no valid support for totalitarian philosophies from this quarter. It is one thing to say that liberty is not enough—quite another to seek to replace it with something else. Cf. Nicholas Berdyaev, *The Fate of Man in the Modern World* (London: Student Christian Movement Press, 1935), esp. pp. 41–

The critic of liberal philosophy often retorts that his use of compulsion is purely incidental. The main force of his criticism is directed against the materialistic and utilitarian philosophy of liberalism that is forever talking of happiness and pleasure, and especially of material comforts, as though these values were the finest things in life, overlooking the fact that honor, courage, nobility of character, loyalty, devotion to duty, and willingness to sacrifice one's self for a greater end are of superior worth. To many men of good will this line of talk has considerable persuasive force. But its force is more rhetorical than rational. A moment's reflection will reveal that there is no necessary connection between the philosophy of liberal democracy which we have been defending and materialism or hedonism. We have made it clear that the happiness which accompanies attainment of one's ends is not to be confused with mere pleasure.[21] Furthermore, we must distinguish between happiness as result and happiness as aim. Happiness probably cannot be obtained in highest measure by those who make their own happiness their chief concern. There is no necessary connection between liberal democracy and a theory that makes the chief end of life a "self-centered and untroubled prosperity."[22] On the contrary, the democratic doctrine of equality makes considerable demands upon one's concern for others. In short, the argument is directed against a libertarian philosophy which is no part of liberal democracy *per se*, and not against true liberalism.

Freedom, then, is absolutely fundamental to all else that is of value; and it cannot fulfill its mission unless it extends to the most important decisions governing our lives. As Professor Murphy says, it "is not a peripheral accessory of a bourgeois culture, to be weighed against the competing charms of security, national

---

58, and note in particular the statement: "There are too many lovers of their own liberty in the world. These include all Communists, all Fascists, all National Socialists and all others possessed by the demon of the will to power." (pp. 45–46).

[21] See above, p. 42, note 9.

[22] See Hans J. Morgenthau, *Scientific Man vs. Power Politics* (Chicago. The University of Chicago Press, 1946), p. 171.

aggrandizement or 'charismatic' submission to a presumably inspired leader, when the comparative convenience of various forms of government is being discussed. It guarantees the conditions under which and the area within which we act as morally responsible persons." [23]

INDIRECT VALUES. We have yet to consider the value of liberty from the standpoint of society. The key proposition under this heading is that liberty is the key to progress. Advancement has come about largely through experimentation. Other things being equal, the more people are free to experiment, the greater are the chances of discovering better ways of doing things than have hitherto prevailed. All history testifies that if one or a few are given the power to decide what ideas may be expressed and tested, they will use that power to prevent new developments. In primitive societies, the rule of custom and taboo effectively maintains the *status quo*. Among civilized states, China has been the classic example of an authoritarian society in which progress was effectively stifled for centuries. Western civilization, too, provides us with countless examples of attempts on the part of those in power to muzzle heretics, whether in the field of religion, science, or politics, in spite of the obvious fact that all significant new ideas begin as heresies.[24]

As our discussion suggests, it is in the field of expression of opinion that the point we are making has greatest application.

[23] Arthur E. Murphy, *The Uses of Reason* (New York: The Macmillan Company, 1943), p. 199.

[24] "The progressive societies are those which most decisively have trusted themselves to . . . the way of persuasion."—Alfred North Whitehead, *Adventures of Ideas* (New York: The Macmillan Company, 1933), p. 109. Even more pertinent are the following sentences from the great historian of freedom of thought, J. B. Bury: "History shows that knowledge grew when speculation was perfectly free in Greece, and in modern times, since restrictions on inquiry have been entirely removed, it has advanced with a velocity which would have seemed diabolical to the slaves of the medieval Church. Then it is obvious that in order to readjust social customs, institutions, and methods to new needs and circumstances, there must be unlimited freedom of canvassing and criticising them, of expressing the most unpopular opinions, no matter how offensive to prevailing sentiment they may be."—*A History of Freedom of Thought* (New York: Henry Holt and Company, 1913), p. 240.

The fundamentals of the case for a maximum of freedom in the realm of speech and opinion may be briefly put: Progress depends upon the discovery of truth; truth, among fallible human beings, may be approximated only where the atmosphere is congenial to the development of new ideas, where such ideas may be freely expressed, and where prevailing ideas and institutions may be subjected to criticism from all quarters. If an idea is false, it should not be protected; if it is true, in the long run it will be able to stand up under attack better than its false rivals. Argument may seldom avail to convince a participant in the debate, but the nonparticipating bystanders are more likely to be persuaded by the side which is supported by the most valid reasoning, other things being equal. Other factors will, of course, enter in. A glib tongue may more than offset acute analysis. But glib tongues may be on either side of the argument, and there is no reason to expect them to be overwhelmingly on the side of falsehood. They may be trusted to cancel one another out.

This reasoning is subjected to at least four lines of attack. In the first place, it is argued that this theory would make Hamlets of us all. In the world of practical affairs it is essential to *assume* certain things to be true as a basis for action. To delay, to take no action at all, is frequently far worse than to take action that falls considerably short of the ideal. All of this may easily be admitted by the defenders of free trade in ideas. We must nearly always act before there is unanimous agreement. But this does not mean that criticism must be stopped. In fact, it is reasonably safe to take action at an early date precisely because our errors are subject to subsequent correction in the light of criticism. There is, however, the further argument that the opportunity for unlimited debate of public policies tends to divide opinion into so many different camps that agreement on any positive proposal becomes next to impossible. This is a serious criticism which must be considered in due course; but it more properly comes under the heading of particular institutional devices for implementing democratic ideals than under a consideration of the validity of those ideals themselves. We shall return to this point in Chapter XII.

In the second place, it may be argued that words are more than the vehicles of ideas; they are incitements to action. This is, indeed, both true and significant. As a matter of fact, it may plausibly be contended that, in a democracy, the case for free speech covers the use of words of advocacy only to persuade persons to exercise their legal rights, through the ballot and otherwise.[25] Against this statement of the principle, the argument under consideration would have no application. In practice, however, the importance of avoiding infringements of the proper sphere of free speech and the danger of abuse of a test involving such a vague concept as the purpose of the advocate justify the establishment of a stronger presumption in favor of freedom to speak or write than its supporting principle itself would call for. Such a presumption is supplied, for example, by the familiar "clear and present danger" test. At the same time, that test offers ample protection for the safety of the commonwealth. One might go even further and say that, as long as the persons who in fact commit illegal acts, and those who clearly and directly incited them to the commission of these acts, are punishable, a healthy democracy has nothing to fear—and an unhealthy democracy would have little to gain by drawing the line sooner.

A third criticism may also be dismissed briefly. It may be said that there are at least some things so clearly false that it is safe to ban them. But surely if this is true no good purpose can be served by doing so. Undoubtedly there are some people who are still concerned to proclaim that the earth is flat. What useful end would be served by silencing them, however, it is hard to see. To go beyond such obvious cases as this would transcend the assumption upon which this attack is based.

Finally, and most important, it may be argued that the

---

[25] It is worthy of note that Mill himself, in his classic defense of freedom of thought, declared that "opinions lose their immunity when the circumstances in which they are expressed are such as to constitute their expression a positive instigation to some mischievous act."—John Stuart Mill, "On Liberty," *op. cit.*, p. 114.

whole case for freedom of opinion is based upon false rational- ism. It assumes that men are rational beings who respond to rea- son and tend on the whole to act in accordance with what their reason approves. The facts, our critic maintains, fly in the face of this assumption. Man is notoriously subject to prejudice and sus- ceptible to emotional appeals. The old art of influencing man's conduct by the use of symbols and other appeals to his irrational nature has now been reduced to a science. It would be easy to elaborate on this statement; but anyone who has read a political party platform, listened to a campaign speech, or reflected for a moment upon the kinds of advertising which most advertisers be- lieve to be effective will not need further demonstration.

This is all very true. But the answer cannot be found in the direction of regimented opinion. The classic arguments against this alternative remain sound. To go along that path is to give up all hope of getting progressively nearer to the truth. Rather, we must place our dependence upon the fact stressed above: namely, that irrational appeals under liberal-democratic institu- tions are not the monopoly of any party or group. They can be made in support of all positions. If we see to it—and this is of prime importance—that every group has effective opportunity to make use of whatever techniques of opinion formation are avail- able to other groups, we may be reasonably sure that such ap- peals will cancel each other out. It may even be that some tech- niques, some types of appeal, should be denied to all. This possi- bility raises practical questions that we need not examine here.[26] It remains true that without allowing a free play of rational criticism we can have no hope of discovering the truth.

But, our critic may protest, all this discussion about "truth" begs the question. Questions relating to public affairs generally resolve themselves into questions of value, and there is no such thing as "the truth" in the realm of values. In the preceding chapter we rejected the utterly nihilistic version of this attack. However, the critic may take a middle ground. As was pointed out in the discussion of positivism, he may deny that there are

[26] See below, pp. 254–260.

any universally accepted or valid values and still admit a large measure of agreement as to the nature of the good.[27] If this is his position, he will contend that there is no truth in matters of value judgment as between those who disagree.

Even if we admit the accuracy of this analysis, however, the case for freedom of expression is not invalidated. Whether or not there is ultimate and complete agreement of interest, it is certain that thorough discussion will frequently dissipate an apparent conflict. The union wants higher rates of pay to compensate for the seasonal nature of the work. The employers resist the demand in the interest of profits. Discussion may lead to the discovery that there is a way to overcome unemployment during the off season by a rearrangement of production schedules. Reflection, stimulated by discussion, may even go a long way toward narrowing the divergences among preferences for such things as leisure and more material goods. I may feel very strongly that I have enough leisure now and prefer to take my share of added productivity in cash. But after listening to persons with more experience or better imaginations describe ways of using my leisure that had not occurred to me, or the value of which I had not appreciated, I may change my mind. This sort of thing is such a common experience that we tend to take it for granted. Taking it for granted, and so forgetting it, we may accept too easily the argument of the man who tells us that our conflicts of preference are not resolvable by discussion. On the contrary, as John Dewey has said, "Instead of there being no disputing about tastes, they are the only thing worth disputing about, if by 'dispute' is signified discussion involving reflective inquiry." [28]

[27] This view is not confined to the positivists. Professor Perry, for example, holds that there may be cases where there is an ultimate conflict of interest between one individual and others and that in such cases there is no way of determining the greatest good.

[28] John Dewey, *The Quest for Certainty* (New York: Minton, Balch & Company, 1929), p. 262.

We should perhaps remind ourselves that up to this point our discussion of freedom of expression, like our discussion of liberty in general, has been concerned to prove that it is *in itself* an essential feature of an ideal

The resolution of conflicts by discussion is by no means entirely a matter of discovering that the initial objectives of the parties can be reconciled. Those objectives may be changed. It is far from true that the behavior of each of us reflects a constant and unchangeable set of attitudes. In point of fact, our systems of values are not that neat and consistent. We all subscribe to many values and principles which conflict with one another. At any given moment certain values will be kept below the threshold of consciousness by the fact that an incompatible value is ascendant. But the submerged values (or, more properly, "valuations") are there nonetheless, capable of being appealed to by others, perhaps successfully. For example, my initial opposition to an increase in the borough tax rate on grounds of personal financial interest may be overcome by an appeal to my belief in the importance to society of good schools. Incidentally, it is worthy of notice that, since the obvious way to win over an opponent or to justify oneself is to appeal to valuations that are widely accepted, the tendency of the whole process is to raise to the conscious level the more general valuations and so to widen the area of community and give it a more substantial basis. People's desire to be, or at least to appear, rational (consistent) facilitates the process.[29]

3. Concluding Considerations

Little has been said here about particular liberties of action because in this respect the doctrine of liberalism can hardly be more specific than to express a general presumption in favor of liberty. It is obvious that each individual's liberty must be subject

---

society. It may also be valuable or even indispensable in a secondary fashion. For the democrat this is most surely the case. Democratic processes are mere form without substance unless the public opinion upon which democratic government depends is the product of the widest possible access to facts and opportunity for discussion. This needs no elaboration. If the case for democracy to be developed in succeeding chapters is sound, then the case for freedom of expression receives still further support.

[29] An excellent brief discussion of this subject is to be found in Appendix I, "A Methodological Note on Valuations and Beliefs," of Gunnar Myrdal, *An American Dilemma—The Negro Problem and Modern Democracy* (New York: Harper & Brothers, 1944), II, 1027–1034, esp. 1027–1031.

to all sorts of restrictions both in favor of the liberty of others and in behalf of other interests. Some discussion of specific liberties as against government will appear below.[30] However, liberal doctrine is frequently attacked in certain general ways which demand notice before this chapter is concluded, if only, as in some cases, to show that the answer will appear elsewhere.

It is said, for example, that order is just as important as liberty and that they are opposing principles. Generally speaking, they are not opposing principles; herein lies the fallacy of the argument. In the first place, a substantial degree of order is absolutely essential for liberty. It is sufficiently obvious that the regime of order which compels me to obey traffic regulations really frees me from the much greater frustration I would experience if each driver were allowed to fend for himself at busy intersections. One does not have to be a Hobbesian to recognize that life in a society in which each is free to follow his own impulses without any sort of control would be "nasty, brutish, and short." Order, in other words, far from being opposed to liberty, is a condition of liberty. It is also a condition for other elements of well-being and for the sense of community that is in turn essential to that self-development which is the goal of liberty. Two conditions may be visualized under which order and liberty might be said to conflict. The first obtains if the instrumental role of order is lost sight of and order is thought of as an end-in-itself, or if some other aspect of well-geing to which it is instrumental, such as material prosperity, comes to be thought of as an end-in-itself. Here the conflict is based entirely upon the misconception of confusing means and ends. The second case arises where the minimum requirements for order essential for the maintenance of independence (liberty for the group), or for preventing disintegration of the political community,[31] or for securing the means of subsistence for all, require the temporary relinquishment

---

[30] Chap. VI.

[31] The argument that the ideals and institutions of political liberalism tend to destroy the unity of society on which essential order must rest will be fully considered in Chap. XII.

of the means to the good life (liberty) in order to retain life itself and the opportunity for its fulfillment in the future.[32] It would, of course, be self-defeating to insist on liberty to the extent of destroying one of its own essential conditions.

It is also sometimes said that liberty is bad because it permits the unscrupulous to get on top. But obviously this would be applicable only to a regime which tolerated unscrupulous practices. As against a Spencerian version of laissez faire, the criticism is eminently sound; but the liberty to be a quack until your patients find you out is no part of the ideal of freedom herein defended. It is also contended in some quarters that too much liberty allows the more able to take advantage of the less able. In part this is the problem of working out the mutual relationships between the two ideals of liberty and equality. More specifically, it boils down to a claim that too much of certain kinds of liberty now may result in depriving a great many people of liberty later on. This is clearly not an attack upon liberty as such. Finally, and in direct opposition to the last argument, it is frequently maintained that liberty for all will degenerate into liberty for those of mediocre ability to dominate over the able few. The validity of this contention will be appraised in Chapter XI.

[32] The point is well put by Eduard Heimann: "The nature of man is such as to require order for his physical life and freedom for his spiritual life. Order is more fundamental, freedom is higher."—*Freedom and Order: Lessons from the War* (New York: Charles Scribner's Sons, 1947), p. 10.

CHAPTER V

THE IDEAL OF
SOCIAL DEMOCRACY:
II. EQUALITY AND FRATERNITY

Equality, in some sense, is basic to any conception of democracy. Some would say that it is *the* basic element. Others would accord this position to liberty, saying that equality is a necessary condition for liberty. As long as we are agreed that both are essential, we need not attempt to resolve this controversy.[1]

1. Erroneous Concepts of Democratic Equality

It is a favorite though cheap device of antidemocrats to pretend to believe that democratic doctrine asserts some factual equality of all mankind, such as equality of ability. The words of the Declaration of Independence, "all men are created equal," give fleeting, but only fleeting, support to this view. Such was not the

[1] It may be suggested that differences of opinion on this point arise from the fact that some of the disputants are thinking about what is essential to democracy, per se, while others are thinking about what is essential to man. If the first point of view is adopted, it seems fairly clear that equality takes primacy. One can imagine a democracy—although not a liberal democracy—in which there was little liberty, but a democracy without equality would indeed be a contradiction in terms. From the second point of view, however, what has been said in the preceding chapter supports the priority of liberty. Better liberty for some but not all, than equality without liberty, the equality of slavery, if such a dilemma can be imagined. The remarks of R. H. Tawney, great exponent of equality, are of interest in this connection: "The spiritual energy of human beings, in all the wealth of their infinite diversities, is the end of which external arrangements, whether political or economic, are merely means. Hence institutions which guarantee to men the opportunity of becoming the best of which they are capable are the supreme political good, and *liberty is rightly preferred to equality, when the two are in conflict.*"—*Equality* (New York: Harcourt, Brace and Company, 1929), p. 220. Italics mine.

meaning of the authors of the Declaration. It was in respect of the possession of the "unalienable rights" of life, liberty, and the pursuit of happiness that they were equal.[2] This was made explicit in the more carefully phrased Declaration of Rights incorporated in the French Constitution of 1791. The first article of that statement of democratic principles declared, "Men are born and live free and equal as regards their rights." Nothing in the history of liberal-democratic thought or action supports any other interpretation of this cardinal dogma of liberal democracy. Equality of voting power, as we shall see, is supported as a means of recognizing and protecting equality of rights, not on the theory that all voters will or can make equal contributions to the commonweal.

But "equality of rights" is still vague. Just what does it mean? That men are equally entitled to life and to liberty? Undoubtedly so. But this does not mean that no man may be denied liberty, else why our jails? "Equality of opportunity" is a concept frequently used in this connection and often held to be the real basis of democracy, as opposed to absolute equality. Not that all men should have the same rewards, but that they should have the same chances. Jefferson did not proclaim a right to happiness, but only to the *pursuit* of happiness—the opportunity. Differences in reward and in well-being, it is reasoned, will then depend upon effort and ability. At first blush, this is likely to appeal to our sense of justice, and we are inclined to say that this is part of the social democratic concept of distributive justice.

Further thought reveals that the concept does not always yield results that would generally be considered equitable or democratic. Where lack of an equal opportunity keeps the underdog down, we all tend to feel injustice. But what we may easily overlook is that our sense of justice often calls for more than is provided by equality of opportunity. If the least able and the most able are given an equal start in the race for success, the former

[2] The subject of rights will be dealt with in the next chapter. For present purposes, a "right" may be defined simply as a claim to which a person is entitled.

will fare badly indeed. Our principle has betrayed us into giving to ability a greater reward than we had bargained for. When does the process stop? As between two youths of twenty who have equal opportunities, in a few years one is likely to have got so far ahead in the race that he will find open to him many opportunities for even greater progress which are not available to the other. Furthermore, the success of runners in the race of life is governed by other factors than effort and ability, even if they start on a par with each other. Luck inevitably enters in. Why should not man step in to equalize the capricious dispensations of Dame Fortune? And, moreover, to what do we owe ability, if not to fortune? Why should some be entitled to special deserts by virtue of having been blessed at birth with superior mental or physical equipment? [3] Finally, the principle of equality of opportunity is subject to an even more devastating attack. It is self-defeating. Equality of opportunity for one generation is incompatible with an equal chance for members of the next generation, unless the institution of the family is to be completely scrapped. For, quite apart from inherited wealth, the justification of which is open to debate, it is inevitable that the children of the successful family will have advantages in terms of training, contacts, and the like, which will give them a head start as against children of less successful families. We are forced to conclude that equality of opportunity is little more than a useful rule of thumb; certainly it is not the defining principle of social democracy. Perhaps its basic shortcoming is that it takes no account of need.

2. *Equality of consideration*

What, then, of "equality of consideration"? This is in fact the principle of equality of individuals as subjects-of-ends—the principle of impartiality, we might call it—which we defended in Chapter III. It means, as we saw, that in considering the respective claims of two individuals we should treat them alike, equally, in

---

[3] See Herbert Spiegelberg, "A Defense of Human Equality," *Philosophical Review*, LIII (Mar., 1944), 101–124.

the absence of some relevant basis for distinction. This, it will appear, is a purely formal, procedural principle. It can be given some content, however, from the ethical basis which has already been established—the principle of satisfaction as fundamental to what is good. For example, we might be justified in allowing X a larger income than Y on the grounds that he had a larger family to support. Other things being equal, the fact of the larger family would indicate that X would need a larger income to achieve (or for his family to achieve) satisfaction equal to Y's. Again, we might justify allowing X a larger income on the ground that he made a greater contribution to society and that the extra income was required to induce or to enable him to make that contribution. Here again it would be increased satisfaction—in this case of others—that would be the test. On these principles, then, need and contribution to society would be relevant to the question of a just reward. Race, on the other hand, would not.

It would seem to be clear that social democracy's equality of rights includes at least as much as does the principle of equality of consideration as interpreted above. The liberal-democratic principle of equality before the law, for instance, provides an example of its application. This principle means that the law must be impartially administered and that the substance of the law itself must be impartial, that it must not discriminate between individuals except on the basis of differences which are relevant to a legitimate purpose.

As will be argued in the next chapter, the case for political democracy can be adequately defended on the basis of the ethical principles established thus far, without reference to anything more.[4] Democracy is more likely to preserve the impartiality principle than any other form of government. Furthermore, since all justification of unequal treatment ultimately goes back to individual satisfaction, it is imperative that all should have an equal opportunity to present their claims. Nevertheless, it is rightly felt that more than this is included in the concept of social democracy, or the democratic way of life. The latter includes a sub-

[4] See below, pp. 105–115.

stantive concept which goes beyond anything described above. And, since the belief in the values of social democracy adds so much to the support people will give to political democracy, it will be worth our while to devote some attention to their justification, even though the case for political democracy does not stand or fall thereby.

What is the substantive content of the social democratic principle of equality of consideration? Let us begin with the principle of impartial maximization of satisfaction, as interpreted above. Consideration should be given to the nature and extent of my needs and also to what will induce or enable me to contribute most to the satisfaction of the needs of others. A law that prevents city dwellers from supplementing their income by raising chickens in their back yards would properly be upheld as not violating the equal protection of the laws even though I, a city dweller, have greater need for the extra income than my country cousin who suffers under no such restriction. My need for the comforts this income would provide must be balanced against my neighbors' need for relief from disturbance by early morning cackling. But surely a demand that I should give up my life—say for a scientific experiment—in order that others (even though a great many others) might enjoy more comfort, would violate the democratic equality principle. We feel that here we touch something sacred and final. This is what we mean when we speak of the "dignity" of the individual. This, too, is the distinguishing feature of democratic equality of consideration. Professor Perry puts it this way. "Justice," he declares, "imputes a certain inviolability to the claims of that unit of life which we term loosely a human, personal, moral, free or rational being. There is some sense in which you are a finality; making it improper for me to dispose of you, even if it be my sincere intention to promote thereby the well-being of humanity." [5]

It may be suggested that this principle grows directly out of the ethical foundations outlined earlier. The good arises out of

[5] Ralph Barton Perry, *The Moral Economy* (New York: Charles Scribner's Sons, 1909), p. 64.

the satisfaction of persons as subjects-of-ends. *As subjects-of-ends,* they are all alike, it may be said. In accordance with the rule of reason, then, they must be treated alike. The life of one is equal to the life of another. The complete satisfaction of one is equal to the complete satisfaction of another, although (be it noted) this may require much more in the way of material well-being for one than for another. If there is not enough to go around, then each, *as subject-of-ends* (that is, for the moment leaving out of account each person's capacity as means to the ends of others), is entitled to the same proportion of total satisfaction as all the others. The claims of one individual, as subject-of-ends, are on a plane of equality with those of all others as long as they represent needs which are equally essential to the satisfaction of the individuals concerned.[6]

When analyzed in this fashion, the democratic interpretation of the principle of equality of consideration, which we may call the principle of equal satisfaction of equally central needs, will be widely accepted as self-evident.[7] It may even be suggested that it is implicit in the (practical) reasoning process itself [8] and therefore cannot be rationally doubted.[9]

We might conclude the discussion of equality and of the ethical case for the liberal-democratic way of life at this point. We have argued that what is good for man is to satisfy his ends—self-

[6] For this analysis I have been greatly assisted by a thesis written by Barbara Schinnerer Tovey, entitled "An Essay on the Ethical Bases of Equalitarianism in Recent Democratic Theory" (Swarthmore College, 1945).

[7] There are many ways of expressing and attempting to justify the democratic principle of justice. They include such statements as the following: that equal rights flow from equal worth; that all men are of equal value, or are morally equal; that all men are equal in the sight of God; that the value of the individual is infinite; and that the individual soul is ultimate, and an end-in-itself. Although I do not agree with the literal meaning of all of these propositions, it seems plausible that what is really meant by such expressions is the equality principle as interpreted and defended here and in Chap. III.

[8] This position is persuasively supported by W. D. Lamont in *The Principles of Moral Judgment* (Oxford: The Clarendon Press, 1946), pp. 184–193.

[9] See above, pp. 44–45.

regarding, other-regarding, and mixed—to the fullest extent possible, subject to the inescapable rule of reason, interpreting the latter now as including the principle of equal satisfaction of equally central needs. As was mentioned above,[10] however, there is an additional argument for the democratic principle of equality—the argument of harmony between individual and social interests—which merits examination. This inquiry will also give us an opportunity to give some consideration of the position of those who, like Plato and Aristotle, would seem to disagree with the equalitarian principle which has been supported here.

3. Harmony of Interests

We turn, then, to an exploration of the area of conflict, if any, between the course of action which will yield the individual most satisfaction and that which is demanded by the equality principle. It may be slight or even nonexistent, especially in the political realm. Professor Perry, for instance, appears to take this view. He maintains that only a life lived justly can be fully satisfying. In a recent volume, he supports this point in the following words:

Treat another as inferior and you place him in a dilemma. He must either suffer humiliation or show resentment. You either break his will or antagonize it. Feel superior and you do something equally injurious to yourself; you acquire a narrowing insensibility and a stagnant complacency. Arrogance and contempt are sterile, both in him who gives and in him who receives; in self abasement life is shrivelled and degraded. The most enlivening and fertilizing of social relationships is hopeful confidence and esteem, felt stoutheartedly by each man for himself and generously by each man toward his fellows.[11]

This analysis seems to me to be essentially sound and to carry with it no little conviction. It is in the nature of the case, to be sure, that its persuasiveness for each individual will depend upon that individual's own experience and his interpretation of

[10] Above, p. 47.
[11] Ralph Barton Perry, *Puritanism and Democracy* (New York: The Vanguard Press, 1944), pp. 581–582.

the experience of others. Further investigation of the sort of things that tend to promote human happiness and satisfaction will aid us in making our own evaluations of this argument. In a world in which competition and conflict are so prevalent, it is easy to overlook the fact that man is preponderantly a social animal. A moment's thought, however, is sufficient to demonstrate that he is dependent upon society for the satisfaction of his psychological needs even more than for his physical needs. Short of actual physical torture, solitary confinement is one of the most severe punishments that can be inflicted upon man. He is sympathetic, as well as ambitious, as Rousseau was quick to see, and as even that incorrigible egoist, Thomas Hobbes, admitted. His simplest joys are multiplied on being shared or enjoyed in company. Everyone likes to be amused, yet a joke that will leave us without a smile in cold print will elicit uproarious laughter when told to a group. We do not need to inquire into *how far* it remains true that "it is more blessed to give than to receive" to know that often the profoundest and most enduring enjoyments come from observing, and especially from being the cause of joy in others. Likewise, the sight of suffering, mental or physical, causes us pain. Man requires human affection—what more barren than a life without it?—and needs, as well, to give affection to others.[12]

Furthermore, the socializing effects of the sympathetic nature of man are buttressed from an unexpected source—his desire for approval. To win the respect and commendation of others, it may safely be asserted, is a universal yearning of human nature. One of the most effective devices in the training of children in societies at all stages of civilization is the manifestation of ap-

[12] A fuller treatment of this crucial point may be found in W. T. Stace, *The Concept of Morals* (New York: The Macmillan Company, 1937), Chaps. 11 and 12, especially pp. 262–277, and also in the same author's *The Destiny of Western Man* (New York: Harcourt, Brace and Company, 1942), Chap. 12. For support from a psychologist (and a psychoanalyist) for the view that man's fullest satisfaction comes from productive activity rather than destruction and must be based on respect for others, see Erich Fromm, *Man for Himself* (New York: Rinehart & Company, 1947), pp. 210–230.

proval for the favored line of conduct and of disapproval for conduct which offends against the rules of the society in question. Anyone who has owned a dog or a horse knows that this is a trait which extends even beyond the human domain. The importance of this psychological law is so great and so obvious that probably anyone would feel safe in predicting that there is no such thing as a truly happy individual who does not command the love and respect of most of those who know him. And how better can one secure the approbation, the respect, and the love of others than by treating them as equals, that is, in accordance with the principle of equal rights? How else can one create that complete community which elicits the most widespread energies and the most cooperative behavior? The democratic principle, in other words, nourishes the environment most favorable to the flowering of the individual self or soul.[13]

Even Plato asserted the primacy of this ideal. He gives us one of the most remarkable statements of communal ethics—one going far beyond the requirements of democratic theory—to be found in the annals of political philosophy:

The first and highest form of the state and of the government and of the law is that in which there prevails most widely the ancient saying, that "Friends have all things in common." Whether there is anywhere now, or ever will be, this communion of women and children and property, in which the private and individual is altogether banished from life, and things which are by nature private, such as eyes and ears and hands, have become common, and in some way see and hear and act in common, and all men express praise and blame and feel joy and sorrow on the same occasions, and whatever laws there are unite the city to the utmost,—whether all this is possible or not, I say that no man, acting upon any other principle, will

[13] T. V. Smith has made the point that the concept of the self, which is the modern, secular substitute for the soul, is more flexible and dynamic than the latter and is therefore even more satisfactory as a basis of democratic doctrine. *The American Philosophy of Equality* (Chicago: The University of Chicago Press, 1927), pp. 246–249. Erich Fromm also makes a useful point in this connection. He argues that the idea of the self and its satisfaction as the end of human activity is not "selfish" in the usual sense of that term when it is realized that the ends of the self are other-regarding just as much as they are self-regarding.—*Man for Himself*, pp. 119–141.

ever constitute a state which will be truer or better or more exalted in virtue.[14]

In modern times, Matthew Arnold has put the case in this fashion: "Can it be denied, that to live in a society of equals tends in general to make a man's spirits expand, and his faculties work easily and actively; while, to live in a society of superiors, although it may occasionally be a very good discipline, yet in general tends to tame the spirit and to make the play of his faculties less secure and active?"[15] In another essay he goes even further and argues that it is to the interest of each individual to live in a society of equals. "The well-being of the many comes out more and more distinctly, in proportion as time goes on," he declares, "as the object we must pursue. An individual or a class, concentrating their efforts upon their own well-being exclusively, do but beget troubles both for others and for themselves also."[16]

All this, it may be objected, falls short of proving the point at issue. Few would deny that man is a social and even a communal animal. To say that his welfare requires love and fellowship is obvious, but not enough to establish the case for democracy. Even Plato, as we have seen, felt the need of an affectionate, communal life for those fully developed men of virtue and wisdom who were to constitute the elite of his ideal state; but this did not prevent him from virtually quarantining them from the bulk of inferior men who could never aspire to enter into their comradeship. Aristotle proclaimed that man was a social animal and that out of this fact arose the state; but he favored an aristocratic rather than a democratic ideal, and even attempted to justify slavery.

[14] Plato, "The Laws," Bk. V, 739 in *The Dialogues of Plato,* trans. and ed. Benjamin Jowett, (3d. ed., 5 vols.; London: Oxford University Press, 1892), V, 121.

[15] Matthew Arnold "Democracy," in *Mixed Essays, Irish Essays and Others* (New York: The Macmillan Company, 1883), p. 8.

[16] "Equality," *ibid.,* p. 52.

4. Consideration of Counterarguments

It may be that Plato and Aristotle simply failed to carry their principles to the logical conclusion. But it is also possible that the human needs which comprise the social side of man are subject to the law of diminishing returns. Man needs friends, but it is not clear that ten friends are twice as good as five. And it is very clear indeed that sympathy weakens as its object grows more remote—one is tempted to say in proportion to the square of the distance. We crave approval and shun disapproval but, once we have established an inner circle of psychological security, we are devilishly ingenious about devising means to insulate ourselves from the effects of the disapprobation of outsiders.

Furthermore, there are other basic psychological drives which foster antidemocratic tendencies. In the first place, there is plain self-interest. All too often our sympathy for the sufferer does not extend to making any substantial concession of our own privileges for his betterment. Even more fundamental is the desire to feel superior. Few can have failed to observe how this trait appears to permeate every level of society. It is no less characteristic of the lower levels than of the higher; and it has been pointed out that few things are more disruptive of social cohesion than developments that tend to deprive a group of privileges or social standing which it has long enjoyed.[17] Failure to appreciate this fact was one of the cardinal errors in the social theory of Marxism.

Before attempting to appraise these objections, it will be well to remind ourselves of just what we found to be involved in the case for social democracy. It did not include absolute equality of treatment. On the contrary, it left considerable room for differences. Different treatment on the basis of different needs is elementary. There is nothing in the ideal which is incompatible

---

[17] Cf. Hans Speier, "Social Stratification," in Max Ascoli and Fritz Lehman, *Political and Economic Democracy* (New York: W. W. Norton & Company, 1937), pp. 255–270, esp. pp. 262–270.

with permitting greater reward for greater effort, and this reward may properly take the form of social recognition. Differences in contribution to society growing out of different abilities may also, within reasonable limits, form a proper basis for differential rewards. The democratic ideal has been transgressed only when we violate that minimum of equality which posits, not equal worth, but an equal right to realize one's good to the fullest. Such a violation is most clearly illustrated in an instance where on person is denied life so that others may live more bountifully, but the case is essentially the same wherever an individual claims that his superiority entitles him to a fuller realization of his potentialities than the next person is entitled to. Stated in this way, the ideal of social democracy leaves plenty of room for the desire to excel and to receive special recognition. It is doubtful whether anything that falls short of this ideal can do full justice to man's social nature.

That man has many antisocial desires is obvious. But frequently his uncriticized desires will lead him astray. He may think he wants wealth, only to discover, too late, that the single-purposed pursuit of gain to which he had to devote himself to acquire wealth so constricted his potentialities and range of enjoyment that the door has been forever closed to that fullness of life which was his original object. He may crave power only to discover that it is the sort of craving that feeds on itself and so even in being satisfied creates greater dissatisfaction than before. He may never learn in time, if he relies entirely upon his own experience, what is to be found in the accumulated wisdom of the ages, namely, that he can secure an integration, a satisfying and fulfilling response to the totality of his needs only by committing himself to an ideal beyond himself. As one psychologist has put it: "Only an object of loyalty that requires the support of the whole self can serve as an integrating purpose. No object less than the democratic ideal of love of man can do this. Around this ideal an individual can easily organize his various needs, and the pursuit of each need becomes of double significance because it is subsumed under a master motive." [18] In other words, there is a sound reason for preferring those desires which take account of the claims of others to those which are more self-centered: the former are more harmonious and their gratification leads to more lasting happiness. The words of the popular song of a generation ago, "I want to be happy, but I can't be happy 'till I make you happy too," have wider application than their author intended.

The ever-increasing acceptance in practice of equalitarianism may be taken as additional evidence that it satisfies fundamental human needs. Over a century ago Tocqueville declared that "the gradual development of the principle of equality is a providential fact. . . . It is universal, it is durable, it constantly eludes all human interference, and all events as well as all men contribute to its progress." [19] This is no transitory development following in the wake of the French Revolution. The aristocratic doctrines of Plato and Aristotle gave way in the following centuries to the equalitarian doctrines of the later Stoics. The religion of Christianity supplied powerful reinforcement to this trend. It is true, of course, that for a long time the idea had little influence on practice. The demands for order were so great, and the conditions for maintaining it so difficult, in the days of the Roman Empire and its successor, the Holy Roman Empire, that liberty and equality gained scant recognition. However, the ideas were never allowed to die, and, what is more important for the present discussion, their suppression in practice merely added power to the explosion which eventually occurred. The period of the Renaissance marks the beginning of that series of movements and events which brought the individual man once more to the fore. And, while the accentuation of the individual naturally enough laid primary stress, at first, on the battle of liberty, the equalitarian implications of individualism gradually made themselves felt.

---

[18] Charles C. Josey, *The Psychological Battlefront of Democracy* (Indianapolis: The Butler University Press, 1944), p. 69.

[19] Alexis de Tocqueville, *Democracy in America*, trans. Henry Reeve, ed. Phillips Bradley (2 vols.; New York: Alfred A. Knopf, Inc., 1945), I, cx.

In our own day, the general equalitarian trend is too obvious for comment. In certain cases it has assumed a distorted form. In the Soviet Union, for instance, overemphasis on things material, in line with Marxist philosophy, has led to an almost complete neglect of liberty and to a blindness to the significance of power and of political rights. The emergence of a liberal philosophy and of liberal institutions from a background of ignorance, poverty, and despotism is not likely to be either easy or expeditious.

Even fascism—in large measure a movement of reaction on the part of those who had lost the special privileges or relative advantages they had previously enjoyed—based its appeal upon a kind of equalitarianism at the same time that it condemned liberals for their doctrine of equality. The very name of National Socialism is witness to this fact. Nazis made much of their gestures toward social democracy in eliminating certain vestiges of feudal privileges. Mussolini, in 1937, declared that Germany and Italy were the world's greatest and soundest democracies.[20] But, insofar as their equalitarianism was anything more than a sham, it was, like Plato's, limited to a special group. It was the fatal divisiveness of this limitation that brought about their downfall.

This provides us with the final argument in defense of the contention that man's social nature requires the indefinite extension of equal rights for its satisfaction. Anything less than complete extension of equal rights tends to produce a division within human society that is certain to result in strife. Social harmony and denial of equal rights do not mix. The only kind of harmony—if it can be called that—which is compatible with denial of this democratic fundamental is an imposed harmony. Insofar as we have had harmony at all, this is exactly what we have had during most of recorded history, to be sure. But it can be had only at a tremendous sacrifice of liberty, the value of which has already been established.

Before leaving the subject of equality, we should say a word about the line of attack upon this doctrine which has come to be

[20] Quoted by Sidney Hook, *Reason, Social Myths and Democracy* (New York: The John Day Company, 1940), p. 283.

known as "social Darwinism."[21] Nietzsche—and the fascists after him—relied heavily upon this theory. The great fallacy of this argument is to assume that the principles which do in fact prevail in nature are those which ought to prevail in civilized society. Yet when the assumption is stated thus baldly hardly anyone would support it. If the natural order is the right one, why should we establish police forces to interfere with the survival of the fittest? Surely, if the appeal to the principles of evolution can prove anything for our purposes, it proves that man has succeeded in bringing all other living creatures under his control not by superior brute force but by virtue of his reason. Even if struggle and domination of the weak by the strong does, as alleged, characterize the animal world, this proves nothing about what will lead to the greatest fulfillment of the ends of rational beings. So falls this attack upon the equality principle; it never really comes to grips with the problem.

5. Fraternity

The third ideal of the liberal-democratic trinity, fraternity, is so closely related to equality that it is appropriate to couple the treatment of the two. No painstaking definition is required. It is the spirit of brotherhood, of treating others not simply as though they had rights equal to ours but with loving concern for their welfare. Vital though this spirit is not only to the success of liberal-democratic institutions but to the peace and happiness of the world, we dismiss it very briefly here. We may safely do this for two reasons: because the philosophical basis for it has already been developed in our discussion of equality, and because it is less specifically a political concept than the other two.

It is clear, of course, that fraternity grows directly out of those social aspects of human nature which have just been discussed. But it goes much further than the demand for the rather mechanical rule of equal rights. It goes beyond anything that can be reduced to rule or demanded as of right. This leads to the second point. Unlike liberty and equality, fraternity is not directly

[21] See above, pp. 34–35.

related to any of the democratic rights. These rights do not include fraternity; furthermore their rational justification stands
without reference to such a concept. Its supreme importance,
however, comes from the fact that it is the spirit without which
those values would soon be lost sight of. A society in which people cease to be conscious of their rights and to demand their fulfillment is far along the road to tyranny. But a society in which
insistence upon rights is not accompanied by a consideration for
the rights of others, and also by a willingness to be accommodat-
ing in making those mutual adjustments without which social
life is impossible, is no less surely headed for speedy disintegration.

As has been often remarked, the ideal liberty can be attained
only in a community, a true community, infused with the spirit
of equality and of fraternity.[22] Only here can liberty flower into
that rich development of the self which is its ultimate object.
Only here can that supreme index of the liberal spirit, toleration,
be fully maintained. Whether we like it or not, our fates on this
planet are inextricably intertwined; and, as Herbert Spencer declared, "No one can be perfectly free till all are free; no one can
be perfectly moral till all are moral; no one can be perfectly
happy till all are happy." [23]

This last statement indicates how far wrong are those who
claim that the liberal ideal is atomistic. In truth, there is today
no major social philosophy which subscribes to social atomism.
Communism, fascism, and liberal democracy, at least in principle,
all deny it. As usual, however, the fascists have here succeeded in
combining opposites. While making their appeal on the basis of
unity and harmony and attacking liberalism for its alleged social

[22] Two remarks by John Dewey express the point well. "Regarded as
an idea," he writes, "democracy is not an alternative to other principles of
associated life. It is the idea of community life itself." And again, "The
clear consciousness of a communal life, in all its implications, constitutes
the idea of democracy."—*The Public and Its Problems* (New York: Henry
Holt and Company, 1927), pp. 148, 149.

[23] Herbert Spencer, *The Evanescence of Evil*, quoted in Norman
Cousins (ed.), *A Treasury of Democracy* (New York: Coward-McCann,
Inc., 1942), p. 126.

atomism, they have succeeded also in attracting to their ranks in large numbers those cynics whose attitude is, "Why should *I* work for the social welfare? Why should I not live on the capital of other people's good will?"

CHAPTER VI

THE CASE FOR POLITICAL DEMOCRACY

We have sought to establish the liberal-democratic ideals of liberty, equality, and fraternity as fundamental to the best way of life. If our arguments are sound, it would seem that the case for a liberal-democratic system of government is already established in principle. A social system whose ideals did not extend to the political realm would be too truncated to be worthy of the name. But it would not do to drop the matter with this simple statement. It is vital that we should know in considerable detail exactly what kind of political system is required for the attainment of the liberal ideals, and that we should understand the reasons for each of the requirements.

Moreover, in dealing with political democracy, we must have regard for another point of view—that of practicability. Politics, as Aristotle remarked, is a science of the second best. The closest approximation of the ideal that is attainable is not necessarily the best practical form of government. Aristotle himself believed that aristocracy would be the ideal form of government; but his prescription for the best practical government was a mixed form, combining elements of democracy and of oligarchy. So it might be that liberal democracy in its attainable form is not the most desirable possibility.[1]

[1] For the purposes of the argument to be presented in this chapter it will be assumed that a certain minimum of satisfactory operation of democratic governments—comparable to what has been achieved in English-speaking countries—can at least be maintained in the future. Arguments against this assumption will be set forth and appraised in the chapters that follow.

1. Meaning of Political Democracy

First, it will be well to review what we mean by liberal-democratic government, arranging the elements in a slightly different fashion from that which was followed in Chapter I, and going into rather more detail in certain particulars. Around the edges of the concept there is, of course, a twilight zone within which there may be disagreement as to what is and what is not essential. For the present purpose we shall be fairly dogmatic and not waste time trying to make certain that to which no certainty attaches.

For neatness's sake, we may think of liberal democracy as composed of a system of powers and a system of liberties, although in fact either could be expressed as the converse of the other. The powers are the powers of self-government. If democracy means anything it means government by the people. Without attempting to put too fine a point on it, "the people" includes all sane adults save those criminals whose antisocial behavior has disqualified them.[2] "Government by the people" means that the major policies of the government should be determined by the people or by their representatives freely elected at reasonably frequent intervals, and that the administration should be conducted by those who are accountable to the people or their representatives. In all voting each should count for one and none for more than one.

The system of liberties (historically prior to self-government) is slightly more complicated. One group has to do mainly with the realm of ideas. This category includes freedom of religious belief and observance; freedom of speech and of the press and of

[2] It should be clear that we are defining democracy by an ideal standard. Few if any governments may fully meet the test, but we normally call governments democratic if they approximate it in reasonable degree. Our ideas of what is "reasonable" in this regard change from age to age. It was once, but is no longer believed reasonable to exclude women. In the United States, the poll tax, once accepted without question, is now widely challenged as undemocratic. The question of the justification in democratic terms of an honestly administered literacy test has not become a real issue and is not likely to as long as we have free, compulsory education for all.

access to the facts; and the right of assembly and of free association. In general, the difficult problem of precise definition may be passed by here with the simple statement that substantially the meanings given these rights by the United States Supreme Court may be accepted as adequate. The phrases "access to the facts," and "free association," however, do not appear in the American Constitution. By the former we mean that every citizen shall be free to consult the records of official transactions, such as legislative debates and enactments and judicial judgments, and, broadly, that he shall be provided with an education which will equip him for responsible citizenship. "Free association" generally means the right to meet together and to organize for the accomplishment of legitimate purposes.

The second group of liberties may be roughly described as those which concern themselves with physical freedom. Here we have, first of all, the right to life, the right to be protected against physical violence. Here also is included a reasonable freedom of action, of movement from place to place, of choice of occupation, of contract (including the right to have others compelled to keep their contracts), and of the use and disposal of property. The use of the word "reasonable" here is indicative of the fact that the second division of this group of liberties is both more difficult to define and more susceptible to change with changing conditions than the other liberties enumerated. In the past, especially in the nineteenth century, various formulas were devised for marking out that area of freedom of action which governments should respect, but today the inadequacy of all such attempts is generally recognized. About all we can say is that political liberalism sets high store by such liberty and holds that it should be limited only for the sake of social considerations of equal value.

Finally, there is a highly important area of freedom which finds protection under the principle known as the rule of law. This principle may be defined as follows: First, no one should be detained or punished except for a violation of law—law existing at the time of the act in question. Second, this law must be the same for all, including government officials. Third, violations of the law shall be determined only in accordance wtih a fixed and regular procedure designed to secure a fair and impartial judgment. This principle should be interpreted broadly to include protection against the harassments of unreasonable searches, seizures, and questionings, and the spyings of secret police. Fourth, punishments must bear some reasonable relationship to the enormity of the crime. All of these rules pertain exclusively to the domain of criminal law. The fifth and last point is set off from the others in that it seeks to apply the general principle of the rule of law to the rest of the field of governmental activity. This canon of political liberalism states that the legislative and administrative acts of government shall make no discrimination between persons similarly situated and that the application of the laws shall be fair and impartial.[3]

For the protection of these liberties there are various devices, some of which, like the writ of habeas corpus, are thought of as cornerstones of our freedom. Nevertheless they remain mere mechanical contrivances for which there may well be substitutes which would be equally efficacious. Accordingly, we cannot say that they are themselves essential institutions in a liberal-democratic state. The case is essentially the same with the separation of powers. Doubtless it is true that a government in which all authority was placed in the hands of a single individual, even though he might have to submit himself to periodic election, would seem so ill designed to carry out the principles of political liberalism that we should hesitate to admit it to the category of liberal-democratic forms of government. Beyond this point, however, the ways in which power may be distributed so as to offer protection against its abuse are so numerous and various that it would be fatuous to select any particular one as a *sine qua non*.

[3] This formulation is more inclusive than the traditional Anglo-American rules, as cast in classic form by Albert Venn Dicey—*The Law of the Constitution* (9th ed.; London: Macmillan & Co., 1939). It is supported, however, by the trend of British and American jurisprudence in the twentieth century.

2. Rights

A government by the people in which the system of liberties just described is maintained comprises our conception of liberal democracy. But before we proceed to consider the validity of this ideal, we must digress to give some attention to a subject we have so far largely avoided, that of rights. In describing the limitations placed upon government in a liberal democracy we have spoken chiefly of "liberties." Liberal philosophy has sought to give its creed more definite form and greater strength by specifying certain liberties as "rights." No subject in political philosophy has been the occasion of more confusion than this. No aspect of democratic doctrine has been subject to more attack. The rights asserted have been designed as simple, inflexible protections for the individual. Hence they were bound to be targets for criticism in a complicated and rapidly changing society in which the individual must needs be increasingly curbed in the interests of the group. On the other hand, they are inevitably infused with a high emotional content, a fact that contributes to the confusion which constantly attends the subject.

Eschewing refinements, a right may be defined simply as a power or a privilege to which a person is entitled.[4] The word "entitled" in the definition may refer to either moral or legal justification; and accordingly rights may be classified as "moral rights" or "legal rights." Moral rights may or may not also be legal rights, and vice versa. Some moral rights could not be enforced by law. For example, a child may have a right to his parents' affection, but a law requiring parents to love their children would be an absurdity. On the other hand, if there is a moral right to freedom of speech, that is clearly a matter for legislation. Certain rights may even be so important that their legal

---

[4] For a useful analysis of the definition of rights, see J. P. Plamenatz, *Consent, Freedom, and Political Obligation* (London: Oxford University Press, 1938), Chap. 4. For a different theory of rights from that presented here, see A. C. Ewing, *The Individual, the State, and World Government* (New York: The Macmillan Company, 1947), Chap. 2.

formulation should be protected against alteration by simple majorities, as in the case of constitutional rights in the United States. On the other hand, many legal rights, such as my right to dispose of my broken glassware on the town dump, are mere matters of convenience to which I have no ethical claim in the absence of law.

The "natural rights," of which the democratic philosophers of an earlier day had so much to say, belong within the category of moral or ethical rights. A natural right may be defined as a moral right which is inherent in man as such and which is therefore fixed and immutable.

Is there any basis for claiming that there are any "natural rights" in this sense? The eighteenth-century notion of natural rights as those rights which existed in a state of nature will not withstand critical inspection and is now nowhere seriously entertained. The argument from self-evidence, although many would still hold it to be sound, does not command general acceptance, as we have seen.[5] Proceeding, however, from the ethical foundation we attempted to establish in Chapter III, we may conclude that, if a right is a power or a privilege which an individual ought to have, then everyone ought to have those powers and privileges which are necessary for him to approach as nearly as possible to the goal of happiness or satisfaction, subject to his respect for the principle of equal rights for all. This much may safely be asserted to be a natural right.[6] The equality principle itself may be said to constitute a natural right—the natural right to equal consideration. We have argued further that this assumption implies that the needs of one person should be considered as of equal importance with the equally central needs of another. These two principles or natural rights may quite properly be designated respectively as the rights of liberty and of equality. It is sometimes said that they are purely formal, without specific content;

[5] Ewing defends the view that there are self-evident natural rights, but that they are not absolute. Ewing, *op. cit.*, Chap. 2.
[6] For a statement of a parallel position to which I owe a great deal, see William Ernest Hocking, *Present Status of the Philosophy of Law and of Rights* (New Haven: Yale University Press, 1926), pp. 71–74.

but this is not true. The principle of equality before the law, that of no punishment without offense, the prohibition of ex post facto laws, and the requirement of prompt and fair trial for those accused of crime are direct logical derivatives of one or the other of these principles or of the two in combination. For the most part, however, life is too complicated and ever-changing to permit formulation of the conditions of the good life in terms of eternally valid rules. Nevertheless, there are many rules which can be laid down as being generally (although perhaps not without exception) valid corollaries of the natural rights, at least for a given age and culture. These might appropriately be called "presumptive rights." Possibly even freedom of speech—certainly any specific definition of it—falls in this category; the same may be said of property rights.

Besides the distinction between legal and moral rights, and the subsidiary category of natural rights, there is an important distinction between negative and positive rights. By a "positive right" is meant a right to have society, generally acting through government, take certain steps—going beyond preventing interference by other individuals—in behalf of the holder of the right. A right to public support in case of dire need would be such a right.

The rights upon which liberal democratic doctrine has been concerned to insist have generally been negative rights—the right to be free from interference, either by other private individuals or by government officials. The basic rights of free speech, free press, freedom of religion, and freedom of assembly are all of this kind. So also with property rights, the right to come and go as one wills, to choose one's occupation freely, and the right to a fair trial. This is a product of the theory which held that government was the chief enemy of liberty and that the individual, unaided by government, was the best promoter of his own interests. But this theory is not a necessary component of the democratic philosophy. As we shall see later on, one may believe in liberty and the development of the individual as basic goods and yet hold that a great deal of positive action by government is required to achieve these ends. Proponents of such a positive liberal philosophy will lay stress on rights as powers as well as on rights as privileges. Thus the negative right to educate our children in accordance with our own beliefs might be supplemented by the right to have the state provide our children with a free education. The American Constitution includes the first, under the right of free speech, but says nothing about the second. Yet today education is generally recognized as so vital both to effective citizenship and to the good life of the individual that most people who subscribe to the doctrine of liberal democracy would say that everyone has a right to a free basic education.

Nevertheless there is a greater presumption in favor of the validity of an asserted negative right than there is for an asserted positive right. This proposition flows from the key position of liberty and from the centrality of self-direction to the concept of liberty. The point appears more clearly if we consider the relationship between rights and duties. A right on my part implies a duty on the part of someone else. My right to privacy within my house implies the duty of others to stay out unless invited in. It also implies the duty of certain government officials to take whatever steps may be necessary to prevent others from entering my house against my will. My right to have contracts enforced carries with it the right to have government officials compel you to take action which you may have promised me you would take. Such rights as these do not compel private individuals to take positive action to which they have not freely consented. But if I have, for instance, a right to public support in case of need, that means that others must make positive contributions to me, and I, of course, must be ready to do the same for them. If my claims should then be extended beyond this fairly minimal level to (let us say) practically everything that seemed essential to the good life, my obligations would mount in proportion and I would soon find that under the guise of seeking to increase my real freedom I had virtually enslaved myself. For instance, the right to work, if carried far enough, might entail abandonment of the right to choose one's occupation, as well as the right not to work.[7]

3. *The Case for Political Democracy*

We may now get on with our consideration of the case for the political aspects of liberal democracy. The major outlines of that system are frequently formulated as rights: the rights to self-government, to freedom of belief and of expression, to reasonable freedom of action, and the numerous more specific rights which we have lumped together under "the rule of law." We shall follow that practice here with the understanding that they are generally not absolute, but presumptive rights. Their validity, therefore, will often depend as much upon calculations of probability as upon logical deduction.

THE RIGHT TO SELF-GOVERNMENT. Is the exercise of political power a condition for each individual's attainment of maximum satisfaction? It appears to be so, for a number of reasons. In the first place, a share in political power gives a tremendous enlargement to the area of self-determination. In our discussion of liberty we saw that freedom to determine our own actions was essential to that full and harmonious development of our powers in which we find our most complete satisfaction. But insofar as individual liberty must be regulated by government, the only way we can achieve this self-determination is by sharing in political power. And the area of state regulation is constantly increasing. To take a homely example, the farmer who a few years ago was completely free to plant what he pleased must now take care to obey various restrictions, such as not planting more than a specified amount of crops which are in surplus supply. The only way he can regain the freedom he has lost is by sharing in govern-

---

[7] Cf. E. H. Carr's statement regarding the proposal for an international declaration of "the Rights of Man." "If the new declaration of the rights of man is to include provisions for social services, for maintenance in childhood, in old age, in incapacity, or in unemployment," he writes, "it becomes clear that no society can guarantee the enjoyment of such rights unless it in turn has the right to call upon and direct the productive capacities of the individuals enjoying them."—"The Rights of Man," *United Nations Weekly Bulletin*, III, No. 17 (Oct. 2, 1947), 522.

ment. It should be noted in passing that there are numerous ways in which he can exercise this power of collective self-determination. Formal political activity at the polls and through political parties is only one possibility. In many cases, as in the example cited, there is an opportunity for popular participation at the administrative level. Furthermore, individuals can and do associate themselves for political activity in other ways than in political parties. In expressing himself on subjects affected by governmental regulation at a meeting of the Grange, the Farmers Union, or the Farm Bureau, the farmer may exert more political influence than he does at the polls. It must be noted however, that these kinds of influence gain their effectiveness largely from the ultimate political power which resides in the ballot.

Second, as we have seen, true harmonious happiness can be attained only through the attainment of community, for man is a communal animal. A community in turn will grow only where its members have a highly developed sense of community interest, where their sensibilities have been extended and their moral horizons enlarged, where they have developed a feeling of responsibility for the whole and where they are willing to work in its behalf—where, in short, there is public spirit. And how better can these ends be attained than by popular participation in and responsibility for government?[8] It is a common experience that people tend to take an interest in things for which they are given responsibility, and that the converse holds as well. But the process also works in a less obvious fashion. In considering public questions, and especially in attempting to influence others with respect to such questions, we inevitably appeal to the broader evaluative principles, such as the equality principle itself, simply because they are held more widely and valued more highly than other principles. This process tends to reinforce our commitment

[8] The classic statement of this argument was enunciated by John Stuart Mill. See his "Representative Government," Chap. 3, in *Utilitarianism, Liberty, and Representative Government*, "Everyman's Library" (New York: E. P. Dutton & Co., 1910).

to those principles and so to improve community relations.[9] (A caveat must be entered here. It is not argued that self-goverment will always have these beneficent results; but only that it tends to have them and that without it they tend to be lacking.)

The last clause suggests certain further observations. It may be said that a sense of community has often been known to develop—for example, in primitive societies—in the complete absence of self-government. This is very true. It brings out the fact that there is an important distinction between large and small societies. Where members of a group live close together, practically within sight of one another and having almost daily contact, a sense of community develops quite naturally without reference to the form of government or other outside stimulus. But in a large and dispersed society, such as characterizes modern states, this is not the case. There positive measures must be taken to ensure the development of public spirit.[10] If the stimulation of responsible citizenship is not used to achieve this effect, greater resort will be had to nationalism, and to emotionalism generally. The fascist states provide a clear illustration of this phenomenon. It is a fact of common knowledge that dictators find themselves forced to resort to ever new and more drastic stratagems to whip up the flagging interest of their "citizenry"; and as for idealism generally, and especially the standard of honor which is proudly announced as the spirit of fascist dictatorships, it soon gives way to cynicism.

Self-respect as well as public spirit is dependent upon the possession of political power. To be deprived of political power, to be judged unworthy of participating in public affairs, and to

[9] See Gunnar Myrdal, *An American Dilemma—The Negro Problem and Modern Democracy* (New York: Harper & Brothers, 1944), II, 1029.

[10] The very existence of political liberty is highly favorable to its development. That sage student of political behavior, Machiavelli, observed that a liberal regime is the most conducive to public-spiritedness. See especially *The Discourses*, Bk. I, Chap. LVIII, and Bk. III, Chap. IX. (Niccolò Machiavelli, *The Prince and the Discourses*, ed. Max Lerner [New York: The Modern Library, 1940].) Cf. also Diana Spearman, *Modern Dictatorship* (New York: Columbia University Press, 1939), p. 223.

be compelled to obey the commands of others whom one has had no share in selecting—these things are degrading, they crush one's self-respect and tend thereby to prevent one from achieving the very capabilities that are judged lacking. A man seldom climbs beyond his own idea of his capacities; and his self-evaluation is largely determined by the evaluation placed upon him by society.

Finally, political power is important to each of us as a protection against mistreatment and tyranny. As Bertrand Russell has said, "If you are going to have people with self-respect, who are not viewed with contempt, you must endow them with their share of power, for power is the one thing which in the long run brings the respect of others in the mass; and any class which is destitute of power will be despised and accused of every kind of crime, and harried and ill-treated and subjected to cruelty." [11] It is not necessarily true, as used to be asserted, that each man is the best judge of his own interest. But he must be the judge of what ultimately gives him satisfaction, and he needs power to make this judgment effective. He is, normally, the best *respecter* of his own interest and the best defender of his own rights. Insofar as men are self-seeking, they cannot be trusted, unchecked, to handle the affairs of others. On the other hand, insofar as they give more thought to the welfare of the whole than to their own well-being, surely they can be trusted with political power. Democracy is not an absolute guarantee that human rights will be protected and human interests advanced, but it is the best guarantee we have.[12]

Once more the positive values of self-government show up most clearly by contrast with the situation under democracy's opposite (and its only practical alternative today), autocracy, in its modern form of permanent dictatorship. Modern dictatorship

[11] New York *Times*, October 23, 1927, Sec. 1, p. 12, col. 1; quoted in Edward M. Sait, *Democracy* (New York: Appleton-Century-Crofts, Inc., 1929), p. 96.

[12] In other words, we are suggesting that man has sufficient commitment to the general welfare to justify giving him a share in political power, but also that he is sufficiently selfish that other men must have the protection of an equal share in power. The possibility of an aristocracy, in which the virtuous would rule, will be considered below (pp. 118–120).

is born of impatience with liberty and with the checks, the delays, and the technicalities attendant upon the rule of law. Its campaigning is composed very largely of attacks upon these features of liberalism. Insistence upon action is its keynote, action at any cost. Constitutionalism and popular control are alike anathema to dictatorship.

Not only, that is to say, does dictatorship involve placing fallible human beings in possession of uncontrolled power, but it also does away with all objective tests of the proper exercise of power. From the earliest times this has been recognized as the perfect setting for tyranny.[13]

It is bad enough that everything should depend upon the unguided good will of those in power, but this is not all. There is an inner dynamic in modern authoritarianism which makes it almost a certainty that the worst rather than the best elements will ascend to the seats of power. Thus the principle of aristocracy is stood on its head, and talk about rule by the "elite" becomes bitter irony. It can readily be seen why this is so. In the first place, the dictator, or "Leader," must have a powerful group of supporters, organized along military lines. Only by their efforts can he attain power and only by their continued adherence can he keep it. How can he secure the unquestioning allegiance and fanatical support of such a group? In practice, two methods have proved most successful. One is the appeal to self-interest. This produces the class party, committed to the pursuit of class aims. It will se-

[13] Cf. Herodotus: "How indeed is it possible that monarchy should be a well-adjusted thing, when it allows a man to do as he likes without being answerable? Such licence is enough to stir strange and unwonted thoughts in the heart of the worthiest of men. Give a person this power, and straightway his manifold good things puff him up with pride, while envy is so natural to human kind that it cannot but arise in him. But pride and envy together include all wickedness: both leading on to deeds of savage violence. . . . [Kings] are jealous of the most virtuous among their subjects, and wish their death; while they take delight in the meanest and basest, being ever ready to listen to the tales of slanderers. . . . But the worst of all is, that he sets aside the laws of the land, puts men to death without trial, and rapes women."—Herodotus, "The Persian Wars," Bk. III, Chap. 80, trans. George Rawlinson in Francis R. B. Godolphin (ed.), *The Greek Historians* (2 vols.; New York: Random House, Inc., 1942, I, 199). By permission of Random House, Inc., publishers.

cure the support of many who believe that the interests of their class and of the society as a whole are identical. But it will inevitably attract many—vastly more than those of the first group—whose horizon is limited by the boundaries of their class. And all must dogmatically commit themselves to class-defined goals.

The other method—more likely to succeed in advanced industrial societies because of their variety of economic interests—is that of seeking emotional and idealistic bases of unity. What is the simplest and most effective way of producing a closely knit and militant group along the latter lines? Broadly speaking, there are again two possible methods. One is to proclaim the ideal of universality and to appeal to the motives of love and sympathy. The other is to seek unity within a limited group by setting it in opposition to other groups. This means an appeal not to love but to hatred, not to sympathy but to envy, to religious and racial bigotry, to narrow self-interest, and to jingoistic nationalism. That the latter is the path most likely to succeed is known to every demagogue and to every observer of fascist movements.

Before proceeding further we must deal with a possible objection. Democratic parties as well as the monolithic parties of dictatorships must seek bases of unity. Is it not also true of them, it may be asked, that they will find appeals to the baser passions most effective? It is sometimes true; but there are vastly significant differences in the two situations. First, it is of the essence of liberalism to provide constitutional checks—those devices so reviled by authoritarian regimes—against the very abuses which might otherwise arise. Second, there is all the difference in the world between a militant movement seeking that degree of unity and submission to authority which the dictatorial pattern requires and a loosely knit democratic political party where discipline is weak, where at most unity is sought on but a few points, and where the absence of revolutionary urgency allows unity to be sought through the gradual processes of integrating subgroup loyalties.[14] Third, it must be remembered that dictators, too, must

[14] See below, Chapter XI, *passim.*

seek the support of the most stupid and ignorant. The great difference is that they foreclose the processes by which stupidity may be leavened and ignorance enlightened. The irrationality of the masses is thereby accentuated. Max Ascoli puts part of the answer very well when he says: "It is hard to condemn the new regimes in the name of democracy, because they boldly accentuate the elements and tendencies that every democracy has in itself, but it is even harder to condemn democracy in the name of the new regimes, because they aggravate with a pitiless exaggeration the most unbearable features of democracy." [15] To this we must add that the heart of liberal democracy is to be found in the protection which it provides against this exaggeration while the totalitarian regimes are based upon repudiation of these safeguards. In summary, as Reinhold Niebuhr has aptly remarked, "Man's capacity for justice makes democracy possible; but man's inclination to injustice makes democracy necessary." [16]

So we return to the conclusion, peculiarly true today, that if the masses of the people are deprived of political power, the worst rather than the best elements will be on top. The stage is set for tyranny at its worst. Because of the deterioration of communal ethical standards, an inevitable consequence of the fomenting of hatred between groups, there will not be even a moral check on the pressures impelling the dictator to rely on the method of terrorism, of secret police, of concentration camps, of arbitrary rule with its purges and its subjective criteria of justice. Standards of decent human relationships even in small friendly and familiar groups will tend to be undermined by fears of being denounced—with or without justification—for disloyalty or sabotage. Where all must profess a prescribed belief, deceitfulness and hypocrisy become the order of the day. Where ad-

[15] Max Ascoli, *Intelligence in Politics* (New York: W. W. Norton & Company, 1936), pp. 75–76.
[16] Reinhold Niebuhr, *The Children of Light and the Children of Darkness: A Vindication of Democracy and a Critique of Its Traditional Defence* (New York: Charles Scribner's Sons, 1944), p. xi. Note that this liberal position cannot be charged with the rosy optimism of the Enlightenment.

vancement and preferment may be had by informing, scarcely anyone will be trusted.[17]

THE RIGHT TO EQUALITY OF POLITICAL POWER. We have been giving reasons why every citizen should share in political power. These are not necessarily reasons, however, why they should share *equally*. Why should not those who have more ability than the average, or a greater stake in the conduct of government because they have more property (or more children!), have more than one vote? The equality principle, as developed in the preceding chapter, calls only for an equal response to equally central needs. It is impossible to prove that this standard can be most nearly attained in each particular case by an absolutely equal distribution of voting power. But neither is it possible to prove that an unequal distribution of power would approach the standard more closely. In fact, the presumption is strongly to the contrary because each has the same right, at the minimum, to preserve his life and the same right, at the other end of the scale, to complete fulfillment. Therefore, it is safe to assume that on the average the needs which government will be called upon to satisfy will be equally important for each of its citizens. How better guarantee an equal response in each case than by giving equal political power?

Moreover, at least one of the arguments used above regarding the right to political participation is also applicable here— the argument from self-respect. Equality of the vote is an important symbol. It stands in the minds of all for that basic minimum of equality which we have called the equality principle and which is generally known as equal rights. To give me but one vote when my neighbor has two is to tell me and announce to the world that I am but half a man. It is a blow to my self-respect and a discouragement to my moral ambition.

It may be contended, however, that this reasoning gives too little weight to the effect of a man's vote on the rest of society.

[17] The record of modern dictatorships illustrating and substantiating these points is too notorious to need recital. The theoretical analysis above is given to show that this record is by no means accidental.

A vote cannot be considered merely as a means of protecting and advancing the interests of the voter; it affects everyone in the state. Surely it is to my interest, other things being equal, that policies should be determined by those who have superior intelligence. Even John Stuart Mill thought this point of sufficient importance to justify inequality of voting power.

That there is merit in this contention cannot be denied; but there are three considerations which appear to the writer to clinch the argument against it. In the first place, it must be remembered that we are dealing now not with the whole of the political power an individual may possess, but only with that residual element of which he cannot be deprived. With its assistance, the man of exceptional ability or concern for the public interest may win for himself an influence on public affairs commensurate with his merit. Furthermore, there are, of course, especially on the administrative side of government, abundant opportunities for intelligence and competence to be brought to bear on the affairs of government other than through the ballot box.[18]

Second, the argument for differential voting power assumes that it is possible to identify those who possess the moral and intellectual capacities for political power in exceptional degree and to see that they and they only are given the politically superior status. Intelligence and information can, it is true, be measured with some degree of accuracy; but the equally important element of character, of commitment to the public interest, has so far defied measurement. Few since Plato have dared to think that this vital element of good citizenship could be tested with sufficient objectivity to justify society in permitting any group to devise and administer such a test.[19]

Finally, the great vice of any such system is that it would permit the minority to rule, and misrule, the majority. The salu-

[18] These points will be further developed below, Chap. XI.

[19] On the failure of proponents of aristocracy to wrestle effectively with this problem, see Charles E. Merriam, *Systematic Politics* (Chicago: The University of Chicago Press, 1945), pp. 188 ff.

tary effect of a check on the abuse of power by those whom it affects is lessened. Acton's adage that "all power corrupts" is pertinent. Responsibility attentuated, however so little, weakens by that much the protection against tyranny. Once the rule of equal votes is abandoned, there is no longer any assurance that the principle of equality of consideration itself, and its political counterpart, the rule of law, will be respected.

To this argument it may be replied that there is never any complete assurance against tyranny. There is, after all, such a thing as the tyranny of the majority. Aristocracy, it is true, weakens the defenses of the masses against the minority, but democracy exposes those of superior merit and ability, who are always in the minority, to the tyranny of the masses.[20] There is here, however, an important distinction which is often overlooked. In a democracy "the majority" is not a fixed group, set off from the rest by suffrage regulations or otherwise. One who is among the majority today is likely to be in the minority tomorrow. Even in such a moderate aristocracy as we are considering, however, the very fact of differential voting arrangements sets apart a certain group from the others. Its members are encouraged to think of the others as inferior. Under such circumstances, almost inevitably even that degree of respect to which the majority is entitled by aristocratic principles ceases to be accorded to them. If it be argued that the minority might not act as a unit, politically, the answer is that unless they do so the chief potential advantage of the aristocratic principle is lost. The politically favored either act together or oppose one another. That is to say, they are either irresponsible or ineffective.[21]

[20] Thus a modern critic of democracy writes: "The very people who tell us that human nature can not resist the strain of autocratic power require even more of human nature in their schemes for a successful democracy."— M. Alderton Pink, *A Realist Looks at Democracy* (London: Ernest Benn, Ltd., 1930), p. 211.

[21] If some of the arguments used here seem overdrawn, as applied to a very mild application of the principle of differential voting on the basis of ability, it must be pointed out that as the disadvantages of the aristocratic principle are minimized by watering it down and applying it in very limited form, the advantages suffer a proportionate diminution.

Summing up, it would appear that a consideration of the most defensible alternative to the rule of equal votes reinforces the positive arguments in favor of that principle. Relying as we must upon the laws of probability,[22] we must accept the rule of "one man, one vote" as a practical absolute, a presumptive right.[23]

OTHER LIBERAL-DEMOCRATIC RIGHTS. Having established, it is believed, the case for the equal right of self-government, the completion of our defense of liberal democracy in the political sphere is comparatively simple. The various democratic liberties are but direct applications to the political realm of aspects of the democratic way of life which we have already established. So it is, for example, with freedom of belief and expression of opinion. It needs only to be added here—and it is an important addition—that the case for freedom of speech and the press is immeasurably strengthened by the addition of the right of self-government. That right demands for its fulfillment free elections and the maximum opportunity for citizens to gain the facts and engage in the discussions necessary for reaching sound judgments on public issues. Even apart from the ballot, criticism plays an important role in checking the abuse of authority.[24] The same arguments support the right of assembly, which is a device for spreading knowledge, aiding in the formation of opinion, and organizing for its most effective expression.

The guarantees of equal protection of the laws, fair and speedy trial, and others lumped together above under the heading

[22] Cf. Niebuhr, *op. cit.*, pp. 71–73, for a discussion of the inevitable relativity of principles of political morality.

[23] At this point it is fitting to remind the reader that, for the purposes of this chapter, we are assuming that democratic government can maintain a certain minimum of satisfactory operation (see above, p. 97). It should be further pointed out that the evidence and arguments supporting the positive contributions that the average man, as voter, can and does make to society will be discussed in Chap. XI (see especially pp. 221–232, 252–253).

[24] As Reinhold Niebuhr says, ". . . . there is no historical reality, whether it be church or government, whether it be the reason of wise men or specialists, which is not involved in the flux and relativity of human existence; which is not subject to error and sin, and which is not tempted to exaggerate its errors and sins when they are made immune to criticism." —*Op. cit.*, pp. 70–71.

of the rule of law, all comprise straightforward applications to the political realm of the principles of liberty and equality. But here again the distinctively political right of self-government reinforces the case, because in the absence of such guarantees a government in power could discriminate against its political opponents and so intimidate them that they would fear to exercise their political rights against the government. Without the writ of habeas corpus, for example, an unscrupulous government could arrest opposition political leaders during political campaigns and thereby disrupt the organization of their competitors for power. This is but a mild example of what could happen and of what does happen under governments lacking effective guarantees against this kind of abuse.

Finally, the rights to a reasonable freedom of action, of movement from place to place, of choice of occupation, of contract, and of the use and disposal of property are in general clear corollaries of the general case for the maximization of liberty. However, a few words of explanation with regard to the last two are in order. A constant process in any society is the arrangement of the terms on which exchanges of goods and services shall be made. Either these terms must be fixed by voluntary agreement between the parties or they must be imposed from without. It is obvious that in a liberal society the former is to be preferred, *other things being equal.* Contracts enable individuals to go ahead and produce with the assurance that they will be able to make a certain exchange for their goods (or services) when they are produced (or rendered). In other words, by enlarging the area within which one can anticipate the actions of others and so diminishing the role of unpredictable factors, they greatly increase the area of effective self-determination, or liberty.

The institution of private property performs a similar function. It enables the individual to extend his power and so to increase his effective liberty. In this way, by distributing among many individuals power that would otherwise have to be exercised in some collective fashion, it avoids the threat of tyranny that always attends the concentration of power. It is entirely conceivable, however, that in a democratic society this concentration of economic power in the hands of political authorities could be kept under popular control. It is also possible that any other system will result in irresponsible concentration of power in a few private hands, as well as in the inefficient operation of the economy. These are not questions which we are called upon to consider at this point.[25] The principles of liberal democracy extend only to a "reasonable" freedom in the use and disposal of private property. In doing so they merely insist that the right to own property is a kind of freedom and that its values should be carefully weighed against other methods of protecting and enlarging the scope for the exercise and growth of human faculties.

4. *Appropriate Legal Status for Rights*

It is clear that the rights we have been discussing are capable of being cast into legal form. Whether or not they should be given that extra rigidity and stability that attends constitutional rights in this country is a matter of expediency. Much will depend upon the strength of public opinion in support of these rights and also upon the probable effect on such public opinion of giving the rights constitutional form. What should be insisted upon is that liberal democracy must be a *constitutional* democracy, that there must be effective restraints of some kind—legal or moral—upon the government and even upon the electorate. It is important to point out the fallacy in the reasoning of those who contend that to give rights a special status violates liberal-democratic principles.[26] Of course, if democracy were to be defined in terms of majority rule, meaning by that phrase the right of the majority to do whatever it pleases, any limitation upon the majority would be undemocratic. But no absolute right of majority

[25] They will be given some attention in Chap. XIV.
[26] See the argument of Willmoore Kendall in "The Majority Principle and the Scientific Élite." *Southern Review*, IV (Summer, 1938—Spring 1939), 463–473. This also appears to be the position of Professor Herman Finer, who declares that "in a democracy right is what the majority make it to be."—*Road to Reaction* (Boston: Little, Brown & Company, 1945), p. 60.

rule has been established, nor in the writer's opinion can it be established.[27] From our argument that there is an equal right of self-government it would follow that votes should count equally. But this right of self-government itself was derived from the basic rights of liberty and equality. Because it was the most apt instrument for the realization of these values it became entitled to the status of a right. The liberties that liberal democracy includes are fully as basic to the ultimate goal as is the power of self-government. In fact, in no small measure the latter is justified by its tendency to protect the former. Surely, then, the right of the majority cannot be advanced against one of the rights it is designed to protect.

This proposition is especially true of those rights, like the right of freedom of expression, which are basic to the operation of the democratic process itself. To allow democracy to destroy its own foundation would be self-defeating. Worse than this, the act of abolishing free speech is practically irreversible. It is a one-way street. Freedom of speech and of the press and of other political activities once lost, the avenues for regaining them without resort to violence are also gone. The right of the majority, in other words, does not exist in the absence of full opportunity for minorities to win over the majority, and therefore does not extend to the abolishment of that opportunity.

5. Concluding Remarks

If we have accomplished our aim in this chapter, we have established as presumptive rights the characteristic elements of liberal democracy. This means that these elements are essential conditions for the best way of life. It does not mean that they are necessarily sufficient conditions—that given these the best society will automatically follow. There are certain other conditions, to be discussed in the chapter on "Democratic Prerequisites." [28] In any case, the argument is based upon probabilities, not certain-

[27] Mr. Kendall assumes it to be self-evident, stating that it is incapable of proof or disproof.—*Op. cit.*, p. 465. See also Edwin Mims, Jr., *The Majority of the People* (New York: Modern Age Books, 1941).

[28] Chap. X.

ties. For this reason we have considered certain possible alternatives (dictatorship and a highly modified aristocracy) and have concluded that they would be far less likely than liberal democracy to provide the needed conditions. In conclusion we should show that there is reason to suppose we have considered the only other real possibilities. What about an hereditary aristocracy, or a mixture of democracy and aristocracy, such as England once enjoyed? This would appear to be the best combination for anyone seeking a rival for liberal democracy. Believers in aristocracy often cite the British aristocracy, in a vague and general sort of way, as an example of a good aristocracy. If space were available it would be fairly easy to show that, by almost any conceivable standards, democracy has done a better job of government in England than aristocracy ever did. A noted English historian concludes that democracy has produced "more wise legislation and administration than any other form of government" and has shown "greater vigor, greater ability, greater justice, and greater enlightenment" than either autocracy or aristocracy.[29] As a matter of fact, most of those who refer favorably to the English aristocracy are thinking of the latter half of the nineteenth century, when the principle of aristocracy had already been given up. But the sort of government provided by leaders selected from aristocratic families when they are responsible to the people is, of course, no indication of what would be the case if they did not enjoy their power by sufferance of the majority. Good or bad, such a system was necessarily temporary, tiding over the transition from aristocracy to democracy.

Furthermore, it was also inevitable that aristocracy should have been abandoned. The easygoing aristocracies of the past, benevolent even when inefficient, could not be re-created even if

[29] Edward P. Cheyney, *Law in History and Other Essays* (New York: Alfred A. Knopf, Inc., 1927), title essay, pp. 1–29, at p. 19. See also his "Historical Tests of Democracy," in which he compares three periods of English history (1600–1618, representing autocracy; 1800–1818, representing aristocracy; and 1900–1918, representing democracy) with respect to financial affairs, the conduct of war, relations with its principal dependency (Ireland), the encouragement of literature and learning, and service to humane progress.—*Ibid.*, pp. 90–129.

it were judged desirable to re-establish them. They governed easily because they governed in a relatively static society where little government was needed. Where most affairs were controlled either by tradition or by the mechanism of the market, the problem of government was simple. Even the sharp divisions of interest between the rich and the poor were not felt as such in a society where status was accepted as part of the law of nature. Today all that is changed. Modern technology and universal education have created a revolution in popular attitudes. People en-masse today would not for a moment willingly give up political power—at least not unless they were completely frustrated by inability to solve their problems democratically. It would have to be taken from them by violence. They would have to be put down and kept down by repressive methods. This would not be aristocracy as is meant by its proponents. This alternative, if it is to be taken seriously at all, should be discussed under the head of dictatorship; for, regardless of form, this is what it is.[30]

Old-fashioned monarchies, like old-fashioned aristocracies, are today among the museum pieces of forms of government. For the kind of society with which we are concerned, therefore, the only real alternative to some type of democracy [31] is dictatorship.

This concludes our ethical reappraisal of liberal democracy. We are concerned, however, not only with its value but also with its prospects. We have been assuming that it can be made to work in the future at least as well as it has in the past; but this assumption cannot be allowed to go unexamined. As we shall see in the course of the next three chapters, many developments cast doubt upon it.

---

[30] As a matter of fact, the wiser heads among the proponents of aristocracy realize this. What they are really doing is appealing to democracy to rid itself of its excesses. Faguet, for example, declares that it is necessary to put the brake on democracy. Then he hastens to add: "When I say put the brake on democracy, it must be understood that I mean that it should put the brake on itself, for nothing else can stop it, when once it has made up its mind."—Émile Faguet, *The Cult of Incompetence*, trans. Beatrice Barstow (New York: E. P. Dutton & Co., 1911), p. 226.

[31] Including under this heading the system of differential voting, or modified aristocracy, which was considered above.

PART THREE

ALTERED FOUNDATIONS

CHAPTER VII

THE SHIFTING
CLIMATE OF OPINION:
THE PRESENT STATUS OF
THE LIBERAL MYTH

Our reappraisal of the ethical foundations of liberal democracy has shown that the liberal ideal is still sound. Neither the attack on rationalism nor other philosophical developments have destroyed its validity. Yet liberal institutions in the second quarter of the twentieth century have been on the defensive. Gone is that unbounded faith in the free intelligence of the individual which characterized the earlier liberals. Buoyancy has given way to defeatism, pessimism, and cynicism. This contrast can be overdone. By no means everyone in the nineteenth century was convinced that the future was rosy—certainly not in England and not even in the United States; and many are hopeful today. But clearly there was a dominant note of optimism as to the future of liberal institutions a century ago which is now lacking. Anyone who doubts this has forgotten the unbounded optimism which characterized the liberals of the last century. The dominant tone of that period was struck by Renan when he proclaimed, in one of his early writings: "We believe in humanity in its godlike destinies, in its imperishable future . . . ; we believe in the dignity of man, in the goodness of nature, in the rectitude of his heart, in his right to attain the perfect state. . . ." [1] The same man, forty years later, with a strong foretaste of twen-

---

[1] Ernest Renan, *The Future of Science*, trans. Albert D. Vandam and C. B. Pitman (Boston: Roberts Brothers, 1891), p. 56. For this reference I am indebted to Christopher Dawson, *Enquiries into Religion and Culture* (New York: Sheed & Ward, 1933), p. 153.

tieth century disillusionment, wrote as follows: ". . . it is possible that the ruin of idealistic beliefs may be fated to follow hard upon the ruin of supernatural beliefs and that the real abasement of the morality of humanity will date from the day it has seen the reality of things. Chimeras have succeeded in obtaining from the good gorilla an astonishing moral effort; do away with the chimeras and part of the factitious energy they aroused will disappear."[2]

As Mr. Laski has remarked, liberalism is hardly less a habit of mind or a mood than a doctrine.[3] It is, in the political sense of the word, a myth—one of those great sets of beliefs which determine as much as they express the character of a whole civilization.[4] If this myth disintegrates, it will cease to govern the behavior of men whether or not the propositions it embodies are valid.

In what respects, then, has the myth of liberalism been on the wane? What accounts for the change? What does it signify for the future? These questions we must examine.[5] Certainly part of the change has been a decline in confidence in the rationality of human behavior and so in the workability of democratic institutions. We have considered the attacks on rationalism inso-

[2] Renan, *op cit.*, p. xviii, cited in Dawson, *op. cit.*, p. 153.
[3] Harold J. Laski, *The Rise of European Liberalism* (London: George Allen & Unwin, Ltd., 1936), pp. 15–16.
[4] Cf. Gaetano Mosca, *The Ruling Class*, trans. Hannah D. Kahn, ed. Arthur Livingston (New York: McGraw-Hill Book Company, 1939), esp. Chap. 3. Mosca uses the term "political formula" rather than "myth."
[5] The present chapter will deal with the changes in opinion and with the causes of the changes only insofar as those causes may be explained in ideological terms. The following chapter will deal with the movement of events which has tended to undermine liberal democracy, often by way of contributing to the changes of opinion discussed in the present chapter. In spite of this causal relationship, which would suggest a reversal of the order of this chapter and the next, it has seemed best to adhere to the order used because of the very intimate relationship between the next chapter and that which follows it. This sequence makes it necessary to warn the reader, however, that some of the material causes of the ideological changes that are discussed in the present chapter will be considered in due course. Their omission here does not imply denial of their importance. The prospects of the liberal myth will be dealt with in succeeding chapters, especially Chap. XIII.

far as they bear on the case for the liberal-democratic ideal, but we have not yet examined these attacks as they bear on the practicability of that ideal.

1. Doubts as to the Workability of Liberal-Democratic Institutions

Believers in liberal democracy have generally given credence to the existence of a natural harmony of interests. Those who did not adhere to the "unseen hand" doctrine, believing in a harmony of self-interest, narrowly conceived, placed their confidence in human sympathy. Like John Stuart Mill, they assumed that man was such a social animal, so sympathetic toward the needs and interests of others that—quite apart from consideration of "objective" right—he would be led to subordinate his special interests to the general welfare. Even more essentially, they have assumed that men generally act rationally, that is on the basis of a considered judgment as to the ends they should pursue and of a careful calculation of the means best designed to attain these ends. Both the assumption of harmony of interests and that of rational behavior have been subjected to serious criticism during the past century.

One of the most powerful attacks on the notion of harmony of interests is that which was delivered by Karl Marx. Ultimately, to be sure, Marx himself believed in a natural social harmony. After all, his ideas were strongly influenced by the stream of English Utilitarian thought. But for Marx this harmony of interests was something which could not be achieved as long as society permitted private ownership of the instruments of production. This institution introduces into society a fatal division—fatal, among other things, to democracy. As long as men are divided among owners and workers, rich and poor, exploiters and exploited, there can be no general community of interest. In such circumstances it is only so long as the masses can be deceived as to their true interest that anything resembling democracy can work under capitalism. And this, of course, is no true democracy, for the ruling capitalists are forced to use their power at every turn to prevent the institutions of democracy from functioning properly lest they lose their dominating position. Thus, while liberty, equality, and fraternity remain the ultimate goals for Marxists, and the usual democratic forms of government, or something essentially like them (though lacking coercive organs), will presumably characterize the ideal communist society, the operation of these ideals and institutions in capitalistic regimes is reviled and derided.

The most direct impact of this line of analysis is upon the liberal-democratic belief in the possibility of peaceful change by the ordinary processes of constitutional government. Marx taught not only that democratic institutions under capitalism are necessarily perverted to antidemocratic purposes but also that capitalism itself, which is the root of the evil, cannot be eliminated by democratic processes.[6] Furthermore, it is held by followers of Marx that the revolution must be followed by the "dictatorship of the proletariat," a more or less lengthy period of authoritarian rule by a small minority (though for the benefit of the majority). Regardless of ultimate objectives, therefore, the main emphasis in Marxist teaching has been toward the belittlement of democracy as it is known today and toward the glorification of a kind of dictatorship. And indeed, if Marx was right, not only is our democracy a sham but it is destined to become increasingly unworkable until revolution abolishes the capitalist system.

In this connection, further reference should be made to the ideas of Nietzsche. Although he was not primarily a political theorist, and can hardly be said to have formulated his ideal systematically, his belief in the will-to-power as the dominant characteristic of man was certainly at odds with the liberal assumptions under discussion. (It should be remarked parenthetically that he represents only the most extreme version of a line of thought which stems from his compatriot Schopenhauer.) Both his glorification of will as opposed to reason and his romantic idealization

---

[6] Or at the very least Marx believed that such elimination was so improbable that the supporters of the proletariat should proceed on the assumption that they could accomplish their aims only by revoluton.

of struggle and conflict for their own sakes are ideas that have had great influence in modern times. They are more significant for their bearing on attitudes toward democracy than for any direct light they throw on the question of its workability. (But, of course, the former affect the latter.)

Fully as serious for liberal democracy are the criticisms of those who deny that men generally behave rationally, or even that rational conduct can be counted on to prevail on the whole. During the past seventy-five years or so, students of psychology and sociology have persistently cast doubt upon this assumption. For example, the French sociologist Gabriel Tarde brilliantly expounded the thesis that man is predominantly an imitator.[7] Imitation, as Tarde uses the term, may be either conscious or unconscious; but in any case it is more likely than not that nonlogical influences will determine what is imitated. Tarde himself was not primarily concerned with either the desirability or the practicability of democracy. He was inclined to believe that Tocqueville was right in predicting the continued spread of equalitarianism and was also of a mind to believe that this development threatened liberty. But he recognized that this trend might someday be reversed and even contemplated the possibility that imitation, so to speak, might run itself into the ground and cease to dominate the social scene. For our purposes, however, the significant point is that Tarde cast serious doubt upon democratic rationalism. It was left to others—who were not wanting—to seize upon this aspect of his theories and use it to discredit democratic dogmas.

Among those others was another Frenchman, the social psychologist, Gustave Le Bon.[8] Le Bon dealt especially with the behavior of men in "crowds." Like Tarde with imitation, however, he gave to the term "crowd" a technical meaning. Not all aggre-

---

[7] Gabriel Tarde, *Les Lois de l'imitation: étude sociologique* (5th ed., Paris: F. Alcan, 1907). The first edition of this book appeared in 1880. Several years before this, Walter Bagehot, in his *Physics and Politics* (London: H. S. King & Co., 1872), developed the theme that man is primarily an imitator and that society is and should be preserved by minimizing liberty and protecting the "cake of custom."

[8] Le Bon's most popular work, *La Psychologie des foules,* was first published in Paris, in 1895, by Félix Alcan.

gations of persons composed crowds in his sense of the word; on the other hand, a crowd might be composed of scattered individuals. For our purposes, however, we need note only that crowd behavior was a kind of behavior which he believed was widely characteristic of people's political conduct. Its most significant feature is the subordination of reason to sentiment and emotion. The behavior of a crowd may be morally either good or bad, but it will always be "intellectually inferior to the isolated individual." [9] In a crowd, individual personality vanishes, and by processes of suggestion and contagion the feelings and ideas of all turn in the same direction. The heart of Le Bon's position is summarized in his own words in the following passage:

> We have shown that crowds do not reason, that they accept or reject ideas as a whole, that they tolerate neither discussion nor contradiction, and that the suggestions brought to bear on them invade the entire field of their understanding and tend at once to transform themselves into acts. We have shown that crowds suitably influenced are ready to sacrifice themselves for the ideal with which they have been inspired. We have also seen that they only entertain violent and extreme sentiments, that in their case sympathy quickly becomes adoration, and antipathy almost as soon as it is aroused is transformed into hatred. [10]

The incompatibility of this picture with that of the rational voter, thoughtfully discussing and considering issues in terms of personal, group, and national interests, and exerting his political influence accordingly, needs no elaboration.

Curiously enough, the third writer who calls for comment under the present heading was also of French nationality. He is Georges Sorel, whose *Reflections on Violence* [11] appeared in the first French edition in 1906. Sorel was strongly under the influence of the irrationalist philosopher Henri Bergson. [12] He attacked

[9] Gustave Le Bon, *The Crowd—A Study of the Popular Mind* (London: George Allen & Unwin, Ltd., 1896), p. 37.

[10] *Ibid.*, p. 81.

[11] Georges Sorel, *Reflections on Violence,* trans. T. E. Hulme (3d ed.; New York: The Viking Press, 1912).

[12] Although Bergson was not concerned with political philosophy, his mystical emphasis upon intuition and upon "life force" as basic, with reason as its handmaiden, places him along with Schopenhauer and Nietzsche as one of the chief philosophical sources of irrationalist political theorists.

what he called "intellectualist philosophy" in politics, claiming that it was unable to explain the fact that men continually sacrifice their lives for such ideals as honor and national glory. To assume that men act from a calculation of consequences, he insisted, is quite contrary to the facts. Men, in the mass, always act under the impetus of a powerful "myth." They envisage themselves as participants in a great battle in which they are destined to be successful. Such a myth was Marx's catastrophic revolution and the syndicalists' general strike. It is of no moment to discuss the truth or falsity of these myths in terms of conventional academic analysis. Their significance lies in the very fact that men will act in response to them regardless of rational considerations. Sorel utilized this theory to support his belief in direct action for the attainment of syndicalist objectives. This doctrine was in complete opposition to the liberal belief in constitutional change. Its broader significance, however, lay in its emphasis upon the irrational character of political behavior. Even more directly than any of the preceding philosophers of irrationalism, Sorel contributed to the *Weltanschauung* and even to specific proposals of fascism.[13]

Perhaps the most fundamental blow that has yet been struck at liberal rationalism stems from the writing of Sigmund Freud, a man whose work was chiefly in the field of individual psychology. What may be the ultimate consequence for liberalism of the fertile vein of investigation being pursued by the psychoanalysts remains to be seen. But that the immediate impact and the net result up to the present time have been unfavorable can hardly be doubted. Man's mind can never again, since Freud, be visualized in such simple terms as was possible before. Freud's discovery of the subconscious mind, which, like the submerged portion of the iceberg, is far weightier than the part exposed to view, has had revolutionary consequences. Man is now presented as a creature whose behavior is determined by powerful driving forces welling up from within, beside which the restraints of

[13] To be sure, his most immediate influence was on the syndicalist movement.

"reason" are virtually helpless. Reason provides the justifications for actions whose true motives lie hidden even from ourselves, in the subconscious. We are the less able to control them because we are not aware of what is motivating us. These drives can be, and often are, repressed; but then they come out in other, and often socially less desirable, forms. Man is irrational, according to Freud, not only in the sense that he does not regularly use reason to discover the means to achieve a deliberately selected end, but more fundamentally in the sense that many of his drives are anti-social, and many of them mutually incompatible.[14] In short, Freud attacks both of the liberal assumptions under review—rationality of conduct and harmony of interests.

2. *Other Factors Tending to Undermine Confidence in Liberal Democracy*

How much validity these various criticisms have, to what extent they prove the liberal-democratic state to be impracticable, it will remain for subsequent chapters to discuss. The prospects of democracy, however, are affected not only by the facts of human nature but also by the faith or lack of faith which men have in it, and by the reigning attitudes toward the values which it seeks to embody. We have just seen certain developments which undoubtedly have had an unfavorable impact upon the liberal-democratic myth. We must now proceed more directly to a consideration of the changes in that myth.

RELATIVISM AND SKEPTICISM. Before considering the effects of the doubts as to the rationality of human behavior, we shall go back and refer to certain consequences of ethical relativism and of relativism more generally. Political liberalism, as we have seen, emerged on the crest of a great wave of confidence in the power of reason to disclose certain absolute rights. Even if it can now be supported, as we have argued, on less absolutist reasoning, there might be a long and disastrous lag between popu-

[14] ". . . the tendency to aggression is an innate, independent, instinctual disposition in man . . . ."—*Civilization and Its Discontents*, trans. Joan Riviere (3d ed.; New York: Jonathan Cape & Harrison Smith, 1930), p. 102.

lar loss of confidence in the old theory and popular acceptance of the substitute.

That the trend of thought during the past century has been relativistic, i.e., away from all absolutes, can hardly be doubted. In a general way, this may be said to represent the impact of natural science. Both its method and some of its conclusions tend in this direction. The method is based upon skepticism. All propositions must be doubted. Nothing must be taken on faith. Even the basic scientific assumption of the unity of the universe has come to be increasingly treated as a purely heuristic principle, advanced in a very tentative fashion.[15] This outlook is productive of popular attitudes which are unfavorable to any myths, and therefore particularly devastating in their effect upon current complexes of belief.

More specifically, social relativism has been fostered primarily by the theory of evolution in biological science and by that of relativity in physical science. The impact of each has been felt far beyond the borders of its special province. It is perhaps not too much to say that together they have formed the scientific world view of our generation, dominating the climate of opinion of the age.[16] The idea of a fixed, immutable, and universal law of nature, discoverable by reason, could hardly remain untouched by evolutionary doctrine. Belief in the gradual evolution of the species, of continuous change in the most fundamental characteristics of all living things, including man himself, tended to weaken the belief in unchanging principles of right and wrong. It is possible, of course, that there are laws of right conduct which, like the law of survival of the fittest, remain constant in the midst of change. Possibly, indeed, there are certain rules which are always conducive to survival, and a sound ethical system might in fact be the embodiment of such rules. Such was the position of Herbert Spencer. But it may seem equally plausible to

[15] It should be clearly understood that no question as to the validity of this method is being raised.

[16] John Herman Randall, Jr., *The Making of the Modern Mind* (rev. ed.; Boston: Houghton Mifflin Company, 1940), p. 458.

hold that beliefs which represent the most successful adaptations to one type of environment may give way to quite different principles under altered conditions. Philosophers like Nietzsche, finding the struggle for power dominant in nature, have sought to raise this law of the jungle to the level of a normative principle. With Nietzsche, reason is completely displaced by will, specifically the "will-to-power," as the basis of ethics. Regardless of the validity or invalidity of Nietzschean ethics (which was discussed in Chapter V), it can hardly be doubted that it has contributed to an erosion of popular confidence in the ethical superiority of liberal democracy.

Einstein and the theory of relativity have also contributed powerfully to the disintegration of the belief in an objective good, ascertainable by reason. Newton's discovery of universal physical laws had encouraged the belief in natural laws governing politics. Einstein's demonstration of the parochial nature of Newton's laws constituted a further blow to the idea of absolutes in the social order. Einstein appeared to attack the finality, the stabilizing quality, of two of our most basic physical concepts, space and time. Even these, it seems, are relative. The Newtonian laws apply only within certain finite limits. Geometries based upon assumptions contrary to what had been believed self-evident truth (the postulates of Euclid) now no longer are treated as fantastic. Under certain circumstances they may be "true," i.e., useful. On both the macrocosmic and the microcosmic levels there appear to be discontinuities in the erstwhile universal laws of physics. The fact that physicists and mathematicians alike continue to search for unifying principles, and in fact appear to be convinced that there are and "must be" (query: Why?) such principles, is generally overlooked. Some, it is true, have grasped at the principle of indeterminism as a support for their desire to believe in some of the old moral "truths"; but for the most part the effect of these developments has been to discredit belief in any and all kinds of finality, of objectivity, and of universality.

Even the laws of logic themselves have not escaped the corrosive effects of this attitude borrowed from the natural sciences.

Carl Becker put the matter in his usual brilliant manner, as follows:

Logic was formerly visualized as something outside us, something existing independently which, if we were willing, could take us by the hand and lead us into the paths of truth. We now suspect that it is something the mind has created to conceal its timidity and keep up its courage, a hocus-pocus designed to give formal validity to conclusions we are willing to accept if everybody else in our set will too.[17]

Such an attitude, it may be argued, is the *reductio ad absurdum* of whole movement. When we doubt the first principles of our reasoning, we doubt all our conclusions, including our doubts! But even the self-defeating quality of complete skepticism does not disprove its validity. Furthermore, it is possible that only the last stage, the application of skepticism to the laws of logic, was faulty. In any case, regardless of its validity, skepticism is part of the intellectual milieu which today colors our thinking in general, and especially our thinking about principles of ethics and politics.

Not only did skepticism raise doubts as to the effectiveness of reason; even its desirability was brought into question. The natural reaction to skepticism was romanticism. In moderation this amounts only to giving a proper emphasis to emotion and feeling, with insistence that intellectual values are not the only ones.[18] It tended, however, to go much further than this and to amount to belittlement of reason, and to an assertion that there is a fundamental conflict between rationality and vital forces. In the following passage the view is clearly expressed by one who holds it:

We admire the man whose reason is capable of more than scheming, whose logic is not the mere rationalization of his desires, and who can follow through an argument to its conclusion even though that conclusion is not one favorable to himself, his party, his country, or his species. But intelligence as detached as this is a vital liability. It puts the man or the race which possesses it at a disadvantage in dealing

[17] Carl L. Becker, *The Heavenly City of the Eighteenth-Century Philosophers* (New Haven: Yale University Press, 1932), p. 25.

[18] See José Ortega y Gasset, *The Modern Theme*, trans. James Cleugh (London: The C. W. Daniel Company, 1931).

with those whose intelligence faithfully serves their purpose by enabling them to scheme for their ends and to justify to themselves their desires.[19]

It needs no elaboration to show how such disillusionment sets the stage for the romantic anti-intellectualism and hero-worship of fascism.[20]

If we consider together the natural effects on popular beliefs and attitudes of the ideas advanced by such men as Freud, Nietzsche, and Ortega, we might almost wonder that any liberal beliefs survive. Their combined effect has been to cast doubt both upon the ethical doctrines which underlay the natural rights theory of democracy and upon the psychological assumptions which underlay Utilitarian and pragmatic theories of democracy. The net result of these writers and others like them has undoubtedly been to cast a shadow of pessimism and even despair. Especially has the incubus of the psychology of the unconscious contributed to the sickness of liberalism. This effect is exemplified in some of the writings of the political psychiatrist, Harold Lasswell, who contends that social life inevitably deals blows to the ego, which lead to accumulations of personal insecurity, which in turn manifest themselves in the form of "irrational" aggressions.[21]

Equally significant for its effect upon popular attitudes is the modern emphasis upon "rationalization." Man, the rational being, has, in his own estimation, been lowered from this estate to that of the inveterate rationalizer. The idea that much self-proclaimed rational behavior is really fake—that is, pursued for reasons different from those the actor proclaims and also different from what he believes himself to be moved by—was by no means original with Freud, although he and his followers have done much to popularize it. It had already made itself felt in the realm

[19] Joseph Wood Krutch, *The Modern Temper* (New York: Harcourt, Brace and Company, 1929), pp. 42–43.

[20] See, for example, Rohan d'O. Butler, *The Roots of National Socialism* (New York: E. P. Dutton & Co., 1942), Chap. 2; and Peter Viereck, *Metapolitics—From the Romantics to Hitler* (New York: Alfred A. Knopf, Inc., 1941), esp. Chaps. 1–7.

[21] See Harold D. Lasswell, *World Politics and Personal Insecurity* (New York: McGraw-Hill Book Company, 1935).

of liberal political theory, as, for example, in the works of Graham Wallas[22] and Robert Michels.[23] The best example, perhaps, is provided by the Italian sociologist Vilfredo Pareto, who attempted, in four ponderous volumes, to build a science of society upon the recognition of the fact of rationalization.[24] His elaborate conceptual framework for explaining human behavior in terms of "residues," "derivatives," and "derivations" boils down to little more than this. It reflected and no doubt encouraged the cynical view of human nature, and (incidentally) its attempt to provide a science of human relations failed miserably.

Perhaps the most logical conclusion to be drawn from the belief that there is no rational pattern of human ends to bind society together was drawn by Nietzsche and by the fascists after him: the race is to the strong and may the devil take the hindmost. Certainly the aggrandizement of force, the glorification of struggle for its own sake, and the renunciation of duty to mankind make as much sense as anything in such a world. But on the whole, that has not been the popular line of thought in the strongholds of liberalism—possibly because the concept of a right that is distinct from might had too strong a hold on the minds of the masses. Nevertheless it is an ever-present danger wherever and whenever liberalism threatens to lose its appeal. And in large areas of the world which once, at least, wore the mask of liberalism, it gained—perhaps still retains—something like general acceptance.

In most of the Western world, however, it has not been the nihilists but those more moderate relativists, the Marxists, who have had the greatest influence.[25] Their denial that the interests of

[22] See Graham Wallas, *Human Nature in Politics* (3d ed.; New York: Alfred A. Knopf, Inc., 1921).

[23] See Robert Michels, *Political Parties,* trans. Eden and Cedar Paul (New York: Hearst's International Library Company, 1915).

[24] Vilfredo Pareto, *The Mind and Society,* trans. Andrew Bongiorno and Arthur Livingston, ed. Arthur Livingston (4 vols.; New York: Harcourt, Brace and Company, 1935).

[25] On a previous page in this chapter (above, p. 126), it was pointed out that Marx's theory raised a direct question as to the practicability of liberal democracy. The point here is that, regardless of the validity of his

the classes can be reconciled, together with their messianic assertion that the weak would ultimately prevail—by violence—has proved more widely acceptable. Yet clearly it is no more favorable to the liberal-democratic belief in a common good attainable by peaceful methods. Only a small minority in Britain or in America has yielded completely to the doctrine; but many have been sufficiently affected to blind them to instances of common interest between classes and to examples of class yielding to class without resort to violence.

Moreover, the effect of Marxian relativism upon liberal-democratic attitudes goes far beyond the matter of faith or lack of faith in the possibility of peaceful reform. Marxism teaches that all institutions, all beliefs, all principles, are relative to the particular historical circumstances out of which they arose and the interests which they were designed to protect or advance. Abstract principles are meaningless. They must be understood as the expression of certain interests. As the interests change, so do the principles. The principles are to be valued by reference only to the interests which, at a particular stage of historical development, they support. This approach is applied right down the line to all liberal, or "bourgeois" institutions and beliefs. Democracy itself has no absolute claim to our allegiance. "Rights," "freedom," "justice," "equality," are likewise terms which cannot be accepted as representing things of value without inquiring "For whom?" and "For what?" Freedom of speech must not mean freedom for fascists to speak. "Formal" freedoms and "formal" equality may not be worth preserving if they are rendered ineffective by economic pressures and inequalities. The logical conclusion of this line of attack, or so at least it may be argued, might be to make such reforms as would make the "formal" principles actually effective; but the Marxist tendency is to belittle the formal principles and institutions themselves. Even the liberal tends to become

argument, the effect on popular thought tends to be dispiriting and to arouse skepticism about liberal-democratic institutions. The danger in this situation, of course, is that, even though Marx's teaching as to the *inherent* unworkability of liberal-democratic institutions may be false, the very effect of his teaching might be to make them unworkable.

confused and his defenses weakened by the growing list of qualifications and exceptions to his absolutes. Regardless of whether or
not the defenses of liberty, equality, and other democratic rights
set forth in previous chapters are sound, the impact of this movement has greatly weakened the assurance of their supporters.
As E. H. Carr has said, ". . . . the serious thing about the contemporary revolution is not that Marxism has kindled and inflamed the resentments of the under-privileged against the existing order and helped to make them articulate: the serious thing is
that it has undermined the self-confidence of the privileged by
sapping their own faith in the sincerity and efficacy of the principles on which their moral authority rested." [26]

More generally, and quite apart from Marxism, skepticism as
to human rationality, perhaps imparted by theorists, perhaps by
the ever-present example of the effectiveness of modern propaganda and advertising appeals to emotion, sentiment, prejudice,
and illogical association, has undermined people's confidence in
the rational appeal as a means of settling human differences.
When cigarettes are sold by pictures of bathing beauties, political candidates will likewise relegate reason to second or third
place as a method of persuasion. When the ideal of objectivity
and impartiality is gone, discussion, the lifeblood of democracy,
becomes only another means of attaining one's end, and a rather
ineffectual one at that. In the absence of faith in ultimate rationality, there is no basis for believing that in the end "truth"
will win out—a truth that will be to my advantage as well as
yours. Optimism loses its foundation; and so do tolerance and the
willingness to abide by majority decisions and constitutional restraints.[27] Thus both this view and the Marxist view lead to a "we
or they" type of reasoning which destroys the prospects of unity

[26] Edward Hallett Carr, *The Soviet Impact on the Western World* (New
York: The Macmillan Company, 1947), pp. 94–95. Carr's discussion of the
subject of the paragraph above is excellent and I have drawn upon it
heavily, especially pp. 90–95.

[27] Cf. Melvin Rader, *No Compromise—The Conflict between Two
Worlds* (New York: The Macmillan Company, 1939), p. 141. "When men
cease to reason they begin to fight."

by agreement because it preaches the impossibility of attaining it and therefore the futility of making the effort without which it surely cannot be attained.

MATERIALISM AND SECULARISM. Relativism and general skepticism are not the only ideological factors in contemporary society tending to destroy faith in, and enthusiasm for, liberal democracy. It would appear that materialism and secularism have tended to have a similar effect. Before the close of the nineteenth century, Lecky remarked that materialism and lack of enthusiasm tend to go together.[28] He found no dearth of contemporary evidence to support this generalization. ". . . when we look back," he wrote, "to the cheerful alacrity with which, in some former ages, men sacrificed all their material and intellectual interests to what they believed to be right, and when we realize the unclouded assurance that was their reward, it is impossible to deny that we have lost something in our progress." [29] Secularism, which is one aspect of materialism, and which gives the dominant tone to society today, deprives the liberal tradition of useful support. This is true for more reasons than one. First, in spite of the fact that rationalism arose partly in revolt against the church, it continued to find support in, and to rely heavily upon, a belief in natural law, which in turn tended to rest upon faith in a divine order. Furthermore, it appears to be a fact that the bulk of mankind still demands some kind of religion. When it is lost to many people in the usual form, they experience a spiritual vacuum, a lack which is soon filled by one of the great political religions. These political religions, whether of the right or of the left, are patently not democratic. They demand that the individual bow down to a god which is yet not a god, but an all-too-human tyranny. How specific is this need for some kind of religion it is hard to tell. It seems clear, however, that there is a side of man's nature we may broadly designate "spiritual" and "heroic" that de-

[28] W. E. H. Lecky, *The History of the Rise and Influence of Rationalism in Europe* (2 vols.; New York: Appleton-Century-Crofts, Inc., 1890), II, 373.
[29] *Ibid.*, p. 375.

mands fulfillment. If it is starved it will provoke a sharp reaction. But it may well be that democracies can develop programs and ideals that will give ample recognition to this side of human nature.[30]

Materialism may also be unfavorable to democracy in ways other than its effect on enthusiasm. Unity is threatened by the substitution of the goal of material gain for spiritual salvation. The love of God unites at least those who are agreed about the way in which that love should be expressed, while the love of material goods might almost be said to be inherently divisive. Two people, or two billion, can love the same God and will have a greater respect for each other because they do, but they cannot all enjoy the same meal or ride in the same automobile. Moreover, preoccupation with material progress seems to feed upon itself. Each increment of material welfare appears only to create insatiable demands for more. Further, emphasis upon material things rather than ideas tends to detract from the disinterested pursuit of truth and from disinterestedness generally, again leaving liberal institutions bereft of an important prop.

One aspect of the unfavorable effects of materialism has perhaps never been better put than by Tocqueville. He wrote as follows:

When men have once allowed themselves to think no more of what is to befall them after life, they readily lapse into that complete and brutal indifference to futurity which is but too conformable to some propensities of mankind. As soon as they have lost the habit of placing their chief hopes upon remote events, they naturally seek to gratify without delay their smallest desires; and no sooner do they despair of living forever, than they are disposed to act as if they were to exist but for a single day.[31]

He goes on to argue that, where social democracy prevails, the danger is increased because the attendant equality of opportunity

[30] See Chap. XII.
[31] Alexis de Tocqueville, *Democracy in America*, trans. Henry Reeve, ed. Phillips Bradley (2 vols.; New York: Alfred A. Knopf, Inc., 1945), II, 149–150. By permission of Alfred A. Knopf, Inc., authorized publishers.

gives greater scope for materialistic striving and consequent instability.

Moreover, not only unity and disinterestedness but also liberty itself is threatened by materialism; for wherever it appears that material well-being will be advanced by sacrificing liberty, materialistically minded people will, of course, be ready to make the sacrifice. Liberty is a spiritual value—it has to do especially with things of the mind—and people who are more concerned with comfort are obviously less likely to exert themselves to stave off the encroachments of the power hungry, and less likely to risk loss of their material goods. Yet historically, liberty has been obtained and preserved only by the "eternal vigilance" and exertions of those willing to risk everything for its preservation. It can hardly be doubted, either, that over a period of time a life of comparative security and comfort softens the spirit of independence, makes one less inclined to run risks and less inclined to see serious threats to one's own liberty in acts which restrict the conduct of others.[32]

THE DECLINE OF INDIVIDUALISM. Another view of what is happening to the liberal ideology may be seen by examining that group of ideas and attitudes known as individualism. There can be no doubt that this focus of attention upon the individual, sometimes referred to as "ego consciousness," was one of the characteristic and basic elements of all aspects of the liberal movement. The "rights of man" were rights to be enjoyed by individuals, all individuals alike; and they were rights—"life," "liberty," "property"—which emphasized the individual, private nature of the ultimate human satisfactions and also the individualistic means for attaining those ultimate ends. There can hardly be any question that this focus of attention is shifting. Leonard Woolf, for example, in his masterly study of the development of the climate of opinion during the nineteenth century, depicts the rise of a new communal psychology which is sharply opposed to

---

[32] We are dealing in this paragraph with materialism in two senses: materialism as a system of values, and materialism as a life of material comfort. Since they both relate to the problem at hand, there seems to be no harm in treating them together.

individualism.[33] Another analyst of the modern temper selects as one of its three chief characteristics (along with "experimentalism" and "emphasis upon impulse rather than reason") a "sense of social cooperation," and of community, as contrasted with "the ideal of saving one's soul in medievalism and with the complacent individualism of the early industrial era . . . ." [34] Writing two years or more before Hitler's accession to power, he declared that "the modern mind envisages the group-life of any community or association as a reality which cannot be understood in terms of a collection of separate units." In fact, he adds, "the devotion of men to a group-life more inclusive than egoism or altruism would imply is so obvious as to be almost a danger." [35]

But possibly the individualism of the early political liberals was one-sided. The true values which it enshrined may be in no wise threatened but even reinforced by a proper recognition of social elements it inclined to overlook. The subject certainly deserves further analysis. Just what do we mean by this individualism which we say has been basic to liberal culture? For one thing, it seems clear that we mean self-reliance—the belief that a man should stand or fall on the basis of his own merits and efforts. In the sphere of religion, this might take the form of Protestantism—a protest against the authority of the church and the necessity of priestly intermediation between the ordinary man and his God—or the more extreme forms of agnosticism or atheism, denying completely the necessity for human dependence upon supernatural forces. Except insofar as the loss of religion may have made some people more susceptible to the lure of political religions—a phenomenon which was discussed above[36]—this area discloses no threat to liberalism. A few prominent intellectuals of liberal persuasion have joined the Catholic Church, convinced of the inadequacy of their previous liberalism;

[33] Leonard Woolf, *After the Deluge* (2 vols.; New York: Harcourt, Brace and Company, 1931, 1939), I, 290 ff.

[34] C. Delisle Burns, *Modern Civilization on Trial* (New York: The Macmillan Company, 1931), p. 315.

[35] *Ibid.* The quotations are to be found, respectively, at p. 316 and p. 318.

[36] Above, p. 138.

but there are not enough of them to indicate a clear trend in this direction. On the other hand might be cited the marked increase in the number and following of revivalist movements in the United States.[37] Whatever else may be said of these movements —they are certainly antirationalistic and may be an alternative outlet to the political religions mentioned above—their central emphasis upon the salvation of the individual soul cannot be said to be anti-individualistic.

In the field of social relations the philosophy of self-reliance called for an end of hereditary class distinctions and for greater social mobility. Here again in the greater part of the Western world there has been no tendency to reverse the movement. The Nazis, to be sure, while attacking the remnants of the old feudal social distinctions, tried to create a new hereditary peasantry. There is little to indicate that this represents a general trend in Western culture, although the tendency of some trade unions to favor seniority over merit as a standard for measuring reward is a danger signal.

In the economic realm, self-reliance stood for freedom of contract, freedom of trade, and free enterprise—the abolition of feudal obligations, of the guild system, and of mercantilistic trade restrictions. Here is where the great change has taken place. As will be pointed out in detail in the next chapter, the exigencies of industrialism have necessarily subordinated individual self-reliance in the economic sphere to reliance upon various forms of group and collective activity. In this respect, certainly, the old liberal myth is waning—or at least it is changing. The great question from our present point of view is whether political individualism can stand without economic individualism.[38] If so, the tarnishing of the myth, its loss of drawing power (as far, at least, as it proceeds from this cause), may be only a temporary phenomenon.

Finally, in the political realm itself, self-reliance meant the

[37] See Eduard C. Lindeman, "Trouble at the Grass Roots," *Survey Graphic*, XXXIII (June, 1944), pp. 280–282.
[38] This question will be examined in Chap. XIV.

demand for individual liberty against government and for political power—a demand which eventuated in the overthrow of despotism and the substitution of constitutionalism and democracy. We shall have occasion in the following chapter to speak in some detail of attitudes toward individual rights as they have been affected by changing economic conditions. Here, however, it is pertinent to remark the general statement, so frequently heard, that people today are much less concerned about liberty and much more with security than was true in the heyday of liberalism. This is undoubtedly true, but there is little evidence that it applies to political or civil liberty, as contrasted with economic liberty—certainly not if a bare minimum of security is maintained. It is a fact, of course, that in Germany and Italy and in certain other countries where democratic institutions had never taken deep root, under conditions of grave and prolonged crisis, large numbers of people willingly saw themselves deprived of political power and rights in return for the promise (among other things) of security. It is also a fact that France has, since the war, yielded at last to the demand for female suffrage, and that in the United States the slow process of enfranchising the Negroes in fact as well as in form is proceeding with improved (though laggard) pace.[39]

As to civil liberties, even in Great Britain, where liberty relies for its protection upon ordinary acts of legislation, backed up by strong public sentiment, democracy has shown no sign of minimizing these protections of personal freedom. Even when the nation was faced with the grave threat of invasion, the actual administration of emergency legislation granting powers to curtail civil liberties was remarkably liberal.

In the United States, where civil liberties receive constitutional protections, enforced by the judiciary, the record is, on the

[39] See O. Douglas Weeks, "The White Primary: 1944–1948," *American Political Science Review*, XLII (June, 1948), 500–510; Donald S. Strong, "The Rise of Negro Voting in Texas," *American Political Science Review*, XLII (June, 1948), pp. 510–522; and Gunnar Myrdal, *An American Dilemma: The Negro Problem and Modern Democracy* (2 vols.; New York: Harper & Brothers, 1944), Vol. I, Chaps. 22–23.

whole, also encouraging. Throughout most of the thirties, while the Supreme Court was busy paring down property rights, it was equally assiduous in maintaining and even enlarging the area of civil liberty. The war record in the United States, as in England, was exceptionally good—with the notable exception of our treatment of Japanese-Americans. The American Civil Liberties Union, a zealous guardian of personal rights, reported that both the war and the immediate postwar periods were remarkable (especially as contrasted with the record of World War I) for the low incidence of repressive measures. For the past three years, however, the reports have noted an unfavorable trend arising out of the "cold war" between the United States and the Soviet Union and of the activities of Communists everywhere in support of the latter country's policies.[40] The tension between the two great powers is continuing to create a problem of unexampled difficulty because of the fact that the Communist party is at once a political party and at the same time (it is generally believed) responsive to the dictates of an outside power that would like to bring about the overthrow of the United States government. It must be sadly recorded that the United States is currently undergoing a case of Red hysteria. Smear tactics by political investigating committees are nothing new in American life, but the widespread activities of secret, unidentifiable investigators, accumulating scraps of gossip as "evidence"—this is a new and dangerous development. Private quizzing of neighbors along such lines as "Does he own an album of Paul Robeson records?"—this and the new spirit which tolerates and accepts it are alien to the American tradition. For short periods of time, however, the United States has had such attacks of hysteria before; so there is ground for hope that this one may be similarly

[40] See the following reports of the American Civil Liberties Union: *The Bill of Rights in War* (New York: The Union, 1942); *Freedom in Wartime* (New York: The Union, 1943); *In Defense of Our Liberties* (New York: The Union, 1944); *From War to Peace—American Liberties, 1945-46* (New York: The Union, 1946); *In Times of Challenge—U.S. Liberties, 1946-47* (New York: The Union, 1947); *Our Uncertain Liberties—U.S. Liberties, 1947-48* (New York: The Union, 1948); and *In the Shadow of Fear—American Liberties, 1948-49* (New York: The Union, 1949).

short-lived. In fact, nothing has yet developed that is comparable in intensity to the anti-liberal hysteria after World War I, with its "Palmer raids," mass arrests, and deportations. It is reassuring to note that there is little, if any, evidence of direct interference in the central fields of expression of ideas—whether by speech, press, or radio. And in the field of political rights the trend continues to be toward improvement.[41]

There is encouraging evidence that public opinion distinguishes between civil and political liberty, on the one hand, and economic liberty, on the other hand. An indication of this fact is to be found in a poll of the opinions of high school students taken by *Fortune Magazine,* in the autumn of 1942. Students were asked which of the following they were "most willing to give up" and which they were "least willing to give up": freedom of speech, freedom of religion, the right to vote, trial by jury, the right to change jobs, or the right to earn over $3,000 per year if they could. Less than 3 per cent listed either of the first two freedoms as ones they would be most willing to give up, while 82.5 per cent indicated one or the other of these as the freedom they would be least willing to part with. On the other hand, approximately 60 per cent were most willing to give up the right to earn over $3,000 per year if they could, while another 20.8 per cent would sacrifice the right to change jobs first of all. Thus over 80 per cent would give up their economic liberties first, 6.4 per cent refused to commit themselves, leaving only a total of 13 per cent who would part first with any of the political or civil liberties.[42] Whether the distinction between the two kinds of liberties can be maintained in practice is another question which must be considered in the proper place. For the time being, the significant point is that it is not the distinctively political side of this aspect of individualism which is on the wane.[43]

[41] See, for example, the report of the American Civil Liberties Union for 1948–1949, *op. cit.,* p. 3.

[42] *Fortune,* XXVI (Nov., 1942), 8.

[43] Perhaps the optimism of this paragraph calls for some qualification. If it had been written in the depth of the depression, its tenor would have been less sanguine. Even today it can hardly be denied that the current

There is another side of individualism, more important from the point of view of democratic belief than that of self-reliance. This is the notion variously denominated as the "sacredness," "dignity," "infinite value," or "absolute value" of the individual. Actually it is a fusion of the theory that all value must be measured in terms of individual experience with the belief in equality of rights; but it is commonly thought of as a single doctrine, and as the most vital part of the democratic creed. Frequently it is identified with the Kantian principle that each person should be treated as an end-in-himself. Perhaps an even more pivotal part of the concept is the belief that one individual should not be compelled to undergo serious suffering so that others—even many others—might have more pleasure. This is the principle of equally central needs, which was discussed in a previous chapter.[44] From this key notion of the absolute value (or perhaps better, the "presumptive equality") of individuals springs the whole array of democratic rights of the individual—pre-eminently the rights to life and liberty; and, of course, also the belief that all people—regardless of ability, birth, or social or economic status—are equally entitled to these freedoms.

In passing, it may be noted that the general attitude of humanitarianism implicit in this focal democratic dogma may act as a limitation upon certain aspects of economic individualism. This lends support to the position that the modification of economic individualism may be in no wise incompatible with the essence of the democratic myth. We may now add that it may even be required by it.

What, if anything, is happening to this key concept? There

---

emphasis on "freedom from want" betokens a concern for security so great that it might well lead to the voluntary abdication of political and civil liberty if it appeared that the choice had to be made. Cf. Hermann Rauschning, *Time of Delirium*, trans. Richard and Clara Winston (New York: Appleton-Century-Crofts, Inc., 1946), esp. pp. 172–174. It was remarked on a previous page that the materialistic trend of the age tends to bring about a depreciation in the value placed upon liberty (above, p. 140). If this effect has not extended to civil and political liberties, it does not follow that it would not do so if those liberties came into conflict with material welfare.
[44] Above, pp. 84–85.

are a priori reasons for thinking it must be on the decline. Secularism tends to deprive all moral values of their atmosphere of sanctity. The attack upon rationalism has further contributed to lowering their prestige. Utilitarianism and other rationalistic supports of ethical norms have likewise been depreciated. With mingled truth and exaggeration, Professor Sorokin declares

More and more, present-day ethical values are looked upon as mere "rationalizations," "derivations," or "beautiful speech reactions" veiling the egotistic interests, pecuniary motives, and acquisitive propensities of individuals and groups. Increasingly they are regarded as a smoke screen masking prosaic interests, selfish lusts, and, in particular, greed for material values. . . . Ethical and juridical norms have both become mere rouge and powder to deck out a fairly unattractive body of Marxian economic interests, Paretian "residues," Freudian "libido," Ratzenhoger "interests," the psychologists' and sociologists' "complexes," "drives," and "prepotent reflexes." [45]

Over against this argument, however, is another a priori consideration, based upon sociological rather than ideological factors, which tends in the opposite direction. In all "advanced" industrial countries the size of the family has greatly declined. It is quite possible that one tendency resulting from this change will be to enhance the value placed upon the individual. Such is the argument advanced, for instance, by Professor Robert MacIver.[46] The mutual contradiction between these speculative arguments emphasizes the importance of securing concrete evidence before making generalizations.

It is obvious that in countries dominated by totalitarian regimes the value of human life has been cheapened, and it is significant that it is from such countries that Sorokin draws the bulk of his supporting evidence. There is little to indicate, however, that the decline in respect for human life and other individual rights preceded the accession to power of their dictatorial governments. In any case, the question is not what happened in

[45] Pitirim A. Sorokin, *The Crisis of Our Age*, p. 157. Copyright, 1941, by E. P. Dutton & Co. Reprinted by permission of E. P. Dutton & Co.
[46] Robert M. MacIver, *The Web of Government* (New York: The Macmillan Company, 1947), p. 310.

Germany or Italy, where democratic myths which had never become more than partially developed broke down in the face of crisis situations, or in Russia where no such myth ever existed, but what is happening in countries where the myth has been most fully developed. As has already been indicated, in the United States and in England, equalitarianism is still on the rise and regard for civil and political liberties is likewise in the ascendant. We continue to insist that it is better that many criminals should escape unpunished than that one man should suffer the injustice of being punished for a crime he did not commit. This is a key application of the principle of absolute value. We view with great suspicion proposals for compulsory sterilization of the socially undesirable, although the fact that such procedure in the case of certain types of mental defectives has come to be permitted in some states might be viewed as a slight trend away from the notion of individual "sacredness." Euthanasia continues to be generally condemned, and punished, although it is possible that there is an incipient alteration in attitudes on this matter. Opinion polls indicate that it is more widely approved among the young than among the old, but whether this is indicative of a trend or merely of a very understandable change in attitude produced by advancing age it is impossible to say.[47] In any case it is not at all clear that a change of attitude toward euthanasia carried out only at the request of the individual concerned, would indicate any change in respect for the individual.

3. In Conclusion

Before concluding this survey of ideological influences, we must note that the emphasis on factors in the realm of ideas tending to weaken the liberal-democratic myth should not be overdone. The course of events probably has had more to do with it.[48] Depression and unemployment cast a wet blanket over the

[47] A poll released by the American Institute of Public Opinion in June, 1947, found 54 per cent of the people opposed to euthanasia for incurables, by doctors, at patients' and families' request. Approval was recorded by 37 per cent.—*Public Opinion Quarterly,* XI (Fall, 1947), 477.

[48] See the following chapter.

confident optimism of an earlier day. But it was not entirely the fact that this depression was worse and more prolonged than others had been; here ideas and events worked hand in hand. Millions of people who had not accepted Marxist dogma were yet sufficiently influenced by its ideas to come readily to the conclusion that capitalism was contracting, its expansive days gone, never to return. The theory that American prosperity had been a phenomenon of youth and that now we must restrict ourselves to the more abstemious diet characteristic of a mature economy gained wide if not general acceptance. To be sure, these notions relate to economic rather than to political conditions; but so closely were economic and political liberalism woven together in the past that anything which tended to discredit one inevitably discredited the other as well.

Furthermore, in England and America, the sight of fascist successes abroad had a depressing effect on the ardor of many democrats. The fact that both of the influences just referred to (depression and the spectacle of fascist triumphs), have now been eliminated may be taken as encouraging for the prospects of the liberal-democratic myth. Moreover, the authoritarian and totalitarian regimes of the twentieth century have had at least this value: they have furnished the world a gigantic demonstration of what tyranny is like. We have been reminded of the depths of degradation to which men in positions of absolute power can and will sink. Any notion that civilization has softened the nature of tyranny has been fully disproved. Time and again, too, we have seen how the suppression of particular liberties— such as freedom of expression and the right to form political parties—has been the prelude to other despotic practices.

The war itself served to quicken our love for liberty. Ironically enough, the present "cold war" between the Western states and the totalitarian Soviet Union has the same immediate effect, in spite of the fact that it carries with it one of the most serious challenges to that freedom, which is even now making itself felt in terms of spy scares, loyalty tests, and investigations conducted in an atmosphere of hysteria.

Furthermore, democratic self-confidence is being boosted by the realization that democracies have dealt more successfully with the great problems that face the world today than have other types of government. Whatever may have been the errors of liberal foreign policies, few would challenge the statement that totalitarian regimes have proved to be greater threats to world peace than their democratic counterparts. Not only that, but even in domestic affairs, totalitarianism failed to bring either prosperity or permanent security. At best, the fear of unemployment has given way to the fear of "liquidation." During the period of the recrudescence of authoritarianism, nowhere in the world has such progress been made as in liberal-democratic countries. This statement will stand whether we speak of the material well-being of the masses, of personal security and liberty, or of equality of rights.[49]

[49] The last two items, of course, are not subject to precise measurement, but no observer pretending to impartiality could doubt the statement made. It has been of the essence of the authoritarian regimes to curtail liberty and deny rights. During this period even the darkest chapter of American liberalism—our treatment of the Negro—has witnessed striking improvement, whether the test be the lynching record, opportunity to vote, or equality of employment opportunities. With regard to the material well-being of the masses, certain significant figures are reported by the International Labour Office. The data indicate that, even during the bitter thirties, real weekly wages in industry in the United States (on a 48-hour-week basis) increased by 17.2%, while Germany and Italy experienced 7% and 2% increases, respectively, during the same period.—*International Labour Review*, LV (May, 1947), 470–472. Comparable figures for Great Britain are not available. Comparisons with the Soviet Union are extremely hazardous both because of the difficulty of getting reliable data and because her economy was so completely disorganized during and immediately after the revolution. Thus, while with most countries 1929 is a useful guide point for comparisons because it was the predepression peak, in the case of the Soviet Union production at this time was at an extremely low point. For the period 1913 to 1937, Colin Clark estimates a slightly greater rate of increase in the *per capita* national income (on the basis of a 48-hour-week) in the United States than in Russia. (See Colin Clark, *The Conditions of Economic Progress* [London: Macmillan & Co., 1940], chart facing p. 148.) Clark also notes that at an earlier period in its growth—which would be more properly comparable with Russia during the 1913 to 1937 period—American development was considerably more rapid.—*Ibid.*, p. 147. Other estimates made by reputable authorities are much more unfavorable to Russia, showing a decided *decline* in real wages in Russia for the period in question. See, for example, the estimates by Leonard E. Hubbard, *Soviet Labour and Industry* (London: Macmillan & Co., 1942), Chap. 12.

To be sure, the facts are one thing and the popular realization of those facts is another. It is certainly true that even in the United States we have not completely recovered from the shock that was administered to our self-confidence by the decline of liberal democracy in so many parts of the world between the wars, and by the great depression. There can be no doubt, however, that in the United States there is far less defeatism and far more confidence in the prospects of liberal democracy than prevailed during the thirties. In England the severity of the economic pinch resulting largely from the wartime liquidation of capital is hardly compatible with bouyancy of spirits, to say the least. This being so, the obvious determination of the great bulk of Englishmen to retain all their civil and political liberties, while substituting a measure of socialism for the old ideal of economic liberalism, and their resolution to keep the latter change from seriously interfering with liberty of action are highly encouraging signs. In short, the evidence suggests, although it does not prove, that enthusiasm for liberal democracy may be in for a lasting revival, and that the ideological factors tending to undermine it may have little effect as long as political and economic success prevail.

Nevertheless, in spite of what has just been said, we can but conclude that the enthusiasm and optimism which characterized the earlier years of the liberal movement have declined. This fact in itself tends to weaken liberal institutions. Moreover, one cause for this decline has been a growing conviction that man is a less rational animal than was once assumed. In subsequent chapters we must examine the actual operation of the democratic process to see whether or not it is hopelessly and inevitably vitiated by human irrationality.

In addition to the weakening of democratic faith there has been a great shift in popular attitudes toward the individual. There can be no doubt that we are today less "ego conscious" and more aware of the fact that man is necessarily a social being than was true a century ago. It is not clear, however, that this change has affected those aspects of individualism which are essential to political liberalism. The great change has been in the economic field; it has no direct significance for liberal democracy. Whether there are indirect relations, whether liberal democracy can stand without liberal economics, presents a problem which must be postponed until we have examined the economic changes in some detail. This in large part will be the task of the following chapter.

CHAPTER VIII

THE MOVEMENT OF EVENTS

Liberalism arose out of a particular social milieu just as much as it did out of a body of abstract ideas. Social conditions as well as ideas have continued to change, and anyone who is concerned with the future of liberal democracy must examine the nature of these changes and appraise their bearing on political institutions. As a preface to such an examination, it is pertinent to note certain significant aspects of the environment in the early days of liberal democracy. In the first place, we were in the horse-and-buggy era, technologically speaking, when modern democracy came into being. As someone has remarked, Voltaire or even Jefferson would have been more at home in the material culture of predynastic Egypt than they would be in a modern metropolis. Industrially, capitalism was in the small-enterprise stage, with the individually owned business predominant. Representatives of the middle classes were achieving the positions of leadership and control, economically and politically. Laissez faire was the ideal of the rising classes and to a large degree characterized the policy of governments in the countries under consideration. The activities of government were thus kept at a minimum. Decentralization added to this effect as far as concerned the central government. Although between England and the United States there were vast differences, economically and industrially as well as socially, neither was dominated by the Big City.

1. Increase in the Rate of Change

It is obvious that most of these conditions have changed. It may be noted at the outset that the very Industrial Revolution which made democracy possible, by undermining the position of the old ruling class and by providing the common man with military might and (thanks to the printing press) with the education to enable him to use his new-found force effectively—this same Industrial Revolution has by no means ceased its revolutionizing activity but has gone on to transform completely the environment of even a century ago. One of its most significant consequences for democracy is the very fact of change itself, and especially the increasing *rate* of change. Today there are often more inventions in a single year than there were in a thousand years before the middle of the eighteenth century. We no longer leave invention to chance; we have institutionalized it. Society sees to it that an ever-increasing proportion of its members devote their time to the advancement of both pure and applied science. Thus the revolutionizing process seems destined to go on apace. Thirty years ago, Henry Adams estimated that the pace of progress doubled every ten years.

Of the direct effects of this trend upon the tasks of government, we shall have something to say in the next chapter. Here we shall concentrate upon the social and institutional developments which follow in its wake and which are in turn fraught with political significance. The broadest of these is the phenomenon known as "cultural lag." Human beings change their beliefs, their habits, their institutionalized behavior but slowly. Once a particular individual has adapted himself to a given culture, he seems to have little capacity to adjust himself to changed conditions.[1] The gap between generations, between father and son, is nothing new, but anyone who has brought up children during the past decade cannot but be aware of the fact that there is a greater breach between the standards and values of the young today than there was between him and his parents, or (even more) than that between them and their parents. Doubtless the full explanation of this fact is not a simple one, but that the motion picture, the automobile, and the radio have been leading influences seems clear enough.

[1] Cf. Abram Kardiner, *The Psychological Frontiers of Society* (New York: Columbia University Press, 1945), p. 421.

2. Urbanism

Another potent factor in the changed quality of society today may be summed up in the word "urbanism." Even in Britain at the beginning of the nineteenth century the urban population made up only 17 per cent of the total, as contrasted with 54 per cent in 1891.[2] In the United States, of course, the shift is even more striking. In a century and a half we have changed from a country in which less than 4 per cent of the people were urbanites[3] to one where close to half of the people fall in that category.[4]

The sociological consequences of urbanism are intertwined with those of the broader phenomenon, industrialism, which is the cause of urbanism itself. However, it is worth isolating certain effects which may be primarily attributed to the fact of city life. One of the most important of these is the loss of relative self-sufficiency. On the farm, to a large extent, the family group makes up an economically and socially self-sufficient unit. Such outside needs as it has are met in large measure by the still small, face-to-face group of the neighborhood. In this community of neighbors are fulfilled most of the material, intellectual, and spiritual needs of its members. The community is made up of a group of families whose identity changes but little from generation to generation. A man's place among his fellows is determined partly by his own reputation and partly by the standing which his family has attained over the generations. He is thus provided with a sense of security and a feeling of responsibility, both highly stabilizing factors. The large city, by contrast, is made up of racially and socially heterogeneous groups of people, almost every detail of whose lives are entangled in the seamless web of a society that extends far beyond the bounds of their own acquaintanceship,

[2] Adna Ferrin Weber, *The Growth of Cities in the Nineteenth Century* (New York: The Macmillan Company, 1899), p. 47.

[3] *Ibid.*, p. 1.

[4] In 1940, the census figures show that 47.6 per cent of the population were in cities of over 10,000.

indeed, beyond the effective limits of their imaginations. People who share a common area of living small enough to admit of community life are not united by occupational ties or by the need to act as a group for the provision of any of their collective needs. A greatly increased rate of residual mobility is a further hindrance to the development of communal ties and of the sense of responsibility which such ties breed. Even the smallest and most central of primary groups, the family, tends to disintegrate under the centrifugal force of numerous, exciting outside sources of amusement and recreation and in the absence of common family work for self-support. Add to these factors the heightened pace and intensity of city life and it is no wonder that the city dweller tends to be psychologically far less secure than his rural counterpart. Insecurity always weakens the sense of responsibility and breeds a short-run view. The urbanite is likely to be indifferent to politics when times are good, and to go to extremes and to fall victim to demagoguery when they are bad.[5]

3. Increasing Division of Labor

Other aspects and consequences of industrialism have had perhaps even more significant effects upon our political society than has urbanism. One of the most fundamental principles of the Industrial Revolution is that of the division of labor. The effects of this development in terms of increased output and of the mode of production known as "mass production" are well known. Equally significant from the political point of view is the fractionalization of experience which is its inevitable accompaniment. The smaller the role which each individual worker plays in the total productive process, the narrower his outlook on life tends to become. He becomes a specialist who sees the world

[5] In the words of one sociologist, ". . . life among the masses of a large town tends to make people much more subject to suggestions, uncontrolled outbursts of impulses and psychic regressions than those who are organically integrated and held firm in the smaller type of group."—Karl Mannheim, *Man and Society in an Age of Reconstruction* (New York: Harcourt, Brace and Company, 1940), p. 60. The sociological literature on the effects of city life is vast. See Lewis Mumford, *The Culture of Cities* (New York: Harcourt, Brace and Company, 1938), for an effective interpretation.

from the point of view of his activity. An airplane pilot may have a bird's-eye view of the landscape, but his views on matters of national politics are likely to reflect the particularized interests of his own calling. The technician, the machine operator, and the assembly-line laborer have little in their daily work experience to contribute to breadth of outlook.

At the same time, however, hours of work have declined and leisure time activities may bring contact with people from varying occupations. In this way it might be anticipated that some of the narrowing effect of specialized occupations would be offset. No doubt it is; but men and women who work together or at the same kind of activity tend to mix together in informal social life. Their common interests are their vocational interests and the almost inevitable result of such association is to underline their vocational, special-interest points of view, to accentuate rather than to counteract the very tendency we have been discussing. Furthermore, they form organizations along functional lines. Whether the purposes are social or economic and political, once more the tendency is to rigidify the attitudes that are particularistic at the expense of those that are shared with the community as a whole. The general interest suffers. The dispersive[6] character of modern interest-groups, each organized for its own advancement, carries with it a threat to the democratic method of securing the general welfare that is all too obvious. The group self-interest is further encouraged by the fact that the paid officials of these associations inevitably feel under pressure to justify their existence and expand their organization by doing everything possible to emphasize and exaggerate the extent to which the interests of the group in question are at odds with those of other groups. The story is told of a man who visited the national headquarters of a pressure organization just after it had achieved the legislative triumph for which it had been

[6] I have borrowed the term from Ernest Griffith, whose volume, *The Impasse of Democracy: A Study of the Modern Government in Action*, (New York: Harrison-Hilton Books, Inc., 1939), contains a great deal of valuable material pertinent to the discussion in the text. See esp. Chap. 3.

created. Instead of finding the jubilation which he had naïvely anticipated, he was greeted by an atmosphere of general gloom —they had worked themselves out of employment. True or not, the story illustrates a basic fact which cannot help have its effect on all such organizations.

Yet it is possible to exaggerate the threat to liberal institutions which interest-group organization involves. If it appears a rather far cry from Rousseau's conception of the General Will, it is much closer to Bentham's or Mill's view of the interplay of individual interests, with groups substituted for individuals. Certainly pluralistic strife among groups is far better for democracy than a dualistic struggle between two sharply defined classes. The chief question in the former case is whether or not it can be kept from producing such deep and manifold divisions in public opinion that agreement on positive policy becomes impossible. This is a question we shall have to examine in a later chapter.[7] It should be pointed out now, however, that, if we are concerned about actual historical developments, we should beware of comparing the contemporary facts of politics with past visions of what it ought to be or even with rose-tinted versions of what it was. We may well be suspicious of any account of any government at any time in which all who shared in power conducted themselves with singleness of purpose to discover and achieve the general welfare. At the very origin of the American republic, James Madison showed himself well aware of the group nature of politics and of the close tie between economic interest and political behavior. In a famous passage, he wrote:

A zeal for different opinions concerning religion, concerning government, and many other points, as well of speculation as of practice; an attachment to different leaders ambitiously contending for preeminence and power; or to persons of other descriptions whose fortunes have been interesting to the human passions, have, in turn, divided mankind into parties, inflamed them with mutual animosity, and rendered them much more disposed to vex and oppress each other than to co-operate for their common good. So strong is this propensity

[7] See below, Chap. XII.

of mankind to fall into mutual animosities, that where no substantial occasion presents itself, the most frivolous and fanciful distinctions have been sufficient to kindle their unfriendly passions and excite their most violent conflicts. But the most common and durable source of factions has been the various and unequal distribution of property.[8]

As explained above, the greater variety of interests today may be a protection rather than a threat.

Another feature of the division of labor is that of "round-aboutness." Nowadays very few workers produce things directly for the ultimate consumer. Instead, for example, they may help process ore to be used to make metal from which to fashion a part for a machine to make another machine which will in turn produce a part to be assembled with other parts to produce the ultimate item of consumer goods. This is just another way of indicating the almost endless interrelatedness of the modern economic world. Anything which stops production at any point along the line is likely to hold up the whole process from beginning to end. If, say, steel or railroads are involved, practically the whole economy will be affected in a very short time. Apart from such direct relationships as exist between the manufacture of steel and of automobiles, anything that throws large numbers of men out of employment soon extends its effects through the economic system by way of curtailed purchasing power and shattered business "confidence."

One indirect effect of this fact of economic unity is that, as people become aware of it, it tends to offset the fractionalization of experience discussed above. And there are many signs that people are becoming aware of it. The great depression had as its most immediate consequence a marked accentuation of movements for group self-defense; but it also served to point the moral of economic interrelatedness, and the experience of those years has been used with telling effect in popular education during the subsequent years. For instance, there is certainly far more realization in the United States at the present time that

---

[8] Alexander Hamilton, John Jay, and James Madison, *The Federalist*, No. 10 (New York: The Modern Library, 1941), p. 56.

a poverty-stricken Europe means lack of markets, possibly even a nose dive into economic collapse, for the United States, than there was following the First World War. Since the war, too, the the wave of nation-wide strikes has contributed powerful tuition along the same line. Possibly the division of labor is itself providing the answer to the problem it has raised.

To be sure, the division of labor has created other problems. One of the most important of these is that it has tremendously increased the responsibility which the state must assume for keeping the great machine going. In the depression of the nineties, big business came to the aid of government; today the shoe is on the other foot. The staunchest defenders of private enterprise now admit that in the last analysis government must accept the responsibility for keeping capital and labor employed. There are differences of opinion as to the methods which should be used and as to the time at which government should intervene, but on the general proposition there is practically universal agreement. The problems for democracy created by this development will be discussed in the following chapter.

4. Economic Instability

The word "depression," not long absent from almost any economic discussion, has already been mentioned. One of the most striking characteristics of modern industrialism is its instability, its fluctuating, cyclical character. It has improved the average person's material well-being immeasurably, but it has greatly diminished the predictability of his economic future. We have (unintentionally) traded low-level economic security for high-level economic insecurity. This must be added to the reasons for psychological insecurity mentioned above in order to get a true picture of the unstabilizing factors in modern society. Individuals who live under the constant threat of indefinite unemployment, through no fault of their own, from conditions over which they have little or no control, are likely to be willing to pay a high price for relief from this threat. And if they become convinced that abandonment of liberty and democracy will bring them security, no one should be surprised if they make that choice. The strain of unemployment is not made easier by the memory of past prosperity or even by the hope of a return to that condition at some indefinite time in the future. The very disparity between potential and actual productivity which characterizes our periods of low employment heightens the sense of the intolerability of the crisis. Under such circumstances people are in no mood to be "philosophical" about their troubles, nor are they likely to be tolerant of inefficiency, slowness, or ineffectiveness on the part of their government, whether it is democratic or not. The strain on constitutional morality approaches the breaking point. If either majority decisions or minority rights appear to block the path to recovery respect for the orderly processes of government is not to be counted upon.[9]

5. Altered Role and Nature of the Middle Class

Many would argue that we have so far omitted all consideration of the most important changes that have come about—the alterations in the role and the nature of the middle class. Political liberalism did not displace despotism without a struggle; and that struggle was in general the successful revolt of the groups somewhat loosely designated "the middle class" against the old feudal aristocracy. Under the influence of Marxian thought, it has become popular today to say that the political institutions of liberalism reflected the needs of this class and that as the middle class is progressively forced to share its power with the laboring class it may be anticipated that another set of political forms and ideas will have to be developed. Typical of this approach is that of the late Harold Laski, who declared, "This it is which explains the declining authority of liberal doctrine in our epoch. It was so preoccupied with the political forms it had created that it

[9] The point being made here is very closely related to what was said in the preceding chapter in discussing the effects of materialism (above, p. 140). It was there pointed out that people who value material things more highly will necessarily value liberty less highly when the two come into conflict. It is argued here that the insecurity of modern society is likely to produce such conflicts.

failed adequately to take account of their dependence upon the economic foundation they expressed." [10]

In England and the United States, liberal democracy did develop largely under middle-class leadership, and, even more, as a result of middle-class pressure. It was the rising commercial and industrial classes, on both sides of the Atlantic, who pushed aside the old rulers and broadened the bases of representation. In large measure, also, it was they who continued this process until true political democracy was attained; but it is significant that in some cases it was the leaders of the old ruling groups who insisted on extending a share of political power to even larger, and socially and economically lower groups in the effort to gain support against their middle-class rivals. Once the movement was well under way, in other words, it tended to lose its distinctive class character as the various groups bid against each other for popular support. In fact, it may be said that in England and America democracy was even more the product of the disintegration of classes than it was of the victory of one class over another. If anyone doubts that there has been such a change, let him but reflect on the tremendous alteration that has taken place with regard to the general conception of the right of the masses to happiness. In the eighteenth century, by all save a few, it was taken for granted that the masses were not entitled to happiness —certainly not to happiness of the same order as was vouchsafed their "betters." [11] Perhaps nowhere better than in the field of

---

[10] Harold J. Laski, *The Rise of European Liberalism* (London: George Allen & Unwin, Ltd., 1936), pp. 243–244.

[11] Cf. Leonard Woolf, *After the Deluge* (2 vols.; New York: Harcourt, Brace and Company, 1931, 1939), I, 191ff. Note, for example, the words used by Hannah More, a philanthropist, in addressing a group of poor women with reference to the famine that was current. She was at pains to point out that the great misfortune which had struck them was not without its advantages; for, she said, ". . . . [it] has also enabled you to . . . observe the benefits flowing from the distinction of rank and fortune, which has enabled the high so liberally to assist the low . . . ." "We trust the poor in general," she later remarked, "especially those who are well instructed, have received what has been done for them as a matter of favour, not of right . . . ."—*Ibid.*, p. 193. Surely this attitude, then commonplace, is far removed from anything imaginable today.

amusement and recreation is the great change which has taken place evident. Today millions are spent for public parks, public tennis courts, picnic grounds. and similar facilities. Travel is no longer the perquisite of the privileged few. Different "classes" of railway accommodations are approaching extinction in England, while the modern "tourist-type" American railroad coach provides comparative luxury for all. Vast economic differences, of course, there are, but the notion of class status either as something determined by birth or as a fact that carries with it, *ipso facto,* the right to greater happiness than others enjoy is well-nigh a thing of the past in these countries, and especially in the United States. Perhaps nothing is more indicative of this than the fact that approximately 80 per cent of Americans consider themselves as members of the "middle class." [12]

It appears, then, that, even though political liberalism was ushered in on the shoulders of the middle class, the liberal democracy which grew out of it was by no means exclusively a middle-class product. In part it reflected the rise of the laboring class and in part the manner of its coming evidenced the disintegration of hard and fast class lines. Furthermore, Laski's analysis is too general to be of much use. Even if the forms of political liberalism were created to aid the middle class in the exercise of political power and in the enjoyment of liberty and equality of opportunity under a rule of law, it does not follow that those forms might not be equally well suited to enable a broadened constituency to enjoy the same privileges. [13]

[12] Conclusion reached by *Fortune* on the basis of a poll conducted in 1940. The figure given includes persons who listed themselves as belonging to the "working" class but who shifted to "middle class" when asked to choose between "upper," "middle," and "lower." "The Fortune Survey: XXVII: The People of the U.S.A.—A Self-Portrait," *Fortune,* XXI (Feb., 1940), 14, 20. Another study shows that nearly 75 per cent of Americans identify themselves with some part of the middle *income* class and nearly 90 per cent with some part of the middle *social* class. Hadley Cantril, "Identification with Social and Economic Class," *Journal of Abnormal and Social Psychology* XXXVIII (Jan., 1943), 78.

[13] Laski, of course, was concerned even more with the economic institutions of liberalism than with its political institutions. Whether or not his thesis in this connection has more validity we need not inquire, since it is with the political institutions of liberalism that we are concerned.

Moreover, it is not to be assumed that the middle class is dead. As far as numbers are concerned, Marx's prediction that the middle class would decline in size has not been borne out by the facts. True, it is very hard to document this statement because of the difficulty of defining and identifying the middle class. The most reliable English estimates show an increase in the percentage of the occupied population falling in the middle class from 18.8 in 1881 to 26.9 in 1931 and an increase for the professions from 3.8 to 4.4 per cent for the same years.[14] In the United States, except for farmers, who are decreasing in numbers, practically all middle-class groups are increasing relative to the population as a whole. Members of the "professional" category increased from 4.4 per cent of the total gainfully employed in 1910 to 6.5 per cent in 1940, while clerks and related groups increased from 10.2 per cent to 17.2 per cent during the same period. The statistics for "proprietors, managers, and officials" are divided in the census tabulations into three categories: the first, "farmers (owners and tenants)" shows a decline from 16.5 per cent to 10.1 per cent; the second, "wholesale and retail dealers," indicates an increase from 3.3 to 3.7 per cent; and the third, "other proprietors, managers, and officials," shows an increase from 3.2 to 3.7 per cent. Finally, semiskilled workers have increased from 14.7 per cent to 21.0 per cent (skilled workers having shown no change), whereas unskilled labor declined sharply from 36.0 per cent to 25.9 per cent.[15] (All comparisons are for the years 1910 and 1940.) There is no indication in these figures of a decline in the middle class. If clerks be included as middle-class elements, along with professionals, proprietors, man-

---

[14] Figures, respectively, from Arthur L. Bowley, *Wages and Income in the United Kingdom since 1860* (Cambridge: Cambridge University Press, 1937), pp. 128–129, and F. D. Klingender, *The Condition of Clerical Labour in Britain* (London: Martin Lawrence, Ltd., 1935), p. xxi.

[15] U.S. Department of Commerce, Bureau of the Census, *Sixteenth Census of the United States: 1940, Population: Comparative Occupation Statistics for the United States, 1870 to 1940* (Washington, D. C.: Government Printing Office, 1943), p. 187.

agers, and officials, this class is increasing in proportion to the total employed population, in spite of the rapid relative decline of farmers.

Moreover, the great increase in the semiskilled group at the expense of the unskilled is also significant. It is not unrelated to the pertinent phenomenon designated by Alfred Bingham as the "bourgeoisification" of the proletariat.[16] Briefly, he means by this the tendency for the rising standard of real wages, and the availability to ever-increasing numbers of people of automobiles, bathtubs, cosmetics, stylish clothes, "luxury" accommodations, and numerous other erstwhile indicia of middle-class status, to produce all the symptoms of middle-class psychology in persons who, by Marxian analysis, should be numbered among the proletariat. Taken together, these phenomena explain the very high percentage of Americans who, as indicated above,[17] consider themselves members of the middle class. Clearly there is no ground for predicting a decline in liberal democracy in England or America on the basis of a decline in the middle class.

But, it is contended, the middle class is changing in character. Instead of being composed largely of small property owners having a strong stake in the existing order, the middle class is becoming predominantly propertyless.[18] This statement clearly contains elements of truth, but it is grossly exaggerated. The proportion of farm owners is declining. What is happening to businessmen is not so clear. As the figures cited above show, however, the only group of independent businessmen for which the census figures for the United States provide the facts is steadily increasing.[19] Clearly there has been in the United States a net relative decrease of independent enterprisers, owing to the decline in agriculture; but against this decline must be set a tre-

[16] Alfred M. Bingham, *Insurgent America* (New York: Harper & Brothers, 1935), Chap. 3, esp. pp. 28–29.

[17] Above, p. 163.

[18] This claim is made, for example, by Lewis Corey in *The Crisis of the Middle Class* (New York: Covici-Friede, Inc., 1935), pp. 14–15.

[19] Above, p. 164.

mendous growth in the number of individuals owning stock in corporate enterprise.[20] Although comparable statistics are not readily available for Great Britain, Professor Durbin has compiled figures showing rapid growth of small property holders and of their holdings as indicated by savings bank accounts and membership in building societies, retail cooperatives, industrial and provident societies, and friendly societies.[21] In short, the statement concerning the increased tendency of the middle class to be shorn of its property contains, at best, but a kernel of truth. That kernel is that in the United States the relative growth of other than agricultural portions of the population has been so great that there has been a net relative decline of individual enterprisers. This shift, however, is probably more than offset, in the United States as well as in Great Britain, by the growth of other forms of ownership. Finally, even insofar as it is true that democracy rests on a middle-class base and that the interests of that base are changing, it does not follow in any case that the fundamental nature of democracy is changing, but only that its policies are likely to change.

A slightly different line of argument is to the effect that the middle class once was an economically unified group whose self-conscious pursuit of its class interests gave to democracy both the drive and the cohesion which made it a success. Today, by contrast, the argument runs, the middle class is made up of highly heterogeneous elements with little to hold them together or to produce in them a consciousness of class destiny. The assumption of earlier unity is probably exaggerated (cf. Madison's statement quoted above page 157), but no matter; the description of present-day variety of interest is certainly true. The underlying assumption that democracy thrives on any kind of class consciousness and class solidarity, however, is thoroughly fal-

[20] Figures for the United States are given in Adolf A. Berle, Jr., and Gardiner C. Means, *The Modern Corporation and Private Property* (New York: Commerce Clearing House, Inc., 1932), p. 55.

[21] E. F. M. Durbin, *The Politics of Democratic Socialism: An Essay on Social Policy* (London: Routledge and Kegan Paul, Ltd., 1940), pp. 372–373.

lacious. Democracy is pre-eminently the form of government fitted for a society in which there is a high degree of plurality of interests. A pluralistic society in which class lines are blurred and groups, functional and otherwise, proliferate—a society, in other words, such as we have in Britain and America today—can operate only in the flexible framework of democratic institutions.[22]

In short, the middle class has changed, but not in a way which need cause alarm for believers in democracy. It is tending to grow. If the line of theorists from Aristotle down to the present who have associated middle-class dominance with political stability are right, this is all to the good. It has changed in composition, but an analysis of these changes reveals no occasion for alarm. To be sure, if—as Marxists still tend to assume, despite the evidence to the contrary—economic developments should turn against the middle groups and tend to push them down toward the proletariat, they might well turn to radically antidemocratic means to save themselves. But in the absence of better support for this thesis than has yet appeared it would be idle to pursue the line of speculation.

6. *Labor's Growth in Power and Class Consciousness*

In spite of all that has been said about the growth of the middle classes, it is, of course, true that in Great Britain, and to a lesser extent in the United States, there has been a growth of political consciousness, and so of political power, among members of the laboring class. In Britain this has proceeded so far that a party built on trade-union foundations has achieved political dominance. It is to be noted, however, that this position has been realized by securing considerable middle-class support. In any case, the same development is persuasive evidence that labor's aims can be obtained within the framework of the democratic system.[23]

[22] It may, of course, be contended that this pluralism threatens to degenerate into anarchy and that an authoritarian form of government is required to check this tendency. This argument will be considered in Chap. XII.

[23] Whether a completely socialized state would be likely to remain democratic is another question, which will be discussed below (Chap. XIV).

Organization of labor has, of course, increased its economic power as well as its political self-consciousness. This development has reached the point in the United States where three giant aggregations of unions, the American Federation of Labor, the railroad brotherhoods, and the Congress of Industrial Organizations are in a position to dominate the labor market in a way which cannot be matched by any existing combination on the employer side. This fact raises a threat of economic strife between Big Business and Big Labor on a scale which might shake the foundations of any state.[24]

7. The Changed Nature of Warfare

There is another sphere in which the changes have been perhaps even more portentous. That is the sphere of warfare. Here again a controlling factor is to be found in technology. The fact that the conduct of war demands complete regimentation of the economic life of a country is not the core of the problem. It has been found possible to submit to this, for limited periods, and still to maintain democratic controls and a large measure of civil liberties. But the specter of atomic bombs, carried by guided missiles operating from almost unlimited distances, has revolutionized the situation. Once other nations have this weapon at their command and this fact is known to us, the pressure for maintaining wartime controls at all times, so that our whole economy may be geared to strategic rather than economic objectives, will be tremendous. At first sight this situation seems to call for economic rather than political regimentation. It might even aid in solving the political problem of obtaining common agreement, because the objective of military readiness would overshadow all else. It may well be doubted, however, whether the degree of economic control and direction by the state which modern war involves would prove permanently compatible with democratic processes. The great danger about the present situation is that modern weapons give the aggressor such an advantage that even

[24] See below, pp. 287–288, for a discussion of the problem.

the *threat* of total war tends to impose the same requirements as does war itself. A government that feels the necessity of adequate preparation against attack by atom bombs must possess the power to compel decentralization of its industries and, in general, to direct the whole field of economic activity with reference to strategic considerations.

Furthermore, there is another factor, perhaps even more menacing to liberal democracy, involved in international anarchy under modern conditions. The so-called "fifth column" as a first-class instrument of war has been perfected during the last decade. It involves a powerful threat to civil liberties and to the deliberative processes. Governments that will tolerate free speech, including free criticism, when it comes from domestic sources are understandably less inclined to be tolerant when they have reason to suspect that the criticism is part of a campaign to divide and weaken the country as a prelude to military attack. Peoples who are convinced of the soundness of a policy of allowing free expression to all points of view, on the theory that this is the way to the advancement of truth and to the attainment of uncoerced agreement, may well take a second thought when it is discovered that at least some who would make use of this liberty are opposed not only to the government but to the country. Historically, we have found that liberty, to be preserved, must be jealously guarded. We have opposed even what might seem to be reasonable restrictions because of the danger of abuse. While it has been admitted in principle that one had no right to use his liberty directly to subvert the government, we have been rightly chary about allowing the government to decide what was "subversive," short of overt illegal acts or words creating a "clear and present danger" of producing such acts. But now we, in the United States, in fear of fifth-column activities, are making membership in the Communist party a disqualification for public employment, and are even tending to extend this beyond party membership to people tainted by association with those believed to be "subversive." The great threat which this whole development holds for civil liberties and the potential abuses it creates are plain to be seen.[25] So also, unfortunately, is the logic behind it. And so is the psychology which is bound to continue and enlarge it as long as the world remains internationally anarchic. How much of this kind of insecurity democracy can withstand is one of the great unanswered questions of the age, second in importance only to the question of how much it is going to be called upon to withstand.

8. Developments in Education

One final point about the changing social scene must not go unnoted, for its implications for democracy are tremendous, and wholly favorable. Reference was made at the beginning of the chapter to the many evidences of increasing social democracy, especially in the United States—to the democratization of forms of transportation, of recreation, and of dress. We should now add a reference to the phenomenal growth in popular education. The development has been so great and so obvious as to need little documentation. It is worthy of note, however, that illiteracy declined in England from an estimated 33.7 per cent for men and 49.5 per cent for women in 1839 to 5 and 5.7 per cent respectively in 1893.[26] The over-all figures for the United States show a drop from 20 per cent in 1870 to 4.3 per cent in 1930.[27] The growth of popular education has, in recent years, been even more spectacular above the level of primary instruction. For example, it has been estimated that in the United States in 1890 less than 6 per cent of the children of appropriate age were attending secondary schools, while by 1930 the figure had risen to

---

[25] Freedom of movement from place to place, freedom from unreasonable searches and seizures, and other similar liberal devices are threatened equally with freedom of speech and the press. A hair-raising elaboration of the whole threat to civil liberties is set forth in an article by Linden A. Mander, "Civil Liberty after the War," *American Political Science Review,* XL (Feb., 1946), 70–79.

[26] Helen Sullivan, "Literacy and Illiteracy," in *Encyclopedia of the Social Sciences* (New York: The Macmillan Company, 1930), IX, 519.

[27] U.S. Department of Commerce, Bureau of the Census, *Fifteenth Census of the United States: 1930, Population* (Washington, D. C.: Government Printing Office, 1933), II, 1223.

about 50 per cent,[28] and by 1940 it was over 80 per cent.[29] The growth in the numbers of those attending colleges and universities has been even more striking. The figures themselves would be enough to indicate that education—even higher education—is no longer a prerogative of a privileged class. Although in this respect the development in England has been slower and has not yet gone so far as in the United States, there, too, the rapid development of state-supported schools, and the increase in scholarships to private schools and to the great universities have gone far toward providing equality of educational opportunity to all of a stated level of ability.

Democracy is certainly not guaranteed by a high educational level among the citizenry, but at least it is given a good foundation. And equalization of educational opportunities helps to undermine those economic and social distinctions which are so inimical to the healthy operation of democratic political institutions.

9. Summary

We may briefly summarize the major aspects of the changing social scene which have been noticed as having significance for liberal-democratic institutions. They are of varying import. First we noted that the increased rate of change has imposed increased strains on society in general and, of course, on government, in particular. Next came a group of phenomena which shared the characteristic of being atomistic, that is, of contributing to social disintegration and so of tending to undermine that element of popular consensus without which democratic institutions cannot succeed. Among these we noted the increased tensions, the psychological instability, and the social irresponsibility that are produced by city living. The specialized experience of those who work in a society characterized by a high degree of division of labor and the further dispersive effects

[28] George S. Counts, "Education: History," in *Encyclopedia of the Social Sciences* (New York: The Macmillan Company, 1930), V, 412.
[29] See U.S. Department of Commerce, Bureau of the Census, *Sixteenth Census of the United States: 1940, Population* (Washington, D. C.: Government Printing Office, 1943) II, *Characteristics of the Population,* 11.

of the occupational associations which proliferate in such a society contribute to the same result. The economic interrelatedness which is also a product of the division of labor has somewhat contradictory consequences. On the one hand, it tremendously increases the cost to society of anything which interferes with the smooth operation of the economic system. Government is inevitably held responsible for seeing to it that such interferences are kept at a minimum, with consequences which will be explored in the following chapter. On the other hand, as people become more aware of the importance to all of keeping the productive machine going, they tend to support concerted action to check the disruptive effect of pressure groups. It cannot be said that this tendency has yet gone very far in the United States, but there is some evidence to suggest that the dispersive consequences of modern industrialism may yet be checked by forces springing from the same ultimate source. Distinct from the atomistic trends, but closely related, is the economic instability characteristic of the cyclical nature of a capitalistic economy. This brings another source of impatience, another strain upon the social and political fabric. The radically changed nature of modern warfare harbors conflicting potentialities for democracy. On the one hand, the threat of attack from without tends to unite the people of a country and so to counteract, in some measure, the atomistic trends in modern society. On the other hand, it carries with it a very serious threat to that very kernel of liberal democracy, civil liberty. The final item was, uniquely, entirely on the credit side of the ledger. The tremendous spread of popular education is surely favorable to democracy and to liberalism. This we may say while still admitting that the almost unlimited reliance which James Mill and many of his contemporaries placed upon education as a panacea for all social ills was grossly exaggerated.

In addition to the points recapitulated in the preceding paragraph, we examined the Marxist contention that liberal democracy is dependent upon the continued strength of the old-style, capitalistic middle class, and that this type of middle class is on the wane. This contention was found wanting in such vital particulars that it provides no grounds for concern.

The net result of this survey cannot be put in a word or a sentence. It is clear that recent changes in social conditions carry with them certain threats to liberal democracy. Just how they impinge on the practical operation of government, and just how, if at all, democracy may hope to cope with them, will be the task of succeeding chapters to consider. Even at this point, however, it is meet to issue a note of warning. The social scene will continue to change, sometimes in ways we little dream of now. What seem to be inescapable trends today may be reversed tomorrow. Twenty years ago, Professor Chester C. Maxey wrote: "Mass production . . . is so recent an addition to our social equipment that we have yet to plumb its possibilities and discover all its consequences. Already, however, we have seen it virtually destroy the labor movement of the last century and enslave millions of men and women to the dreary lockstep of mechanical production." [30] Four years later began the greatest period of growth which organized labor in this country has ever known. Its wildest dreams of the time when Maxey wrote have now been surpassed. Prophecy is indeed a hazardous adventure.

[30] Chester C. Maxey, *Urban Democracy* (Boston: D. C. Heath and Company, 1929), p. 398.

CHAPTER IX

TRENDS IN
THE ROLE AND OPERATION
OF GOVERNMENT

1. The Changed Role and Nature of Government

It will be the task of the present chapter to survey the impact, on the institutions of government, of the material, social, and ideological changes described in the two preceding chapters. The first and most obvious consequence has been the great increase in the functions of government and in the extent of its activities. The particular factors which have brought this about are numerous. During the nineteenth century, when liberal democracy was developing most rapidly, laissez-faire ideas tended to keep the role of government at a minimum. This was true both in England and in the United States. The cost of government did not increase as rapidly as national income. The twentieth century has witnessed a sharp reversal in this trend. Partly this is a matter of the decline of individualistic philosophy and the rise of collectivism. Thus public provision for education has grown in relation to provision for private education; and the privately constructed toll road has given way almost completely to state-supported roads. But more frequently the increase involves the assumption of responsibilities by the state which were previously borne by no one. The over-all growth of educational facilities and services, for example, dwarfs the shift from private to public; and the same is true of the development of highways. A technological development, the automobile, is responsible for the latter, while the former is attributable to the advancing democratic consideration for the well-being of the common man, as well as to the belief that popular education is itself the key to the satisfactory functioning of democracy. Consideration for the welfare of the common man has combined with the irregularity of employment and city living which have come with industrialism to lead to vast expenditures for "social security"—that is, old-age annuities and compensation for involuntary unemployment, whether from industrial accidents, ill-health, or lack of work.

The phenomenon of urbanism has contributed greatly to the cost of government, which is to say to the size and complexity of governmental establishments. The more concentrated the population, the greater is the cost of providing protection, sanitation, and similar services.[1] The following examples from a list of typical new city activities during the period 1915–1929 illustrate new functions necessitated by urbanism as well as those arising from changed ideas as to the proper role of government:[2]

> Traffic lights
> Auto patrol
> Police teletype
> Municipal employment agency
> Inspection of swimming pools
> Maintenance of children's clinic
> Inspection of food handlers
> Installation of safety zones
> Classes for mental defectives
> Playgrounds and golf courses

The most effective way of measuring this growth in activity is in terms of cost. In 1913, all units of government in the United States spent $2,919,000,000; the corresponding figure for 1936 was $17,047,000,000. To be sure, the purchasing power of the dollar had changed in the meantime, so that an appropriate ad-

---

[1] For example, in 1929, in American cities of 30,000–49,999, the per capita expenditure for operation and maintenance of general departments amounted to $19.13 (in 1915 dollars); this figure was higher for each succeeding group of cities ranked according to size until the figure of $30.41 was reached for cities of 500,000 and over.—The President's Research Committee on Social Trends, *Recent Social Trends in the United States* (2 vols.; New York: McGraw-Hill Book Company, Inc., 1933), II, 1312.

[2] *Ibid.*, p. 1313.

justment must be made. Reduced to the common denominator of 1926 dollars, the figures cited read $4,182,000,000 for 1913, and $21,098,000,000 for 1936.[3] The latter figure is still more than five times as great as the former. Even if a further adjustment be made for the growth in population, the 1936 figure remains slightly more than four times the amount for 1913.[4] Another way to consider the matter is to think of governmental expenditures in terms of their relationship to total national income. In 1913, the country devoted just over 8 per cent of its national income to governmental activity; in 1936 the figure was nearly 27 per cent.[5] This is something over a threefold increase. If we are thinking of the vastness of the business of government, the earlier figures, showing something like a 500 per cent growth, are more significant. If, on the other hand, we have in mind the relative part played by government among other activities it is the threefold-plus increase that is pertinent. However we look at it, the change that has taken place within less than a quarter of a century is prodigious. In itself it has rendered the task of self-government ever so much more difficult. If the trend were to be projected far into the future, some of our present problems might soon look small by comparison.

The growth in governmental expenditures is a good index of the services performed by government and of its welfare activities, but it tells little of what from our point of view is even more important—the expansion of regulatory activities. Here even more than in the matter of welfare activities, the passing of the laissez-faire ideas and practices that characterized the days of economic liberalism has transformed the task of government and greatly restricted the area of economic liberty. Laissez faire first broke down in the matter of decent working conditions. Govern-

[3] Harold M. Groves, *Financing Government* (New York: Henry Holt and Company, 1939), p. 509.

[4] The application of population figures to the statistics in the text gives per capita expenditures in 1926 dollars of $40.13 for 1913 and $164.76 for 1936.

[5] Groves, *op. cit.*, p. 509.

ment soon had to compel industry to take necessary measures for the health and safety of labor. Then consumers, too, demanded and secured the protection of government through regulatory measures against fraud, misleading advertising, shoddy materials, and the like. A free economic system showed signs of committing suicide via the monopoly route, so governments intervened to outlaw monopolies, monopolistic practices, and methods of competition thought likely to lead to monopoly. Key markets (such as that for securities) were subjected to careful policing. At the same time, in the case of so-called "natural monopolies," such as public utilities, railroads, and communications, governments undertook to regulate the charges and other aspects of their business life in great detail. The scope of freedom of contract was greatly limited in the field of management-labor relations by governmental determination of minimum wages and maximum hours and support for collective bargaining. A further group of depression-born activities was not strictly regulatory but was designed to influence the whole framework within which the competitive economy functions. This category included loans to farmers, homeowners, and business corporations, make-work and public works projects designed to assist the unemployed, and pump-priming expenditures calculated to give a boost to business by putting cash in the pockets of consumers and by providing markets for the products of heavy industry.

In Great Britain a similar, although less rapid, development has been taking place. Public expenditures grew by nearly 270 per cent between 1913 and 1935. Making allowance for the change in value of the pound, the rise was still 245 per cent, as compared to a 9 per cent increase in population.[6] In Britain, as in the United States, the period between the wars was marked by a rapid extension of governmental "intervention" in the economic sphere. The developments are well summarized by Mr. Durbin, as follows:

[6] Ursula K. Hicks, *The Finance of British Government, 1920–1936* (London: Oxford University Press, 1938), p. 24.

. . . . the government has come to control or influence the foreign exchange market through the exchange Equalization Fund, the foreign loan market through the informal machinery of control set up in 1931, the short-term money market as the supplier of Treasury Bills, and the long-term capital market through its control of credit policy, and of the short-term rate of interest. It has brought a large fraction of the agricultural industry within its sphere of influence by subsidies to, or marketing boards for, milk, pigs, bacon, hops, potatoes, beet, wheat, and other cereals. The list of industries now brought into some kind of subordinate relationship to the government is extraordinarily long—shipping, aviation, electricity, broadcasting, road transport, coal, iron and steel, railways and parts of the textile trades.[7]

Furthermore, both in England and in the United States, but especially in the latter because of the greater degree of decentralization previously prevailing, there has been a steady and rapid movement toward centralization of government. Again we may find evidence of this in budgetary data. From 1915 to 1929, combined governmental expenditures increased 239 per cent in 1933 dollars, but the expenditures of the federal government increased by 289 per cent. During this period a large part of the centralizing movement was from local to state governments, as is indicated by the fact that the increase for state governments was even greater than for the federal government, 299 per cent, while city outlay grew by only 216 per cent and other local government expenditures increased by 205 per cent.[8] During the thirties there was practically no increase at the local level, while state and federal expenditures considerably more than doubled.[9]

[7] E. F. M. Durbin, *The Politics of Democratic Socialism* (London: Routledge, and Kegan Paul, Ltd., 1940), p. 97.

[8] *Recent Social Trends*, II, 1324.

[9] See United States Department of Commerce, Bureau of the Census, *Financing Federal, State, and Local Governments: 1941*, "State and Local Government Special Study," No. 20 (Washington, D. C.: 1942), p. 71. The figures for state and federal expenditures used in deriving the statement in the text were secured independently from the *Statistical Abstract of the United States*, because the 1941 figures used in the Special Study included large defense expenditures.—*Statistical Abstract of the United States: 1942* (Washington, D. C.: Government Printing Office, 1943), p. 250, and *Statistical Abstract of the United States: 1941* (Washington, D. C.: Government Printing Office, 1942), p. 179.

It is not merely that interstate business, which once was the exception, has now become the rule, and that the scope of governmental regulation has had to keep pace with this expansion. The new[10] concept of utilizing government to influence the general level of the economy's operation requires centralized control. Nothing less than nation-wide scope can be effective.

In Britain the change has been less spectacular—partly because there there was no problem concerning the legal competence of the central government to take over functions previously exercised locally—but no less real. Increasingly Parliament has had to supplement by national appropriations the funds derived from local rates; and just as regularly such action has been accompanied by increased control from Westminster. Long before such striking examples as the Town and Country Planning Act of the Labour government, local government autonomy had been becoming more and more circumscribed. It is the policy of the present government to carry the process of centralized control over the economy much further than anything that has been heretofore witnessed either in England or in the United States. The nationalization of the Bank of England and the control of investment (by means of licensing new capital issues) are key instances of this policy.[11]

2. *Effects on Electorate, Legislature, and Executive*

How have these developments affected the operation of democratic governments? In the first place, they tend to bewilder the electorate. The immensity of the government machine itself and the enormity and complexity of the tasks it must undertake are challenges to the imagination and the intelligence of the most talented, let alone those of the average, distracted citizen. In the nineteenth century, much attention was given to the question of who should possess political power. Today the question is

[10] The concept is "new" in a relative sense only. In the days of mercantilism, the state was equally concerned with the health of the economy as a whole, and took positive steps to control it.

[11] The latter was first put into effect as a temporary war measure before the Labour government came to power.

not who should have it but what should be done with it—a far more difficult problem. It requires no great intelligence to see the arguments in favor of, say, extending the public school system; but the pros and cons of agricultural subsidies and the proper bases (if any) for "parity prices" involve technical problems that the average person is not equipped to handle.

Furthermore, centralization intensifies this effect. In a small community, natural human sympathy may be counted on to curb the drive of individual selfishness, but where distance as well as complexity dulls the perception of consequences, self-interest tends to become less enlightened and sympathy attenuated. It is an axiom that democracy thrives on local self-government. Democracy dies, it has been said, five miles from the parish pump. People are interested in things that are close to them, things they can see with their own eyes. They feel responsibility for conditions which they see are within their control, and the remedies for which they can see in operation. They gain experience in the democratic process through participation in the regulation of community activities.[12]

To this picture of electoral bewilderment and declining political responsibility resulting from changes in governmental functions and organization, we must add the factors making for psychological instability and social disintegration which were described in the preceding chapter.

Nor is bewilderment confined to the electorate. Legislatures are by no means immune from its debilitating effects. Increasingly unable to cope with the complex problems with which they are confronted, they have resorted more and more frequently to the device of delegating their authority to the executive or to administrative agencies. This is by now an old story both in England and in the United States. Volumes are written fulminating against "administrative despotism," bar associations protest, and, most of all, legislators themselves declaim against the powers exercised by administrators, but the process goes on with no

[12] That there is another side to these arguments will be seen below (pp. 312–315).

prospect of reversal.[13] It has not yet reached the point where Congress has delegated to the President full authority to take such measures as are appropriate for the general welfare. But, without mentioning wartime legislation, we may by way of a typical example, refer to powers that have been granted to the Secretary of Agriculture as to what commodities shall be given governmental market support, and (within very broad limits) what shall be the extent of this support. Even the Eightieth Congress, dominated by Republicans committed to a return to legislative government and for partisan reasons set against delegating authority to an administration controlled by the opposing party, authorized the President to lend or grant up to $400,000,000 to Greece and Turkey upon terms and conditions to be determined by him. Legislation empowering administrative authorities to fix reasonable rates for transportation and communication facilities, to grant or deny permission for radio broadcasting and to set the conditions for obtaining such permission, and to make safety regulations in great detail for the operation of commercial aircraft, along with many other laws involving equally sweeping delegations of power, is now a generally accepted part of our legal system.

The war, of course, brought vast extensions of executive power both by way of legislative delegation and also by way of enlargement of the powers exercised by the executive in his own right. The powers wielded, for example, by the War Production Board and the Office of Price Administration gave to these executive arms almost unlimited control over the heart of our economic system—as to what should be produced and at what price it should be sold. It is not being suggested that these grants of power were unwarranted by the facts. But it is pertinent to

[13] See J. Roland Pennock, *Administration and the Rule of Law* (New York: Rinehart & Company, 1941), Chaps. 2 and 3, and literature cited there, for a description of developments in the United States and for the reasons why the trend is inescapable. For recent English experience, see Carleton Kemp Allen, *Law and Orders: An Inquiry into the Nature and Scope of Delegated Legislation and Executive Powers in England* (London: Stevens & Sons, Ltd., 1945).

note that in this vast area of governmental control opened up by the exigencies of war the legislature practically abdicated to the executive, subject to its right to take back what it had granted at any time. As each war calls for greater delegations of authority than the last, so also does each advance in peacetime control of the economy. Increasing control and increasing executive dominance go hand in hand.

The extraordinary powers exercised by the President in his own right were generally based upon his position as commander in chief and hence are less likely than claims based upon the executive power to point the way to comparable peacetime extensions of presidential authority. But one cannot be sure of this. Take, for example, President Roosevelt's message to Congress on September 7, 1942, demanding that Congress should modify the Emergency Price Control Act in a certain way, and stating that if Congress failed to take the requested action by a stated date he would act by himself.[14] In effect he was saying to Congress that, unless it repealed a certain statutory provision, he would nevertheless order it to be disregarded.[15] "The President has the powers," he declared, "under the Constitution and under Congressional acts, to take measures necessary to avert a disaster which would interfere with the winning of the war."[16] No acts of Congress granting the powers in question were cited. It would appear that the justification, if any, for this claim of authority is to be found in his powers as commander-in-chief. This fact might seem to limit these powers to periods when the country is engaged in war, but suppose the President should hold that such action was necessary to avert an economic collapse that would endanger our preparedness for possible war? In the example cited, the President did not have to make good his threat, although it is at least possible that the very threat itself moved Congress to do what it might not otherwise have done.

---

[14] New York *Times*, Sept. 8, 1942, p. 14, col. 6.

[15] See Edward S. Corwin, *Total War and the Constitution* (New York: Alfred A. Knopf, Inc., 1947), p. 63.

[16] New York *Times, loc. cit.*

Certainly this newest development of executive power opens new vistas as to the extent to which executive dominance over the legislature may possibly go, even in peacetime, in the United States. Thus far it is only a threat—and not an immediate one—rather than an actuality.

Furthermore, even such matters as are still determined by act of Congress have in recent years with increasing frequency been settled by legislation proposed in detail by, and even drafted by, the executive branch. Practically all the great legislative accomplishments of the New Deal followed this course. Frequently, during the early days of the New Deal, in the then current atmosphere of crisis, such legislation was disposed of with very little debate and with little or no opportunity for amendment. It has been seriously proposed that steps should be taken to further this process, as by providing a preferred place on the calender for officially proposed legislation and by prohibiting amendments, limiting the legislature to the task of saying yes or no.[17]

In England, both legislative delegation of authority and executive dominance of the legislature have gone much further than in the United States. It has become notorious that legislation not introduced by the government (private members' bills) has practically no chance of adoption. When such a bill is taken up by the government and put through, it is a matter of wide remark. (The present Labour government has continued the wartime practice of allowing no time for consideration of private member legislation, although it promises that this is only a temporary measure.)

To be sure, one must beware of seeking to make too much of legislative adoption of executive proposals. In the United States, the practice grew up under the combined influence of the greatest economic crisis we have ever experienced and the leadership of the strongest personality to occupy the White House in recent times. From 1946 to 1948 with a Democratic President and a Republican Congress, and with the country in a "back-to-

[17] William H. Hessler, *Our Ineffective State* (New York: Henry Holt and Company, 1937), pp. 138 ff.

normalcy" mood, the picture became quite different. What the future may bring depends upon many unknowns, but most of all upon whether or not we have a recurrence of depression in anything like the proportions of the early thirties. In England, it is in the nature of the cabinet form of government that the executive should take the leadership in formulating legislation, and that may be expected to continue. Also, as long as the present Labour government is engaged in the task of putting into effect its program of socialization, we may expect the amount of time given to Parliamentary debate and amendment to be highly restricted. It is worthy of note, however, that the process being pursued is a rather far cry from what was anticipated not only by some of the enemies of socialism but by some of the socialist leaders themselves. A few years ago, for example, Sir Stafford Cripps (now Chancellor of the Exchequer), wrote that the first step of a Labour government would be to "call Parliament together at the earliest moment and place before it an Emergency Powers Bill to be passed through all its stages on the first day. This Bill will be wide enough in its terms," he continued, "to allow all that will be immediately necessary to be done by ministerial orders." [18] Actually nothing of the sort has happened. The Labour program has been put through Parliament a step at a time in thoroughly orthodox fashion. Debate has been extensive even if less ample than the Opposition would have liked, and on frequent occasion bills have been amended before passage to take account of objections raised in Parliament.

Nevertheless, after allowance has been made for these qualifications, there can be little doubt that the combined effect of declining legislative control and mounting executive and administrative power has brought about a fall in the prestige of legislatures. In the United States there is the added fact that the executive branch can act with relative unity and dispatch while

---

[18] Sir Stafford Cripps, "Can Socialism Come by Constitutional Methods?" in Christopher Addison, C. R. Attlee, H. N. Brailsford, and Others, *Problems of a Socialist Government* (London: Victor Gollancz, Ltd., 1933), p. 43, quoted in Allen, *op. cit.*, p. 293.

the legislative process is characterized by delays, seemingly endless talk, and disagreements which not infrequently prevent the taking of any positive action on a particular subject. This situation is fostered by the dispersive trends in American politics referred to in the preceding chapter. The net result is that the legislature in modern democratic governments has taken second place in popular estimation as well as in political power. Traditionally the legislature above all stands for the democratic element. It has been the very heart of representative government. Its relative decline in importance and prestige therefore cannot help be a matter of concern for the supporters of liberal democracy.

It is generally thought, too, that this shift in emphasis from the legislature to the executive is part of a broad tendency in democratic states for the people to pay more attention to personalities and less to issues, and in particular to line up behind one or two strong leaders and to be willing to commit their fate to the hands of such a leader with little effort to direct or control his actions. This has been the pattern in the countries which have succumbed to dictatorship of one kind or another and there was considerable evidence of a similar trend in the United States under President Franklin D. Roosevelt. Again it is necessary to warn against exaggeration. Many of President Roosevelt's measures were, of course, far less popular than he was; but a poll conducted in August, 1939, long after the New Deal had passed its prime, indicated that 55.2 per cent of the people approved the New Deal, on balance.[19] In England, except for the war years, there has been much less indication of such a tendency, but it is undoubtedly true that during recent decades the Prime Minister has gained in power and stature as compared with the other members of his cabinet. Both countries have manifested a strong and healthy reaction to this type of leadership following the war. If in the years to come serious crises are unresolved by legislative action, we may anticipate that even democratic nations will turn with messianic hopes to new deliverers. In such

[19] *Fortune*, XX (Nov., 1939), 168.

an event much will depend upon the presence or absence of democratic good faith on the part of the successful leaders. But it will not be entirely a matter of chance. The type of leader most likely to gain popular acceptance will depend upon the strength of popular democratic convictions, which in turn will be influenced by the success or lack of success with which democratic institutions have been operating.

3. *The Changing Role of the Judiciary in the United States*

Fully as important as the changing balance of power between legislature and executive, as far as the United States is concerned, is the changing role of the judiciary. In fact, an examination of this change, and still more of the factors which have brought it about, will shed a great deal of light on the way in which the developments discussed in the two preceding chapters tend to affect constitutionalism generally, whether it is maintained by the institution of judicial review, or by the separation of powers, or by popular, legislative, and executive self-restraint. In spite of any diminution in legislative control, there can hardly be any doubt that popular determination of broad matters of policy has been increasing. Whether the manner of the increase in popular control carries with it an ultimate threat to the democratic process is another question. Many believe it does. For the protection of the liberties which are an essential part of liberal democracy and ultimately for the protection of equality itself, liberalism developed a series of restraints upon political power which are summed up in the word "constitutionalism." These restraints take the form of set procedures for the exercise of power, and of individual "rights" of person and of property. It is in the United States that these elements of modern constitutionalism have been most fully developed, codified, and committed to an independent judiciary for enforcement even as against the joint action of the other two branches of government. This has been generally accepted as the high-water mark and the epitome of political liberalism. Whether democracy is to continue to be united with the essence of political liberalism is a question often thought to be tied up with the future of judicially enforced constitutional rights and restrictions. What has been the impact on this system of the changed attitudes and conditions outlined in previous pages?

There can be no doubt that a number of factors are tending to weaken the system as it has operated in the past. In the first place, as has been pointed out, both materialism and economic insecurity have tended to produce a decline in popular concern for liberty. Another factor is to be found in certain abuses of constitutionalism, especially in its use to defend vested interests. Freedom of contract, similarly protected, has often operated very unequally in fact because of the great differences in bargaining power between employers and (until recently) weak, unorganized labor. Thus, in the name of constitutional rights, legislatures were estopped from directly attacking the sweat shop by minimum-wage legislation, and even the movement for maximum-hour laws made its way slowly and with numerous setbacks against the judicial philosophy of freedom of contract. These are but striking examples of the ways in which restraints designed to ensure the rule of law were interpreted as guarantees of economic as well as political liberalism. After a considerable lag, the passing of laissez-faire philosophy in public policy has been reflected in judicial behavior, but not before the whole system of judicially protected rights had suffered considerable loss of caste.

This discrediting of the judiciary which resulted from the practice of giving protection to property rights in ways no longer believed compatible either with the general welfare or, for that matter, with true equality of opportunity, is an example of a broader problem. The law must accommodate itself to changing conditions, and it has been one of the virtues of the common-law system that the courts played a vital role in this process. Unfortunately, they have had to perform this lawmaking process in defiance of one of the cherished theories of constitutionalism, namely, that the courts operated mechanically, as logical machines, to discover, interpret according to the rules of logic, and apply the law. There has always been a large fictitious element in this theory. By resort to interpretations to equity, and to both special and general fictions, English and American courts have been developing the law to meet changing circumstances in accordance with their own conceptions of justice, as long as they have been in operation.[20] But in large measure the theory of American constitutionalism has been that the function of judges was a mechanical rather than a discretionary one and that therefore they could properly be entrusted with the task of checking the arbitrary exercise of political power whether by executives or legislatures, subject only to the overwhelming voice of the people as expressed through the amending power. The increasing rate of change in modern times has inevitably focused the spotlight of attention upon the legislative role of judges, especially the judges of our highest court. Whether they stuck to precedents—which in the light of current thought were obviously themselves the product of an outmoded philosophy rather than of the Constitution itself—or whether they abandoned the rule of *stare decisis* and reversed themselves, thus openly admitting their positive role, the effect upon judicial prestige was much the same.

Furthermore, the very idea of a system of "rights"—clearly defined areas of personal freedom within which no one, whether private citizen or agent of the state, dares tread—is more difficult to maintain under the complicated conditions of modern society. In the days of the pre-eminence of Lockean philosophy, no one doubted the "natural rights" of life, liberty, and property. Today the concept is subject to two different kinds of attack. First, there is the practical problem of definition. While the philosophy of laissez-faire prevailed, this question hardly arose; but with the growth of governmental intervention it came to the fore. Analysis, stimulated by the practical problems of government today, soon brings out the fact that our traditional "liberties" are at best little more than slogans serving as useful practical absolutes in

[20] See Roscoe Pound, *The Spirit of the Common Law* (Boston: The Marshall Jones Company, 1921), Chap. 7.

normal times. We speak of "liberty of speech," but we do not, and we never did, mean absolute liberty to say anything at all. The law of libel and slander has always been an acknowledged limitation. Likewise it has always been recognized that the right of free speech did not include the right to induce others to violate the law—to commit murder, for example. The problem of definition has always been with us, and even Justice Holmes's famous formula to the effect that speech should be subject to interference only where there was a "clear and present danger" that it would produce evils of the sort the government had a right to prevent has not always been adhered to by the Supreme Court. Yet it is only recently that people who consider themselves liberals have explicitly recognized that the formula is at best an attempt to devise a rule of thumb which, taken generally, will give a useful balance to the various social values involved.[21]

It leaves many relevant questions out of account. How great is the danger of immediate overt action? How serious will the consequences be if such action does ensue? Should the threat of large-scale rebellion be treated as on a par with the danger of a minor, local riot? Is the balance altered by the need for national unity in time of war? How important is liberty of speech in the particular context? Is the right to criticize a judge while a case is pending as important as the right to question the policies of the party in power? [22] Once it is acknowledged that the right of free speech is not absolute, all these questions become important. No law or constitution can frame rules that will permit courts to take account of such considerations without exercising a large amount of judgment, of measurement of social values, and of calculation of probable consequences.

[21] See David Riesman, "Civil Liberties in a Period of Transition," in Carl J. Friedrich and Edward S. Mason (eds.), *Public Policy*, "A Yearbook of the Graduate School of Public Administration," Harvard University (1942), III, 33–96.

[22] Most of these problems are nicely illustrated in the situation that arises when, for instance, a newspaper editor is charged with contempt of court for criticizing a judge's conduct of a case while that case is still pending. See *Bridges* v. *California*, 314 U. S. 252 (1941).

In addition to the practical problem of definition, the very essence of natural rights philosophy has been undermined. Both the relativistic and the skeptical trend in philosophy and the example of countries in which freedom of expression has been successfully used to dupe and divide the people as a prelude to dictatorship have contributed to this result. This experience has brought home the fact that, regardless of definition, liberty of speech is not an absolute but a means, though a crucial one, to the enjoyment of certain ends. Both of these things—the conventional nature of its definition and the ultimately relative nature of the right itself—are what is meant by calling it a "practical absolute" (or a "presumptive right"). Such practical absolutes generally should be sustained even in particular instances where the immediate values might seem to be maximized by modifying them, simply because of the danger involved in allowing discretion in such matters to governmental officials. Such power is likely to be abused at the expense of liberty partly because the values inherent in liberty are typically of the long-run variety, easily discounted by shortsighted mortals, and partly because it is generally to the personal interest of persons in positions of authority to be on the side of order and the *status quo* rather than on that of liberty. This principle is the very essence of constitutionalism, and yet it suffers from what appears to be an inherent weakness: that it must pretend to a greater absolutism than it actually possesses.

Another source of difficulty for the old constitutionalism arises where new rights achieve recognition—rights which may conflict with previously recognized rights—or where a broadened sense of justice or a realization of the importance of nongovernmental restraints on liberty leads to a modification of old interpretations of rights. For instance, it used to be considered part of the proper liberty of an employer to hire and fire at will. This was his right. But it also has come to be recognized that workingmen have a right to unite with each other to bargain collectively with their employers. It further appears that the mere absence of governmental restriction does not ensure them of this right. Employers may use their power of dismissal and of re-fusing to hire "blacklisted" laborers to intimidate would-be or-ganizers. In this way the legal right of labor to organize and bar-gain collectively was for a period rendered practically ineffec-tive in large areas. Once it is accepted that it is the substance and not the form with which the state should be concerned, it follows that, in the situation just outlined, the employer's right to hire and fire should be limited by the worker's right of collec-tive bargaining. This is but one example among many of how changing concepts and conditions have forced modification in the old structure of constitutional rights.

Still another source of weakness appears in the concept of "property." In the United States a large part of our system of constitutional restraints has revolved around this legal concept. Property should not be taken without "due process of law." The obligation of contracts should not be impaired. These principles were elaborated into a vast structure of rules designed to protect particular vested interests as well as the property system as a whole. In the nineteenth century, relatively few people doubted that the protection of these interests and of this system was to the advantage of society. It was not then possible to raise the cry of "human rights" as opposed to "property rights" because it was generally accepted that there was no opposition between the two. In the security of property lay the best security of persons, for persons could acquire property and in this way provide both for their own protection and for the general welfare. So it was reasoned. But today this is no longer accepted as a matter of course. Property has lost prestige. Where a century ago its pos-session created a presumption of personal worth, today it is be-coming a matter for apology. It must justify itself by its works. This popular frame of mind has contributed to the rapid modifi-cation of the old constitutionally protected rights of property. In-sofar as this modification limits the rights of property holders to interfere with the realization of the equally valid rights of others, it is all to the good. But at the same time it means removing one of the constitutional restraints upon government. This raises the question, which must be considered in its proper place, as to whether some substitute is being provided. It is not merely, it should be noted, a question of providing other constitutional rules to do like service in preserving personal freedom; it is also the problem of supplying the new rules with social support comparable in effectiveness to that which used to be supplied by the sanctity of the whole system of property rights and the economic and political power of self-defense which went with the possession of property.

To the role of factors we have been mentioning as contributing to the decline in the support for constitutional rights must be added a general growth of impatience with checks. In part, this is but the converse of the need and demand for strong, "positive" government. Governments based upon checks and balances (and the related separation of powers) are widely felt to be outmoded in a day when less and less is entrusted to the beneficent operation of the laws of supply and demand and more and more is controlled by the state. Furthermore, the continued advance of the ideal of equality obviously contributes to impatience with a system of rights and other instruments of obstructionism, the effect of which is to protect vested interests in inequality. This source of impatience has led many who are intent upon obtaining legal recognition for previously neglected economic rights to speak with belittlement of some of the essential elements of liberal democracy.[23] Beyond this there appears to be a broader, more elusive impatience which characterizes the spirit of the age. It is part of the modern temper. It may come from the fact that we have become used to rapid technological and attendant social changes and so are less willing to brook delay in general. Whatever the causes, it is symptomatic that reformers now seek to avoid resort to constitutional amendment in cases where a generation ago this method would have been taken for granted. A case in point is the movement for federal legislation

---

[23] Cf. Henry Wallace's rather slighting reference to "Bill-of-Rights democracy."— New York *Times*, Nov. 9, 1942, p. 19, col. 4. (Address to the Congress of Soviet-American Friendship.)

abolishing state poll taxes. There are strong arguments against the constitutionality of such legislation by the federal government. It is difficult to see in what respect, constitutionally, it is in a different category from the enfranchisement of women; yet, so far as I know, it was not even proposed to seek the latter objective by means of ordinary legislation at the national level.[24]

Even more generally it may be said that the present age is one in which people easily slip into a "we or they" type of reasoning. It seems that increasingly the logic of Marx and of Hitler, the belittlers of compromise and of "bourgeois" legalism, is accepted by men who are neither Marxists nor fascists. Just as in the field of international relations, a new, rude diplomacy has displaced the silken glove which once concealed the iron hand, so in the field of domestic affairs it is increasingly common for invective to displace appeals to reason and for persuasion to give way to threats. How far this is owing to the decline of belief in any absolute rationality in human affairs (disbelief, that is to say, in the existence of objective truth in matters of value), how far to the factors contributing to intolerance mentioned previously,[25] and how far to the trends enumerated above, we need not inquire. It is the fact of a tendency to weaken constitutionalism that concerns us.

Finally, among the factors tending to weaken constitutionalism, we may mention legal functionalism. By legal functionalism, we mean to designate generally theories which deny the existence of a body of law apart from the rules enforced by the courts or (in the more extreme versions) apart from the court decisions themselves, and which assert that judges do (must,

[24] In connection with this impatience with checks it is pertinent to recall that constitutionalism is much older than democracy. It originated in the efforts of nobles to restrain kings. It was further developed by the representatives of the people, still for use against monarchs. When parliamentary sovereignty was attained in England, the powers and pretensions of the courts to enforce constitutional restraints were abandoned. In the United States these powers were further developed by those who feared democracy. Whatever may be the merits of the case, then, it is not strange that emphasis on the democratic element in liberal democracy carries with it at least a threat to constitutionalism.

[25] Above, pp. 155–156.

should) govern their decisions by reference to the consequences. Such theories tend also to deny, at least by implication, the existence of any objective standards of justice to guide judges in their work. A corollary of these theories (and also an indication of their wide acceptance) is to be found in the changed concept of the role of public legal counsel, notably the Attorney General in the United States. Formerly the opinions of the Attorney General (and to a lesser extent those of other official counselors at law) were accorded quasi-judicial status. They were supposed to represent his honest attempt to state "the law." Today it is the prevailing philosophy that it is his job to find a way to accomplish the aims of his superior.[26] His opinions are accepted and evaluated in this light.

The idea of the positive role of judges, of judicial legislation, that is, as contrasted with the mechanical view of the judge as one who merely applies the rules of logic to known rules of law to obtain the correct result, is by no means new. But in the doctrine of political liberalism it has up to now been decidedly minimized. The "men of Massachusetts" and the men of Philadelphia believed in a "government of laws, not men." Written into the Constitution of Massachusetts, this slogan aptly described the temper of the period. The separation of powers and especially the independence of the judiciary were designed to implement this conception. Nor was this a purely American phenomenon. The great wave of legal codification that swept over Continental Europe in the wake of the French Revolution was in essence a search for the same goal of legal certainty independent of judicial idiosyncrasy. It was inspired by the same belief that the application of law was, or at least could be made, a practically automatic process. Although in England the movement for codification of laws and constitutions did not prevail,

---

[26] For a case in point, see Attorney General Jackson's opinion in support of President Roosevelt's prewar transfer of fifty destroyers in exchange for naval bases, and Professor Corwin's comment thereon in a letter to the New York *Times.—Official Opinions of the Attorneys General of the United States* (Washington, D. C.: Government Printing Office, 1941), XXXIX, 484–496; New York *Times*, Oct. 13, 1940, Sec. 4, p. 6.

the doctrine of the supremacy of law was even more revered than on the Continent. Especially in England this doctrine included the belief that the judiciary was in possession of tools that enabled it to supplant discretion by logical exegesis. This is the meaning of Lord Coke's famous reply to King James to the effect that judges discovered the law not by ordinary reason but by an "artificial reason" which was the product of legal training. To be sure, England never developed the institution of judicial review, but the margin by which the trend in this direction was defeated was probably a narrow one. As a result, even to this day, English constitutional theory includes, and the English people apparently equally cherish, the two mutually opposing doctrines of the sovereignty of Parliament and the supremacy of the law.[27]

The idea of judicial legislation has been minimized in the liberal tradition not only by the theory of the mechanical nature of the judicial process but also by the belief in the existence of objective standards for judicial guidance. As we have seen, popular thought in both England and America in the seventeenth and eighteenth centuries was saturated with the doctrine of natural law. In such a mental climate whether judges had some leeway in interpreting the law was relatively unimportant, for in any case it was only a question of applying to new situations the fixed principles of immutable natural justice, known to all although possibly appearing with particular clarity to those learned in the law. Blackstone was only following Coke and the whole tradition of the English common law in insisting that "the first and primary end of human laws is to maintain and regulate [the] *absolute* rights of individuals," "which were vested in them by the immutable laws of nature." [28] The theory persisted in the

[27] The classic statement of these opposing principles is to be found in Albert V. Dicey's *The Law of the Constitution* (9th ed.; London: Macmillan & Co., 1939), Chap. 13.

[28] William Blackstone, *Commentaries on the Laws of England* (4 vols.; Philadelphia: W. Childs, 1862), Bk. I, Chap, 1, §124, as quoted by Daniel J. Boorstin, *The Mysterious Science of the Law* (Cambridge, Mass.: Harvard University Press, 1941), p. 163.

United States, not least in the intellectual trappings of the judiciary, long after Bentham's attack (following Hume) on natural law philosophy had pretty well destroyed it in England.[29] In fact, it had its greatest development after 1870 in the interpretation of the "due process of law" clause of the Fourteenth Amendment. The similar clause in the Fifth Amendment, applying only to the federal government, had been interpreted as governing only matters of procedure. But the proponents of a growing tendency to read natural law—and particularly natural rights—into our constitutional law seized upon the new amendment as a heaven-sent opportunity. In a short time it was interpreted to apply to the *substance* of state legislation. Laws must be reasonable and not interfere with "fundamental rights." The Fourteenth Amendment, said Justice Field, "was intended to give practical effect to the declaration of 1776 of inalienable rights, rights which are the gift of the Creator, which the law does not confer, but only recognizes." [30] In this fashion most of the individualistic concepts of natural law theory were read into American constitutional law. The trend was still strong as late as the 1920's, when price-fixing and minimum-wage laws were invalidated on the grounds that such acts interfered with the natural rights of freedom of contract and freedom of the businessman (except where the business was "affected with a public interest") to charge what he pleased for his product.[31]

Nevertheless, as was explained above, the notion of absolute natural rights has been gradually giving way, both in England and in the United States, for a long time. The social utilitarianism which had taken its place, however, still provided judges with a standard, although a much less precise one than the old doc-

[29] See Charles Grove Haines, *The Revival of Natural Law Concepts* (Cambridge, Mass.: Harvard University Press, 1930), Pts. II, III; and Benjamin F. Wright, *American Interpretations of Natural Law, A Study in the History of Political Thought* (Cambridge, Mass.: Harvard University Press, 1931).

[30] *Slaughter-House Cases*, 16 Wallace 36 (1872), at 105, cited in Haines, *op. cit.*, p. 175, n. 4.

[31] See *Adkins* v. *Children's Hospital*, 261 U.S. 525 (1923) and *Ribnik* v. *McBride*, 277 U. S. 350 (1928).

trine of natural rights. It was relativistic in the sense that it necessitated judgment as to the relative claims of individual and society, but not completely relativistic in the sense of denying all standards outside the mind of the individual judge.

Modern judicial functionalism, or "skeptical realism," goes much further than this. Starting from the recognition that the law leaves an abundance of opportunity for the exercise of judicial discretion, and impressed by the fact that personal factors often play a determining role in the exercise of that discretion, the tendency of much modern legal theory had been to concentrate on the law that *is*, without regard for legal ideals, and to define this entirely in terms of judicial decisions.[32] It has been the practice of analytical jurists from the time of Austin to insist on a rigid separation between the *is* and the *ought* and to confine their attention to the former, although this procedure has not generally been adopted by practicing judges. Austin, however, continued to think of the law as a body of rules. These rules were created (commanded) by the sovereign and were enforced by the courts because the sovereign (at least by implication) so ordered. Justice Oliver Wendell Holmes, Jr., generally looked upon as the father of realistic jurisprudence, led the way in shifting attention from legislature to court and from the body of law as a whole to particular decisions. Both trends are exemplified by his famous definition of law as prediction of judicial behavior. "The prophecies of what the courts will do in fact, and nothing more pretentious," he declared, "are what I mean by the law."[33] Although, as has frequently been pointed out, Holmes in fact on many occasions showed that he had a broader concept of law, this definition, to quote Dr. Friedmann, "came to something like a gospel for the followers of realism in jurisprudence who, however great their scepticism and sarcasm in regard to other jurists and their doctrines, followed this and some similar statements

[32] For what immediately follows, the best secondary source is W. Friedmann's *Legal Theory* (London: Stevens & Sons, Ltd., 1947).

[33] Oliver Wendell Holmes, Jr., "The Path of the Law," in *Collected Legal Papers* (New York: Harcourt, Brace and Company, 1920), p. 173.

of Mr. Justice Holmes with almost religious fervour." [34] Similarly, his oft-quoted statement that "The Life of the law has not been logic: it has been experience" [35] was subsequently used by many to go much further than Holmes did in denying logic its proper role in the development of law. As a consequence of the movement initiated by Holmes and John Chipman Gray[36] of the Harvard Law School, "conceptualism" has become outmoded in American legal thinking, and decidedly the preponderance of the leaders of legal thought in this country may aptly be described as "functionalists" or "realists."

Gray continued to think of rules of law (created by courts), and Holmes, in spite of his vigorous denial that the common law was a "brooding omnipresence in the sky," [37] also considered that it was a body of rules, albeit consisting of predictions of what courts would do. But some of their followers were not content to stop at this point. Jerome Frank is representative of the most extreme realists when he gives the following "rough definition" of law: "For any particular lay person," he writes, "the law, with respect to any particular set of facts, is a decision of a court with respect to those facts so far as that decision affects that particular person. Until a court has passed on those facts," he continues, "no law on that subject is yet in existence." [38] Furthermore, Frank contends, judicial "reasoning," that which appears in the published opinions, is more rationalization than honest reasoning. Precedents can generally be found to support whatever conclusion the judge desires to reach, and the normal procedure is for a judge to begin with his conclusion and then find reasons to support it.[39]

Inevitably theories such as we have been discussing under-

[34] Friedmann, *op. cit.*, p. 185.

[35] Oliver Wendell Holmes, Jr., *The Common Law* (Boston: Little, Brown & Company, 1938), p. 1.

[36] See John Chipman Gray, *The Nature and Sources of the Law* (New York: The Macmillan Company, 1909, 1921), Chaps, 4, 9, and 10.

[37] *Southern Pacific Co.* v. *Jensen*, 244 U. S. 205 (1917), at 222.

[38] Jerome Frank, *Law and the Modern Mind* (New York: Brentano's, Inc., 1930), p. 46.

[39] *Ibid.*, Chaps. 12, 14.

mine popular confidence in the courts as instruments of justice. If judges cannot maintain a measure of objectivity and impartiality, there is a strong presumption that no one can. If no one can, then we had better give up dependence upon liberal institutions and use whatever means we can—force if that promises to be most effective—to satisfy our own interests. If not the inevitable conclusion of the realists' line of reasoning, this is at least a plausible one.

It is interesting to note, however, that something in the nature of a reaction appears to be in the making. Some legal theorists today, like Professor Fuller, are sounding the call for yet one more return to natural law.[40] Perhaps more significant is the fact that some of the realists are now stressing what, in their anxiety to make their points, they earlier failed to make clear, namely, that not only do they themselves have ideals and believe that there are general principles of justice, but they also concede that judges are at least in some measure influenced both by legal rules and by legal ideals.[41] This new turn of events is of great significance for the future. But it has not yet had time to have much influence on judicial thinking. Our highest courts have only recently become well saturated with the earlier realism.

4. Consequences for American Constitutionalism

What have been the consequences to American constitutionalism of these various factors tending to weaken the system of judicially protected rights? An interesting illustration of the forces favoring and opposing the institution of judicial review is provided by the attempt made by President Franklin D. Roosevelt to secure legislative authorization for "packing" the Supreme Court. The Court's use of rigid conceptualism to enforce laissez-faire policies had reached its climax during the twenties, and with the accession of Hughes to the Chief Justiceship in

[40] Lon L. Fuller, *The Law in Quest of Itself* (Chicago: The Foundation Press, Inc., 1940).

[41] Cf. K. N. Llewellyn, "On Reading and Using the Newer Jurisprudence," *Columbia Law Review*, XL (Apr., 1940), 581–614. Cf. also Friedmann, *op. cit.*, pp. 193–194.

1930 there began a period of rather rapid modification of many of the old rules in favor of a more realistic appraisal of the needs of the times. However, certain aspects of New Deal legislation, notably the National Industrial Recovery Act and the Agricultural Adjustment Act, had represented more of a break with tradition than a majority of the Court was willing to tolerate, with the result that these important pillars of the New Deal edifice were struck down. The administration undoubtedly feared that even more vital portions of its program, such as the National Labor Relations Act, might be next in line for the judicial ax. The result was the well-known proposal for legislation permitting the appointment of additional justices. Whatever may have been its merits, it was an obvious attempt to override the judicial vetoes by interfering with the independence of the judiciary rather than by resorting to the constitutionally provided mechanism for amendment. Justified or not by the Court's record of writing its own economic views into the law or by the urgency of the situation, it was indeed a manifestation of impatience with the previously accepted methods of procedure under our constitutional system. The attempt to dress the proposal up as a retirement measure was such a thin disguise as to add to the general impression that its backers felt a cynical contempt at least for the mechanics and for some of the traditions of American constitutionalism.[42]

Probably at no previous time in the nation's history—certainly not since judicial review was once well established in popular acceptance—would such a measure have had as good a chance of enactment. Does this indicate a disintegration in the strength of our constitutional morality? It is a difficult question to answer. Perhaps the provocation had never before been so great.

[42] There was considerable argument at the time as to whether or not this was the first attempt to pack the Supreme Court. The question is one of definition and of degree. Clearly it was the most brazen. Perhaps the Court had been indulging in even more brazen instances of judicial legislation in opposition to the fairly clear temper of the majority of the people; that is neither here nor there. The fact is that never before had a President attempted to coerce the Supreme Court into altering its views by threatening to add to its membership.

It must be remembered, too, that this happened at a time when a strong occupant of the White House had a Congress willing, on most matters, to do his personal bidding. Polls indicate that the measure did not command the support of a majority of the nation at any time. We must also bear in mind that the Supreme Court has gone through other periods of popular disrepute and lived to regain its place in popular esteem. The same may happen again.[43] One may hazard the guess, however, that should future crises bring Court and representatives of the people into conflict, an unyielding Court will be risking its own destruction. In a large measure it has been ever thus;[44] but it seems likely that patience with what will appear as judicial obstructionism will be shorter in the future than it has been in the past. A twenty-year lag in the accomplishment of the public will, such as featured the history of the federal income tax, is not likely to be repeated.

It has been often remarked that the defeat of the President's Court plan was an instance of a campaign won though the battle was lost. Not only did the Court proceed to uphold the remainder of the New Deal program (the Wagner Act while the plan was still pending and before any new appointments had been made), but during the decade and more since then not a single piece of any presidential legislative program has been invalidated. The newly constituted Court has adopted a policy of judicial self-abnegation, especially with reference to federal legislation. Furthermore, substantive due process of law as the great source of protection for vested interests and business liberty has in effect been read out of the Constitution, just as it had been read into it over half a century before. In its oversight of the work of admin-

[43] There is no indication, however, that such a reversal of the tide has yet set in, but rather the contrary. In June, 1946, the American Institute of Public Opinion reported the results of a poll in which persons were asked the question: "Has your attitude toward the Supreme Court changed in recent years?" Approximately 30 per cent answered "yes"; 45 per cent "no." Of the former group, 90 per cent said that their opinion of the Court was lower than it had been.—*Public Opinion Quarterly*, X (Fall, 1936), 436.

[44] See Dean Alfange, *The Supreme Court and the National Will* (New York: Doubleday & Company, 1937).

istrative agencies, the Court has retreated from its earlier insistence upon passing on the merits of their decisions to a policy of accepting these decisions as final if only the elements of fair procedure have been observed and if the law has not clearly been misinterpreted.[45]

Not only has the Court greatly enlarged the presumption of validity which it attaches to administrative and legislative action (both federal and state), but in doing so it has reversed many of its former decisions. This decline in observance of the rule of *stare decisis* itself constitutes a weakening, other things being equal, of the structure of constitutionalism.[46] A decision that has been reversed can be reversed again, and as the process continues it becomes increasingly apparent that what is happening is not the rule of law but, as the common jibe goes, the rule of lawyers—of nine very human men, whether old or young.

At this point it should be noted that it is not the substance of the changes in our constitutional law but the method of bringing them about which is primarily of concern here. The substance has consisted partly of ridding our constitutional law of laissez-faire aspects which were never essential elements of it, partly of a general modification of concepts of private property rights, and partly of enlarging the scope of federal powers at the expense of the states. The significance of federal centralization and of the depreciation of property rights has already been discussed. It must be recognized, too, that shifts in policy on the part of the Court are nothing new in its history. The product of Taney's court was very different from Marshall's, for example.[47] In the process of swinging from one orientation to another it has fre-

---

[45] This rather cavalier treatment of the complicated and still evolving subject of the judicial review of administrative determinations covers a multitude of variations not relevant for present purposes. See J. Roland Pennock, *Administration and the Rule of Law* (New York: Rinehart & Company, 1941), Chaps. 6, 7, for a fuller treatment.

[46] The Court has always maintained that *stare decisis* was not an absolute rule and that in constitutional cases in particular it should not be given too great weight. Nevertheless the change during the past decade is very marked.

[47] See the works of Professor Edward S. Corwin, esp. his *The Commerce Power versus States Rights* (Princeton: Princeton University Press, 1936).

quently reversed itself and even more frequently accomplished the same result by means of a distinction here and a none too subtle twist there. Nor is the decline in invalidation of legislation anything to remark about. No federal laws were declared unconstitutional by the Supreme Court between 1803 and 1856. The significant fact is that there were far more and far more important reversals between 1937 and 1947 than in any similar previous period.[48] Even this may be partly accounted for by the abnormal exercise of the judicial veto in the period just preceding this[49] and by the extraordinary severity of the economic crisis that precipitated the New Deal legislation. The fact to be noted is that the Court, the bar generally, and to a large extent the lay public, have become far more aware of judicial legislation than ever before. To what extent this is the product of advancing doctrines of judicial functionalism, to what extent the effect of practices forced on the Court by the situation, we need not inquire. The change is nowhere better evidenced than by the official Court opinions themselves. Time and again, and in more unvarnished terms than ever in the past, occupants of the bench have accused their brethren of reading into the law their own views on matters of public policy. For example, Justice Jackson, protesting against the action of a majority of the Court on one occasion, spoke as follows: "To force the hands of Congress is no more the proper function of the judiciary than to tie the hands of Congress. To use my office, at a time like this and with so little justification in necessity, to dislocate the functions and revenues

[48] Exact figures in support of this statement are not available, but no one familiar with the work of the Court can doubt its truth. In 1932, Mr. Justice Brandeis, in a dissenting opinion dealing with the question of the application of the rule of *stare decisis* by the Supreme Court to its own decisions, listed in a footnote 13 instances of self-reversal since the Court's establishment. *Burnet* v. *Coronado Oil & Gas Co.,* 285 U. S. 393, at 406, n. 1. This list was supplemented for subsequent years down to 1944 by Mr. Justice Reed. He listed 15 instances during this period, all of them actually occurring during the seven years beginning with the 1936–1937 term of court. *Smith* v. *Allwright,* 321 U. S. 649 (1944), at 665, n. 10.

[49] During the first two decades of this century, 16 federal statutes were invalidated, while 35 were declared null and void during the succeeding twenty years.

of the states and to catapult Congress into immediate and undivided responsibility for supervision of the nation's insurance businesses, is more than I can reconcile with my view of the function of this Court in our society.",[50] On another occasion, Justice Frankfurter was moved to declare: "If ever there was an intrusion by this Court into a field that belongs to Congress, and which it has seen fit not to enter, this is it." [51]

There are increasing evidences that the period of judicial self-abnegation that followed upon the Court-packing threat of 1937 is drawing to a close, at least as far as state legislation is concerned, but this does not mean the return to a more rigid "rule of law." The trend is toward deciding each case "on its merits." This necessarily leads the Court into overt policy making. In general the policy the Court is pursuing is a "liberal" one in the sense that it is favorable both to formal liberty and to substantive liberty where the latter is being interfered with or threatened by asserted rights of property. But it is nonetheless a modification of the ideal of government according to settled rule and one which might well threaten the independence of the Court at some time in the future. One of the clearest illustrations of the present Court's functionalism is to be found in its treatment of the decisions of the Interstate Commerce Commission. In the past that commission has enjoyed an enviable record with the Court. Of late, however, there has been a marked change, and this in spite of the trend toward allowing greater finality to administrative decisions. A study of the cases leaves little doubt that this development is not the product of a change on the part of the commission but rather of the attitude on the part of a majority of the Court toward the policies being pursued by the commission. Virtually the same Court that has gone to great lengths to uphold the actions of certain New Deal commissions against charges that their decisions were not adequately backed

[50] *U. S.* v. *South-Eastern Underwriters Assoc.,* 322 U. S. 533 (1944), at 594–595.
[51] *Cloverleaf Butter Co.* v. *Patterson,* 315 U. S. 148 (1942), at 178–179.

up by "findings" [52] has taken a very different attitude regarding this legal requirement when it was dealing with a decision of the Interstate Commerce Commission (which it suspected of favoring the railroad interests at the expense of rival forms of transportation).[53]

Before concluding this discussion of the impact of ideas and events on our system of judicially protected rights, it should be repeated, with emphasis, that the basic liberties of liberal democracy have fared well, exceptionally well, at the hands of the Supreme Court during recent years,[54] although it should also be pointed out that the war brought a substantial paring down of some of the old judicial landmarks regarding the effect of the war power on civil liberties.[55] The judiciary will probably continue to play a somewhat diminished role in American government, but it is not clear that this will necessarily be a loss to constitutionalism. At the same time, there can hardly be any doubt that the Court has lost in objectivity. Making due allowances for the fact that the Court has always been influenced by the preconceptions of its members, it seems clear that neither respect for precedent nor the desire to be consistent exercises as great a brake on judicial legislation as it did in the past. This is a natural consequence

[52] *Securities and Exchange Commission* v. *Chenery Corp.*, 332 U. S. 194 (1947). See the dissenting opinion at p. 209 *et seq.*

[53] *Interstate Commerce Commission* v. *Mechling*, 330 U. S. 567 (1947).

[54] Even here qualifications are required. It is worthy of note that the greatest extensions of the constitutional protection of freedom of speech have been on behalf of labor. At least one decision raises the question—it was raised by a member of the Court itself—whether the Court is equally jealous of the right of employers to free speech. See *Thomas* v. *Collins*, 323 U. S. 516 (1945).

[55] See Corwin, *Total War and the Constitution*, and Eugene V. Rostow, "The Japanese American Cases—a Disaster," *Yale Law Journal*, LIV (June, 1945), 489–533. The Court's validation of the military trial of the Japanese General Homma brought forth the following shocked outcry from Mr. Justice Murphy: "Either we conduct such a trial as this in the noble spirit and atmosphere of our Constitution or we abandon all pretense to justice, let the ages slip away and descend to the level of revengeful blood purges. Apparently the die has been cast in favor of the latter course. But I, for one, shall have no part in it, not even through silent acquiescence." —*Homma* v. *Patterson*, 327 U. S. 759 (1946).

of the various developments, philosophical and practical, which have been traced in the preceding pages. What this means is that in the future even more than in the past the protection of liberty and the avoidance of arbitrary government will depend upon strong popular support for freedom.

It is meet, however, to say a word at this point in reply to those who think it obvious that the change is for the good. The roll of those who in recent years have denounced judicial review as undemocratic and undesirable is a long one.[56] Most recently Jerome Frank, quoted above as a representative of the legal realists, and now a federal judge, has declared that "the concept of governmental guardians cannot be reconciled with the basic concept of a democracy." [57] "In recent years," Frank continues, "the Supreme Court has boldly abandoned the papa role. The Justices have openly acknowledged their human fallibilities, have discarded the 'opportune lie' that judges possess some sort of semi-divinity." In doing so, he concludes, "the Court has set a splendid example." [58]

It is this attitude, so widely held by many professed liberals today, that is alarming. Democratic in the original sense such a development undoubtedly is. But if democracy is to avoid its ancient excesses and ultimate degeneration into tyranny it must not forsake its nineteenth-century marriage to political liberalism. Liberalism had learned the truth with which all the great political seers from Aristotle to Montesquieu were familiar: that liberty and security against the abuses of despotism are best found in mixed governments, characterized by certain checks on the direct and immediate power of the people. One of the earliest and most fundamental of political discoveries was that the unattainable ideal of human impartiality can be most nearly approximated by inculcating certain indivuals with professional standards and

[56] See, for example, Henry Steele Commager, *Majority Rule and Minority Rights* (New York: Oxford University Press, 1943), and Edwin Mims, Jr., *The Majority of the People* (New York: Modern Age Books, 1941).
[57] Jerome Frank, "Self-Guardianship and Democracy, an Editorial," *American Scholar*, XVI (Summer, 1947), 266.
[58] *Ibid.*

then by so circumstancing them that they are protected from political pressure. It is this discovery rather than the belief that judges possess "semi-divinity" that underlies liberal reliance upon courts. The reasoning upon which Judge Frank's remarks appear to be based would lead straight to the abolition of judicial guardianship over even our most basic civil liberties, submitting such matters to the will of legislative majorities and even of direct popular majorities. (For why should legislators any more than judges be set up as guardians of the people?) Liberalism must always be willing to take chances on the political intelligence and good will of the people; but a liberalism which closes its eyes to the tendency for unchecked power to be abused, whether exercised by one despot or a hundred million (to paraphrase Jefferson), is flirting with self-destruction. No institution can preserve liberty in the absence of support in popular sentiment. But institutions can act as shock absorbers to tide over a popular reaction that does not represent the settled desires of the people. Also, institutions mold sentiments as well as reflecting them; and a system of judicially protected rights is perhaps one of the best means of holding up to the emulation of all the ideal of equal treatment of equals.

5. Summary

It will be well to summarize some of the conclusions of this chapter along with those of the two preceding chapters. It is clear that there have been fundamental changes in the reigning ideas and in social and economic conditions that threaten the continued health of liberal democracy even in the countries where it has its deepest roots. Some of these changes tend to produce an electorate that is bewildered, divided, and unstable; that is declining in self-reliance and less inclined to have confidence either in the capacity of the individual to manage his own affairs or of democracy to do it for him; and that is less firmly committed to liberal-democratic values and to democratic constitutionalism as the means for preserving these values. At the same time, the requirements of the socio-economic situation call for governments which can make quick decisions on complicated problems, and act on them positively and energetically. In the face of these demands, we find that legislatures, which have traditionally been the very heart of democratic institutions, have declined in prestige and probably in effectiveness, and that the judiciary, which, especially in the United States, has been the heart of constitutionalism, is suffering a similar declination. On the other hand, the executive, traditionally viewed with jealousy by liberals and democrats, has become the dominant branch of government. There is more than a little in this picture to encourage the belief that liberal democracy is giving way to out-and-out "majoritarianism" and that this in turn will be quickly followed by that plebiscitary democracy that is characteristically the forerunner of tyranny (the democratic totalitarians notwithstanding).

We have noted as we went along that these trends may be exaggerated (and have been by critics from both the right and the left) and that there are certain countervailing factors. In the ensuing chapters we shall examine more carefully the workability and viability of liberal democracy under modern conditions. After a consideration of the prerequisites of democracy, we shall consider in succeeding chapters the problems of the competency of public opinion for the tasks imposed upon it by democracy, the problems of unity, and of the prospects for liberty.

PART FOUR

PRACTICABILITY
AND PROSPECTS

CHAPTER X

DEMOCRATIC
PREREQUISITES

We are considering in this volume the desirability, workability, and prospects of liberal democracy for modern industrial societies and especially for the English-speaking countries. Few, if any, would be so rash as to maintain that democratic institutions are universally applicable. This is not to deny
that they would be desirable anywhere they could be made to
work. If our reasoning in earlier chapters is sound, they would.
But the institutions of government, like all institutions, are part
of a culture pattern. They must be appropriate to the culture of
which they are a part. Bills of rights will remain scraps of paper
in societies where there is no respect for the individual or no
spirit of toleration. Elections cannot secure the expression of
public opinion where there is no "public" that can have opinions.

At the same time it must be remembered that it is part of
the purpose of government to support and to alter the very culture of which it is a manifestation. To a degree, then, democracy
may create its own prerequisites. It should also be noted that, as
societies develop and especially as the sphere of governmental
activities is enlarged, the nature of these prerequisites undergoes
modification. A degree of public spirit which suffices for democratic government in one society or at one period may be wholly
inadequate under other circumstances. In speaking, then, of the
prerequisites of democracy, we must make clear that this is no
static concept. Within limits, a government that lacks them may
bring them into being, and one that has them may cease to have
them, not because conditions have deteriorated, but because the
needs have grown.[1]

[1] There are innumerable treatments of the essential conditions of democracy. John Stuart Mill's classic statement of the case for representative gov-

First of all, democracy cannot be foisted upon people. They must have the desire to be self-governing. And it is important to note that continual frustration may stamp out the aspiration where once it has flourished. Accompanying the desire for self-government must go the willingness to assume the responsibilities it entails. Democratic rights cannot be realized without the acceptance of their correlative duties; with the right to self-government go the duties of active citizenship. Nor is it enough that citizens should express interest in government. A third prerequisite is that this interest must be backed up by at least a minimum of information and intelligence. As in the case of the other conditions, this is a matter of degree and it is impossible to define the lower limit if for no other reason than because it will vary according to the nature of the problems the government in question has to meet. At least it is clear that no country is ready for democracy until the great bulk of its citizens are able to read and write.

A fourth requirement is less easily defined than the foregoing but no less essential. It is that compound variously known as civic or public spirit.[2] Democrats no longer believe with Jeremy Bentham that a society made up of completely self-seeking individuals can operate a democratic government successfully. A democratic society must be infused with a certain amount of group feeling, of loyalty to the whole and to its ideals. A goodly proportion of its members must have enough concern for the general welfare to be willing to put themselves out somewhat for

ernment is accompanied by a discussion of these conditions. ("On Representative Government," in *Utilitarianism, Liberty and Representative Government,* "Everyman's Library" [New York: E. P. Dutton & Co., 1910], Chap. 4.) For typical modern treatments of the subject, see Francis W. Coker, *Recent Political Thought* (New York: Appleton-Century-Crofts, Inc., 1934), pp. 372–373; and Carl L. Becker, *Modern Democracy* (New Haven: Yale University Press, 1941), pp. 11 ff. No attempt is made in this chapter to give a treatment of the subject such as would be called for in a book on all phases of democracy. It is dealt with here only so far as is essential to a discussion of the workability and prospects of liberal democracy.

[2] As was pointed out above (p. 106), it is one of the virtues of democracy that it tends to develop public spirit. It is still true, however, that a certain minimum of this spirit must be present before self-government can get a successful start.

its benefit and, more particularly, to cast their ballots for candidates who show signs of such motivation in preference to those who pander solely to the selfish interests of special groups. Moreover, citizens of a democracy must be tolerant of others with whose opinions and beliefs they do not agree, and they must be prepared to modify their own views and to compromise in the interests of securing agreement upon a program for united action. Although such compromises will generally be to the long-run interests of those who make them, in point of fact most people are too intent upon the short run and too lacking in the ability to visualize their long-run interests to allow us to depend upon self-interest as the sole source of social cohesion. An added element of sympathy and of loyalty is essential.[3]

A prerequisite closely related to public spirit is that of agreement upon fundamentals. Mill long ago observed that "in all political societies which have had a durable existence, there has been some fixed point; something which men agreed in holding sacred; which, wherever freedom of discussion was recognized principle, it was of course lawful to contest in theory, but which no one could either fear or hope to see shaken in practice; which, in short (except perhaps during some temporary crisis), was in the common estimation placed beyond discussion." [4] Mosca makes the same point in discussing the "political formula," [5] while other writers refer simply to the necessity for an underlying consensus to give cohesion to the body politic. It should be noted that this is a prerequisite for any form of government, not just for democracy. It is worthy of special mention here, however, inasmuch as the freedom of discussion that liberal democracy both permits and encourages peculiarly exposes it to attack. Furthermore, the political formula that underlies liberal

[3] It will be observed that what is discussed above as "public spirit" is the positive statement of what is sometimes referred to, negatively, as the absence of a factionalism unqualified by mutual tolerance and forbearance.

[4] John Stuart Mill, "Coleridge," in *Dissertations and Discussions: Political, Philosophical and Historical* in *The Works of John Stuart Mill* (New York: E. P. Dutton & Co., 1905), ser. 1, IV, 342.

[5] Gaetano Mosca, *The Ruling Class*, trans. Hannah D. Kahn, ed. Arthur Livingston (New York: McGraw-Hill Book Company, Inc., 1939), pp. 70–71.

democracy is unique in its insistence upon democratic and constitutional methods that cannot be maintained when there is violent disagreement. As we shall see below, there are those who believe that this fact, too, renders it especially vulnerable at the present time.[6]

Finally, the successful operation of democracy depends upon a reasonable degree of international order and security. This is even more important for the liberal democratic form of government than for others, for reasons which were elaborated above (Chapter VIII).

Attacks upon the practicability of democracy in large measure consist of arguments that the prerequisites—and especially those of intelligence, public spirit, and agreement upon fundamentals—cannot be met. These three will be dealt with in the following chapters, but we shall consider at this point whether or not the first two prerequisites are likely to be present.

As to the desire to be self-governing, if our arguments about the natural inclination of man to be free and to control his own life are correct, this should be no great problem. And in fact history discloses a general growth of the desire to be self-governing as men are freed from the domination of tradition and provided with a minimum of education. Some peoples feel it more strongly than others. Some may lose it as a result of frustration. But the rising tide of independence movements among the subject peoples of the world today leaves no room for dispute as to the prevalence of the desire. Here is no unattainable condition. Nor is there any indication that it tends to decline after democracy has reached a certain stage of development. In Italy and Germany it was clearly the failure of democracy to cope with the problems it faced that weakened the desire for self-government

---

[6] As Professor Friedrich has pointed out, this subject of underlying agreement is a matter of degree and a matter of how evenly balanced are the elements in the society that are in disagreement. Furthermore, a strong commitment to a constitutional procedure for resolving differences will go a long way toward overriding religious or economic differences. See Carl J. Friedrich, *Constitutional Government and Democracy* (Boston: Little, Brown & Company, 1941), pp. 158–169, 586–589.

rather than the reverse. Popular interest in government, as measured by voting, was close to an all-time high just before Hitler succeeded in smashing the Weimar republic.[7] Voting statistics in Great Britain and the United States also reveal no secular decline in political interest, but rather the contrary.[8]

As to the willingness to assume the responsibilities of self-government, there can be no doubt that this condition has been attained in the leading democracies of the world. It is frequently argued, however, that democracies have witnessed a general decline in the matter of willingness to fight, to risk one's life for the defense of his country. This is a natural consequence, so the argument runs, of democratic philosophy, which stresses the well-being, and especially the comfort, of the individual. The result is softness and a tendency to leave disagreeable obligations to the other fellow. There is a certain plausibility to this argument both from a theoretical point of view and also in the light of the spirit that characterized the United States and other democracies during most of the twenties and thirties. But there is no necessary relationship between materialism and debasing love of creature comforts on the one hand and democracy on the other. If democratic countries have been especially prone to be softened by prosperity, it is because the democratic countries in question have been especially prosperous. We have already seen that any relationship between democratic philosophy and a selfish individualism is not only accidental but runs counter to the ideals of equality and fraternity which are as essential to democracy as the love of liberty.

[7] See Sydney L. W. Mellon, "The German People and the Postwar World," *American Political Science Review*, XXXVII (Aug., 1943), 612–613.

[8] From 1924 to 1940, inclusive, the total number of votes for President increased substantially at each successive election. The 1940 vote, four million above 1936, has not been quite equaled since then, but the 1944 and 1948 totals were both substantially above the previous (1936) high. In Great Britain, General Election statistics since the enlargement of the electorate in 1929 show a marked constancy with respect to the total number of votes up to the war. Considerable caution must be used in interpreting any such statistics. A relatively low actual vote is perfectly compatible with a strong insistence on the *right* to vote. It may indicate only a general satisfaction with the way things are going.

An examination of the course of events also serves to show the weakness of the argument. If the French debacle is pointed to as an instance of democratic decadence, we need not argue the merits of that interpretation—although it is a debatable one; it is sufficient to direct our gaze across the channel at Great Britain. Here a democracy which has had plenty of time and relative prosperity on which to grow soft—the home of that very individualism which is supposed to be the enemy of patriotic self-sacrifice—proved more than equal to the occasion and set an example to the world. Again, if the military virtues were exemplified by Germany, not all the posturing of Mussolini, not all the militant preachments of Italian Fascism served to create a heroic army for Hitler's axis partner. We may safely conclude that neither theoretical nor practical arguments provide ground for believing that democracy is doomed to perish for lack of the will to defend itself.

CHAPTER XI

IS POPULAR
GOVERNMENT INCOMPETENT?

We may remind ourselves that traditional democratic theory—especially the Utilitarian variety—made these three assumptions: (1) that men are sufficiently concerned and intelligent to discover what policies are to their interest; (2) that they are rational enough to act in accordance with their conclusions; and (3) that men's interests are also rational in the sense that they harmonize and support a policy which is in the best interest of the whole. If these are sound, one need not be concerned about the third and fourth democratic prerequisites—informed intelligence and public spirit; they would be amply met. But, as we have seen, skepticism has attacked all three of these assumptions. The cheerful optimism with which prevailing opinion in the last century affirmed them is scarcely to be found anywhere today.

We can briefly summarize the contentions of those numerous critics who challenge the competence of the public to perform the tasks required of it in a democracy. Walter Lippmann is typical of those who contend that the information at the disposal of the average voter is hopelessly inadequate and too distorted to enable him, with the best will in the world, to perform his duties intelligently. Numerous investigations bear out the paucity of the average citizen's information on important issues.[1] Other

---

[1] For instance, according to an American poll conducted in 1946 by the National Opinion Research Center, 79 per cent of those polled did not have a reasonably accurate idea of the contents of the Bill of Rights. Thirty-one per cent were not even sure they had ever heard of it. (Poll taken August, 1945.)—*Opinion News*, VII, No. 3 (Aug. 6, 1946), 3. Other polls indicated that 34 per cent of the people could not name either of their senators.—*The Gallup Political Almanac for 1946*, compiled by the American Institute of Public Opinion (Princeton: 1946), p. 212.

writers like Mr. M. Alderton Pink (whose views belie his name) insist that the intelligence of the average voter is too feeble to cope with the problems of government.[2] Here again there is all too much evidence in support of the view expressed. No documentation is needed to support the statement that the intelligence of the great bulk of the population, as measured by any standard intelligence tests, is separated from that of the ablest by a very wide gap. Moreover, a host of writers have emphasized the fact, now well recognized, that men are moved more by appeals to emotion, sentiment, and prejudice than by appeals to reason. In this connection the names of Pareto and Wallas come readily to mind, while that of Freud might seem to clinch the argument, with the addition of a note of the mysterious and inevitable. According to a seasoned observer, the American politician has long since learned this lesson and generalized its implications for practical politics in the form of the rule: "Give them 'hokum.'"[3] Nine times out of ten, he asserts, it works.

Finally,[4] various writers, notably the Swiss, Robert Michels, have argued that on account of these shortcomings, because of the necessity of organization and leadership, and also because of the superior training and ability of the leaders, real democratic control by the rank and file is in fact impossible.[5]

[2] M. Alderton Pink, *A Realist Looks at Democracy* (London: Ernest Benn, Ltd., 1930), p. 68. Recently, Mr. Pink seems to have revised his views in favor of a more optimistic appraisal of democracy. See his *The Challenge to Democracy* (London: Faber and Faber, Ltd., 1946).

[3] Frank R. Kent, *Political Behavior* (New York: William Morrow & Company, 1928), p. 146. An attempt has been made by Professor George W. Hartmann to confirm these generalizations by means of scientific procedures. His evidence gave strong support to the theory that "rational" propaganda is much less effective than "emotional" propaganda in a political campaign.— George W. Hartmann, "A Field Experiment on the Comparative Effectiveness of 'Emotional' and 'Rational' Political Leaflets in Determining Election Results," *Journal of Abnormal and Social Psychology*, XXXI (Apr.–June, 1936), 99–114.

[4] Two other criticisms (that democracy is opposed to quality and that democratic foreign policy is inferior to that of dictatorships) will be dealt with separately below (pp. 242–246, 249–252).

[5] Robert Michels, *Political Parties*, trans. Eden and Cedar Paul (New York: Hearst's International Library Company, 1915). See also Gaetano Mosca, *The Ruling Class*, trans. Hannah D. Kahn, ed. Arthur Livingston

This picture of man as ignorant, misinformed, stupid, irrational, and incapable of enforcing a collective judgment might seem to be more than enough for an attack upon the sovereignty of public opinion; but this is not all. Man as an individual is indeed a weak vessel for self-government; but when acting in association with others he degenerates, so it is contended. Ever since Le Bon described the tendency of men in crowds to become even less rational than usual and to submit to the domination of (frequently) daemonic subconscious motivations, students of social psychology have contributed to the rising tide of criticism of democracy. Politics is the realm in which we seek compensation for our more or less frustrated private motives, where "fear autisms" and "wish autisms" rather than reason rule our actions.[6] Even individuals in small groups not under the influence of crowd psychology and acting with a fair degree of deliberation, manifest, it is said, a weakened sense of responsibility, a lower energy of thought, and a greater sensitiveness to nonlogical influences than do the same persons acting singly.[7] Furthermore, political behavior is especially susceptible to nonrational influences because of the difficulties of rational analysis in a field where it is extremely difficult to isolate and to measure consequences and where these consequences seem so much more remote from the individual than in the fields of social or business relationships.[8] Political man, as Hitler argued and demonstrated, is the creature of propaganda.

1. Consideration of Attacks upon Public Opinion

This, then, is the raw material for that public opinion which democracy seeks to enthrone. Can it possibly be equal to the task

(New York: McGraw-Hill Book Company, 1939); and Vilfredo Pareto, *The Mind and Society,* trans. by Andrew Bongiorno and Arthur Livingston, ed. Arthur Livingston (4 vols.; New York: Harcourt, Brace and Company, 1935).

[6] H. W. Wright, "Intellect versus Emotion in Political Cooperation," *Ethics,* LVI (1945), 19–20.

[7] Joseph A. Schumpeter, *Capitalism, Socialism, and Democracy* (2d ed.; New York: Harper & Brothers, 1947), pp. 256–264.

[8] *Ibid.,* pp. 261f.

of government in ever more complicated and technical industrial societies? One is inclined to reel before the attack and surrender without so much as striking a blow. A moment's reflection, however, suggests that if things were really as bad as this democracy could hardly have achieved that measure of success which has attended it in the past. Surely there must be another side to the picture. And in fact there is. Many of the criticisms of man's shortcomings are exaggerations and half-truths. Men are "inclined" to be governed by their passions in political matters, yes; also men are inclined to drink and to slothfulness—why, then, are they not all wastrels? The confidence of the nineteenth century in human reason and intelligence was exaggerated but not entirely without foundation. It is interesting and reassuring to note the studied judgment of one of America's foremost practicing students of public opinion, Mr. Elmo Roper:

The result of five years of asking the American public what it thinks about this or that, and what it wants in this or that product, is to make me more convinced than I ever was before that, given an *intelligent* and *free press* and an equally *intelligent* and *free radio* for the purpose of disseminating information, the judgment of the majority of our citizens will result in a government far more generally satisfactory than can possibly be had through a government run solely by individuals or groups, even though the intelligence quotient of some small group might be higher than the intelligence quotient of the voters as a whole.[9]

Another source of encouragement derives from a comparison of some criticisms of democracy with others. It is charged that men are selfish rather than socially motivated. But insofar as they act selfishly they are at least guided by a kind of rationality. Again, it is said that the average man is not interested in politics and at the same time that he demands too much control of the details of government. Democracy is at one time identified with

[9] National Municipal League, *Democracy Must Think*, Forty-fourth Annual Conference on Government (New York: Columbia University Press, 1939), p. 13. By permission of Columbia University Press, publishers.

mob rule and at another damned for being "atomistic." [10] Some critics condemn it because it must inevitably lead to socialism, while others savagely attack it on account of its defense of capitalism. The ambivalence of these attacks may properly arouse the suspicion that at least some of the critics are not solely motivated by a scientific search for truth. However this may be, the pairs of criticisms mentioned are not cumulative but tend rather to be mutually destructive.

ANALYSIS OF ARGUMENTS BASED ON HUMAN IGNORANCE AND STUPIDITY. Let us look more carefully at some of the considerations bearing upon the average man's ability for self-government. Is he too stupid and ill-informed to perform his part with tolerable efficiency? Must democracy always degenerate into oligarchy? Much misunderstanding of the democratic process is based upon a highly oversimplified view of the way government in a liberal-democratic state operates. When Mr. Lippmann debunks the "sovereign, omnicompetent citizen," he is dealing with a straw man. Possibly the rosy optimism of James Mill gave some support to the idea that democracy involved such a concept, but certainly John Stuart Mill and most subsequent defenders of democracy have been subject to no such illusions. One does not need to be a social psychologist to know that the man in the street is not equipped to judge whether or not processor subsidies are a desirable means of price control or whether the "prudent investment" theory of evaluating public-utility properties is superior to the "reproduction cost" formula. But the obvious fact which critics of democracy so often overlook is that ordinary citizens are not called upon to answer such questions. These are matters for legislatures and expert administrative agencies.

In point of fact, the governmental machine is a highly complicated and delicately articulated mechanism in which decisions are made at a great many different levels, corresponding roughly to the nature of the issues. From the electorate itself one ascends

[10] These two charges are only partly incompatible. A properly integrated group has a far deeper and more pervading unity than that which characterizes the mob.

the scale through the legislature, legislative committees and sub-committees, and thence, generally through the chief executive or some part of his office, to a head of a department or other administrative agency, and finally to a series of specialists within the administrative agencies.

There is a twofold significance to this process. In the first place, the scale is one of increasing specialization and so, normally, of increasing expertness. In addition to this, however, at each level there is opportunity for advice, persuasion, argument, and disclosure of facts by experts and by the representatives of specially interested groups. Practically wherever a decision is made, the person or persons who make it do so after having been exposed to rival streams of propaganda and after having heard the views—sometimes conflicting—of those whose training and specialized experience give them superiority in the technical aspects of the problem. In all walks of life, the most useful debates are not those which are designed with the idea that one of the contenders will convince his opponent, but rather those where the idea is to enable third parties to come to sounder conclusions than they might otherwise reach. It is just such debates as this which characterize almost all stages of the political process. The fact that congressional debates change few votes need not be a matter for either surprise or dismay. Far more important is what goes on in the congressman's mind as he listens to the arguments of lobbyists or hears the testimony of witnesses at committee hearings.

We see, then, in a general way, that only very broad policy decisions are made directly by the electorate, and that these broad decisions are refined and made more specific at successive stages, at each of which there is opportunity for deliberation, expert knowledge, and analysis to be brought to bear on the problems being considered. We have not yet discovered with any precision, however, just what is the nature of the broad policy decisions that the public does make. Until we do this we cannot be sure that the public is in a position to exercise any real control.

Accordingly, we must now consider the question raised by Michels and others as to the possibility of popular control.

In the first instance, it is the party system which is the effective agency of popular control in modern democracies. Unanticipated by the early theorists of democracy, political parties have proved to be the *sine qua non* of popular government. An unorganized multitude is politically powerless. Political parties are the organizations of the people for the control of the government. No single index of the health of a democracy equals that of the efficient functioning of the party system. There is the pulse of democracy.

About our parties we hear much complaint. Sometimes it is declared that they are as alike as peas in a pod and hence give the voter no effective choice. Others complain that they are irresponsible oligarchies, not representative of those whom they are supposed to represent; while still others deplore the character of party functionaries, the professional politicians, declaring that instead of being committed to the public interest they are unprincipled and self-seeking. Much of this criticism is based upon a misconception of the nature and role of parties. Primarily they are alternative governments. Their existence means that there is an organization to put up candidates to compete with those of the party in power and to take over the task of government if they are successful at the polls.[11] In this way competition is brought into effective operation; and it has the same invigorating effect in politics as it has in trade. Under normal conditions the party in power knows it would require only a relatively small decline in its popularity to displace it from the seats of authority. Every act of its leaders must be carefully weighed with this fact in mind. This certainly gives popular control.[12] At the same time,

[11] The discussion that follows will be phrased in terms of a two-party system, such as we have in the United States, but the essential arguments are applicable also to a multiparty system.

[12] In the United States, a shift of 5 per cent of the electorate is normally enough to oust the party in power. Four times this number, 20 per cent of the voters, are reported as considering themselves independents.—*Gallup Political Almanac for 1946*, p. 205.

all that is required of the public, as a minimum, is to know in a general way whether or not it is satisfied with things as they are.

This opportunity to choose between the ins and the outs, which is the very heart of the party system, was completely overlooked by Michels. His analysis, based as it was upon a study of the internal organization of parties, made a great deal of the fact that the rank and file were always at the mercy of the leaders and could not themselves perform the functions that the leaders performed. But when the picture is revised to include a set of rival leaders, its aspect is radically changed. The rank and file now hold the threat of political eclipse over those in power.

Indeed, the difference today between political parties in a one-party system and in a conventional democratic party system is familiar to all. It is more than a difference in degree; it is a difference in kind. Anyone who is familiar with both and yet is tempted to speak of the impossibility of controlling our political parties need only be reminded of their totalitarian counterparts to be forced to acknowledge a tremendous disparity. Anyone, too, who observes how fearful are our party leaders of doing anything that would give to the other party a good "issue" must recognize that the competitive system provides a potent control.

How does the system work in practice? The fact is that in the United States there are at times substantial differences between the two parties as to what they support. In 1932, for instance, the Democratic party stood for vigorous and positive action by the government as contrasted with the greater reliance placed by the Republicans upon the "natural" forces of competition. More specifically, the former differed from its rivals by favoring repeal of prohibition, reduction of tariffs, and government ownership of railroads, power companies, and banks.[13] In varying degrees, a similar situation generally prevails. In 1948,

[13] These statements are based upon analysis of party platforms and campaign speeches.

Many critics of the party system seem to assume that the parties should be diametrically opposed to each other on all points. Such a condition would render democracy completely unworkable for lack of adequate common agreement.

for instance, the same general difference of orientation existed as did in 1932. After an initial period of swinging toward the center, following his accession to office, President Truman reasserted Democratic commitment to New Deal philosophy. In contrast to the Republicans, he and his party, in the 1948 campaign, stood for repeal of the Taft-Hartley Act, allocation of key materials and, if necessary, reimposition of price controls, stronger support for the trade agreements program, and greater expenditures for social services.[14]

It appears from this analysis that in fact the public has an opportunity to express itself on rather more than the simple matter of satisfaction or dissatisfaction, which was proposed above as the minimum. Immediately certain questions suggest themselves. Do most of the voters have clearly formulated ideas on these issues? If so, are they going to be frustrated by finding that they agree with one party on one issue and the other on another—as a 1932 voter would have been if he had favored prohibition and low tariffs? Fortunately, we have some very useful information bearing on these and similar questions derived from replies to questionnaires supplied by 8,419 voters in 37 states and representing nearly all walks of life. Voters were asked to state approval, disapproval, or uncertainty regarding twelve major issues of the campaign. There were two propositions regarding each issue, separated from each other in the questionnaire, and so worded that acceptance of one logically implied rejection of the other.[15] There was, of course, evidence of both doubt and confusion in the minds of many voters. But it is perhaps reassuring rather than the contrary to note that not more than one eighth of

[14] It should be noted in passing that even if at any given time there were no difference between the positions of the two major parties, it would not prove that there was no popular control. On the contrary, the most likely interpretation would be that the leaders of both parties formed an identical estimate of the desires of the majority of the people. This would be the natural outcome of perfect competition. In politics as in economics, the result of perfect competition appears the same as that of complete monopoly.

[15] In several cases the statements were not exact contradictories. See Samuel P. Hayes, Jr., "The Inter-Relations of Political Attitudes: II. Consistency in Voters' Attitudes," *Journal of Social Psychology*, X (Aug., 1939), 361.

the answers involved absolute contradictions.[16] Excluding also the attitudes of doubt, there remain about two thirds of the attitudes expressed which were well enough formulated to serve as the basis for rational political judgment.[17] It is important to remember in this connection that voters need not be clear on each of the twelve issues in order to make an intelligent choice.

This last point is reinforced when we consider the second question raised above. In fact, most voters are not frustrated in the manner suggested because actually attitudes toward various issues tend to group themselves in clusters, so that most people who manifest one attitude of the cluster will also display the others.[18] Thus, in 1932, Democrats in general were more favorable than Republicans to each of the following: substantial tariff reduction, prohibition repeal, veterans' relief, liberal issuance of money, unemployment relief, government ownership, recognition of the U.S.S.R., membership in the World Court, and taxing the rich. The differences between the major parties on these issues averaged about 12 per cent.[19]

It will be noted that the Democratic attitudes listed above (pp. 224 f.) correspond to the general position of the Democratic party in 1932. Hayes concludes that "the platforms and speeches of the political leadership during the 1932 campaign were closely representative of the desires of the electorate." [20] And if further proof is needed that the electorate in 1932 was expressing

[16] *Ibid.*, p. 374. The sample was an unweighted cross section of the population. The group with the poorest record from this point of view (male, Democratic factory workers) scored 21.8 per cent contradictions.

[17] Samuel P. Hayes, Jr., "Voters' Attitudes Toward Men and Issues," *Journal of Social Psychology,* VII (May, 1936), 167.

[18] Samuel P. Hayes, Jr., "The Inter-Relations of Political Attitudes: III. General Factors in Political Attitudes," *Journal of Social Psychology,* IX (Aug., 1939), 379–398.

[19] Samuel P. Hayes, Jr., "The Inter-Relations of Political Attitudes: I. Attitudes Toward Candidates and Specific Policies," *Journal of Social Psychology,* VIII (Nov., 1937), 466–477. The average difference between Democrats and Socialists was 18 per cent (p. 477). The "average difference" refers to the percentage of members of each party who approved the various policies in question (p. 460, n. 2).

[20] Hayes, "Voters' Attitudes toward Men and Issues," *loc. cit.,* p. 175. See also pp. 176–79.

its opinion on broad questions of policy, it may be noted that in general those who switched parties between 1928 and 1932 moved to the party whose attitudes were more congenial to their own in the latter year.[21]

Finally comes the question, "Did the voters get what they voted for?" The answer is that in general they get what the party leaders had indicated they favored. The prohibition amendment was repealed, tariffs were lowered, albeit slowly, the currency was inflated, the government went into the power business (but not railroads or banks), we recognized the Soviet Union, and progressively graduated taxation measures were enacted. There were exceptions. Notably, expenditures were not drastically curtailed, but, on the contrary, were greatly increased. Judging by subsequent election results and also by opinion polls,[22] however, the party leadership did not permanently defy the membership in this respect but rather won them over to its policy.[23]

Popular control—or, what is but the same thing looked at from the other end, the politicians' opportunity to evaluate the force and direction of public opinion—does not end with the elec-

[21] Hayes, "The Inter-Relations of Political Attitudes: IV. Political Attitudes and Party Regularity," *Journal of Social Psychology,* X (Nov., 1939), 550–551.

[22] For data supporting this statement, see Jay H. Topkis, "How Bad Is Congress?" *Political Science Quarterly,* LXII (Dec., 1947), 535.

[23] Data are not available for an analysis of the operation of the political process in Great Britain similar in extent to the treatment above of the American election of 1932. Certain facts relating to the General Election of 1945, however, are available and tends to bear out the conclusions drawn from American experience. In April, 1945, a poll showed that 51 per cent of those who were asked whether they would approve or disapprove of the nationalization of the land replied affirmatively and only 30 per cent in the negative. The following month, 39 per cent indicated approval of nationalization of the Bank of England, as compared with 20 per cent registering disapproval. Following the election, in December, voters were asked whether they approved or disapproved of the government's idea "of nationalizing coal, transport, electricity and so on." This time 59 per cent approved as compared with 25 per cent who disapproved. It has frequently been said that the British people were merely voting against wartime shortages and controls, but these poll results do not confirm that interpretation but rather suggest that voters were expressing their approval of major aspects of the Labour party's program. (Data supplied the author by Dr. Henry Durant, Director of the British Institute of Public Opinion, by letter dated Oct. 11, 1948.)

tion. In the United States a vast network of professional political workers keeps constant tab on the state of public opinion and reports their findings to party headquarters. Legislators and chief executives receive tons of correspondence from voters indicating their stand on this or that issue. Finally, and perhaps most important of all, there are the "pressure groups." Just as political parties, wholly unplanned for by the early framers of constitutional governments, grew up to supplement the formal machinery in a way that is now of vital importance, so also there have grown up countless associations whose purpose it is to protect and advance some special interest of their members. In the United States there are several hundred such organizations large enough to maintain headquarters in the national capital.[24] They may be as broadly based as the CIO or the Chamber of Commerce of the United States, or they may represent as specific an interest as the National Association of Mushroom Growers. They may be organized, like those named above, for the advancement of the economic interests of their members; or, like the Federal Council of Churches of America, the People's Lobby, or the National Popular Government League, they may be "general welfare" organizations. In any case they are constantly at work striving, both by means of evidence and argument and by means of a show of voting strength, to influence the conduct of legislators and administrators. They form an invaluable supplement to the party system.

Pressure groups are especially useful in aiding the legislator or public official to judge the intensity of public opinion on particular issues. A few years ago the civil service unions staged a campaign to secure the repeal of a depression-born law making it illegal for both husband and wife to be on the payrolls of the federal government. A public opinion poll indicated that something like 75 per cent of the public favored the retention of the law. Congress proceeded to repeal it. The congressmen were un-

---

[24] For the third quarter of 1947, 547 lobbyists filed a report with the Clerk of the House of Representatives, as required by law.—*Congressional Record*, XCIII (80th Cong., 1st Sess.), 10617–10644.

doubtedly correct in judging that the great bulk of the people who indicated approval of the law did not feel at all strongly about the matter, while the opposition did.

This last point deserves emphasis. Fascist critics of democracy have made the point that the interests of the majority do not necessarily coincide with the interest of the whole.[25] The latter, the argument runs, must take account of the *intensity* of individual interests as well as their number. To take a simple example, suppose that five out of six occupants of a room are too warm and desire to have a window opened. The sixth, however, is just recuperating from a severe case of pneumonia and it is vital that he be kept warm. Regardless of what the five may favor, it is obvious that the paramount interest of the group is to keep the room warm. (In terms of our earlier analysis his need for the conditions for health is more central than their need for comfort.) If the operation of democracy were such that each issue was settled by direct popular vote, there would be point to the criticism; but in fact the process of government, as described above, in a rough but quite effective way makes provision for this problem. Legislators must judge not what a referendum on the question before them would indicate but rather how the next election will be affected by their treatment of the issue. For this the intensity of the voters' feelings is all-important.

Administrative agencies may be made responsive to public opinion in other ways than by organized pressure. The agencies may themselves seek the advice and assistance of the specialized publics they serve. In the United States the Department of Agriculture has done this to a marked extent. For instance it has sought the advice of representative groups of farmers in administering the farm tenancy program on such questions as the areas in which loans should be made, the proper controls to be set up to ensure their repayment, and what families should receive loans and in what amounts.[26] In this case, too, the organization of local

[25] See Corrado Gini, "The Scientific Basis of Fascism," *Political Science Quarterly*, XLII (Mar., 1927), 112.

[26] M. L. Wilson, *Democracy Has Roots* (New York: Carrick & Evans, Inc., 1939), p. 182.

groups has contributed greatly to popular education in the processes of democracy and in the special problems of the groups in question. The formation of these groups and the development of the informed opinions to which their continual discussions give rise go a long way toward assuring that the larger farmers' organizations will themselves be democratically controlled by an intelligent constituency.[27]

Reference to the problem of ensuring popular control of pressure group organizations may suggest that some further consideration should be given to the question of party organization and control. Michels was undoubtedly quite correct in insisting that party leadership has oligarchic tendencies. As we have already argued, however, this is substantially checked by the fact that the people can always turn to the other party; and, taking the country as a whole, enough people are always ready to do this to exercise a powerful control over the party "machine." Partly for this reason and partly because of the diversity of elements within each of the major parties in the United States, there is actually no party organization on a national scale approaching that degree of integration and control suggested by the use of the term "machine." There is much talk of the domination of presidential nominating conventions by groups of party bosses, of deals in smoke-filled rooms; but it is clear that there is very little reality behind this talk today. The days when a Penrose could dictate the selection of a Harding are no more. Deals, of course, there still are—and always will be. This is part of the democratic process of compromise. But of recent years nominating conventions with remarkable unanimity have selected the candidates whom polls showed to have the strongest support within the party.[28] This is, after all, the final test.

[27] See further *ibid.*, Chap. 7. Another example of effective citizen participation on the local level is to be found in the administration of the social security program. See R. Clyde White, "Local Participation in Social Security Administration," *Public Administration Review*, V (Spring, 1945), 141–147.

[28] This has been true of both major parties for the last three presidential elections with the single exception of the Republican nomination of Willkie in 1940. The exception is curious because Willkie certainly did not repre-

In Great Britain the national party organization is stronger, but the differences between the parties are somewhat greater, so the voter remains assured of control.

In the United States it is only on the local level, where the issues are less complicated and less important and the interests less heterogeneous, and where one party or the other often enjoys a practical monopoly of power, that we have the phenomenon of "boss rule." Even within its limited area of operation, this uniquely American form of degenerate democracy is definitely on the decline. The number of real city, county, or state bosses has steadily decreased, decade by decade. Pennsylvania's Penrose has not been replaced, nor have the Vare brothers of Philadelphia. Tammany Hall is but a shadow of its former self; the Crockers and the Tweeds are no more. Boss Crump, of Memphis, and Frank Hague, of Jersey City, are the latest victims of advancing democracy. Bossism is by no means dead, but in full-blooded form it survives in only a few outposts.

One answer, then, to the charge that public opinion is not competent to govern is to point out that in a liberal democracy it is not called upon to govern in the full sense of that word. The public is like a man who wants a house built for himself. He has a general idea of what he wants and of what he can afford to pay. He then secures the services, in turn, or architect and builder. With their knowledge of the technical possibilities and costs he is able to formulate a much more definite idea of a reasonable plan in view of his desires and means. If the builder falls down on the job he can be dismissed and another obtained. The owner is in complete control, so far as technical and cost limitations permit,

---

sent the party organization and in fact was generally believed to be the popular choice. The explanation is doubtless to be found in two circumstances: the rapidity of Willkie's rise in popularity after he entered the campaign, and the intensity of his support. Only 5 per cent of the Republicans gave Willkie as their preference on May 17. This figure had increased to 17 per cent by June 12, and to 29 per cent by June 20. During the same period, Dewey's support declined from 62 per cent to 47 per cent. The evidence strongly suggests that the convention was not unrepresentative in projecting this trend. Quite probably Willkie led Dewey in popular Republican support on the day he was nominated.

but he could not for a moment do the work himself. So it is with the public and the business of government.

APPRAISAL OF ARGUMENTS BASED ON HUMAN IRRATIONALITY. The analysis above assumes, however, that the owner—to pursue our analogy a little further—is a rational being who knows what he wants and what is likely to prove satisfactory to him when he gets it. If all human conduct is determined by certain irrational and antisocial instincts, such as the life and death instincts, as Freud taught, public opinion cannot be expected to achieve rational results even with a very restricted role.[29] But this part of Freud's theory was hypothetical at best and is not supported by evidence.[30] Recent trends even among psychoanalysts have been to discard it.[31]

One psychoanalyst has gone further and developed the thesis that the most basic human instinct is that of love for others.[32] Another psychologist, Charles C. Josey, speaks for many of his colleagues when he argues that whether the basic tendencies of an individual are to be dominantly social or dominantly antisocial is largely a matter of their early conditioning.[33]

[29] Of course such a theory of human nature is hardly more pessimistic in its outlook for democracy than for any other form of government.

[30] See Gabriel A. Almond, "Politics, Science, and Ethics," *American Political Science Review*, XL (Apr., 1946), 288–289.

[31] See, for example, Erich Fromm, *Escape from Freedom* (New York: Rinehart & Company, Inc., 1941); Karen Horney, *The Neurotic Personality of Our Time* (New York: W. W. Norton & Company, 1937), and, by the same author, *New Ways of Psychoanalysis* (New York: W. W. Norton & Company, 1939), Ranyard West, *Conscience and Society* (New York: Emerson Books, Inc., 1945), pp. 78–98; and Franz Alexander, *Our Age of Unreason: A Study of the Irrational Forces in Social Life* (Philadelphia: J. B. Lippincott Company, 1942).

[32] Ian Suttie, *The Origins of Love and Hate* (London: Routledge and Kegan Paul, Ltd., 1935).

[33] Charles C. Josey, *The Psychological Battlefront of Democracy* (Indianapolis: The Butler University Press, 1944). He writes: ". . . when an individual grows up confident of the love of his family, accepted by the boys and girls of his age, unembittered by exploitation and discrimination, and uncorrupted by special privilege, he becomes as a matter of course a friendly, cooperative person who delights in friendly companionship and in helping others" (p. 44). For evidence tending to confirm the fundamental importance of early educational influences in determining basic character traits, see Abram Kardiner's volumes entitled *The Individual and His Society*

Dr. Franz Alexander, who might be described as a neo-Freudian, speaks of what he calls the "social drift" within the personality.[34] Alexander points out that the well-known tendency of individuals to rationalize their behavior in terms of socially acceptable and "rational" motivations itself bears witness to this "social drift." Other writers have developed this point. Professor Lovejoy, for example, notes that men tend to become trapped by their own expressed ideas—rationalizations or not—because of their dislike of appearing arbitrary and inconsistent. ". . . . an aversion from manifest and admitted irrationality," he writes, "is, after all, by no means the least pervasive or least powerful of emotions in the creature that has long, and with evident gratification, been accustomed to define himself as the rational animal." [35]

Further support for this position may be derived from a study of the composition of political parties. It is well known that in recent years, at least, the Democratic party has pursued policies more nearly answering the demands of the economically less fortunate than have those of the Republican party.[36] In view of this fact it is perhaps not surprising that numerous studies show that the Democratic party draws much more heavily from the

---

—*the Psychodynamics of Primitive Social Organization* (New York: Columbia University Press, 1939) and *The Psychological Frontiers of Society* (New York: Columbia University Press, 1945).

[34] Alexander, *op. cit.*, pp. 111–112.

[35] Arthur O. Lovejoy, "Reflections on the History of Ideas," *Journal of the History of Ideas,* I (Jan., 1940), 19.

See also the position of Professors Krech and Crutchfield in their recent text on social psychology. They write as follows: "From the psychological point of view, man is not quite the irrational being he is often made out to be by the cynic and the propagandist. That he is not is supported by the great extent to which man's beliefs resist change, by the extent to which his beliefs change meaningfully, and by the deep-rooted need for clarification which makes an active search for the facts one of the outstanding features of man's mental life."—David Krech and Richard S. Crutchfield, *Theory and Problems of Social Psychology* (New York: McGraw-Hill Book Company, Inc., 1948), p. 168. They also make the point that the fact of rationalization itself attests man's rationality rather than his irrationality (p. 169).

[36] A sample poll disclosed that, in 1940, 76 per cent of the Democrats and 64 per cent of the Republicans in a representative county believed that the common people would benefit most by the re-election of Roosevelt.—Paul F. Lazarsfeld, Bernard Berelson, and Hazel Gaudet, *The People's Choice* (New York: Duell, Sloan and Pearce, 1944), p. 29.

lower-income groups and less heavily from the high-income groups than does the Republican party.[37] Nevertheless, this fact does indicate that rational self-interest is a major factor in determining party affiliation. Lazarsfeld's study shows that, on the average, this is by far the most significant factor.[38] It is also interesting to note that, in a representative group of voters who switched from Roosevelt in 1936 to Willkie in 1940, 72 per cent had made up their minds to do so before the campaign began (and before the candidates were selected).[39] This fact suggests that campaign propaganda plays a relatively small role in determining the voters' choices.

If, then, the individual as such is not by nature so basically irrational and antisocial as to render cooperative activity doomed to failure, what of the arguments of the crowd psychologists? That crowds sometimes manifest the psychological characteristics attributed to them by Le Bon no careful observer could deny. But Le Bon's generalizations are too sweeping. Other psychologists have reached opposed conclusions. In speaking of the extensive experiments and literature on this subject in recent years, one social psychologist comments: "The most striking thing about all these researches is the lack of agreement between the individual investigators."[40]

Most people have had the opportunity to observe or participate in the deliberations of small groups where Le Bon's principles are virtually reversed. Opinions are critical and diverse instead of being emotional and are all directed in the same way. Frequently, it is clear to all that the end product of group discussion is more rational than were the ideas of any of the members of the group at the outset. A committee may meet after the conclusion of war to consider what should be done about war-

[37] See, for example, *ibid.*, pp. 17–19, and American Institute of Public Opinion poll released on December 8, 1940, reported in *Public Opinion Quarterly*, V (Mar., 1941), 147.

[38] Lazarsfeld and others, *op. cit.*, pp. 17–25.

[39] *Ibid.*, p. 102. It may be that studies of the 1948 election will call for some revision of conclusions based on the 1940 election.

[40] J. F. Brown, *Psychology and the Social Order* (New York: McGraw-Hill Book Company, Inc., 1936), pp. 99–100.

time price control legislation. Some members will favor immediate scrapping of the whole program, while others believe it should be continued indefinitely, and perhaps still others are uncertain. The obvious arguments of those who wish to see the extension of price control will be met by the contention that such regulation is "artificial" and that sooner or later the "natural" laws of economics will assert themselves in any case, and so on. It may then occur to someone that these "natural" laws would lead to greatly increased prices at this particular time because the supply of many products which are greatly in demand has been cut off for so long by the war. Just allow time for an increase in the supply before removing the controls and the price fluctuations can be minimized with consequent benefit to the stability of the economy. But, it will be protested, if only the controls which are limiting profits were removed, production would increase much more rapidly. At this point some member of the group may well suggest the desirability of securing additional information bearing on the question of whether production is now being held up by reason of lack of financial incentive to entrepreneurs. In this way the final product of deliberations, imperfect as it may be, is likely to be far superior to what we might call the average of the ideas of the individual committee members at the outset—possibly better than any of them.

To take another hypothetical case, let us suppose a congressional committee meeting called sometime after the general election of 1948 to consider the subject of labor legislation. It would not be too unrealistic to assume that at the start a large number of the members of the committee would favor outright repeal of the Taft-Hartley Act, while perhaps a few would feel that no change whatsoever was desirable. Again it is not unreasonable to suppose that the introduction of facts and arguments which the respective sides had not known or considered might bring about not just a compromise for the sake of agreement but an actual change of mind on the part of at least some of the members. Some of those who had at first opposed any change in the law might be convinced by the statistics regarding "union shop" votes that the provision of the law dealing with this matter was a waste of the taxpayer's money. On the other hand, it is at least possible that strong reminders of the temper of the country at the time of the 1946 railroad strike might convince members on the other side that it would be desirable to retain provisions designed to protect the public interest in such crises.

Experiments have demonstrated that the kind of thing just described in our hypothetical case does take place. The superiority of group thinking over individual thinking in such situations, it is reported, "is clearly due in part to (1) the larger number of ways of looking at the problem; (2) the larger number of suggestions for a solution; (3) the larger number of effective criticisms of each proposed plan; (4) the patent need to accept social criticism and not be 'bullheaded' (as subjects working alone frequently are)." [41]

Not only may individuals' ideas be made more rational by group deliberation, but their sense of responsibility may be improved. It is a frequent experience to note that the members of a group will be ashamed in the presence of others to approve a suggestion showing scant consideration for some particular interest that they might well have adopted had they been acting in private. Even the person who took the lead in the group for pursuing the more responsible action might not have done so except that he knew it would make a good impression on others —that is, it would increase his prestige. Thus even Schumpeter's argument (above, p. 219) which was alleged to apply to all groups, of whatever size and under whatever conditions, is seen to be a gross overstatement. There is no iron law of the irrationality and irresponsibility of collective decisions. Everything depends upon the conditions, and there is much that democracies can do to furnish the best conditions for their deliberative processes.

A study of the conditions that tend to elevate the mental life

---

[41] Gardner Murphy, Lois Barclay Murphy, and Theodore M. Newcomb, *Experimental Social Psychology* (rev. ed.; New York: Harper & Brothers, 1937), p. 738.

of groups has been made by McDougall. He listed the following as of primary importance: (1) some degree of continuity of existence of the group; (2) individual members of the group should develop some definite ideas as to the nature, composition, functions, and capacities of the group, as a basis for a sentimental attachment to the group as a whole; (3) the group should always be brought into interaction (especially in the form of rivalry) with other groups, similar, but differing in many respects; (4) groups should have their own customs and traditions determining the relations of their members to each other and to the group as a whole; and (5) groups should have a definite structure, expressed in the specialization and differentiation of the functions of its constituents.[42] It will be observed how well these prescriptions conform to the actual characteristics of our legislative bodies and especially of small policy-forming groups, such as legislative committees and the ruling bodies of political parties.

It should be observed, too, that most of the real work of solving the problems with which government deals in the United States, for instance, is done by small groups—groups of administrators and experts, unpaid advisory committees, groups of legislators meeting as legislative committees, or meeting with representatives of the administration, or of special-interest or welfare groups, party policy committees, or the like. Here there is abundant opportunity for the process of group deliberation to operate on a high plane. The final stage, where issues unresolved by less formal processes are fought out on the floor of Congress, captures the public eye and frequently is a much less edifying spectacle. The relative importance of this part of the political process, however, is greatly exaggerated. Most of the time, after all the talk is over, Congress accepts the recommendations of one of its committees, which in turn generally reflect the thinking of many other groups, such as are referred to above. Even when im-

[42] William McDougall, *The Group Mind: A Sketch of the Principles of Collective Psychology with Some Attempt to Apply Them to the Interpretation of National Life and Character* (2d ed.; New York: G. P. Putnam's Sons, 1920), pp. 69–70.

portant amendments are offered and adopted on the floor, they generally reflect a large amount of preliminary group deliberation.

The same qualitative contrast between large and small political arenas may be seen elsewhere. If we change the scene from the center of the political stage to the "grass roots," the bellowing of a Bilbo to his constituents is indeed a disgrace, and the support which he received by his appeals to race prejudice does not speak well for the liberal-democratic process. But all, the while the Fair Employment Practices Committee—a product of that same process—was quietly and effectively working in hundreds of communities to break down the prejudice which has given the Bilbos and Rankins their following.

Less spectacular than demagoguery, but more important and more widespread, is the "due process of policy-making" which goes on in group discussion.[43] People in the United States belong to groups and voluntary organizations almost without number. Between the family at one extreme and the political party at the other are ranged such organizations as labor unions, business associations, Rotary Clubs, fraternal organizations, community welfare councils, parent-teacher associations, and churches. To a greater or less degree most of these organizations concern themselves with matters of public interest—matters which are or may become political issues. Here much of the preliminary discussion goes on which finally eventuates in legislation. Here, too, and perhaps even more importantly, the members of the groups learn to compromise and, better still, to integrate their purposes with the purposes of others.[44] Unions and business groups soon find that their individual members are by no means united on all questions that come before them. Participation in the activities of voluntary groups of all sorts develops in their members senti-

[43] Wilson, *op. cit.*, pp. 111 ff.

[44] On the process of integration, see the significant contribution to political theory by Mary P. Follett, *Creative Experience* (New York: Longmans, Green and Co., 1924), and Henry C. Metcalf and L. Urwick, *Dynamic Administration—The Collected Papers of Mary Parker Follett* (New York: Harper & Brothers, 1942), Chap. 9, and *passim*.

ments of loyalty and the realization not only of the necessity of compromise but also of the individual's long-run interest in the discovery of solutions to problems that are compatbile with the interests of the majority. Furthermore, the bonds of friendship and loyalty engendered by cooperative group activity, the sense of belonging—all these things contribute to the individual's sense of security. Much of the insecurity of modern life arises out of the disintegration of old community groups consequent upon shifts in population and occupation.[45] The re-formation of groups, occupational or otherwise, with established patterns of conduct contributes to individual integration with consequent diminution of irrational behavior. Here is the answer, too, to those who assert that the unsupported individual cannot stand the responsibility of freedom. Alone he cannot—but in the framework of a familiar pattern of cooperative group behavior he finds strength. In these ways, groups, unlike crowds, reduce human irrationality and socialize the individual.

From what has been said it is clear that not every aggregation of people is a crowd. Government by the people need not be government by individuals displaying crowd mentality. Groups may socialize the individual rather than barbarize him. But there are more reasons than this why the government of a democracy need not be crowdlike. Faguet and others of his kind overlook completely the effects of organization and of fixed procedures. Crowd mentality develops where there is nothing to obstruct the rapid contagion of emotional reactions and where the surroundings discourage deliberation and discussion. Government, on the other hand, operates in accordance with fixed rules that have been gradually developed for the purpose of checking undue haste and encouraging criticism. It is unnecessary to describe these devices in detail. The way in which political parties contribute to the process of checking mob rule was

[45] Cf. Emil Lederer, *State of the Masses* (New York: W. W. Norton & Company, 1940), and Elton Mayo, *The Human Problems of an Industrial Civilization* (New York: The Macmillan Company, 1933), pp. 153–166. Reprinted by the Division of Research, Harvard Business School (Boston: 1946).

never more clearly demonstrated than on the occasion of President Truman's message calling on Congress to pass emergency antistrike legislation at the time of the nation-wide railroad strike, in 1946. In nearly every particular the situation was ideal for irrational behavior. Feeling against the strikes was running high in the country and in Congress. The President's address singled out two union leaders and held them up as targets for the discharge of all the accumulated wrath of Congress. It seemed that everyone's patience was exhausted. The House by an overwhelming vote accepted his recommendations without alteration. It appeared that the Senate might follow suit. But at the critical moment a Republican senator who has never been considered a friend of labor and who had been leading the battle on the floor of the Senate for legislation curbing unions, compelled reference of the proposed law to a committee in accordance with the regular procedure. This meant delay. With delay came second thoughts. Many who had been ready to vote the President's proposals into law changed their minds. The upshot was that the bill was defeated. Whether rightly or wrongly we need not inquire. What is clear is that hasty and highly emotional action was checked and the final decision was taken after opportunity for deliberate judgment.

Senator Taft's action was, of course, a partisan one. It seems highly probable that he was much more concerned about the opportunity to gain an advantage for the Republican party and to put its opponents in a hole than he was about the well-being of labor. This assumption, if true, does not detract from our point but merely serves to reinforce it. It is the very genius of party government to operate in just this fashion. The parties pursue their own interests; but in doing so they perform a number of valuable functions, one of which is to serve as a check on crowd psychology.

Practically any number of other, though less spectacular examples of the same process might be adduced. It would not be unfair to assume that Republican support of civil rights legislation is at least as much motivated by the desire to embarrass the

Democrats as by concern for the Negroes. The (first) Hatch Act, a salutary piece of anticorrupt-practice legislation, probably gained essential support from those who were desirous, for personal reasons, of maintaining the power of local party machines as against the national party organization. And so on. Parties and politicians serve the national interest (not all of the time, of course) because the political organization is such as to make it to their interest to do so.

2. Leadership as an Offset to Weaknesses of Public Opinion

We have argued that the relative lack of information and intelligence on the part of the public is not fatal to democracy because the public is called upon to decide only the broadest of questions, and that the irrationality and irresponsibility of crowd behavior may be avoided by proper use of organization, fixed procedures, and informal groups; but so far we have said nothing of leadership. This obviously important factor is sometimes lost sight of by students of public opinion. Even such a clear-sighted philosopher of democracy as John Dewey nodded long enough to remark that public opinion cannot be better than the average intelligence of the public. This is completely false, as the discussion up to this point should have made clear. Public opinion may be far superior to the average intelligence or it may be vastly inferior. In addition to the factors already mentioned, the quality of leadership will have much to do with determining which it shall be. There is nothing mystical about the way this operates. A good leader does not alter the quality of the minds of his followers. But he does analyze problems into their simple elements so that they can be understood by people who could never perform the analysis for themselves. He defines and clarifies the issues and even shows the relevant considerations, which the individuals can then evaluate for themselves in terms of their own interests and experience. Furthermore, he may dramatize an issue in such a way as to give a fillip to weak imaginations. By the power of his own personality he may arouse latent public spiritedness. These are some of the ways in which a good leader may secure an enlightened and relatively unselfish public response. By the same token, a demagogue may do exactly the opposite. He may confuse the issues and convince the people that they can have their cake and eat it too. He can appeal to the basest motives and play upon the crudest prejudices, stir up passions, and reduce the public to a virtual mob.

Much depends, then, upon the quality of leadership which succeeds to power! It is up to democracy to devise institutions that will favor the former type of leader. Since sound policies often require some time to demonstrate their value to the man in the street, institutions that give leaders a long enough lease on life for the consequences of their policies to become evident are greatly to be desired. A four-year term for congressmen would be a great improvement.[46] However, this is not the place to work out the details of an ideal institutional system. The point here is that in able and public-spirited leadership democracy has another resource for offsetting the intellectual and moral limitations of the average citizen.

3. Consideration of the Record of American Democracy

It is relevent here, however, to give some point to the record of democracy with regard to leadership, and to do so specifically in the light of a criticism that was not mentioned above, namely, that democracy is inherently opposed to quality. The masses, it is alleged, have no respect for intellectual or artistic superiority. They are jealous of any such threat to their own mediocrity.[47] Specifically in the field of government, M. Faguet

[46] Further reference to reforms affecting the legislature will be found in Chap. XIII.

[47] Note Guido de Ruggiero's remark that "the democratic dislike of everything inconsistent with its feeling for equality and social uniformity, leads it to reject the consequences of this spontaneous social differentiation, either by an arbitrary degradation of those members that have risen, or by an artificial elevation of those that have remained beneath."—*The History of European Liberalism*, trans. R. G. Collingwood (London: Oxford University Press, 1927), p. 373. Professor Schneider, paraphrasing Santayana, whose views he is expressing, writes: ". . . the democratic state tends to convert democracy into an end instead of a means, and thus brings about a worship of equality and quantity, the worst foe of the spirit."—"Political

argues that the people, instead of seeking representatives with a high degree of ability, elects only representatives who are "its exact counterparts and constant dependents."[48]

If this proposition is sound, the chances of democracy having the benefits of good leadership are poor indeed. But in fact it is infected by the theoretical errors rehearsed in the preceding pages. It is based on the false assumption that in a democracy "the people" acts as a unit, responding to the laws of mass behavior. We might leave the matter at this point; but it will be well once more to turn to the record. We may commence with the American presidential office. Lord Bryce, it will be remembered, devoted a chapter to the question: "Why great men are not chosen Presidents." [49] Is this as true today as when Bryce wrote, over fifty years ago? Standards of greatness inevitably contain a large element of the subjective. A catalogue of great Presidents of the United States, however, is practically certain to include the names of Washington, Jefferson, Lincoln, Theodore Roosevelt, Wilson, and Franklin D. Roosevelt. Some might wish to add the name of Jackson, but probably few would go any further. We can say, then, that from 40 to 50 per cent of our great presidents have come within a period comprising less than the last third of our history. Bryce's charge is certainly less true today than when he made it.

As to the quality of congressmen, it is even more difficult to

---

Implications of Recent Philosophical Movements," in Charles E. Merriam, Harry Elmer Barnes, and Others, *A History of Political Theories—Recent Times* (New York: The Macmillan Company, 1924), p. 353. For concrete evidence that such a development may indeed take place, see Leslie Lipson, *The Politics of Equality—New Zealand's Adventures in Democracy* (Chicago: The University of Chicago Press, 1948), Chap. 15.

[48] Émile Faguet, *The Cult of Incompetence*, trans. Beatrice Barstow (New York: E. P. Dutton & Co., 1911), p. 36. Note the contrast with James Mill's optimistic assumption that "in any group the less wise tend to be governed by the more wise."—"Essay on Government," in Philip Wheelwright (ed.), *Essays on Government, Jurisprudence, Liberty of the Press, and Law of Nations* (New York: Doubleday & Company, Inc., 1935), p. 208.

[49] James Bryce, *The American Commonwealth* (2 vols.; New York: The Macmillan Company, 1893), Vol. I, Chap. 8.

speak, but the following words of a very careful student of the subject, the late Charles A. Beard, are worthy of note:

> As a more than casual student of the *Congressional Record*, I venture this opinion: It is possible to pick out of the *Record* for the past ten years addresses (not orations) which, for breadth of knowledge, technical skill, analytical acumen, close reasoning, and dignified presentation, compare favorably with similar utterances made in the preceding century by the so-called great orators. . . . Considering the complexity of problems before Congress today, and taking account of the distractions which now beset Senators and Representatives, the quality of serious speeches in both houses is amazingly high. There is, to be sure, more trash—bad poetry, demagogic claptrap, and clotted nonsense—in the *Record* of the past ten years than there was in the *Annals of Congress* from 1789 to 1799. Yet after studying the operations of the first Congresses of the United States and the operations of the Seventy-sixth Congress, I am convinced that for disinterestedness, absence of corruption, and concern with the public good, the present body is of higher order.[50]

Rankins and Bilbos or their like continue to find a place in the political scene. It is worthy of note, however, that the most obvious examples of demagogues and incompetents come from states where illiteracy runs highest and other special circumstances conspire to delay the attainment of political maturity. Against their names we can set such examples of able and intelligent legislators (whether or not we agree with their policies) as Senators Douglas, Taft, Vandenberg, Byrd, Morse, and Lehman.

If we turn to the field of administration, the case is clearer. A little over half a century ago the spoils system reigned supreme at all levels of American government. The steady growth of merit systems throughout the country in recent years is common

---

[50] Quoted, without citation, in Robert M. La Follette, Jr., "A Senator Looks at Congress," *Atlantic Monthly*, CLXXII (July, 1943), 92. An interesting British parallel is provided by the testimony of a former cabinet member who sat in Parliament from 1906 to 1931 and was re-elected in 1935. His reply to a question as to the differences between Parliament in 1906 and the same body in 1935 was that he was chiefly impressed "by the lower level of speaking and the *higher level of technical information*" exhibited by the members.—E. F. M. Durbin, *The Politics of Democratic Socialism* (London: Routledge and Kegan Paul, Ltd., 1940), p. 257, note.

knowledge. Today well over 90 per cent of federal positions are under the civil service system, and the movement is making steady headway in cities and states. The mere installation of a civil service system is, of course, no guarantee that the quality of administrative personnel will be improved. But that is clearly the tendency; and no student of the subject doubts that the standards both of training and of intellectual ability of our public servants are today far better than they were a few years ago.[51]

During the nineteenth century the flood tide of democratic sentiment swept away great numbers of appointive offices in state and local government in this country, substituting elective offices for them. In the main these were not policy-making officials or, if they were, they were officials whose policy should be part and parcel of the policy of the chief executive. Accordingly all sound principles called for their appointment rather than election. But democratic extremism prevailed. This was democracy degenerating from an excess of equalitarianism, just as many of its critics, including Tocqueville,[52] had warned it might. The significant point, however, is that the process did not continue to the bitter end of complete democratic ineffectiveness and then give way to tyranny, as was called for by the classical theories of governmental cycles.[53] Instead it proved to be self-limiting. For the past half century, the process has gone no further, and during the last half of that period, at least, the trend has been definitely in the opposite direction. Although a mass of elective offices is still a great incubus over state and local governments in the United States, it is a notable achievement that about half of the states have reorganized their governments in recent years, such

[51] The percentage of the civilian employees of the executive branch subject to the competitive requirements of the Civil Service Act has grown from 63, in June, 1937, to 81, in June, 1947, having increased in every peacetime year in the interim.—*Sixty-fourth Annual Report of the Civil Service Commission* (Washington, D. C.: Government Printing Office, 1948), p. 77.

[52] See Alexis de Tocqueville, *Democracy in America*, trans. Henry Reeves, ed. Phillips Bradley (2 vols.; New York: Alfred A. Knopf, Inc., 1945), Vol. II, Bk. IV, Chaps. 2, 4, esp. p. 295, where he argues that the spirit of equality feeds on equality.

[53] Above, pp. 5–6.

reorganizations being accompanied in practically every instance by a decrease in the number of elective offices.[54]

These reorganizations have brought other advances tending to improve governmental efficiency. Since the turn of the century the federal government and all the states in the union have adopted a budget system.[55] This is a simple and obvious necessity for efficient government, but many critics of democracy would lead one to believe that the trend was away from such devices instead of toward their constant extension and improvement.

Another indication of the trend toward improvement in American government is to be found in the history of political corruption. Here again the growth of democracy originally brought with it excesses. The prevalence of corrupt political machines made Lord Bryce refer to city government as the "dark continent of American politics." The situation in many parts of the country is still not one of which we can be proud. Nevertheless, taking the long view, the record of the last half century has been one of steady improvement.[56]

We have been considering the record of American democracy[57] particularly with reference to the charge that democracy is opposed to quality. It will be well to consult the record a little more broadly with reference to the general question this chapter poses: Is popular government incompetent? For this purpose we may take another look at the American election of 1932 and subsequent events. At that time the country was in the depths of a severe depression. The problems it faced were numerous and complex. In the months and years immediately following, many of the ablest brains in the country were

[54] See W. Brooke Graves, *American State Government* (3d ed.; Boston: D. C. Heath and Company, 1946), p. 416.

[55] *Ibid.*, p. 584.

[56] See above, p. 230, for a reference to the decline of boss rule. The two phenomena—corruption and boss rule—tend to go together.

[57] Until very recently the spirit of equalitarianism has made greater headway in the United States than in Great Britain; hence examples from the United States have dealt with the opposing argument on the ground most favorable to its supporters.

engaged in working out solutions for them. But the people at the polls were not asked either to solve the problems or even to choose between the proposals of rival groups of experts. What they were asked to do was to choose between two different clusters of general principles or attitudes.

Congress, then, following the leadership of the President, set about hewing out the legislative framework for a program to implement this general attitude. Basic legislation and appropriations for work relief and, where necessary, direct relief payments to individuals, were promptly enacted. More permanent legislation to meet the long-run problems followed only after exhaustive studies by experts and frequently after congressional investigations. The Social Security Act was adopted after very extensive study and planning to which most of the nation's experts on the subject contributed. In many cases, even after such a procedure as this, important policy determinations were left to administrative agencies to work out in the light of experience and in the light of all the expert advice which could be obtained. Mistakes were sometimes made, and corrected, as is illustrated by the failure of the NRA.

Were the people too ignorant, stupid, irrational, and boss-ridden to play the modest role assigned to them in this development? The evidence is to the contrary. There are, of course, many who would still contend that a laissez-faire—or more nearly laissez-faire—policy, if it had been persisted in, would have brought recovery sooner than we in fact obtained it. But few economists today would hold that the peculiar combination of laissez faire and government intervention that the Hoover administration was practicing was likely to succeed. Most economists would probably agree that the general direction of policy we pursued at that time was in harmony with the demands of the objective situation. The Social Security Act, the Tennessee Valley Act, regulation of the securities business, and loans to homeowners would now meet with almost universal approval. Doubtless it would have been better if the change had come sooner. Democratic processes are far from perfect; all that we are contending is that voters are not intellectually so ill-equipped as to be unable to make intelligent decisions on the kind of question that is in fact submitted to them in a liberal democracy. This contention finds support in the facts.

Reference to the record is not complete without considering the accomplishments of fascism as well as those of democracy. It is true that we have already found adequate grounds for preferring liberal democracy to other forms of government if it can maintain a tolerable level of accomplishment. Even if fascism could show that it was in some way more efficient—for example, that it accomplished its purposes more quickly and more completely—democracy might well enter a demurrer. The accomplishment of purposes is important, but even more important is the selection of the right purposes and the use of means compatible with the ultimate ends of society. Waiving these vital points for the moment, however, and considering the fascist claims of superiority on their own level, let us look at the record.

Even on the score of efficiency, in the narrowest sense of that word, the evidence is piling up that fascism failed.[58] Studies made since the fall of Germany show that, despite her long tradition of military and administrative efficiency, the conduct of the war under fascist rule was characterized time and again by gross inefficiency. Production was not increased sufficiently and rapidly enough. The government hesitated to inaugurate double shifts in industry. New technological developments were not adopted or were adopted too late. Quarrels over jurisdiction and differences of opinion as to policy among Nazi leaders led to prolonged deadlocks that sometimes were never overcome.[59]

[58] For comparisons of productivity in totalitarian and democratic regimes, see above, p. 150, note 49.

[59] John Kenneth Galbraith points out that similar situations in the United States and in other democratic countries were prevented from becoming so serious by the fact that the press got wind of the difficulty, smoked out the disputants, and, by bringing the pressure of public opinion to bear, compelled the responsible authorities (generally the President, in the United States) to take action to break the deadlock.—John Kenneth Galbraith, "Germany Was Badly Run," *Fortune,* XXXII (Dec., 1945), pp. 173ff. See also "Fascism in Action," *House Document* No. 401 (Washington, D. C.: Government Printing Office, 1947), *passim,* and p. 206.

4. The Special Case of Foreign Policy

It might seem that enough has been said to clinch the argument, but there remains one special problem which cannot be ignored. That is the problem of the conduct of foreign relations. It is repeatedly charged, by the friends as well as the foes of democracy, that dictatorships are vastly superior to democracies in this particular. Their foreign policies, it is alleged, are wisely conceived, in terms of national self-interest, and are skillfully, consistently, and powerfully pursued. The foreign policies of democracies, on the other hand, are said to be weak, muddled, wavering, and inconsistent. Nor, it is said, are the reasons for this hard to find. In internal affairs, the nation, so to speak, is dealing only with itself. International relations, on the other hand, is a competitive game. The race goes to the fastest. A democratic state is therefore bound to be hopelessly outdistanced when its competitors are authoritarian regimes, geared for ruthless and unhesitating action. The people, to whose opinions democratic foreign policy is tied, are too ill-informed and too shortsighted to understand their own interests in the complicated field of international politics. In times of impending crisis they are notoriously ambivalent: they want peace so badly that they are blinded to the fact that they will be unwilling to pay its price. Thus they delay, flirting with fate.

That the challenge is a powerful one no unbiased observer can deny. Nor can the subject be dealt with adequately in brief compass. Books could be, and have been, written on the subject.[60] It is even possible, as was intimated above (page 169), that liberal democracy cannot indefinitely survive in a world in which powerful states continue to be governed by undemocratic regimes. But there is a brighter side to the picture, which is worth examining.

In the first place, and most obviously—once we stop to

[60] See, for example, Carl J. Friedrich, *Foreign Policy in the Making* (New York: W. W. Norton & Company, 1938).

think about it—there is a great deal of exaggeration about both the wisdom and the consistency of the foreign policies of dictatorial regimes. In retrospect, can we say that Hilter's foreign policy—so successful for a brief span—succeeded, from any point of view? Mussolini provides, if anything, an even clearer case. He could have avoided disaster so easily, perhaps while still retaining some or all of his ill-gotten gains; and yet he blundered into the pit—after a great deal of wavering. An examination of the actual operation of German foreign policy under Hitler reveals many inconsistencies of policy, and numerous internal quarrels, with separate agencies working at cross-purposes, spying on each other and withholding important information.[61]

Today the Soviet Union is likely to be cited to prove the astuteness and effectiveness of dictatorial foreign policy. It is an interesting example of how we are prone to overvalue what we do not understand. When the Soviet Union sticks doggedly to a given policy, even though it may be very badly chosen from the point of view of her own national interest, we speak admiringly of her consistency and are inclined to assume wisdom. So it is with the veto power in the United Nations. So also with her failure to accept the American offer of Marshall Plan aid, which has effectively driven Western Europe into the arms of America and has imposed a terrific strain on the unity of the Russian sphere. When, on the other hand, she shifts unexpectedly first from talk of a strong Germany to a policy of division and weakness and then again to support of a strong Germany, we forget about consistency and take it for granted that she is steadily, if deviously, pursuing a single policy, well conceived in the national interest. The probable fact that Stalin, also, has the problem of conciliating conflicting pressures among internationalists, imperialists, and isolationists is too often overlooked.

Two further, closely related facts often escape our notice. The foreign policies of dictatorships have often been consistent and single purposed by reason of the fact that the maintenance of peace was not for them a prime desideratum. In this way

[61] "Fascism in Action," Chap. 3 and p. 206.

they simplified their immediate problem—even while bringing about their own ultimate disaster. Furthermore, it is no mere accident that they behaved in this fashion. It is by now a commonplace that all governments—even dictatorships—rest upon opinion.[62] The difference is that the dictator, with his monopoly of opinion-making tools, is in a position to mold opinion to suit his own purposes. Yet the breadth of the limits within which he must operate has been grossly exaggerated, and nowhere so much as in the field of international relations. The fanatical do-or-die spirit, the unquestioning obedience and readiness to sacrifice, and the complete unity which are the authoritarian substitutes for the less homogeneous product of liberalism's give-and-take—all these call for continuous crusading by the Leader. As we have seen, the crusade is most likely to be effective if it is *against* something or somebody. Internal scapegoats may be found, but they must not be too numerous, or they will constitute a serious break in unity. On the other hand, if they are not numerous enough they will eventually all be crushed or destroyed and so cease to serve their purpose. In any case, it is doubtful if there is any such powerful unifying agent as a foreign enemy. From time immemorial the rivalry between in-group and out-group has been one of the most powerful forces of social cohesion. The consequence of all this is the well-attested historical fact that dictators tend to secure national unity at the price of international disunity.

Finally, we cannot accept without qualification the charges leveled at democratic foreign policy. It is notable that even American foreign policy (allegedly representative of the worst faults of democracy) has tended to be equal to crises as they arose. Since 1942 the American commitment to internationalism is heartening in the extreme. Many shoals are in the waters ahead, but there seems a good chance that we may develop and maintain a policy of internationalism such as has never been

[62] Cf. Hume's statement, "It is . . . on opinion only that government is founded . . . ."—"Of the First Principles of Government," in *Essays: Moral, Political, and Literary*, ed. T. H. Green and T. H. Grose (2 vols.; London: Longmans, Green and Co., 1875), I, 110.

consistently maintained by a nondemocratic regime. In the light of these various considerations the field of foreign policy is certainly not one in which democracies can be contrasted unfavorably with dictatorships, but rather decidedly the contrary.

5. Case for the Common Sense of the Common Man

As we find argument and evidence all pointing to the conclusion that popular government is not inherently incompetent and that in fact its record belies the claims of its critics and its rivals, let us review also the faith in the common sense of the common man upon which defenders of democracy have relied more or less heavily at least ever since the time of Aristotle.[63] True or not, it does no good merely to assert that the common man has some sort of intuition that guides him toward the common good. Are there any reasons, in addition to those set forth in the preceding pages, to assume that his judgments will be sound? The answer is that there are several. In the first place, there is the hackneyed but still valid argument that the wearer knows best where the shoe pinches. In other words, the general welfare is the welfare of all, and what is good for all is a matter about which each member has certain information that no one else can supply. If I want security, it is possible that you may know better than I how to obtain it; but only I can tell whether or not I am happy when I get that security.

Very closely related to the last argument is the consideration that a society at any given time operates in accordance with a vast network of habitual and customary folkways embodying values and beliefs integral to the personalities of its members. It is one of the prime purposes of popular decisions in a democracy to express a judgment as to whether or not a proposed policy, or

[63] Cf. Aristotle's *Politics*, trans. Benjamin Jowett (Oxford: Clarendon Press, 1923). Among modern writers, see J. A. Hobson, *Democracy—and a Changing Civilization* (London: John Lane, Ltd., 1934), pp. 78–83. Carl J. Friedrich, *The New Belief in the Common Man* (Boston: Little, Brown & Company, 1942), *passim*, esp. pp. 31–37, 114–119; and A. D. Lindsay, *The Modern Democratic State* (London: Oxford University Press, 1943), I, 276–279.

one already enacted, comports with this social substratum. No one can express this judgment for the public. And yet it is of vital importance.[64] It is important if the public interest is to be served; on a lower level, it is also important from the point of view of the government in order to indicate what the public will stand for. A government that operates without this indicater is sitting on the safety valve.

Perhaps most important of all, what is meant by the common sense of the common man is not so much anything that any single common man possesses as it is a characteristic of common judgments. We have already seen how it is that common sense may be additive. Group deliberation may yield a product that has benefited from cooperative endeavor in a way that makes it embody more wisdom than is possessed by any one of the deliberators. This additive feature of common sense has a much broader scope than that of group judgments. Decisions that are hammered out of the practical dialectic of conflict between group and group may similarly combine more elements of reason than could be found in any one of the contending groups. The same process extends vertically, through time, as well as on the horizontal plane. Decisions made today can be reversed or modified tomorrow as experience dictates. A priori judgments can be corrected and corrected again in the light of actual experience. A decision based upon passion, prejudice, lack of information, or faulty analysis may usually be changed after the consequences have made themselves manifest. Those irrationalities that do not cancel each other out in the original decision-making process are likely to lead to failures in practice. The process of trial and error is still one of the most effective means for the discovery of truth in public affairs; and it is one for which the democratic process is remarkably well fitted.[65]

[64] Cf. Friedrich, *The New Belief in the Common Man,* pp. 31–37, esp. p. 36.

[65] A good discussion of democratic empiricism appears in J. L. Stocks, *Reason and Intuition—and Other Essays,* ed. Dorothy M. Emmet (New York: Oxford University Press, 1939), Chap. 9, esp. pp. 140–144.

6. Prospects for the Future

Finally, we must consider whether we have given adequate thought to possible future developments that might nullify both the analytical and the historical arguments used in the course of this chapter. The chief point that might be made in this connection would be to stress the effectiveness of modern propaganda techniques, to claim that the methods of appealing to the irrational elements in man will be more fully developed in the future than they have been in the past, and that as a consequence popular government is doomed.

But irrational appeals are nothing new. They are as old as demagoguery. And the technological developments—popular press, radio, and now television—that give them leverage perform the same service for reason.[66] It was pointed out earlier[67] that two principles can safely be relied upon to check the irrational effects of propaganda. One is the mutual canceling out of various appeals to the irrational. The other is the long-run steadying and enlightening effect of rational argument. In accordance with these principles, given a fair opportunity for all sides to appeal to emotions and prejudices as well as to reason, the former will tend to concel each other out, while the latter are cumulative. This is true for the simple reason that the non-rational or irrational may be either "X" or its exact opposite or anything in between; but the rational element, by definition, can be but one thing. This proposition is also supported by studies showing that the effectiveness of propaganda is limited by pre-existing attitudes and values and (what is especially important by present interests.[68]

It follows from what has just been said that as long as we

---

[66] Experience with the first application of television to political conventions encourages the hope that this latest development may put a premium on sincerity (the camera catches people when they least expect it) just as the radio has already curbed high-flying oratory.

[67] Above, pp. 75–77.

[68] See Kimball Young, *Social Psychology* (2d ed.; New York: Appleton-Century-Crofts, Inc., 1944), pp. 508–513, and studies cited there.

have a pluralistic society, a society of manifold interests, with opportunity for all groups to address themselves to each other and to the public in general, we have a powerful defense against being swept off our feet by appeals to emotion and prejudice for any particular interest. The great examples of the power of propaganda that have so impressed us all in recent times come from countries where a single group or party has had a monopoly of the agencies of communication; and where also all possible means have been used to prevent discussion and rational deliberation[69] and to give support to lies by preventing access to the truth. In the absence of such a situation there is every reason to believe that antiliberal movements will fail in the future as they have in the past. The Ku Klux Klan in the United States during the twenties provided an encouraging example of an organization that appeared to have all the advantages of popular prejudice and irrationalism on its side, and that nevertheless was driven to cover and killed as an effective force through the operation of democratic processes. We shall doubtless continue from time to time to have our Father Coughlins, our Bilbos, our Gerald Smiths, and our Huey Longs. If people were reduced to desperation from other causes there is certainly no assurance, perhaps not even room for confidence, that an effective majority would not turn to such a leader. But experience gives absolutely no reason for thinking this will happen unless democracy has already substantially failed.

Moreover, there are positive steps that can be taken to give further opportunity for the operation of the two principles of rational criticism and mutually counterchecking propaganda. In the first place, anything that increases the number of independent agencies of communication and opinion formation is very much in point. A consideration of the means for accomplishing this purpose would call for a book in itself. Fortunately, Morris Ernst has supplied that need. In his *The First Freedom*,[70]

---

[69] On the latter point, see Lederer, *op. cit.*

[70] Morris L. Ernst, *The First Freedom* (New York: The Macmillan Company, 1946). See esp. Chap. 7.

he has proposed numerous extensions of our traditional legislative patterns that would contribute greatly to the goal of a free market in ideas. Common ownership or control of various mediums of opinion formation could and should be prohibited. Monopolistic practices could be further limited by divorcing production of motion pictures from theater ownership, by preventing radio networks from owning individual stations, and by compelling newspaper publishers to stay clear of the business of paper production. Taxation policy might well be bent in the direction of discouraging chain ownership of newspapers, and copyright laws might be revised so as to give less encouragement to monopolistic practices.

Whether our democracy will avail itself of the opportunity to take such steps as these to protect one of its basic elements is, of course, another question. In the absence of legislation the trend has been markedly toward monopoly in this field. The single fact that 92 per cent of the communities in the United States have only one local newspaper is sufficiently striking.[71] It becomes even more serious when it is noted that the percentage of towns having only one newspaper doubled between 1910 and 1940.[72] On the other hand, there have been several important developments in the opposite direction. For instance, the Supreme Court's decision preventing applicants for membership in the Associated Press from being blackballed by those with whom they are in competition is of great significance.[73] So also is the action of the Federal Communications Commission, upheld by the Court, in compelling the abandonment of numerous restrictive practices by the radio networks.[74]

Even more encouraging, because it is not dependent upon legislative action, is the fact that technological developments hold forth great promise of limiting if not acually breaking up monopolistic controls. For example, multiple-address press trans-

[71] Commission on the Freedom of the Press, *A Free and Responsible Press* (Chicago: The University of Chicago Press, 1947), p. 37.
[72] Ernst, *op. cit.*, p. 284.
[73] *Associated Press v. U. S.*, 326 U. S. 1 (1945).
[74] *National Broadcasting Co., Inc., v. U. S.*, 319 U. S. 190 (1943).

mission is capable not only of making the distribution of news much cheaper but of making it "as cheap for the obscure editor in a distant outpost of civilization as for the metropolitan publisher in a European capital." [75] Facsimile newspapers offer still another prospect of independent news sources. In the radio field, frequency modulation is likewise a decentralizing force that cannot be held back indefinitely by the opposition of the unions and of the owners of standard broadcasting facilities.

In addition to the provision of abundant opportunities for the expression of all views, whether by rational argument or emotional appeal, certain more direct attacks upon the propaganda problem are possible. In my opinion the line between the rational and the irrational is far too subjective to justify giving power to any government agency to limit publication on the ground that it does not come within the rationale of freedom of expression. It is one thing, however, to prevent someone from having his say, and quite another to compel him to give similar publicity to opposition views or to make a retraction of any of his own statements that were untruthful. Various proposals along this line have been made. For instance, the Commission on Freedom of the Press recommends, as an alternate to the present (often highly inadequate) remedy for libel, "legislation by which the injured party might obtain a retraction or a restatement of the facts by the offender or an opportunity to reply." [76] Harold Lasswell has suggested that the principle of equal opportunity for all political expressions now enforced in the field of radio might well be extended to the press by what he calls an Instant Reply Plan.[77] The idea is to have newspapers and periodicals (perhaps also books) that publish antidemocratic propaganda give space in the same issue for a reply. Obviously this is the mere germ of an idea. The administrative difficulties would be many and complex. At most it would be partial in its cover-

---

[75] Commission on the Freedom of the Press, *op. cit.*, p. 34.

[76] *Ibid.*, p. 86.

[77] Harold D. Lasswell, *Democracy through Public Opinion*, "Chi Omega Service Fund Studies," No. 4 (Menasha, Wisc.: George Banta Publishing Company, 1941), pp. 107 ff.

age, but anything it accomplished would be that much to the good. Properly developed, it might have a tremendous influence. These suggestions do no more than point the way. That way is in the increase of opportunities for expression rather than in their limitation. Vague and irresponsible charges unsupported by facts may properly be checked—checked, however, by requiring the presentation of substantiating evidence and allowing appropriate opportunity for a reply that will reach the same audience as the charge, rather than by censorship. Just what would be feasible will probably have to be discovered at least partly by trial and error. Certainly the elaboration of a detailed plan would take us far beyond the practicable scope of this book.

There are possibilities of improvement not only in the area of dissemination of information and opinion but also in the mechanisms for discovering the truth and for reconciling differences of opinion. As an example of the first, we might mention the matter of legislative investigating committees. There is undoubtedly a need for some such device both for the purpose of bringing to light facts that might otherwise remain hidden and for the purpose of focusing the light of public attention on some scandalous situation that might otherwise go unchecked. But there can be no excuse for the use of this device as a weapon for gaining partisan advantage even at the expense of distorting the truth and confusing the public. It is as important to protect individuals from being attacked in public without an immediate opportunity to answer and cross-examine their attackers as it is to grant them similar safeguards in a judicial trial. In the latter case their liberty is at stake, but in the former their reputation, and with it their future opportunities to gain a livelihood, is threatened. What is relevant for the present discussion, however, is the equally important consideration that this device be used to clarify rather than distort the facts, to enlighten rather than confuse public opinion. That this problem can be solved has been demonstrated by the British royal commissions. There the job of conducting such investigations is turned over to a group of men who stand apart from party strife and whose impartiality and integrity and zeal for the public good are beyond question. No one who has observed the conduct, say, of the American Congressional Committee on Un-American Activities can claim that we have even approached this standard. There is fortunately no reason to doubt that eventually public opinion will force reform in this area as it previously (in large measure) forced partisanship out of appointments to public office.

Great improvements are also possible in the arena of public debate and deliberation, whether on the floor of legislative assemblies, in committee rooms, or in privately sponsored public meetings. Here, again, liberal democracy British style can give lessons to the United States. The tradition by which the Speaker can and does insist on relevancy in debate and temperance of utterance makes an important contribution to the rationality of deliberation sadly lacking in the United States. Perhaps the point in the American system where reform would be most productive is at committee hearings. Time and again the testimony of one witness is not directly met by his successor on the other side of the case. If someone were present charged with the responsibility of seeing to it that the points made by one side were answered by the other side, if someone pointed out the significance of certain testimony and the irrelevance of other material, a significant advance would be made. A similar technique might be used for many types of discussion of public affairs.[78] The radio, through such programs as America's Town Meeting of the Air" and the "University of Chicago Round Table" in the United States and the "B.B.C. Brains Trust" in Britain, has made a great contribution toward the dignified consideration of public affairs. Television may add to the interest and value of such programs. These random suggestions may serve to suggest that both social and technical inventions give at least as much advantage to the furtherance of rationality in public affairs as to irrationality.

[78] See *Ibid.*, Chap. 7, for amplification of some of these ideas. See also *Democracy Must Think,* cited early in the present chapter.

In this discussion of the competence of popular government, we have not been concerned to evaluate the operation of
particular institutions, legislative, executive, administrative, and
judicial. We have tried to look at the problem more broadly from
the point of view of the capacities of the people and the actual
record of accomplishments, although this has involved some
analysis of the modes by which the electorate operates. We
have attempted to answer the attacks on government by public
opinion by showing that they are frequently doctrinaire; that,
in view of the way popular government in fact operates, it does
not make demands on the public that are incommensurate with
its capacity; that nevertheless the public controls the general direction of policy without dictating the means for its attainment;
that by numerous devices, such as the abundant use of the group
process and the encouragement of able and responsible leadership, it fosters rationality; and, finally, that it has in fact produced commendable results, both absolutely and by comparison
with its totalitarian rivals. As for the future, the dire predictions
of some to the contrary, new developments hold out fully as
much promise of good as of evil; and many suggestions for the
improvement of the democratic process are at hand.

CHAPTER XII

THE PROBLEM
OF UNITY

It is a commonplace that there are at work in every society
both centripetal and centrifugal forces, and that the stability of a state depends upon the maintenance of a balance between the two. Many have suggested, as did Professor Mc-
Dougall, that there is a certain perversity in the affairs of men
which prevents this balance from ever being kept for long:

> In the main, those societies which, in virtue of the strength and social
> efficiency of their system of supernatural beliefs and sanctions, have
> been most stable and capable of enduring have been least tolerant of
> the spirit of inquiry, and therefore least progressive; on the other
> hand, the flourishing skepticism, has been too often the forerunner of
> social decay, as in ancient Greece and Rome. Continued progress has
> been rendered possible only by the fact that the gains achieved by the
> spirit of inquiry have survived the dissolution of the societies in which
> they have been achieved (and to which that spirit has proved fatal)
> through becoming imitatively taken up into the culture of societies in
> which the conservative spirit continued to predominate.[1]

Any analysis of the general state of health of a given culture-
pattern, then, would do well to pay particular attention to the
trends and factors making for disintegration and to those making
for unification and even regimentation. We must ask ourselves,
with reference to liberal democracy, first, what are the prospects of its maintaining the necessary unity and cohesion? Is it
threatened with a breakdown of consensus, a failure, if not of
nerve, at least of common purpose? Second, we must inquire
whether it is in danger of losing its liberal character—its freedom

---

[1] From *An Introduction to Social Psychology*, pp. 326–327, 2nd ed., by
William McDougall. Copyright 1926 by John W. Luce Company. Reprinted
by permission.

of inquiry, its respect for individual differences, its opportunities for freedom of choice, and its restraints upon arbitrary power. The first of these questions will be the concern of this chapter; the second of the one to follow.

Critics of democracy from Plato to the Nazis have charged that its emphasis upon individual liberty is destructive of order— of that degree of cohesion without which no state can survive. Although they are right in insisting on the importance of unity, they overemphasize it. Liberal democracy requires unity, but it must be a loose unity, held together without resort to such powerful tensions as would threaten liberty. People, that is to say, must be reasonable and tolerant of differences, rather than committed to a common pattern of life. It is Aristotle's pluralistic unity rather than Plato's unity of uniformity that characterizes liberal democracy. But unity there must be. Not only the practical necessity of obtaining a minimum of agreement upon public policies but even more the psychological requirements of individuals demand it.

It will be observed that we are dealing here with two of the democratic prerequisites enumerated in Chapter X—public spirit and agreement upon fundamentals. The two are closely related, but the first refers primarily to attitudinal characteristics while the second has an intellectual reference. Not only is the maintenance of these prerequisites always a serious problem for democracy, but many of the modern trends discussed in previous chapters are especially threatening to social cohesion. All of the factors growing out of urbanism and industrialism that have been reviewed as contributing to economic and psychological instability come under this heading. So, too, the increasing rate of change, materialism, and the growth of skepticism as to the rationality of human ends and human behavior. To these may be added the growth, especially in the United States, of national unions with its consequent development of class consciousness and concentration of industrial life.

Not all the trends of modern life, as has been observed above, are in the same direction. To a certain extent they counteract each other. For example, the greater need for unity and for tolerance of differences that is imposed by the requirements of the positive state is in some measure compensated for by the very decline in ego consciousness that it brings with it and that, from another point of view, is also said to constitute a threat to liberal democracy. Similarly, there are offsets to the dispersiveness that results from industrialism's fractionalization of experience. For example, there is the added time for participation in unifying group activities, which, as much as dispersiveness, is a product of industrialization. Furthermore, the increasing popular realization of the fact of world-wide economic interdependence, with its corollaries in terms of the necessity of curbing group particularism, is another item on the credit side of the ledger. Even the growth of working-class consciousness which is both cause and product of the formation of national unions tends to be offset by the increasing pluralization of economic interests that is a parallel feature of advancing specialization.[2]

The last statement in fact contains within it a sufficient answer to the Marxist charge that democratic capitalism is, like Plato's city of the rich and poor, hopelessly divided against itself. But any theory that has gained such a wide following and that has infected so much of the thought of countless numbers who do not subscribe to the system as a whole deserves more than a sentence in the present context even though this is not the place for a full-fledged critique. Let us therefore see just what is the nature of the communist attack and submit it to analysis.

1. Consideration of the Marxian Doctrine of Class Conflict

It is the foundation of the Marxian position that political power is merely a reflection of economic power. Good will and

[2] This development was discussed above (p. 162) with special reference to the middle class, but it is equally true of the working class. By far the greater part of the national income goes to labor. Any given laboring group, therefore, has more to gain if it competes with other laboring groups than if all labor acts as a unit to increase its proportionate share of the whole. Actually, organized labor pursues a policy partly directed toward increasing its share of the total national income at the expense of capital and man-

disinterested thought do not exist as effective social forces.[3] The application of this doctrine to the liberal-democratic state is familiar ground. The liberal state is the state of the *bourgeoisie*. It represents a rationalization of the economic interests of the middle class. The liberty it provides is essentially liberty for the middle class, and when it ceases to serve the interests of that class it will be abolished. Effective political power, regardless of the franchise, remains in the hands of this class. Fundamental change in the class structure or in the system of production that it reflects and perpetuates cannot be brought about by democratic processes, for the great preponderance of property in the possession of the middle class gives it a monopoly of political power. At the same time Marxian economic theory holds that the capitalist system will steadily sharpen the division between the classes and increase the misery of the proletariat. In the resulting class struggle the consensus essential for the satisfactory operation of democratic institutions will disappear, and the popular demands for a change in the economic system will drive the *bourgeoisie to* repressive measures, stamping out the last remnants of popular liberty.[4]

Detailed criticisms of communist doctrine abound.[5] For pres-

---

agerial income and partly aimed (deliberately or not) toward gains at the expense of other units of organized labor or at the expense of unorganized labor.

[3] The scattered and disorganized nature of Marx's writings, plus the fact that much of the time he was writing propagandistically, leaves room for endless disputation as to his real meaning. It appears to be quite clear, however, that the proposition above is essential to Marxism. Without it the whole structure is without support. Of the innumerable volumes dealing with the subject of the Marxian interpretation of history, reference may be made to two quite different views by the same author. See Sidney Hook, *Towards the Understanding of Karl Marx: A Revolutionary Interpretation* (New York: The John Day Company, 1933), and also his *The Hero in History* (New York: The John Day Company, 1943).

[4] These arguments may be found set forth in the books of Harold J. Laski. See especially his *The Rise of Liberalism* (New York: Harper & Brothers, 1936) and *The State in Theory and Practice* (New York: The Viking Press, 1935).

[5] See, for instance, Max Eastman, *Marxism, Is It Science?* (New York: W. W. Norton & Company, 1940) and E. F. M. Durbin, *The Politics of Democratic Socialism* (London: Routledge and Kegan Paul, Ltd., 1940).

ent purposes a few salient points will suffice. In the first place, Marx and his followers vastly underrated the power of the masses short of revolution; and this for a number of reasons. It was a mistake to deny that good will, concern for the general welfare, and particularly for that of oppressed groups, could be an effective force, as the history of the successful struggle by middle-class reformers for factory legislation in Great Britain demonstrates. In the United States, the enactment of legislation for the conservation of natural resources provides another example of a victory of the general welfare over special interests and even of the interests of future generations over present interests. Another very typical mistake Marx made was to allow his emphasis on the class struggle to blind him to the divisions of interest within the classes, and especially within the *bourgeoisie*. Such divisions led middle- and upper-class groups to seek supremacy over their rivals by bidding for support from the lower classes. This they did, notably in England, by successive extensions of the ballot. For a while they were able to keep the newly enfranchised classes subject to their leadership; but here again Marx, and perhaps many capitalists as well, miscalculated. Education and organization under their own leadership have gradually aroused the masses to a consciousness not only of their interests but of how to advance them through the use of the vote. The secret ballot has rendered increasingly ineffectual attempts on the part of employers to control the political behavior of their employees.

A final count under this head finds Marx off base on his own grounds. Even if political power does derive from economic power, it does not follow today that the masses are weak. They have discovered that in unions there is strength. The ownership of property is not the only or necessarily the strongest form of economic power. At best it depends for its effectiveness upon political power. The laws of property are at the mercy of those who vote, and today these laws command much less sanctity than they once did. A man's control over his own labor power, on the other hand, is far less vulnerable than is the power of property. Whatever may have been true in the past, no argument is needed now to demonstrate the enormous political and economic power of organized labor.

Another serious flaw in the communists' analysis resides in their oversimplified and inflexible concepts of "classes" and of "systems of production." By reason of this mode of thought, they conclude that a shift from one system of production to another, with an attendant displacement of a hitherto privileged class, must at some stage involve a sudden, revolutionary change. On both counts they are wrong. The so-called capitalist system of production has been undergoing continuous modification ever since the time of Adam Smith and before. Laissez faire gives way to more and more complicated forms of regulation or to state enterprise, so that not only does capitalism become a very different thing, but the line between it and socialism is blurred almost to the vanishing point. Since systems of production can be displaced by a process of gradual modification, it follows that the class structure of a society can also be revolutionized by such slow stages that one is hardly aware of what is happening until it has happened. A landowning class gives way to a manufacturing and commercial class largely by the processes of sons of landowners becoming businessmen. A "class" has lost power, but no large group of individuals suffered sudden displacement. There was no occasion or opportunity for taking a stand. So it has happened; and so it may happen again.

This last point is reinforced when it is realized that the Marxian economic analysis has proved faulty. Where Marx predicted that the division between *bourgeoisie* and proletariat would become increasingly sharp, exactly the opposite has taken place. Factory workers, the heart of Marx's proletariat, are decreasing in relative numbers both in the United States and in Great Britain. The middle classes, whether defined in terms of amount of income or source of income, are definitely on the increase.[6]

This analysis of specific weaknesses in communist theory finds abundant support in an over-all survey of recent history. In

[6] See above, p. 164.

England a party proclaiming a socialist platform has come into power with a clear parliamentary majority. Now, nearly five years later, there are still no signs of a Tory counterrevolution, as was predicted in some quarters. The Labour party is proceeding to carry out its program of socialization of key industries. In the Scandinavian countries, and even more in New Zealand, labor's demands are being realized by democratic methods. In the United States, although the spirit of free enterprise and the philosophy of rugged individualism still manifest themselves more vigorously than almost anywhere else in the world, no impartial observer can fail to note that the last two decades have witnessed tremendous modification of the power of capital, growth in the power of labor, and increase of collective controls of the economy. To one not blinded by doctrinal obscurantism, there is not the slightest suggestion of any point beyond which this process may not go if its indefinite continuation proves acceptable to the majority of Americans.

2. Possible Roads to Social Unity

The theory that the state is nothing but a manifestation of class struggle is indeed fallacious; but this fact does not mean that democratic unity is assured. Communism feeds upon a supposed unity, rigidity, and intransigence of the so-called ruling classes. These, at least under the circumstances prevailing in many countries, have turned out to be more myth than fact. But fascism feeds upon disunity. We have not yet found the answer to many of the threats of social and political disintegration enumerated in previous chapters. And we know from the experiences of this generation that unless there are effective answers, liberal democracy must perish. When people lose the power of united action, through division into self-seeking groups without common purpose, democratic government is stultified. They turn against it in disgust and despair. In the face of psychological as well as economic insecurity people will turn to Authority. A government which has ceased to serve as an effective "father symbol" will be abandoned. Where the people have no sense of "belonging" they will glady sacrifice liberty in order to get it.[7]

In a broad way it may be said that the roads to social unity are three. First, there is the unity of rational individuals, held together by common recognition that their true long-run interests dictate social behavior. In large measure, this was the theory of the Benthamites. We know today, all too well, that this is a hopelessly oversimplified, even false view of human psychology. The desire of the moment too often overshadows long-run interest even when the latter is perceived. The dislikes and passions aroused in social intercourse and economic competition blind the mind to "interest" and forestall calculation. The frustrations inevitably attendant, in greater or less degree, upon practically all striving build up the raw material for future irrational aggressions. Reason alone is clearly inadequate.

Feeling and sentiment must be brought to the support of reason; even John Stuart Mill recognized this truth. The second path to unity is the exact antithesis of the first. It substitutes sentiment for reason; instead of the individual it places the Great Community, or the State, at the center of things. The difficulty is that the ideal of a single Great Community does violence to the variety of human needs and interests. So it is with any single ideal powerful enough to supersede individual selfishness. George Santayana put the matter thus clearly two generations ago:

What might happen if the human race were immensely improved and exalted there is as yet no saying; but experience has given no example of efficacious devotion to communal ideals except in small cities, held together by close military and religious bonds and having no important relations to anything external. Even this antique virtue was short-lived and sadly thwarted by private and party passion. Where public spirit has held best, as at Sparta or (to take a very different type of communal passion) among the Jesuits, it has been paid for by a notable lack of spontaneity and wisdom; such inhuman devotion to an arbitrary end has made these societies odious. We may

[7] Cf. John Maurice Clark, *Alternative to Serfdom* (New York: Alfred A. Knopf, Inc., 1948), p. 18; and George B. de Huszar, *Practical Applications of Democracy* (New York: Harper & Brothers, 1945), p. 2.

say, therefore, that a zeal sufficient to destroy selfishness is, as men are now constituted, worse than selfishness itself. In pursuing prizes for themselves people benefit their fellows more than in pursuing such narrow and irrational ideals as alone seem to be powerful in the world. . . . an indoctrinated and collective virtue turns easily to fanaticism; it imposes irrational sacrifices prompted by some abstract principle or habit once, perhaps, useful. . . .[8]

Such a total ideal is necessarily narrow and productive of fanaticism; moreover, even it must be supported by indoctrination and suppression, as the historical examples testify. The result is not only to destroy liberty but also to defeat the very ideal of unity itself.[9] A government which sets out to secure unity in this fashion must distinguish between the elite who impose the doctrine and those who are to be indoctrinated. But, as Aristotle long ago pointed out in criticism of Plato, any government by an elite automatically destroys unity by creating a division between rulers and ruled. Moreover, the harder a dictatorship tries to secure unity, the more it defeats its purpose. Resort to oppression and cruelty may secure uniformity, but only at the expense of deep divisions and antagonism, which are destructive of any real unity. As Professor Durbin remarks, "Behind the drilled enthusiasm, the endless repetition of common slogans, and the monotonous tramping of military reviews, there lies a deeper reality of hatred, division and fear."[10] Even security, another of fascism's professed objectives, is destroyed by resort to fear as an agency of control. In fact, for this reason the search for unity may actually produce atomism. This is doubly true because suppression destroys the group life which, as we shall see more fully later, is one of the greatest sources of real social unity. Authoritarian governments cut off the social process at the very point where it is most effective. This argument is underlined

---

[8] George Santayana, *The Life of Reason: Or the Phases of Human Progress* (5 vols.; New York: Charles Scribner's Sons, 1905), II, *Reason in Society*, 133–134. By permission of Charles Scribner's Sons, publishers.

[9] Thus fascism stands condemned in terms of one of its own expressed objectives, unity. It has already been pointed out that it fails in terms of its other chief ideal, efficiency (above, p. 248).

[10] Durbin, *op. cit.*, p. 252.

from the point of view of a social psychologist by Professor Kimball Young, who writes:

. . . . may it not be that severe regimentation would further a sense of individual isolation or social atomism? Would it not result in a certain yearning for intimacy because man cannot live effectively merely as an atom in a mass of atoms, but needs the support and guidance of close and whole-hearted participation? An individual's sense of integrity is born apparently, not of physical massing and specialization of role, but of co-operative and competitive participation both in special groups and in the larger society of one's fellows.[11]

The third way, then, to political unity—and the only way that holds out the promise of permanent success as well as the only way that can hope to attain unity along with liberty—is that of social pluralism. Unity, as Aristotle saw, must be a unity in plurality. People are too different from each other, both in natural endowment and as modified by their specialized vocational activities, to submit willingly to a common set of purposes and ideals. One man finds fulfillment in a church where he can purge his soul by confession and find comfort in submitting to authority, while another craves the opportunity for religious self-expression which he finds in a Quaker Meeting. People discover a large measure of their satisfaction through belonging to this, that, and the other religious, political, social, vocational, and other association; they also find their individuality through the opportunity to select a slightly different pattern of associations from those of their next door neighbor. Sometimes the difference will reflect a divergence in interest or in temperament, sometimes only the desire to assert one's individuality; but the opportunity for such difference is essential to a healthy society.[12]

But the fundamental question here is not whether a freely

[11] Kimball Young, *Social Psychology* (2d ed.; New York: Appleton-Century-Crofts, Inc., 1944), p. 556.

[12] On the whole subject of democracy and social pluralism, see A. D. Lindsay, *I Believe in Democracy* (London: Oxford University Press, 1940), pp. 7–8, and his *The Essentials of Democracy* (Philadelphia: University of Pennsylvania Press, 1929), *passim;* and the works of Robert M. MacIver, for instance, *The Web of Government* (New York: The Macmillan Company, 1947), esp. pp. 192–208, 410–430.

articulating group life is essential to social unity—although the fact that it is is in itself a sufficient answer to the pretensions of totalitarianism; the question here is rather whether such group life is likely under modern conditions to prove compatible with the effective operation of democratic government. We must not overlook the possibility, in other words, that no satisfactory solution is available, that resort to enforced, totalitarian uniformity, while neither productive of true unity nor compatible with freedom, is the only alternative to anarchy and the complete breakdown of civilization. The evidence, however, does not support this conclusion. There are, to be sure, factors making for social and political disintegration. While other factors tend to offset these, we would be foolish to assume that the latter may be counted on to take care of the situation without any action on our part. We shall do well, in other words, to consider what measures may and should be taken by liberal democracies to maintain the bases for democratic consensus.

3. The Record

First, however, we may gain perspective by taking a look at the record. The failure of democracy in Italy, Germany, and France was largely the product of social disunity leading to political chaos. Although in each of these cases special circumstances helped destroy such unity as had existed, and although only in France—and there under the impact of military conquest—did a seasoned and once successful democracy fall, still these experiences have rightly given pause to liberal democrats everywhere. The political manifestation of social disintegration in each of these countries, it should be remembered, took the form of the proliferation of political parties, cabinet instability, and legislative deadlocks. It is an important and highly encouraging fact that these phenomena have not manifested themselves in Britain or the United States.[13] The two-party system, which

[13] The same statement holds true, for the most part, for the British Dominions and for Sweden and Switzerland, to name only countries not overrun by the tides of war.

has done so much in England and the United States to prevent political instability and deadlock, shows no signs of disintegrating. The emergence of the Labour party in England failed to break up the essence of the traditional pattern. Slowly but surely the Liberal party is being squeezed out. Today there is no need to rely upon coalition governments. In the United States no serious rival of the old parties has appeared on the national scene. There will and should be realignments from time to time; and it is possible that in the United States as in England a third party may rise to prominence in the process. But there is no reason to believe that a three-party alignment will prove to be more permanent in the United States than it was in Britain.

Both governments have shown a great capacity to achieve unified and purposive action in times of war and depression. In the United States our particular system of separation of powers, which, of course, is not essential to liberal democracy, encourages disunity and deadlocks. In spite of this fact, there is no sign that political deadlocks are on the increase. In this case, as in others, there are indications that we have learned by experience and that the errors of yesterday need not necessarily be repeated tomorrow. When, during the last two years of President Hoover's administration, executive and legislature were not controlled by the same party, the country was treated to a spectacle of political helplessness well calculated to bring the institutions of democracy into disrepute. In 1947 and 1948, however, when the situation was repeated, the fact of divided political leadership did not result in governmental stalemate. Disagreement between the President and the Congress did not prevent action. A program was adopted—as consistent a one, it may safely be said, as has characterized most periods when the President and the majority of Congress belonged to the same party.

Incidentally, the recently adopted reorganization of Congress is a good omen. Whether it has gone anything like far enough in the direction of equipping and organizing Congress for effective and responsible action is not the question. What is important is the fact that it represents a recognition by Congress itself (no doubt reflecting a more widespread recognition among the people) that it must meet the challenge of contemporary needs if it is to survive. Far more drastic measures can be taken if they prove necessary.[14] There is no ground today for assuming that they will not be taken if they do prove to be necessary. But neither is there ground for asserting that they will be necessary. At most these are devices for channeling such agreement as the underlying sociological condition of the country makes possible. Let us turn, therefore, to a consideration of some of the factors that control this political substratum and of some of the ways in which it may be reinforced.

4. Means for Developing Psychological Health and Social Adjustment

SECURITY. It has now come to be generally recognized that one of the great political imperatives of our age is the provision of economic security. The government and the social system that fails to provide a minimum of economic security which bears a reasonable relationship to what the resources of the country render technically possible are doomed. Here psychological and economic considerations meet. Men's material well-being and their self-esteem are both involved in the assurance that they can go on providing for themselves and their families in something like the fashion to which they have become accustomed. This combination of factors explains why job security has become such a critical item on the agenda of all governments of industrialized

[14] One of the most discussed proposals in this category is the suggestion that the President be given the power of dissolution. See William Yandell Elliott, *The Need for Constitutional Reform: A Program for National Security* (New York: McGraw-Hill Book Company, Inc., 1935), Chap. 9, pp. 198–201; also Thomas K. Finletter, *Can Representative Government Do the Job?* (New York: Harcourt, Brace and Company, 1945). The pros and cons of this proposal are ably discussed in E. Pendleton Herring, *Presidential Leadership—The Political Relations of Congress and the Chief Executive* (New York: Rinehart & Company, 1940), pp. 73–76. See also George B. Galloway, *Congress at the Crossroads* (New York: Thomas Y. Crowell Company, 1947), and Arthur C. Millspaugh, *Toward Efficient Democracy—the Question of Governmental Organization* (Washington, D. C.: The Brookings Institution, 1949).

nations. The battle for "social security"—meaning by that the provision of compensation for those who, for reasons over which they have no control, are unable to support themselves and their dependents—has in large measure been won in England and the United States. Coverage is not yet complete—especially with regard to health risks—and the protection is often less than it should be, but it is fair to say with reference to this particular problem that its back has been broken and that it can no longer be considered a serious threat to social unity and stability.

People desire not only security against starvation and want, however; they want jobs, useful and respected jobs, not "made work." [15] Even more than this, they want, so far as it can be obtained, security in the particular job or kind of job and standard of living they now have, with opportunity for betterment not impaired. This is a large order. No society can hope to provide it in full. How nearly it can be approached is not the problem of this book. Whether in the effort to reach it we shall be driven to steps incompatible with liberty is a question we shall have to consider in a later chapter. There can be no doubt that governments today are "full employment-conscious." There are sharp differences of opinion, especially in the United States, as to the best way to achieve something like full employment. [16] But we may be sure that a government that signally fails in this regard

[15] Harold D. Lasswell, *Democracy through Public Opinion*, "Chi Omega Service Fund Studies," No. 4 (Menasha, Wisc.: George Banta Publishing Company, 1941), p. 167.

[16] Within limits, the level of employment, and especially the level of productivity, and hence the standard of living, is less important than the maintenance of stability or of an even rate of change. Professor Lasswell has pointed out that unevenness of development carries the greatest threat to psychological security: "More upsetting, even, than the speed of social development is the erratic shift in direction from an expanding to a contracting phase, and back again. It is during periods of irregularity that the position of the individual ego is least secure, and crises of deference are most intense. Intelligence is crippled by the surge of emotions connected with the status of the self. We know that human destructiveness springs from endangered self-respect, and from unsound methods of using the mind. When the tempo of social change is least regular, bruises to the ego are most prevalent, and the task of using the mind is most complex."—*Ibid.*, p. 151. By permission of the copyright owner, Chi Omega Fraternity.

will soon find itself displaced. If in the competition of the parties for power, then, a way can be found to prevent mass unemployment for long periods of time, we may be fairly confident that it will be put into effect, whether that way be through gigantic programs of government spending, through government management of heavy industry, or through capital expenditures by private industry encouraged by an appropriate taxation and fiscal policy.[17] It goes without saying that any government which finds a reasonable solution for this problem, which avoids mass unemployment for a long enough period for people generally to become confident that it is not likely to recur, will have built a sturdy foundation under its political edifice. The whole thing, of course, is a matter of degree. How much economic insecurity any given society can tolerate without experiencing a collapse of consensus will in large measure be a function of other conditions of psychological health.

CHILD TRAINING. "Democracy is much more a result of character in a people than of law or learning. Its roots are emotional rather than intellectual. It is fundamentally a consequence of psychological health and the absence of neurosis." So writes Mr. Durbin.[18] A social psychologist, Professor Wright, expresses himself in similar vein in the following manner:

Man's intellect creates, it is true, the structure and framework of the social world as a society of intercommunicating persons who participate in the same or similar experiences. But, except for the influence of human affection, it is not supplied with the range of social experiences that it must have in order to discover in the social world satisfying opportunities for mutual understanding of people and things, for comradeship in practical achievement, and for sympathetic appreciation of the varieties and vicissitudes of life and experience.[19]

[17] As to the latter possibility, see the proposal set forth by Peter F. Drucker in his *Concept of the Corporation* (New York: The John Day Company, 1946), pp. 276–284.

[18] Durbin, *op. cit.*, p. 263.

[19] H. W. Wright, "Intellect versus Emotion in Political Cooperation," *Ethics*, LVI (Oct., 1945), 28–29.

It is Wright's conclusion that provision of the proper atmosphere of loving care and cooperative endeavor for young children will develop tolerant, cooperative citizens. Durbin finds in the minimization of frustration during early childhood and in the avoidance of punishment of children who express resentment at frustration the keys to the development of psychologically healthy members of a well-integrated community.[20] In brief, his prescription (and also Wright's) is that of the supporters of "progressive education." Although there has been somewhat of a reaction against the extremes of the progressive education movement in the United States in favor of greater discipline, certainly the trend toward relaxation of the older pattern of both family and school discipline in the early years still prevails. If the psychologists referred to are right, this should be a good omen for the future of democracy in the United States, and we would do well to push further in the same direction, especially in terms of extending the newer practices to areas where they have not yet penetrated or have not been fully adopted. To be sure, there is still a good deal of disagreement among the psychologists. Durbin himself says that while aggression (the product of early frustrations) is the enemy of tolerance, guilt is the enemy of political responsibility.[21] A sense of guilt, as well as aggressive proclivities, may come from a regime of strict discipline; but, according to some psychologists, it may also be produced by too little discipline. The child who is not punished for his aggressions (which he knows are "wrong") nonetheless develops a sense of guilt. Moreover, some experts in child care have concluded that the happy and emotionally well-balanced child must be a disciplined child—and discipline is not likely to be established without considerable frustration.[22] In short, it would not appear that we have yet discovered, let alone put into affect, the training formula—if there is one—that will produce perfectly cooperative, tolerant,

[20] Durbin, *op. cit.*, p. 66.

[21] *Ibid.*, p. 263.

[22] Cf. statement by the executive director of the Society to Protect Children from Cruelty, Philadelphia *Evening Bulletin,* Sept., 1, 1947, p. 3.

completely socialized individuals. There is some ground for hope that we are on the right track; and this is a fertile field for further study, the political significance of which has not been properly appreciated. Democracies would do well to see that it receives adequate financial support.

Meanwhile, it is probably sound to conclude with Professor Kardiner that "social stability does not . . . depend so much on an intrinsic rightness about living practices as it does upon recognizing the anxieties and discomforts any system is bound to create and introducing appropriate balances." [23] To the word "balances," we might add "outlets." For instance, competition among individuals and among groups provides a valuable outlet for the discharge of aggressive impulses in relatively harmless fashion within the interstices of a pluralistic society.

SOCIAL ADJUSTMENT. Accordingly a more fruitful avenue for the pursuit of social cohesion than methods of child training, at this stage of our knowledge, is to be found in a sociological approach. Not only do social institutions well adapted to the personality type of a given society make for a cohesive society, they also make for a democratic one.[24]

Although it would require a treatise on sociology to deal adequately with the problem of organizing society for the maximization of social adjustment, a few suggestions may be outlined here. We may remark at the outset that one of the sources of social maladjustment discussed above—the shift from rural to urban-industrial living—may be expected to decrease.[25] The move-

[23] Abram Kardiner, *The Psychological Frontiers of Society* (New York: Columbia University Press, 1945), p. 421.

[24] It is reported in an abstract of a paper by Theodore F. Lentz, on "Democraticness, Autocraticness, and the Majority Point of View," that the findings "lend weight to the assumption that the greater the degree of social adjustment of the individual, the greater the faith in the democratic way of life."—*Psychological Bulletin*, XXXIX (Oct., 1942), 594.

[25] Elton Mayo, in one of his slender but richly rewarding volumes, has argued that not only the irrationality but even the acquisitiveness of modern society is a result of this too-rapid shift. Disagreeing with Professor Tawney's argument, he writes: "When Tawney refers to the industrial colonizing movement in eighteenth-century England 'from south and east to north and west,' it does not occur to him to ask whether the change of occupation and

ment from country to city in both Great Britain and the United States has apparently passed its peak.[26] It seems highly unlikely that this particular, and very significant, cause of social maladjustment will ever be as important in these countries in the future as it has been in the past.

No doubt unstabilizing factors are present in city life. As was pointed out in a previous chapter, its greater pace and intensity, its increased population mobility, and its lessened self-sufficiency all tend in this direction.[27] Other aspects of city life, however, are more favorable and tend to offset these disadvantages. Concentrated population centers furnish greater opportunities for the formation of all sorts of groups of like-minded people. Social, vocational, and avocational organizations may in large measure replace community organizations as agencies of sociological adjustment. Much has been done, by both public and private agencies, especially for young people, in the way of the formation of community centers around which are developed recreational and other organizations as needs demand. Much more could be done.

---

the extensive movement away from former settlements may not have contributed something to the disturbance of ordered personal interrelationship and so to the 'moral change' he specifies. It seems that he is affected by the Rousseau method of arguing from the individual to the society. Actually the problem *is not that of the sickness of an acquisitive society; it is that of the acquisitiveness of a sick society.* The acquisitiveness he selects for such unsparing condemnation is itself no more than a symptom of the failing integration which invariably accompanies too rapid social change."—*The Human Problems of an Industrial Civilization* (New York: The Macmillan Company, 1933), p. 153. Reprinted by Division of Research, Harvard Business School (Boston: 1946). This excerpt is used by permission of the Division of Research.

[26] In Britain, where the urban population more than trebled during the first ninety years of the nineteenth century (see above, p. 155), it has been increasing at the rate of less than 1 per cent a decade during the present century.—*Statesman's Yearbook, 1946* (New York: The Macmillan Company, 1946), p. 17. In the United States, a similar though less marked trend is indicated. By decades since 1880, the figures for the percentage of increase of urban population are as follows: 6.9, 4.6, 6.0, 5.5, 5.0, 0.3. The first five and one half years of the current decade show a war-stimulated increase of 3.3 per cent.—*Statistical Abstract of the United States, 1947* (Washington, D. C.: Government Printing Office, 1947), pp. 14–15.

[27] Above, pp. 155–156.

It is difficult to exaggerate the importance of the security and "sense of belonging" that such groups create. If the individual feels he is not facing the world alone but as a member of various groups whose unity gives him strength, his demands on others will be less immoderate. He is much less likely than otherwise to make demands for economic security so great that society cannot meet them.[28]

Furthermore, the problem of the sprawling, overgrown, and formless city may be tackled more directly. The city planning movement has not yet scratched the surface of what is technically possible in terms of breaking up large aggregations of population into sub-urban units so designed that they may become real communities, not just "suburbs." It is being discovered that many of the supposed advantages of industrial centralization under modern transportation and communication conditions are no longer so great, while the advantages of decentralization are increasingly appreciated.[29] What planning for the location of industry, and of recreational facilities and for the distribution of population can do for a community has been illustrated many times over by the Tennessee Valley Authority. David Lilienthal tells, for example, of the replanning of Guntersville, Alabama, which was a by-product of the flooding of part of the city. "What at first seemed a calamity," he says, "was turned into an opportunity, and a community sense of direction has resulted that continues to bear fruit." [30]

It is worthy of note, too, that this new sense of direction was not merely the product of planning but of *democratic* planning. The officials of Guntersville themselves adopted the plan they had worked out in collaboration with state and TVA experts. Thus the democratic method, alleged to be inherently atomistic, may

[28] Cf. Clark, *op. cit.*, p. 18.

[29] See Benton MacKaye, *The New Exploration; a Philosophy of Regional Planning* (New York: Harcourt, Brace and Company, 1928); and Lewis Mumford, *The Culture of Cities* (New York: Harcourt, Brace and Company, 1938), Chaps. 5–7.

[30] David E. Lilienthal, *TVA—Democracy on the March* (New York: Harper & Brothers, 1944), p. 64.

operate as a powerful integrating factor. People take joy in doing things together and in the joint accomplishments that result from such activity. No more powerful means of unleashing human energies and producing *esprit de corps* has been discovered than that of organizing people for voluntary joint endeavor for a common purpose. Whether the project is a barn-raising, the development of a community recreation center, or a war, the unifying or energizing results are much the same. Here again[31] it would appear that it is not liberal democracy but its erstwhile attachment, laissez faire, that is the disintegrating factor.[32]

With this example we see the close relationship between objectives and methods, between what is done and how it is done. Social cohesion is essential for satisfactory functioning of the democratic process. Social cohesion grows out of functional groupings of people—people working together on a common problem. And such group activity is itself the very essence of the democratic process! We seem to be going in a circle! But the reasoning is sound. We were speaking first of the democratic process in the large, viewed as a whole; the second reference is to a minuscule application of the democratic principle within the great democracy. It is indeed true that at least a partial cure for the evils of democracy is more democracy, but not in the way imagined by the early reformers. By democracy they meant voting. Direct elections, direct primaries, initiative, referendum, and recall—these were their remedies. They failed to appreciate that the essence of democratic procedure is not the counting of heads or even the obtaining of consent. Rather it is the processes of discussion, adjustment, and cooperative activity. It once was best typified by the town meeting. The group was small enough to carry on a real discussion, diversified enough in interest to have

---

[31] Cf. the Lewin experiment with groups of children, discussed above, p. 68, note 14.

[32] See Professor Hocking's discussion of what he calls the "commotive" process. William Ernest Hocking, *The Lasting Elements of Individualism* (New Haven: Yale University Press, 1937), pp. 105–115, and the same author's *Man and the State* (New Haven: Yale University Press, 1926), pp. 14 ff. and 163 ff.

real problems for solution, and in a position to take action on the basis of its achieved agreements. All of these conditions are important. Such problem-centered groups, we are coming increasingly to realize, are the greatest single expedient that man has discovered for bringing unity out of discord and for enlisting popular energies. Their use is by no means confined to government. In fact, no democratic government today can succeed unless the great bulk of the work of group discussion is carried on through voluntary associations.[33] But, as we shall see, government itself has before it a wealth of opportunities, of which it is just begining to take advantage, to make use of this device. The town meeting is largely outmoded, but a whole new frontier has been opened up on the administrative policy-making level.[34]

Reference has already been made to the TVA in this connection. Perhaps to most people outside the Tennessee Valley the TVA means large dams and cheap electric power. These, however, are incidental not only to its real purpose but also to its chief accomplishments. It is perhaps the world's greatest example of integrated democratic planning in action. It has transformed the material and spiritual life of thousands of people. And it has

---

[33] One writer, who has written about this aspect of democracy in brilliant fashion, goes so far as to say: "We cannot, I think, ever make our political government, *considered in itself*, really representative. The scale on which it has to operate is too vast—its units, the constituencies, are, if taken in themselves, too big and far too little informed by any public spirit to be really democratic. But if a vigorous nonpolitical democratic life exists, the political machinery may harmonize and coordinate all that partial focussing of public opinion which the nonpolitical associations perform. There can be, and there is increasingly coming to be, a vast deal of public discussion and political education focussed by universities, by churches, and by all kinds of cultural associations."—Lindsay, *The Essentials of Democracy*, p. 81. By permission of University of Pennsylvania Press, publishers.

[34] One of the best discussions of the whole subject of this paragraph is still to be found in the early work of Mary P. Follett, *The New State* (New York: Longmans, Green and Co., 1920). See also her *Creative Experience* (New York: Longmans, Green and Co., 1924) and Henry C. Metcalf and L. Urwick (ed.), *Dynamic Administration—The Collected Papers of Mary Parker Follett* (New York: Harper & Brothers, 1942). A popular little book by G. B. de Huszar, *Practical Applications of Democracy*, cited above, gives many constructive proposals for applying Miss Follett's ideas to the modern state. See also M. L. Wilson, *Democracy Has Roots* (New York: Carrick & Evans, Inc., 1939), esp. Chaps. 4, 7.

done so by strict adherence to the principles set forth by Miss Follett, John Dewey,[35] and others. By discussion, consultation, persuasion, education, it has obtained the voluntary cooperation of private citizens and local and state officials in the plans necessary for its gigantic program of soil conservation, water utilization, and community planning. Nor have these devices merely been used to secure agreement to preconceived plans. The plans themselves have been developed on the spot, in direct contact with the details of the problems they were to solve, with full collaboration of all parties concerned, experts and laymen each contributing what they had to contribute.

Obviously not all parts of any country are suited for the Valley Authority type of treatment. Regional units with common dominant problems are not everywhere to be found. And where there is a common major problem, as in certain British coal mining areas, the lack of a vast undeveloped natural resource may make it much more difficult to achieve spectacular results. But many other agencies of government in the United States have applied the same principles with results that are highly encouraging. The most outstanding example is that of the Department of Agriculture, whose Land Use Planning Committees, spread throughout the agricultural sections of the nation, have achieved great success in accomplishing the integration of conflicting interests.[36]

Other agencies of government are beginning to take advantage of this technique, although few have got to the grass roots so effectively as the ones discussed above. But anyone who has had experience with the work of the Regional War Labor Boards, for

---

[35] Dewey says: ". . . democracy . . . is the idea of community life itself." And further, "Associated or joint activity is a condition of the creation of a community."—*The Public and Its Problems* (New York: Henry Holt and Company, 1927), pp. 148, 151.

[36] See John D. Lewis, "Democratic Planning in Agriculture," *American Political Science Review*, XXXV (Apr., 1941), 232–249 and XXXV (June, 1941), pp. 454–469; also Wilson, *op. cit.*, Chap. 7.

These committees were discussed above in another connection, and examples of the types of questions they have dealt with were enumerated there (above, pp. 229–230).

example, can hardly have failed to observe that the deliberations of the panels made up of representatives of labor, management, and the public, in spite of the fact that they did not have the advantages of a permanent or semipermanent group working over a period of time on a single problem, often achieved real agreement. Unanimous panel reports and unanimous board decisions[37] were a common occurrence.

Even the traditional conflicts between legislature and administration under the separation of powers may be ameliorated by the group-discussion technique. A well-known instance of this method is provided by the cooperation between the State Department and those responsible for leadership of congressional foreign policy matters that was initiated during the war. It was carried out by weekly discussion and planning-committee meetings composed of a bipartisan group of members of the Senate Foreign Relations Committee and State Department experts under the chairmanship of Under Secretary Welles. How much of the subsequent unwonted harmony between executive and legislature on foreign affairs is to be attributed to the use of this device it is, of course, impossible to say; but it is difficult to believe that the result could have been achieved otherwise.

Another, less spectacular but possibly no less significant example is provided by an experiment conducted by the National Housing Agency. At an early date in the career of that agency its administrator, John B. Blandford, Jr., arranged with the chairman of the House Committee on Public Buildings and Grounds for informal, monthly meetings between the members of that committee and staff members of the agency. It appears to be generally agreed that the results have been highly favorable, a great improvement over the usual practice of meeting only when legislation was contemplated. For one thing the meetings made it possible to catch sources of disagreement and misunderstanding at the outset rather than allowing them to accumulate and transform irritation into festering sores. The importance of settling grievances individually and promptly is a lesson that has become

[37] The boards were also composed on a representative basis.

clear (although by no means universally taken to heart) in the field of labor relations, and its validity is not confined to that field.[38] To be sure, the wartime situation was exceptional, and it would be a mistake to jump to the conclusion that any agency of the government under any circumstances could accomplish the same results in the same manner. Nevertheless the experience is inviting and encouraging.[39]

In our discussion of the means of attaining unity and social cohesion in a democracy, we have been carried from an examination of the means of improving the psychological health of individuals to a consideration of more direct methods of attaining integration, and also from the level of nongovernmental activity to the activities of government and even to its very organization. In considering the health of liberal democracy it is important that we should move readily from one of these levels to another, remembering that the democratic prerequisites of public spirit and consensus may be at the same time both cause and effect of sound governmental institutions. Let us return to the nonpolitical level and recall that among the factors generally charged with partial responsibility for the irritability and instability of the inhabitants of the modern city are the conditions of mass-production industry, which is relevant to our concern both because of its effect on the mental health of the community and because the problem of labor-management conflict is itself one of the serious threats to democracy. Great progress has been made in recent years in dealing with these problems. It has been discovered that a man's satisfaction in his work depends a great deal more upon social than upon economic considerations. As was noted above, he needs more than job security; he needs security in a respected job.[40] More broadly, he needs to be taken seriously

[38] See Clinton S. Golden and Harold J. Ruttenberg, *The Dynamics of Industrial Democracy* (New York: Harper & Brothers, 1942), pp. 91–95.

[39] A brief account of the experiment was given by Mr. Blandford in his testimony before the Joint Committee on the Organization of Congress. Joint Committee on the Organization of Congress, "Organization of Congress," Hearings pursuant to H. R. 18 (79th Cong., 1st Sess.), pp. 514–515.

[40] See Drucker, *op. cit.*, pp. 149–153, 163–175.

as a person and given attention. This was first brought out by the famous experiment conducted by Elton Mayo and his associates in the Western Electric Company's Hawthorne plant in Chicago.[41] Change after change in the working conditions in the test unit brought increased productivity. Then came a crucial test. The original working conditions were restored during the twelfth test period. To the amazement of the investigators, production remained at the new high levels. The only plausible explanation seemed to be that it was the attention being given to the workers in the test unit rather than the specific changes in their working conditions that had been the significant factor. This experiment has led to the development of regular interviewing procedures and other techniques designed to take advantage of this discovery. Professor Mayo and his associates have also determined that people crave to be parts of "organic unities"— groups held together by ties of friendship, shared experiences, and interlocking patterns of work. This factor and others have led many companies to break up the old linear assembly line in ways that take account of the importance of establishing psychologically satisfactory working conditions. It has also been discovered that the effectiveness of financial incentive in industry has been overrated. Where it tends to put individual workmen in competition with others in their group it frequently fails to increase production at all, and even when it does it may produce unfortunate psychological and social effects.

The immediate significance of these discoveries, of course, is of concern for industry; and industry has only begun to take advantage of them. But the political implications may be just as important. In the first place, insofar as they contribute to the amelioration of capital-labor strife, they will be minimizing one of the most serious threats to political unity and social cohesion in every industrialized country of the world. Second, insofar as they make for happier, better adjusted people, they will to that extent improve the raw material of public-spiritedness and of

---

[41] Elton Mayo, *The Social Problems of an Industrial Civilization* (Cambridge, Mass.: Harvard University Press, 1945), Chap. 4.

tolerance—the spirit, in other words, without which democracy cannot succeed. In this connection, it is relevant to make one further reference to the Mayo studies. In one instance it was found that, in a particular plant where turnover was high and there were other evidences of poor morale, many of the workers were unhappy in their home lives. It might seem reasonable to suppose that the unsatisfactory domestic situations were at least partly responsible for the bad morale at the plant.[42] The striking discovery was made, however, that when various improvements were made in work relationships at the plant, there was marked improvement in the domestic lives of the workers concerned. This is a clear indication of the carry-over into other aspects of life—one may safely say "all aspects"—of the frame of mind produced by working conditions. Social scientists have long been aware of the socially and politically undesirable effects of many aspects of our technological civilization;[43] but now that it has been discovered that techniques can be developed for overcoming or avoiding many of these effects and that these techniques will also pay employers themselves in terms of greater produc-

---

[42] In fact, the Western Electric study had revealed just such a cause-and-effect relationship.—Mayo, *The Human Problems of an Industrial Civilization,* Chap. 5.

[43] Mayo himself paints the picture in the following words: ". . . the imposition of highly systematized industrial procedures upon all the civilized cultures has brought to relative annihilation the cultural traditions of work and craftsmanship. Simultaneously the development of a high labor mobility and a clash of cultures has seriously damaged the traditional routine of intimate and family life in the United States. Generally the effect has been to induce everywhere a considerable degree of social disorganization; the comfortable non-logic of every social code has been reduced, at least in part, to irrational exasperation—without any prospect of development towards better understanding for the average citizen. . . . The belief of the individual in his social function and solidarity with the group—his capacity for collaboration in work—these are disappearing, destroyed in part by rapid scientific and technical advance. With this belief his sense of security and well-being also vanishes and he begins to manifest those exaggerated demands of life which Durkheim has described."—*Ibid.,* p. 166. (By permission of the Division of Research, Harvard Business School.) It should be mentioned in connection with this passage that taking care to acquaint workers with the purpose of what they are doing and the part it plays in the total process of production is another one of the techniques successfully tried on the basis of Mayo's recommendations.

tion and improved labor relations, we may anticipate that something will be done about developing them, although the process will undoubtedly be a slow one.

Unions are also undoubtedly making an important contribution in this respect. Partly because they are effective weapons in the struggle for security and partly because of their social functions, unions contribute to the psychological security of their members. The social aspect of unionism is not to be disregarded. What the community no longer provides in this respect must be and increasingly can be taken care of by such functional organizations as labor unions. Here, also, is a great opportunity for further development.

DIRECT APPROACH TO THE PROBLEM OF STRIKES. We must shift our level again. Some of the newer techniques for handling labor relations will doubtless have important effects in improving relations between capital and labor as well as in increasing productivity and relieving the social malaise of an industrial society, but one would be naïve indeed to think that it will solve the whole problem of industrial strife. And no one can fail to recognize that such strife presents the greatest single domestic threat to political cohesion and to democracy today. How serious the present situation is no one can say with assurance. After a postwar epidemic of strikes somewhat similar to that which followed the War of 1914–1918, the situation may revert to a level of struggle not incompatible with the continued functioning of democratic institutions.[44] But the emergence of numerous national industrial unions, able to enforce industry-wide collective bargaining, is a new factor, the full implications of which it is too soon to evaluate. In industrial unions great power is in the hands of the upper strata in the labor organization pyramid. This fact almost inevitably means that the question of labor strife or har-

[44] Already (1950) there has been a marked decline in time lost from strikes since the first postwar year. This comparative peace has been purchased, however, by substantial wage increases. What may happen if industrial activity slackens and industry is no longer able to afford wage increases remains to be seen.

mony will be dictated by broader considerations than the conditions in a particular plant or even under a particular employer. Whether it also means that improvements in industry's labor policies of the sort discussed above will have less effect on the success of collective bargaining than might otherwise have been anticipated, or whether it will simply mean that they will become effective only after they have been adopted by a large part of the industry in question remains to be seen.

In any case, it seems probable that government in peacetime will have to take more of a hand in this matter in the future than it has in the past. Intervention might be either in the form of placing limits upon the extent to which labor should be allowed to create monopolies or in the form of compulsory arbitration for key industries. In the latter case, it seems certain that it will be necessary to develop and obtain widespread agreement to certain standards for the determination of wage rates. This job will be immensely complicated, but it may be safely assumed that over-all wage rates will have to be related in some way to over-all production, that differentials between types of work will be related to certain measurements of skill and exertion and to the desirability of the work involved, and that variations from the norms so determined will be related to variations in the production of the industry or plant concerned, especially insofar as these variations are attributable to labor. All of this is more easily said than done, but it does not appear that the problem presents an insuperable bar to that minimum of industrial peace which is essential for the healthy functioning of political democracy.

The Problem of Racial Intolerance. Finally, a word should be said specifically regarding racial intolerance as one of the most serious forms of democratic disunity. Where there is a long-standing tradition of discrimination, as notably in the case of the American Negro, there is a major task of re-education to be done which must be participated in by all the educational agencies which can be mobilized for the task. Tocqueville's "providen-

tial fact" of the trend toward social equality and the natural
sense of fairness that is indigenous to our culture (if not natural to man himself) are powerful factors in support of such a
re-educational movement. Nevertheless, where the prejudice
is as deep-seated and as institutionalized as it is in a large
part of the United States, and where it is believed to coincide
with the economic interest of the dominant racial group, the task
is likely to be difficult and slow to be realized. Insofar as it per-
sists and results in the violation of the principle of equality of
consideration, it constitutes an infringement on one of democracy's fundamental principles. Insofar as it invades the political
realm, to that extent the government fails to be truly democratic.
Nevertheless, *as far as concerns the dominant group*, a liberal-
democratic government may prosper even while a particular
group is excluded from effective participation, even as with the
slaves in democratic Athens. Difficulties are most likely to arise
in the process of change from one condition to another. Thus
when the movement for abolition of racial discrimination gets
under way—as in conformity with democratic ethics it certainly
should—it becomes the task of statesmanship to see to it that the
serious rifts in opinion that are bound to result are minimized,
especially where they tend to follow sectional divisions. Adjustment will be a matter of speeding the education of the laggard
elements of the population and restraining the impetuosity of
those whose passion for justice tends to outrun their recognition
of the importance of maintaining social cohesion. Although the
Negro problem in the United States remains a serious blot on the
nation's democratic pretensions, there can be no doubt that steady
progress is being made toward its solution.[45] The number of
lynchings has markedly declined, a slowly but steadily increasing
number of southern states are allowing Negroes to vote in primaries, educational opportunities are moving in the direction of
equalization, and the same is even truer of employment oppor-

[45] See Gunnar Myrdal, *An American Dilemma—The Negro Problem
and Modern Democracy* (2 vols.; New York: Harper & Brothers, 1944),
passim.

tunities.[46] In the latter connection, Fair Employment Practice Commissions have made a splendid record, showing what can be done by education and persuasion, supported by the coercive power of the state to the extent, and only to the extent, that seems wise in the circumstances of the particular case.[47]

But the kind of racial problem that is most serious for the continued life of a democracy is not that which may accompany a movement to abolish racial discrimination. Such growing pains of democracy are not at all likely to be fatal. The great danger, and one of the besetting evils of our day, is the situation where racial feeling is on the increase. Whether or not it is true there is such a tendency, notably a growth of anti-Semitism, in the United States and in other liberal democracies today, it obviously does not constitute an argument against democracy and in favor of dictatorship. But anyone concerned for the future well-being of democracy must nonetheless view the trend, if it be a trend, with concern, and give thought to the question of how to check it. In my opinion, however, this is not so much a special question as it is identical with the whole problem with which this chapter has been dealing. A psychologically healthy society does not develop these deep fissures in its texture. When they appear they are symptoms of severe social maladjustment or of some crisis[48] that drives people to irrational behavior. Students of Nazism are almost unanimously agreed that the success of Hitler's anti-Semitic propaganda in Germany is to be attributed largely

---

[46] There were well over 100 lynchings a year, on the average, between 1890 and 1900. By contrast, the average figure for the years 1936–1946 was 4.3.—*To Secure These Rights; the Report of the President's Committee on Civil Rights* (Washington, D. C.: Government Printing Office, 1947), pp. 20–25.

[47] See "Antidiscrimination in Employment," Hearings pursuant to S. 984, before a subcommittee of the Senate Committee on Labor and Public Welfare, 80th Cong., 1st Sess. Note especially the statement by the chairman of the New York State Fair Employment Practice Commission, at pp. 325–328, the brief of Joseph L. Bustard, in charge of enforcement of the New Jersey law, at pp. 377–383, and the statement by the chairman of the Massachusetts FEPC, at pp. 425–429. See also Herbert R. Northrup, "Proving Ground for Fair Employment: Some Lessons from New York State's Experience," *Commentary*, IV (Dec., 1947), 552–556.

[48] See below, p. 303.

to the fact that it provided outlet for abnormal aggressive tendencies built up by the combination of military, political, and economic failures that had beset the German people and driven them to despair.[49] There were doubtless other contributory factors. For instance, the large influx of culturally "foreign" Jews from Eastern Europe into Germany following the War of 1914–1918 undoubtedly helped to arouse prejudice. We can hardly doubt that the great movement of Jews following the recent war, outdistancing the slow pace of economic readjustment and cultural assimilation, will in many cases have a similar effect. Barring the addition of the other conditions present in Weimar and Hitlerite Germany, however, there is no reason to anticipate that the unfavorable results will be more than temporary.

5. Maintenance of the Liberal-Democratic Myth

THE PROPER ROLE OF THE STATE IN MYTH-MAKING. Except for passing reference above, we have yet to deal with education and other agencies of opinion formation as devices for promoting democratic unity. We noted in a previous chapter that some aspects of the liberal-democratic "myth" appear to be on the wane. During the interwar period, at least, the peoples of democratic countries showed a definite decline in optimism and in enthusiasm for their way of life and a growing skepticism regarding the potential harmony of human ends. Furthermore, economic and social changes have conspired to accentuate this trend. On the other hand, the success of the totalitarian regimes in indoctrinating youth with their value systems and in enlisting their enthusiastic support of these systems is notorious. The combined effect of these developments has been to cause liberal democrats to reconsider what should be the role of the state with regard to education. Should the state teach democratic ideals in the public schools? Should it require private schools to do likewise? Should it ban criticism of democratic ideals and institutions in the

[49] Cf. Peter Nathan, *The Psychology of Fascism* (London: Faber and Faber, Ltd., 1943); Erich Fromm, *Escape from Freedom* (New York: Rinehart & Company, 1941); and Frederick L. Schuman, *The Nazi Dictatorship* (New York: Alfred A. Knopf, Inc., 1935), pp. 312–318.

schools, on the theory that the liberal doctrine of freedom of criticism and discussion applies only to mature minds? Should it organize the free-time activities of its young citizens, making use of the full gamut of devices of opinion control that have been developed by the dictatorships? Clearly there is a limit beyond which a state cannot go and remain in any sense "liberal." Obviously, too, any state that has ever officially adopted a national anthem or erected a monument to a national hero has entered this field.[50] Where should the line be drawn?

What course of action is open to a liberal democracy? Clearly it cannot do anything that involves monopolizing channels of opinion formation or prohibiting criticism of our institutions. Publicly supported youth organizations, even if there is no compulsion to join, would constitute dangerous infringements on the pluralistic realm of cultural autonomy that is essential to a liberal society. But there are things compatible with the philosophy of liberalism that the schools can and should do. First of all, they can teach the value of truth and of impartiality, of the pursuit of knowledge with scientific objectivity. The case for free

[50] For an account of the various devices long used by the democratic government of Switzerland for indoctrination in democratic traditions, see Robert Clarkson Brooks, *Civic Training in Switzerland; A Study of Democratic Life* (Chicago: The University of Chicago Press, 1930). As a frontispiece, Brooks quotes Bryce's statement that ". . . . the most interesting lesson it [Switzerland] teaches is how traditions and institutions, taken together, may develop in the average man, to an extent never reached before, the qualities which make a good citizen—shrewdness, moderation, common sense and a sense of duty to the community. It is because this has come to pass in Switzerland that democracy is there more truly democratic than in any other country."—James Bryce, *Modern Democracies* (2 vols.; New York: The Macmillan Company, 1921), II, 449. It should be noted, however, that, of the nine devices Brooks enumerated as contributing to this end in Switzerland, one only is wholly subject to government control, the government service. A second, the schools, are, of course, largely public, and civic training may be required in all. A third, political parties, might be termed quasi-governmental organs. But the others—churches, the family, patriotic and other societies, language, literature, and the press, tradition and devotion to locality, and the group designated as "symbolism; cults; art, music, drama"—are almost wholly outside the control of the liberal state.—Brooks, *op. cit.*, p. 423.

See also Charles Edward Merriam, *The Making of Citizens* (Chicago: The University of Chicago Press, 1931).

speech itself is based upon rational analysis, so there can be no violation of the tenets of free speech in "indoctrinating" children with this method. This means that children must be taught to submit existing institutions to criticism and to be skeptical of all dogma; it also means that they must be trained to set store by insitutions that provide full opporunity for free expression of critical thought.

Second, it does not violate the tenets of liberalism to teach or even to glorify the values of liberty. It is important, however, to maintain the distinction between liberty in the broadest sense and particular forms of liberty. Particular institutional devices, even particular "rights" that in one period are valuable protections for liberty may at another period become unessential encumbrances. This does not mean that the great historical, instrumental value of the Bill of Rights should not be emphasized. Its virtues can be stressed while making clear that certain parts (e.g., freedom of speech, press, and religion) are more fundamental than others (e.g., the right to grand jury indictment), and that the whole is subject to amendment by constitutional process. It is, however, the ideal of the free human spirit, as described above,[51] that should be held up as the primary goal.

Much the same may be said with regard to the ideal of equality. In part, as we have seen,[52] and perhaps most fundamentally, the liberal democratic doctrine of equality is implicit in the rational principle itself. Equality before the law, then, and equality of consideration are principles that democracies need have absolutely no qualms about teaching. What about a principle of equal treatment that goes somewhat beyond this and draws for its support upon a broad humanitarianism, upon the belief that the indefinite extension of human love and sympathy will add to human well-being on the whole? Here we pass beyond that which is logically demonstrable. But, for reasons discussed above, the principle appears to me to be highly plausible—so plausible, indeed, that it would seem justifiable for the state through its

[51] See Chap. IV, esp. pp. 58–63.
[52] Above, pp. 84–85.

schools to do whatever can be done to propagate belief in such equality.[53] This area, however, is one in which the family, the church, and various character-building organizations are likely to be more influential than the schools.

What is true for liberty and equality holds as well for a belief in tolerance and in democratic procedures. Here, as always, doing is more effective than preaching. Many schools take advantage of the opportunities for giving children firsthand experience with democratic procedures in the management of school affairs.[54] There is room for vast improvement and expansion of present practices in this area. It should hardly need to be said that schools

[53] It should be borne in mind that anyone who wishes to teach a contrary doctrine should be free to do so.

What is said above rests upon the important distinctions made earlier between propositions that can be proved, those that cannot be proved but for which there are plausible grounds for belief, and those that are supported by little or no evidence. Much misunderstanding, and perhaps also misapplication of liberal doctrine, flows from a failure to observe these distinctions. Thus when it was said above (p. 293) that children ought to be taught to be skeptical of all dogma, what is meant is that they should be taught always to seek the grounds for beliefs, but not that they should be taught to disbelieve in propositions for which there is reasonable support. When Professor Hallowell, for example, declares, "Our children and our students must be taught the precepts of natural law, as we now teach them the rudiments of arithmetic," he is probably not saying anything with which I would disagree.—John H. Hallowell, "Modern Liberalism: An Invitation to Suicide," *South Atlantic Quarterly*, XLVI, Oct., 1947, 465. Much would depend, to be sure, upon what was included in the concept of "natural law," as the discussion in the text should make clear.

[54] One authority writes "Democratic self-government for children effectively encourages real independence of a kind that probably makes for the development of individuals who are less susceptible of being exploited and misled than are individuals who as children were intimidated and rendered submissive by autocratic authority. . . . Modern fascism springs from psychological roots which are as old as the human family and which are by no means confined to the populace of those countries in which fascism has gained official status. The danger of emergence and growth of such a political doctrine . . . comes . . . from a country's own internal educational and economic institutions. No one, I believe, can at present point with certainty to the solution of this important problem; but surely encouragement of greater independence and emotional self-sufficiency in children and practice in the resolution of their social difficulties by democratic techniques is a step in the right direction."—O. H. Mowrer, "Authoritarianism vs. 'Self-Government' in the Management of Children's Aggressive (Anti-Social) Reactions as a Preparation for Citizenship in a Democracy," *Journal of Social Psychology* (Feb., 1939), 125–126.

where racial discrimination is officially practiced are setting poor examples in the matter of democratic living. And schools can do much more than practice nondiscriminatory treatment; they can point out the fact of discrimination wherever it occurs and appeal to children's sense of fairness in an effort to break down prejudice.

Although no attempt has been made here to go into detail as to the means, it is suggested that we have outlined the general area within which the agencies of formal education can effectively operate to create the political myth of liberal democracy. There are those who suggest that in a liberal democracy the public schools should be completely neutral with regard to values, except for the value of the open mind. Willingness, even eagerness, and ability to apply rational criticism to all existing ideals, principles, institutions, and practices should be the single political objective—barring the simple impartation of knowledge—of educational policy. At the other extreme are those who believe that the modern state must determine in detail what is the best pattern of life and of society and should teach its youth to believe in the absolute rightness of this pattern. I have indicated my disagreement with each of these extremes; but the line I would follow falls considerably nearer to the former than to the latter.

One further point about the policy here advocated should be made clear. It is one thing for the state, through its schools and universities, to take an official position in support of certain controverted value judgments outside the basic democratic values themselves; it is quite another for individual teachers to express their own convictions. The latter should be allowed and even encouraged as long as the distinction between fact and opinion is kept clear. Too often teachers, with a false sense of what is required of a liberal, have refused to express any value judgments, being content to point out the variety of existing opinions and to marshal the arguments pro and con. The laudable intention is to allow the student to arrive at his own conclusions on the basis of independent thought. All too frequently, however, the effect is to discourage the formation of opinions on important questions.

The student comes out of the educational process with no sense that he should make up his mind on public issues but rather with the stultifying feeling that to have convictions on such matters betokens a lack of open-mindedness. Instead of taking up where the teacher leaves off—with an enumeration of neatly balanced arguments for and against—he falls into the same pattern of thought. He may even conclude that there is no basis for making such judgments. This is all a great mistake. For the teacher to conceal his own value judgments is in no sense an integral part of the liberal method, although it has doubtless developed from a misconception of what that method entails. We must fight against this error by encouraging teachers to give voice to their convictions—but not by telling them what convictions they should express.

It may appear to some that the educational role we have assigned to the state is too intellectualized, both in content and method. Let us be clear on one point: we do not intend to belittle the importance of myths.[55]

Professor MacIver is undoubtedly right when he says: "Every society is held together by a myth-system. . . . All social relations, the very texture of human society, are myth-born and myth-sustained. . . . Every civilization, every period, every nation, has its characteristic myth-complex. In it lies the secret of social unities and social continuities, and its changes compose the inner history of every society."[56] The point is rather that the great, successful myth systems of the world—such as "the American way"—have been only in small part political. What we have been saying is that no attempt to make up for the disintegration of the system of social myths by concentrating solely on the political level—by developing a political religion—can be permanently successful, much less avoid the destruction of liberty. Fur-

[55] By this term, it will be remembered, we mean the system of beliefs (whether true or false) and values that are fundamental to any given society. In this sense, all that is meant by the phrase "the American way of life" is a myth.

[56] MacIver, *The Web of Government*, pp. 4–5. Cf. also Ernst Cassirer, *The Myth of the State* (New Haven: Yale University Press, 1946).

thermore, deliberate attempts on the part of a government to produce social and political cohesion directly are almost certain to place chief reliance upon whipping up nationalistic and patriotic enthusiasm. In moderation these sentiments are useful and perhaps at present indispensable elements of the healthy body politic, but in excess they are dangerous threats to the peace of the world; moreover, the democracies with which we are presently concerned are in no need of stimulation in this particular.

Conversely, a healthy society is in no need of depending primarily upon the state for the perpetuation of its myth. This will be true as long as the young learn from the precept and example of their elders, from every contact they have with the settled beliefs and institutions of the society in which they find themselves, and as long as societies are free to form associations for all of the manifold purposes that men share with other men. Man is an inveterate myth builder; given halfway satisfactory institutions and social and economic conditions, he will glorify his way of life. Just as most men like foods cooked the way Mother cooked them, think the region of the country in which they spent their youth is superior to all others, prefer the domestic arrangements and minor customs of their own household to those of others, insist upon the superiority of their school and college, and so on throughout the gamut of human relations, so the form and philosophy of government to which they are accustomed will appear in ideal lineaments to the average citizen barring some very powerful countervailing factor.[57] For this reason I disagree with

[57] A recent contribution to the theory of democracy by a social psychologist holds that, while fear and considerations of rational expediency are not enough to bind a people together for cooperative effort, successful communal living itself is the best way to develop powerful sentimental supports against future shocks to the body politic. The author writes as follows: "The outlook is much better . . . if a people already have a memory and a tradition of successful communal effort. It seems to be a principle of rather general validity that people learn to love the activities they habitually and successfully practice, and nothing seems to bind together a group so effectively as the consciousness or memory of having successfully braved dangers or performed difficult tasks together."—Thomas M. French, "The Psychodynamic Problem of Democracy," in Goodwin Watson (ed.), *Civilian Morale.* "Second Yearbook of the Society for the Psychological

those, like the late Karl Mannheim, who believe that democracies must meet the challenge of the disintegration of traditional values and norms by positively seeking new bases of agreement.[58] It is important for democratic leaders to try their hands at formulating revised bills of rights, and the like, that more nearly reflect current valuations and express current needs than did the old ones. Indeed, it is essential that there should be continual efforts at clarification, reinterpretation, and elaboration of democratic methods and potentialities. Such action may even play a significant role in bursting asunder the old outworn doctrine and gaining support for the new. But a government that lays primary emphasis on the formulation of doctrine rather than on the provision of conditions favorable to the growth of sound beliefs is doomed to failure.

SKEPTICISM AND DIMINISHED ENTHUSIASM. Nor does the growth of skepticism as to the rationality of human nature and the harmony of human ends point to a different conclusion. Skepticism does not disintegrate a community, although a disintegrated society may produce skepticism. In a healthy society there is no need to fear its corrosive effects. If measures such as those discussed in the preceding pages succeed in establishing a smoothly functioning social structure, conflicts will not prove to be insoluble, and it will become apparent that man is not hopelessly irrational.[59]

Something of the same sort may be said of the decline in enthusiasm for democracy and of the lessening optimism as to its prospects, which were noted in an earlier chapter. In some measure these were but a natural reaction to the excessive optimism of the early period. More recently they were accentuated by the successes of dictatorship and the failures of democracies in the

---

Study of Social Issues" (Boston: Houghton Mifflin Company, 1942), p. 28. See also T. D. Weldon, *States and Morals* (London: John Murray, Ltd., 1946), for a discussion of the tenaciousness of political traditions.

[58] See Karl Mannheim, *Diagnosis of Our Time* (New York: Oxford University Press, 1944), pp. 30–34.

[59] For an interesting and pertinent discussion of the dynamics of moral ideals, such as the democratic ideal of equality, see Myrdal, *op. cit.*, II, 1027–1031.

interwar period. The goal of equality has lost nothing of its power of attraction. New and more direct applications of democratic procedures are showing great capacity for the enlistment of energy and enthusiasm.

THE ROLE OF RELIGION. Before concluding this discussion of the mythical bases for democratic consensus, a word should be said concerning the role of religion. Many people today believe that without a religious revival, liberal democracy cannot hope to survive. John Middleton Murry, for example, declares that "the dynamic that achieved democracy was, in the main, a dynamic not of interest but of morality and religion." He maintains that "if democracy, being achieved, decays into a mere mechanism for the resolution of the conflict of immediate interests within the social whole, its moral and religious vitality begins also to decay." [60] Mr. Ross Hoffman, in a vein typical of many others writes as follows: "The fundamental disease of the democratic state is the rotting away of its spiritual foundations. It arose in Christendom and could not have appeared anywhere else. It sprang from a belief in the dignity and worth of man which rested ultimately on the mystical dogma of man as God's creature and formed in His image." [61] The general position of those who believe that the fate of democracy is dependent upon the fate of religion, and particularly of Christianity, may be summarized in the following four propositions: (1) that the belief in the individual as the center of value is dependent upon the belief in the existence of the "soul"; (2) that belief in the democratic morality of equality and tolerance cannot be sustained without a religious sanction; (3) that materialism constitutes an integral part of the liberal democratic myth and that it inevitably leads to selfishness and dissensions incompatible with democratic consensus; and (4) that materialism will also

[60] John Middleton Murry, *The Defence of Democracy* (London: Jonathan Cape, Ltd., 1939), pp. 177, 180.

[61] Ross J. S. Hoffman, *The Organic State—An Historical View of Contemporary Politics* (New York: Sheed & Ward, 1939), pp. 114–115. See also the statement on "The Christian in Action," by American Roman Catholic bishops—New York *Times,* Nov. 21, 1948, Dec. 1, p. 63.

produce a sense of emptiness, a spiritual vacuum from which a violent and antidemocratic reaction is inevitable. To these propositions may be added the charge that the spirit of science, always demanding proof, undermines all religion and all belief in undemonstrable principles.[62] Those who take this position are not doing so to criticize the ideal of liberal democracy (although some of them would assert that this ideal is hopelessly entangled in a larger synthesis they are attacking because of other elements in it—notably materialism). Rather they are urging a return to religion and predicting the collapse of democracy and of our whole civilization as the alternative.[63]

Let us assume, at least for the sake of the argument, that the secular trend is likely to continue, that religion will become a less and less effective force in our culture. Let us assume, further, that it has in the past been of some value to liberal democracy in the manner implied by the four propositions listed above. This is not the whole story. Religion has had other consequences, some of which were distinctly unfavorable to democratic unity. Wars of religion, civil as well as international, have played a large part in human history. One need only think of France in

[62] This position is well stated by Eduard Heimann, who writes: "That the world is one and demands to be organized for peace by justice—this is a dogma, whether we trace that oneness to the further dogma that the world emanates from the one Maker who gave it His justice as the means to live in peace, or whether with philosophy we analyze that oneness as ultimately given in the human mind. The dogma of oneness and justice, being dogma, must be accepted or rejected, but cannot be proved or refuted in terms of science. As science in its quest for tangible demonstrable proof moves against dogma, it not only destroys religion but also corrodes the inevitably dogmatic basis of the autonomous ethic."—*Freedom and Order —Lessons from the War* (New York: Charles Scribner's Sons, 1947), p. 267. By permission of Charles Scribner's Sons, publishers.

[63] Note, for example, that Reinhold Niebuhr, a leading exponent of the point of view being discussed, would not alter the ideals of liberal democracy. It is true he believes there is no solution to what he calls the problem of vitality and form within the limits of the dimension in which modern culture sees the problem.—*The Nature and Destiny of Man* (2 vols.; New York: Charles Scribner's Sons, 1941), I, 53. But at the same time he believes in a liberal democratic (but not bourgeois) society as defined here. He merely adds: ". . . no society, not even a democratic one, is great enough or good enough to make itself the final end of human existence."—*The Children of Light and the Children of Darkness* (New York: Charles Scribner's Sons, 1944), p. 133.

the sixteenth century or Germany in the seventeenth. Moreover, the history of religious persecutions forms a large part of the history of most of the great churches. It is true that toleration, and liberty more generally, owe much to religion, but this is an accident. As Father Figgis aptly put it, ". . . . political liberty is the residuary legatee of ecclesiastical animosities." In the struggles between church and state and later between one church and another, liberty and toleration emerged as objectives instrumental to quite different purposes.[64] Even practically universal commitment to a single faith failed to prevent the Middle Ages from being a period more noted for turbulence than for order.

On the other hand, belief in the dignity of the individual and in the obligation of equality of treatment for all is not left without all support in the absence of the religious sanction. The choice need not be between belief in a supernatural religion and corrosive cynicism. All the rational arguments and the democratic psychological tendencies of human nature discussed in earlier chapters remain valid.[65] One does not need to prove that satisfaction of the demands of human nature is "good." This is implicit in the meaning of "good." It cannot be undermined by science; on the contrary, science and logic support it.[66] The discovery that justice has foundations in human nature (including human reason) does not weaken its claim upon us, or its chances of survival.[67]

It is true that a discussion of the foundation of moral prin-

[64] See J. B. Bury, *A History of Freedom of Thought* (New York: Henry Holt and Company, 1913), Chaps. 4, 5.

[65] See above, Chaps. III, V.

[66] It is pertinent to note that a summary of recent contributions as to the psychology of morals includes the following tendencies as characteristic of normal human development: from egocentricity to sociality, from moral inhibition to spontaneous "goodness," from aggression to tolerance and love, and from fear to security.—J. C. Flugel, *Man, Morals and Society: A Psychoanalytical Study* (London: Gerald Duckworth, Ltd., 1945), pp. 242–252.

[67] The opposing argument is thus strongly put by Eduard Heimann: "Religion is the root of spirituality. That is why a humanistic ethic without religion can be short-lived only and will then give way to some crude form of pseudo-religion." With regard to the apparent exception of the Stoics, he contends that "the discrepancy between their pre-eminent place in the history of thought and their complete inability to influence political history only confirms the truth that an autonomous philosophical ethic is no his-

ciples tends to dissolve that aura of sanctity which customarily surrounds them.[68] Similarly, skepticism as to the supernatural foundations of ethics may have a dispiriting effect on some people. But there is much to suggest that this is a transitional rather than a permanent phenomenon. The appeal to history is by no means entirely on the side of the pessimists. It is true that modern democracy stems largely from the ideas of the religious Independents of seventeenth-century England.[69] But it is equally true that the great liberal philosophers of the eighteenth century were not profoundly religious.[70] Nor was the popular movement that gave rise to the French Revolution. English thought in the nineteenth century, when democratic institutions really came into being in that country, was increasingly secular. In fact, one careful student of that period declares that democracy's preoccupation with the goal of earthly happiness is at odds with the central doctrine of the Christian churches. "Democracy is essentially irreligious and anti-Christian," he declares, "because of its fundamental tenet with regard to the importance of, and equal right to, human happiness." [71] This extreme view requires qualifi-

torical force, while religion indisputably is."—*Op. cit.*, pp. 265, 266. (See also the passage quoted above, n. 62.) Against this view it must be argued that, properly interpreted, science does not oppose plausible postulates as to principles of conduct that will most fully satisfy the felt demands of the human psyche. There is, that is to say, no logical conflict between science and sound principles of morality. It is undoubtedly true that misunderstandings of the scientific spirit often prevail and tend to have a dispiriting effect. But, as Professor Stevenson argues, "The proper task, certainly, for those who lament this situation and seek to improve it, is one of revealing the teachings of science for what they are. Nothing can be said for those reformers who share the very confusions that make reform necessary, and whose efforts to provide an emotional orientation to nature are placed in artificial rivalry with the study of nature itself."—Charles L. Stevenson, *Ethics and Language* (New Haven: Yale University Press, 1944), p. 324.

[68] See John Stuart Mill, "Utilitarianism," in Philip Wheelwright (ed.), *Essays on Government, Jurisprudence, Liberty of the Press, and Law of Nations* (New York: Doubleday & Company, 1935), p. 428.

[69] See George Gooch and Harold J. Laski, *English Democratic Ideas in the Seventeenth Century* (2d ed.; Cambridge: Cambridge University Press, 1927).

[70] See Carl L. Becker, *The Heavenly City of the Eighteenth-Century Philosophers* (New Haven: Yale University Press, 1932).

[71] Leonard Woolf, *After the Deluge* (2 vols.; New York: Harcourt, Brace and Company, 1931, 1939), I, 218.

cation, but it does indeed show the weakness in the contention that history proves that the well-being of democracy and the well-being of the Christian religion necessarily go together.

As a final point in this connection, it should be noted that the apparent drawing power of political religions in this age may not indicate, as is frequently argued, that the decline of religion has left a vacuum that must be filled. Rather, the popular demand for a unifying faith may be a reflection of social disintegration and of the need for especially strong cohesive ties in a period of rapid change when the strains upon consensus are tremendous. The dependence of a society upon faith, or upon mythical or magical elements, is largely a function of the extent to which men are unable to solve their problems by rational methods. Malinowski has pointed out that even in primitive societies, where myth is all-pervasive, the magical rites connected with it are used chiefly in situations where the savages' technical knowledge is inadequate. "There is no exaggeration," he writes, "in saying that in all matters where knowledge is sufficient the native relies on it exclusively." [72] The reversion of modern societies to irrational beliefs appears to correspond to the same psychological laws. If this analysis is sound, the answer is to be found partly along the lines of facilitating social adjustment, as suggested above,[73] thus removing the source of a demand for faith so likely to take an antiliberal form.

What has been said assumes that religion is becoming a less effective force and that this trend will continue. This assumption may turn out to be false. Materialism may indeed prove to be an insufficient diet for the human psyche, but there is no logical relationship between materialism and democracy. The latter has proved itself to be equally at home with the strongly spiritual atmosphere of the "Puritans of the Left" and with the hedonism of the Benthamite Liberals. If a reaction against materialism

[72] Bronislaw Malinowski, *The Foundations of Faith and Morals,* in University of Durham, Riddell Memorial Lectures, Ser. 7, 1934–1935 (London: Oxford University Press, 1936), pp. 32–33, quoted in Cassirer, *op. cit.,* p. 278.

[73] Above, pp. 277–287.

sets in, it will be a problem for democratic statesmanship to prevent it from taking an antidemocratic form. There is no reliable formula for this, but, once more, everything that we can do to develop a well-adjusted, smoothly functioning society will be all to the good.

6. Conclusion

In conclusion, no attempt will be made to summarize what has been said in this chapter, but one final point needs to be made. Both Marxians and Freudians and many others, who, without knowing it, are in some measure influenced by one or the other of these doctrines, are constantly referring to contradictions within the pattern of liberal democracy, as though the fact of their existence spelled its certain destruction. But such contradictions should not be a matter for surprise. Life is full of them. Men crave freedom *and* authority. They desire security yet love the thrill of taking risks. They want to be happy, yet if they subordinate everything else to the pursuit of personal happiness they are almost certain to be unhappy. Under these circumstances, it is only natural that society, too, should manifest contradictions. If, for instance, some social institutions are based on the principle that men are concerned about the general well-being, while others appeal to the principle of self-interest, this dualism merely reflects the fact that man is both selfish and altruistic. In most individuals these conflicting desires do not prevent the attainment of a reasonable degree of happiness. Similarly, in society they need not prevent the achievement of a high degree of harmony. In fact, a society that did not make provision both for man's competitive nature and for his cooperative urges would most certainly be radically unsatisfactory.[74]

[74] It will be noted that what we are saying is at odds with the position taken by the widely read psychologist Karen Horney. She denies that there is any biological or innate psychological basis for such conflicts as those mentioned in the text. Rather she believes that personal conflicts, which often manifest themselves as neuroses, are attributable to contradictions imbedded in our culture, such as that between competitiveness and Christian submissiveness.—*The Neurotic Personality of Our Time* (New York: W. W. Norton & Company, 1937), esp. pp. 281–290.

CHAPTER XIII

THE PROSPECT
FOR LIBERTY

It has been one of the major arguments of this volume that liberty, as we have defined it, is an essential of liberal democracy and of the good life. It has been further contended that no other form of government than the democratic holds forth as great assurance of providing a maximum of liberty for its citizens. Moreover, the contentions sometimes advanced to the effect that both the ideal and the practice of liberty are disintegrative forces that lead to an atomism ethically undesirable and practically destructive of the conditions of effective government have been considered and found wanting.[1] It remains to appraise the prospect for retaining liberty as a practical ideal in a world where many forces appear to be working against it.[2] Nor shall we be content with a mere estimate of probabilities; where it is called for we shall endeavor to add prescription to prognosis.[3]

First of all, we must remind ourselves of what we have taken to be the meaning of the term "liberty" for the purposes of

---

[1] The first point was dealt with in considering liberty as an ideal (Chap. IV), whereas the discussion of the latter found its place in the treatment of unity, in the chapter just concluded.

[2] This query might suggest itself: Why single out liberty for such separate treatment and not equality? The answer is that in fact it is liberty which is threatened. No one who has even a nodding acquaintance with the developments of the past quarter century can doubt that it is authoritarianism that presents the great threat to liberal democracy.

[3] It should be pointed out that the proper classification of problems is sometimes rather arbitrary—a matter of how one looks at it. For instance, complete freedom of expression may be a threat to unity. On the other hand, the fact that this is so arouses forces that may threaten liberty. It has seemed more convenient to treat this problem in the present chapter rather than in the preceding one.

this book and consider a little more fully than we have yet done the relationship between liberty and the role of the state. Liberty, we have said, is the opportunity for deliberate self-direction in the formation and accomplishment of one's purposes. The first corollary, then, of the proposition that liberty should be one of our primary concerns is that there should be a minimum of restraint in the realm of expression of ideas and a maximum of education and of access to information. Second, in the realm of action—for example, choosing an occupation, selecting a mate, making contracts, forming associations, acquiring property—restraints and compulsions should be minimized, other things being equal. Third, to the extent that restraints and compulsions backed up by political power are desirable, all should share in the determination of what these shall be. Finally, nothing should be left undone in the effort to secure voluntary acceptance of such restraints and compulsions as it is decided to use.[4]

The implications of the last point call for some elaboration. Frequently restraints whose source is social rather than political receive a wider willing acceptance than do governmental restraints. We may dislike a social convention that effectively prevents us from wearing the kind of clothes we would prefer if left to our own tastes, but it does not fill us with the rebellious indignation that would be our reaction to a state decree governing styles. In fact, the former, of course, leaves us with greater freedom of action. We can retain our liberty by defying public opinion, but to defy the law will certainly cost us our

[4] It may seem that to speak of voluntary acceptance of restraints and compulsions is self-contradictory. The difficulty, however, is verbal. Frequently we are entirely willing to accept a limitation on our action provided others are similarly limited; but most of us would not accept it until we are provided with that assurance of general acceptance which comes only from the sanction of law. (This is the element of truth in Hobbes's statement that there is no justice or injustice in the state of nature.) For instance, although we may chafe somewhat under the requirement to pay taxes, we do not consider a just tax an infringement of our liberty. But if others similarly situated did not have to pay taxes, while we did, we would most certainly consider it a monstrous tyranny. Furthermore, there is often a contrast between our purposes and our momentary desires. I may need to be restrained from driving through a red light even though I should be the last to vote to remove the penalty for such behavior.

liberty in the fullest sense. Similarly, the very indirect (although very effective!) restraints imposed by the market, operating through the price system, generally involve less frustration than does governmental rationing. Here, too, the real choice left by the nongovernmental restraint is greater; it at least allows us to choose whether to go without meat or without butter. In both of the examples cited, however, the difference between the social and the political restraint is partly that in the former case it is harder to identify the responsible parties, and so harder to locate a focus for indignation.

It also follows from the value of voluntary acceptance of constraints and restrictions that there should be a maximum of popular participation in the determination of governmental policy. Other things being equal, this calls for both legislative and administrative decentralization.[5]

Now there are today undeniably numerous trends and conditions that appear to threaten one aspect or another of liberty as here defined. They have been pointed out in earlier chapters. It will be useful to recapitulate them at this point. First there is materialism, with its attendant loss of enthusiasm—especially for liberty. Then there are the various factors making for social disintegration. Third equalitarianism itself, one of the primary elements of liberal democracy, threatens liberty when it is carried too far. Finally, there is the tremendous growth in both the areas and the scope and nature of organized controls.

1. Materialism and Other Disintegrative Forces

The first two of these items we can treat very briefly because they have been discussed elsewhere. In a previous chapter[6] we saw that the oft-lamented loss of esteem for liberty has probably been greatly exaggerated. It was pointed out there that while materialism has contributed to such a development, there is reason to believe that other factors have tended to coun-

---

[5] Not only is participation a key to acceptance, it is also in itself one type of that very self-direction that is the essence of liberty.

[6] Chap. VII.

teract this effect and that there is considerable evidence of a recrudescence of interest in liberty at the present time. There is cause for concern, but certainly not for despair.

Furthermore, governments may take positive, educational action to invigorate the love of liberty. The "Freedom Train" that toured the United States in 1947 is a small example of the sort of thing that can and should be done. We have hardly begun to exploit the possibilities of democratic education for freedom— not of indoctrination with the value of any particular economic system or form of government, but with the value of freedom itself.[7] Any trend toward social disintegration endangers liberty in two quite different ways. First, and most obviously, it erodes the foundations of mutual trust and tolerance. But, more than this, insofar as social disintegration means not only the development of rifts among groups but also the weakening and disappearance of social restraints that tend to produce a measure of conformity to a common social pattern, to that extent it deprives society of an important, perhaps an essential, shock absorber. The point has seldom been better put than by Adolf Löwe in his essay *The Price of Liberty:* "A large-scale society can stand the strain of freedom of action on the part of its members only if the individualization of those members is kept within definite limits. The individual must pay for this freedom by being turned to a certain extent into a type. The price of liberalism as a social principle is the sacrifice of self-indulgence."[8] Herein he finds the secret of English liberty—in a spontaneous collectivism that transcends the boldest dreams of fascism and communism, whereas, as he puts it, the German body politic, with greater individualization, "exhausts its strength between the extremes of

---

[7] This also has been discussed above (pp. 292–295). It might even be suggested that materialism itself, which we have suggested tends to depreciate interest in freedom, could be directly attacked by governments, as by checking the pace of material progress or by limiting advertising. It seems unlikely, however, that materialistically minded people will freely seek to limit their own materialism.

[8] Adolf Löwe, *The Price of Liberty: a German on Contemporary Britain,* trans. Elsa Sinclair, "Day to Day Pamphlets," No. 36 (London: The Hogarth Press, 1937), p. 23.

disintegration and autocracy." [9] It might seem that we have here only a choice between two despotisms, but it involves the critical difference between social and political control discussed above.

That there are powerful disintegrative forces at work in modern society we have been at pains to point out; but we have also shown in the preceding chapter that the means for counteracting these forces are at hand. More perhaps than is true of the forces tending to reinvigorate the love of liberty, they depend upon positive action on the part of government and other social organizations; but such action is already being taken on an important scale, and there is every reason to anticipate that the future will see ever-increasing attention being given to this vital portion of the democratic agenda.

2. *Equalitarianism*

In the case of the growth of equalitarianism as with materialism, it is both the theory and the practice that are threats to liberty. It is clear that the ideal of equality *may* run counter to that of liberty. Where equality is taken to mean absolute equality, it is incompatible with the liberty of each to develop his capacities to the fullest. In this sense the ideal of equality leads straight to the concentration camp, where it is most fully realized. In fact, anyone who ranks equality of status, whether absolute or relative, as the prime value will end up by putting people where they belong for their own good or for the good of society, regardless of pleas for individual autonomy. In other words, where the ideal of equality stems from concern for the individual, it cannot run counter to liberty, for that is basic to the welfare of the individual; but where it becomes an end-in-itself it is antithetical to liberty.

On the practical side, the equalitarian movement may easily have similar consequences. Historically, it has been the middle classes that have been the greatest supporters of liberty because —apart from other reasons—it was to their interest to overthrow feudal and mercantilistic restrictions. Today the equalitarian

[9] *Ibid.*, p. 24.

movement has transferred political power in large measure to those who are further down the economic ladder. Just as it was to the interest of the rising *bourgeoisie* to fight for liberty, so it is to the apparent interest of the working classes to strive (or strike) for security. They have known the ills of both slavery and economic insecurity; but they have known the latter more recently, for it is still with them. It is therefore only natural that this increasingly powerful part of society should tend to minimize the value of liberty whenever it seems to conflict with security.[10]

Insofar as love of liberty is threatened by equalitarianism, the answers are clear enough in principle. It seems likely that demands for absolute equality gain general acceptance chiefly where equality of opportunity is not effectively operating. Certainly in the United States there has in general been a greater degree of equality of opportunity regardless of "class" than in most other countries, and the ideal of absolute economic equality has had singularly little following here. This clearly means that it is a simple rule of self-preservation for liberal democracies to maximize equality of opportunity by such means as improving and further expanding the facilities for free education for all to the extent to which their capacities warrant, continuing and perhaps extending the policy of high and steeply graduated inherit-

[10] Cf. Lecky's argument, stated briefly in the following passage: "Equality is the idol of democracy, but, with the infinitely various capacities and energies of men, this can only be attained by a constant, systematic, stringent repression of their natural development. . . . To place the chief power in the most ignorant classes is to place it in the hands of those who naturally care least for political liberty, and who are most likely to follow with an absolute devotion some strong leader. . . . in all countries and ages it is the upper and middle classes who have chiefly valued constitutional liberty, and those classes it is the work of democracy to dethrone."— W. E. H. Lecky, *Democracy and Liberty* (2 vols., new ed.; New York: Longmans, Green and Co., 1899), I, 256, 259; see generally pp. 256–261. Note also Guido de Ruggiero's remark that "the democratic dislike of everything inconsistent, with its feeling for equality and social uniformity leads it to reject the consequences of this spontaneous social differentiation either by an arbitrary degradation of those members that have risen, or by an artificial elevation of those that have remained beneath."—*The History of European Liberalism*, trans. R. G. Collingwood (London: Oxford University Press, 1927), p. 373.

ance taxes, and facilitating the initiation and development of small enterprises.

Insofar as liberty is threatened by an overpowering interest in security, an obvious remedy is the provision of greater security. Great strides have been made in recent years in the enlargement of "social security" measures. More remains to be done. Furthermore, it is almost universally agreed today that democracies must avoid prolonged mass unemployment in the future if free governments are to survive. Whether this can be accomplished remains to be seen. It is clear, however, that if mass unemployment threatens again, democratic governments will not hesitate to take vigorous action to avert it. This raises the further question of whether such general state management of the economic system as this action might lead to would itself be compatible with liberal democracy. This is a problem to which we shall turn in the next chapter.

3. Centralization

Finally, there is the growth in both the areas and the scope and nature of organized controls.[11] We shall deal first with the enlargement of the areas of control.[12] Decentralization of power, whatever its disadvantages, is generally believed to be favorable to liberty. It is true that a small tyranny may be as great as a large one. In no small measure the reason that centralization of power is feared by lovers of liberty is that it makes practicable an enlargement of the *scope* of control. It is also true that decentralized power amounts to a kind of hedging against abuse of power. It is unlikely that abuse will triumph in all of a number of relatively independent centers. But by the same token it is unlikely that all will escape abuse. For a country as a whole the risk for liberty is greater under centralization, other things being

[11] These developments are in some measure causes of the trends discussed above and in some degree effects of them, although they are also in some degree independent.

[12] The facts regarding this development in Britain and America were set forth in Chap. IX (above, pp. 178–179).

equal, but so also is the possibility of a maximum of freedom. From this point of view, centralization would appear not to affect the balance of probabilities but only the magnitude of what is at stake.

More than this, however, it has been a commonplace of political science that, while centralization may lead to greater efficiency and more effective control, its effects upon political and civil liberty are unfortunate. The central government, remote from the average citizen geographically, tends likewise to be remote in the field of his interests—so the argument runs. It fails to evoke that active participation on the part of the citizen which is at once a tonic to him and a benefit to the government. At the same time the central government becomes so overloaded that it cannot perform its functions efficiently. The combined result of these tendencies, it is frequently alleged, is to produce apoplexy at the center and anemia at the extremities.

That there is truth in these arguments I would be far from denying. It may be suggested, however, that these generalizations of political science are in great need of qualification by that favorite phrase of the economists, "other things being equal." Perhaps even this proviso is not enough. The world is getting smaller, it need hardly be remarked, with the result that the modern equivalent of five miles from the parish pump may be five hundred miles, or more. In large measure, public interest will center on that level of government which does things that affect our lives most vitally. With the increase in the number of matters that cannot in the nature of things be effectively controlled locally, the premises on which the old arguments about centralization rest are automatically modified.

By way of verification of this line of reasoning, it may be pointed out that in the United States national elections invariably call forth a larger vote than do local elections. Let the reader think for himself whether he knows, cares, and thinks more about the activities of his state legislature or of the national legislature. Election statistics show a long-term rise in the proportion of eligible voters who cast their ballots in national elections.[13] This does not seem to betoken the onset of anemia.

What, then, about the apoplexy? That there are serious dangers to liberty (and even to efficiency) inherent in centralization cannot be denied, nor need it be asserted that those dangers have not in some degree materialized. What is, however, very important to make clear is that the remedy for these ills may be found at least in important measure in administrative rather than legislative decentralization. It is often discovered some time after a function has been transferred to the central government that it can be best administered, following an initial period for experimentation and establishment of general policies, with a maximum of decentralization and local participation. In the United States the Tennessee Valley Authority and the Department of Agriculture are outstanding examples of national administrative agencies that have achieved great success in decentralizing their operations and in enlisting local cooperation both in the development and in the application of their policies. They have found this conducive to the highest efficiency and that it provides not only the stimulus to local interest that accompanies actual participation but a very important check on bureaucratic rigidity and infringement of the proper sphere of liberty.[14] In brief, although threats to both political and civil lib-

---

[13] The percentages of the total population of the United States who voted for President at recent elections are as follows:

1920	25
1924	25
1928	31
1932	32
1936	36
1940	38
1944	(not comparable because of large numbers in the armed forces)
1948	33

The last figure is derived from election figures given in the New York *Times* for Dec. 12, 1948, Sec. 4, p. 7. Other figures are from *Information Please Almanac, 1948* (New York: Doubleday Company, 1947), p. 117.

[14] The literature on this subject is almost limitless. See, for example, Rensis Likert, "Democracy in Agriculture—Why and How?" in U. S. Department of Agriculture, *Farmers in a Changing World*, "Yearbook of Agriculture," 1940 (Washington, D. C.: Government Printing Office, 1940), pp. 994–1002, and other articles in Parts 5 and 6 of this volume; and C.

erty are inherent in the centralization movement, they need not be realized. Centralization that is based on sound principles and that constantly seeks out avenues of bringing in citizen participation and influence on the administrative level may increase efficiency without diminishing liberty. There is considerable evidence that in Britain and in the United States the movement is in this direction.

It may be, however, that the real threat to liberty implicit in enlargement in the size of governmental units lies in its effect on the spirit of individualism, on the idea of the autonomy, the rights, the "sacredness" of the individual. The belief in individualism in this sense, as well as the spirit of readiness to defend the belief and what it stands for, is, as we have seen, one of the essential conditions of liberty. Under conditions where significant (and, especially, politically effective) groupings are large, the individual tends to be lost sight of, and the sense of his worth, his "infinite value," tends to decline. Anyone who has experienced the difference between a large school or college and a small one, or between a large factory and a small shop, cannot help realize that the smaller unit is more favorable to consideration of the individual—especially to that vital kind of consideration which takes account of individual differences.

To be sure, in the examples just given, the psychological change takes place in governors who are not democratically held accountable. But even in a democracy, those charged with the job of government must of necessity exercise such a large measure of free discretionary authority that their attitude toward those whom their acts affect is immensely important. Furthermore not only officials but also the mass of the people themselves tend, in an era of mass government, mass education, mass

---

Herman Pritchett, *The Tennessee Valley Authority* (Chapel Hill: University of North Carolina Press, 1943), Chap. 5; R. Clyde White, "Local Participation in Social Security Administration," *Public Administration Review*, V (Spring, 1945), 141–147.

See also Winston W. Crouch, "Trends in British Local Government," *Public Administration Review*, VII (Autumn, 1947), 254–262.

production, and massive pressure groups, to think quantitatively rather than qualitatively. It is not that the whole is conceived of as having a value greater than that of the sum of its parts, although in extreme cases this may happen. Nor is it even that people cease to believe in equality of rights. If anything, the fact of large units seems to be favorable to this belief.[15] But the quality of the rights maintained is affected in two ways. First, viewing people in large numbers is not conducive to appreciation of differences. Distinctions tend to be blurred, and one becomes less conscious of the injuries done to individual needs by submitting all to a common pattern. It is probably also true that one more easily makes all human experience commensurable, being willing, that is to say, to sacrifice the vital interests of a few for a much less important interest of large numbers of people.

This is a highly speculative argument and is for that reason difficult to appraise. We previously examined the evidence and found little reason for believing that respect for the individual as such has significantly declined in the United States or in Great Britain up to this point.[16] The movement under discussion, however, is a relatively recent one, and it is possible that all its effects have not yet manifested themselves. The only answer to the tendency—and it may be a sufficient one—would appear to be constant vigilance to maximize administrative decentralization, to make the fullest use of citizen participation at the administrative level, and in general to find and use every opportunity for the introduction of the group process that we have seen to be such an essential part of liberal democracy.[17] Here, as elsewhere, the answer is not to be found purely in terms of governmental organization and procedure; in no small part the practices of industry and of nongovernmental community organization will play a decisive role.

[15] It is significant that it was not until the city-state had given way to the empire that the ideal of human equality really took hold.

[16] See above, pp. 146–148.

[17] See above, pp. 234–239.

4. Enlarged Scope and Altered Nature of Control

We turn now to the implications for liberty of the enlarged scope and altered nature of governmental controls previously described.[18] We shall consider the effects upon the chief institutions of government—the legislature, the relationship between legislature and executive, and the judiciary and the rights traditionally dependent upon it for enforcement.

EFFECT ON JUDICIALLY PROTECTED RIGHTS.   To begin with the judiciary and judicially protected rights, it seems hardly open to question that the factors discussed above[19] will continue to operate. Such absolute or near-absolute rights as those of property and freedom of contract are not likely to resume their former role in the dynamic society of the present day. The new, positive rights nowadays achieving growing recognition, such as the right to useful work, and to adequate housing and medical care, are much less suited to precise definition or to judicial enforcement than the older, negative rights. Courts are better fitted for preventing action than for compelling it, especially where, as generally is the case, the means to be taken to achieve the desired (or even guaranteed) end is a matter requiring the exercise of discretion. We may take it for granted that the realm of individual freedom of action from governmental restraints is bound to go on decreasing. The problem will be more and more. one of distinguishing between governmental action that curbs liberty and that which increases it on the whole even while imposing certain restraints. This again is not a task for which the courts are a useful instrumentality.

Before going further with this analysis it is fitting to remind ourselves that constitutionalism is by no means to be identified

---

[18] For a description of these developments and for a general consideration of their consequences, without special reference to the prospects of liberty, see Chap. IX.

[19] We shall include here not only the changed nature and scope of governmental controls but also the factors in the realm of ideas, the impact of which on constitutionalism was discussed in Chap. IX.

with the institution of judicial review as developed in the United States. Here the judiciary has rendered a useful service in this connection (although whether the harm it has done is not even greater is an open question), but Great Britain supplies the outstanding example of a country in which civil liberties have been admirably respected through the sheer force of public opinion acting through a sovereign legislature. Whether the American record would be equally good were we suddenly to dispense with judicial review is another question. The judiciary possesses (even yet) an extraordinary prestige in the United States that enables it to act as a shock absorber against waves of intolerance and as a rallying point for the forces in support of civil liberty. When we learn that a public opinion poll finds that 39 per cent of Americans believe that Communists should not be allowed to speak over the radio,[20] we realize that the margin supporting our freedom of speech is uncomfortably thin and that we need all possible supports against sudden attacks at vulnerable points. In any case, liberty of expression is perhaps the one area in the United States in which judicial review appears to be operating with even increasing effectiveness. But the point here is that insofar as the judiciary becomes a less effective check, it is at least possible that its declining effectiveness may be compensated for by a general development of political maturity reflected in such an appreciation of the value of civil liberties as the British public has long manifested.[21]

All of this is not to say, however, that the courts cannot and will not continue to play an important role in protecting areas of freedom vital to liberal democracy. One of the most fundamental principles of constitutional liberty is that of the rule of law. This is much less subject to the blurring effects at-

[20] National Opinion Research Center poll, reported in *Public Opinion Quarterly*, X (Fall, 1946), 409.

[21] For the benefit of any who might think that this is very improbable in view of the poll results referred to above, it should be remarked that we have no significant trend line on public opinion in this matter, and also that it appears not unlikely that the fuller thought and discussion that would be involved in an attempt to take legislative action would operate in favor of maintenance of liberty.

tendant upon the complications of modern society than many other "rights." Courts can continue to insist that, whatever the content of legislation, it must be applied alike to all who are similarly situated. They can continue to stand guard against the punishment of individuals for acts that were not crimes when committed or whose commission has not been proved beyond a reasonable doubt under conditions historically established as essential to a fair trial.

It is true that modern states are forced to depend increasingly upon various types of administrative agencies for the elaboration and application of law, and that such agencies frequently exercise wide discretionary authority. It does not follow, however, that the rule of law has given way to administrative despotism. There are numerous safeguards against the abuse of administrative discretion.[22] The legislature may prescribe judicially enforceable standards or tests to control both the manner in which administrative power is exercised and the uses to which it is put. In many situations it is appropriate for administrative authorities themselves to act by means of promulgating general rules rather than orders of specific application, thus assuring the like treatment of those who are similarly circumstanced. In other cases, where the subject matter of regulation is too protean to admit of treatment by ready-made forms, administrative agencies may still be able to develop, over a period of time, a set of standards to give guidance to themselves and to the interests being regulated. Possibly more important than such devices is the assurance by appropriate means that all affected interests will be given an opportunity to have their say and that decisions will be made only after a careful study of all the evidence and arguments, by experts or on the basis of the recommendations of experts.

Furthermore, much of the talk about administrative lawlessness loses sight of two very important facts: administrative ac-

---

[22] For a fuller treatment of this subject, see J. Roland Pennock, *Administration and the Rule of Law* (New York: Rinehart & Company, Inc., 1941), esp. Chaps. 2, 3.

tion is typically (although not always) prospective rather than retrospective; and in any case, it deals with civil rather than criminal penalties. The strict version of the "rule of law" was formulated as a guarantee against arbitrary punishment. Our administrative agencies do not deal out punishment. They restrain, as when the Federal Trade Commission orders the cement industry to "cease and desist" from the practice of freight absorption; or they direct, as when the National Labor Relations Board orders a business concern to recognize a particular union for purposes of collective bargaining; or they withdraw a privilege, as when the Federal Communications Commission refuses to renew a license for radio broadcasting; or they seek to correct the damage done by illegal action, as when the National Labor Relations Board orders an employer to re-employ a dismissed employee and to give him back pay for the period during which he had been illegally dismissed. These are important actions, of great moment to the people affected. They may even make the difference between financial success and bankruptcy. It is therefore not meant to suggest that we can afford to allow such actions to be arbitrary. Nevertheless it is important to remember that Anglo-American law has traditionally (and, it is believed, rightly) taken greater precautions to ensure against injustice where criminal punishment (which might take away personal liberty) is involved than where the action is one dealing at most with property rights.

Finally, in this connection, it may be observed that the rule of law receives support from a source not yet mentioned and which tends to give it immunity from the trends that have been militating against certain other aspects of constitutionalism. It is supported by that part of the liberal-democratic myth that is in the ascendant, equalitarianism. This statement, it is true, needs qualification. Equalitarianism certainly can work against the very equality of treatment that is the heart of the rule of law. If it is directed toward achieving economic equality at all costs, it may justify almost any means that seem useful. It therefore becomes a task of liberal-democratic statesmanship to maintain and constantly to reinforce the tradition that equality means equality before the law. As suggested above,[23] it seems probable that the concept of justice as relative (that is, relative to merit—demanding equality of opportunity but not equality of rewards) will prevail as long as equality of opportunity is measurably realized.

The case of freedom of expression calls for special comment. In spite of the good record in the United States in recent years, there are reasons for concern. Even during the thirties, there was a noticeable reaction by intellectuals and others against the use of democratic liberties by antiliberal forces with the intent of undermining liberalism itself. It has been traditionally recognized by liberals that incitement to illegal action is properly excluded from the protection of the First Amendment. Just as we do not allow a person who induces a man to commit a murder to go scot-free, so also we recognize the culpability of one who incites to riot or rebellion. The Supreme Court has attempted to define the line between incitement and free speech by the "clear and present danger" test. During recent years the people of the United States have witnessed the interesting spectacle of a Court committed in general to a functional approach and to the belief that all the people's rights are relative, holding up the "clear and present danger" test more than ever as a sufficient basis for decision in cases involving freedom of expression.[24] Liberals may well be encouraged by this fact until they reflect upon the anomaly it but thinly veils. How long can a judiciary that has grown used to thinking of all legal questions as matters of degree be expected to make this exception? More specifically, how long will it refuse to follow the reasoning that

[23] Above, p. 310.

[24] See Vincent M. Barnett, Jr., "Mr. Justice Murphy, Civil Liberties and the Holmes Tradition," *Cornell Law Quarterly*, XXXII (Nov., 1946), 177–221; Robert G. Cushman, " 'Clear and Present Danger' in Free Speech Cases: a Study in Judicial Semantics," in Milton R. Konvitz and Arthur G. Murphy (eds.), *Essays in Political Theory, presented to George H. Sabine* (Ithaca: Cornell University Press, 1948), pp. 311–324; and David Fellman, "Recent Tendencies in Civil Liberties Decisions of the Supreme Court," *Cornell Law Quarterly*, XXXIV (Spring, 1949), 331–351.

led the same bench after the First World War to accept the logic of the "bad tendency" test?[25] This is the argument that any speech or publication, the necessary tendency of which is to lead to illegal action, may be banned. Why jail the little soapbox orator while allowing the author of the arguments he espouses free rein? In my opinion there is an adequate reply to this position in terms of the need for a clear line and the great danger of abuse of any such indefinite standard as the "bad tendency" test; but whether a Court generally confident of its own ability to apply the law in terms of such calculations of degree will continue to do so is a different question.[26]

Another factor calculated to weaken the resistance of defenders of freedom of expression is the increasing use of appeals to the baser emotions and passions, and to prejudice. It is indeed a plausible argument to say that, since the whole justification for freedom of expression is based upon its tendency to favor the formation of rational opinion, it should not be used to defend propaganda that makes no appeal to reason but rather seeks to stir up those passions most likely to interfere with rational proc-

[25] Possibly only while the Court is dominated by those for whom the doctrines of the later Mr. Justice Holmes are (perhaps fortunately) something of a fetish.

[26] Cf. Holmes's oft-quoted dictum, "The power to tax is not the power to destroy while this Court sits."—*Panhandle Oil Co. v. Miss.*, 277 U. S. 218 (1928), at p. 223.

The "clear and present danger" test has come in for considerable criticism of late, both from those who believe it permits too much control and from those who believe it does not allow enough. It is indeed less precise than would be desirable. Granted that the danger must be "clear" and "present," how serious must it be? If *any* words, no matter how important is liberty in the context in question, may be punishable if they involve clear and present danger of even the slightest disorder, it would seem that the protection given by the formula is hardly adequate. On the other hand, if the very life of the nation must be threatened before restrictive action can be taken, the test probably errs in the opposite direction. Until a better test is devised, we must rely upon the Court to prick out a sound line between these extremes. (Dr. Alexander Meiklejohn's attempt to use a distinction between public and private spheres of speech as a substitute for the Court's test does not seem to represent an advance in precision. See his *Free Speech and Its Relation to Self-Government* [New York: Harper & Brothers, 1948]. See also Arthur M. Schlesinger, Jr., *The Vital Center—the Politics of Freedom* [Boston: Houghton Mifflin Company, 1949].)

esses. The argument is reinforced when it is directed against those who are acting in bad faith vis-à-vis democracy, who are seeking to stir up general discontent not with the idea of channeling it into avenues of effective democratic action but with the idea of destroying that unity (by arousing group hatreds) without which democracy cannot effectively function. Examples of such practice both here and abroad have become commonplace, with the result that many have come to echo the idea expressed by an English writer that we must modify our traditional concepts of civil liberties in the direction of distinguishing between "theories and beliefs propounded with intellectual honesty and the typical rubbish of the venal journalist." [27] In this country, Professor Sorokin expresses a like concern. He writes:

> Freedom of speech, of the press, and of thought are the greatest boons when they are not dissociated from moral and social responsibilities. When, however, they degenerate into irresponsible and unbridled propaganda . . . or the means of discrediting and undermining precious values, they become a societal and cultural poison infinitely worse than the denial of freedom of thought and expression.[28]

In view of the threats of judicial relativism and of abuses of freedom of expression, are the judicial and popular bulwarks likely to retain their effectiveness? There can be no absolute assurance of this, but British experience, in addition to the recent history of the American Supreme Court, gives ground for confidence that the courts will continue to set high store by civil liberties. As for public opinion, which is fundamental in the final analysis, it would appear that, on the domestic side, two factors will be determinative. One is the general attitude of tolerance or intolerance; the other is the extent to which freedom of expression is subject to abuse. Fortunately, both are in some measure subject to public control. Much of what was said in the preceding

[27] M. Alderton Pink, *A Realist Looks at Democracy* (London: Ernest Benn, Ltd., 1930), p. 150.

[28] Pitirim Sorokin, *The Crisis of Our Age*, p. 198. Copyright, 1941, by E. P. Dutton & Co. Reprinted by permission of E. P. Dutton & Co., publishers.

chapter about the fostering of psychological health and of social unity is pertinent to the encouragement of attitudes of tolerance.[29] And what was said in the chapter before that concerning devices for improving and purifying public opinion—both by providing real equality of access to the mediums of opinion formation and by taking steps to check the irresponsible dissemination of falsehood and malicious appeals to passion and prejudice —points the way to checking the abuses that would discredit essential freedoms if they were allowed to go unchecked. We have seen, too, that some steps in each of these directions have already been taken—enough to encourage the hope that liberal democracies will use the means at their disposal to protect this *sine qua non* of liberalism.

In addition to these domestic factors, the foreign situation— specifically, the relations of the United States with the Soviet Union—adds a grim imponderable to the situation. There can be no gainsaying the fact that cold warfare, conducted in large measure with ideological weapons, imposes a severe test upon liberal traditions and institutions.

EFFECT ON THE LEGISLATURE AND ON LEGISLATIVE-EXECUTIVE BALANCE. Historically it has been felt, and rightly felt, that the legislature is the palladium of democratic liberties. The fact that there has been a tendency for the legislature to be eclipsed by the executive-administrative branch of government is therefore properly a matter for concern. That there has been such a

[29] The growth of skepticism is not dealt with separately as a threat to tolerance here because it is believed, as was argued in the preceding chapter, that this trend will not get out of hand if a reasonably high level of psychological security is maintained. It should perhaps be remarked, however, that it would be unsafe to dismiss skepticism regarding human rationality as a threat to tolerance on the ground that it in fact provides a strong argument *for* tolerance. Regardless of the validity of the latter argument, it appears probable that the psychological effect of doubts as to the power of reason is to encourage suppression of ideas; while, on the other hand, the more certain a person is that reason will in the end prevail, the more willing he will be to allow free play to discussion and to await the results of this process. Cf. Waldo Beach, "The Basis of Tolerance in a Democratic Society," *Ethics*, LVII (Apr., 1947), 157–169.

trend can hardly be denied.[30] Partly this is a matter merely of the great increase in the numbers of those employed in administration. Partly it is a matter of the remarkable growth in the delegation of discretionary authority to executive or administrative officials that has characterized representative governments generally. Both of these trends are absolutely inescapable, for reasons that need not be elaborated here. In Britain, it is also a matter of strengthened party discipline, which has limited the independence of the member of Parliament, that is to say his power as an individual, and has at least seemed to weaken Parliament as a whole as compared with the cabinet. These trends have appeared to weaken the legislature in two different ways: by increasing the power of the executive, which might then in some measure be used against the legislature itself, and by lowering the prestige and the self-respect of the legislature, with the long-run consequence that it becomes less attractive to potential candidates for legislative office.

Closer analysis, however, suggests that in part the weakening of the legislature is more apparent than real, and that in part it can be counteracted. Except as it adds to the prestige of the administrative branch, the mere matter of numbers has no significant bearing on this problem. It may increase the power of the administration at the polls, but that is a question to be considered in the next chapter. Far more important is the matter of the vast grants of discretionary authority nowadays made to administrative officials and chief executives. These grants may be effective both by increasing the relative prestige of the administrative branch and by giving it power that it may use to influence the electorate and so, indirectly, the legislature itself. Before we jump to the conclusion that this process has markedly altered the balance of power, however, we must consider other aspects of the situation. One of these is the fact that the total effective power of government has increased tremendously. The development of the positive state has added powers to both legislative and executive branches. In the case of the executive

[30] See above, pp. 180–186.

branch, the added powers are more obvious because they are accompanied by a growth in personnel and because they involve the exercise of discretionary authority by officials who formerly had virtually no such authority. When the government embarks upon a river-development program, for example, attention is naturally concentrated upon the administrative agency that carries it out; but it was Congress that determined the project should be undertaken. It is Congress, too, that makes the all-important annual appropriations, not infrequently hedging them about with conditions as to policy and all too frequently even as to legislative detail. When Congress is in a spending mood and budget balancing is out of favor, the importance of this aspect of legislative control is easily minimized; but in a period of retrenchment it becomes very obvious who controls the purse strings and how pervasive and complete that control is. It might well be likened to the power to open or close the valves of a desert irrigation system.[31]

It is true the power of the legislature is sometimes more apparent than real. Most modern regulatory statutes, for example, delegate to administrative agencies vast discretionary authority that in practice would be completely beyond the resources of the legislature to exercise itself. But, on the other hand, administrative power is often subject to a similar discount. In the case of an administrator who has the legal authority to allocate certain funds for housing projects, let us assume that the question of further appropriations for his agency is about to come up and that a close vote is in prospect. Let us assume further that certain wavering congressmen hold the balance of power and that their judgment on the matter might be substantially affected by revising the hitherto prevailing standards for the allocation of these funds in such a way that the districts of the congressmen in question might be benefited. That this is by no means an unrealistic example anyone with experience in the field will testify.

[31] The extent to which this continuing control is actually exercised has been demonstrated by Professor Arthur Macmahon in "Congressional Oversight of Administration: The Power of the Purse," *Political Science Quarterly*, LVIII (June, 1943), 161–190, and LVIII (Sept., 1943), 380–414.

Is it an example of the power of administration to control the legislature, or the reverse? Perhaps this illustrates better the power of a few congressmen than of Congress as a whole. A better case is the actual one of the OPA and grade labeling. It was clear that those charged with administration of the Price Control Act felt that it would be a great assistance to them in carrying out their mandate from Congress to require grade labeling of certain products. It is equally clear that they were prevented from doing so by the hostility of Congress to this particular device. Instances of this sort could be multiplied indefinitely.

Our examples on this point have all been drawn from American government. The nature of the cabinet system as it operates in Great Britain is such that it is a great deal more difficult to tell who is in the driver's seat. Superficially at least, the appearance is that the cabinet is in the dominant position. But then, of course, the cabinet is really a committee of the legislature. Is the cabinet, in turn, dominated by the administration, that is, by the civil service? It is sometimes charged that it is, but it seems fairly clear that this is certainly not the rule in matters of major policy. In a day when the government in England, responding, of course, to an electoral mandate, is making such momentous decisions as are involved in the nationalization of the coal mines, of the Bank of England, and of the transport system, it seems hardly necessary to labor this point. The experience of the present government in England also throws light on the question whether the Commons as such is now only a pawn in the hands of the cabinet. In spite of its tremendous majority in the House, that government has on several occasions had to modify its proposals in order to satisfy its own parliamentary supporters.[32] It is to such relatively obscure and back-

[32] For example, even the present Labour Government, with its huge majority, had to yield to pressure from the rank and file on the matter of abolishing capital punishment, in 1948. The coalition government, in 1944, made substantial modifications in the Education Bill as a result of opposition in the House of Commons. For earlier instances, see Harold J. Laski, *Parliamentary Government in England* (New York: The Viking Press, 1938), pp. 127–128.

stage maneuvers as these, rather than to the record of votes, that we must look for evidence as to the legislative-executive balance in Great Britain. And when we make such an examination, while it is clear that with the growth of party discipline the individual member of Parliament has lost much of his independence, it is by no means clear that the parties are any less subject to the rank and file of their parliamentary membership than in the past.

All of this is not to deny that changes are taking place in the kind of problems with which legislatures must deal or that these changes call for periodic alterations in their organization and procedure. Such a reorganization has recently been undertaken in the United States. Whether it has gone far enough is open to question, as is also the advisability of certain of the steps actually taken.[33] The provision of technical staffs for Congressional committees constitutes both a recognition of the fact that such assistance is necessary if congressmen are going to have the knowledge that will enable them to hold their own in dealings with representatives of the administration and an important step toward redressing the balance in this matter. But this is not the place to engage in a discussion of the merits of this particular act. Congress has made a step toward ridding itself of some of its nonlegislative functions and toward equipping itself to deal more effectively with broad questions of policy. There is much more that it could do. The point here is simply that there is much that can be done and that there is no reason to believe that, by successive changes, the legislature cannot retain its position as a major partner in the determination of national policy.

Britain's more flexible system allows similar changes to take place more gradually and with less general notice. Yet even in England there is talk of the need for legislative reform and no

---

[33] For a good critical review of the Legislative Reorganization Act of 1946 and also of various studies on which in large measure it was based, see Joseph P. Harris, "The Reorganization of Congress," *Public Administration Review*, VI (Summer, 1946), 267–282. For a fuller discussion of the subject see George B. Galloway, *Congress at the Crossroads* (New York: Thomas Y. Crowell Company, 1947).

dearth of suggestions as to how it should be achieved.[34] It is certainly true that the problem of combining effective parliamentary control of the purse with the principle of responsible government remains unsolved there, with results that call forth a great deal of complaint.[35] On the other hand, with reference to the fundamental problem of the ability of Parliament to continue to attract men of high caliber, the most basic fact remains unchanged: membership in Parliament continues to be the only avenue to a ministerial post. This in itself assures a certain rough equivalence of talent between government and legislature.

5. Conclusion

In conclusion, it is unnecessary to recapitulate what has been said regarding the threats to liberty inherent in materialism, equalitarianism, social disintegration, and the growth of governmental power. In general we have found that the trends allegedly unfavorable to liberty have been exaggerated, that countervailing trends are often overlooked, and that, furthermore, various remedies for particular ill effects of the trends in question are available. In short, new problems for liberalism are constantly arising, and many of the old ones are becoming more acute; at the same time new devices for meeting these problems keep coming to the fore. The evidence, on balance, does not support the belief that essential liberties are declining or must decline.

A final proviso is in order. We have argued that psychologically healthy individuals in well-adjusted communities tend to give loyal support to democratic institutions. The converse of this proposition is that when men are driven to despair by conditions that seem to be beyond their control, they will seek surcease from their woes and relief from responsibility by turning to Authority. The point is well put by Professor MacIver in words difficult to improve upon:

[34] See William I. Jennings, *Paliamentary Reform* (London: Victor Gollancz, Ltd., 1934), Chaps. 4, 9.

[35] See Ramsay Muir, *How Britain Is Governed* (New York: Richard R. Smith, Inc., 1930), pp. 218–235.

When men are too sorely tried, when their hopes are shattered, when their livelihood is rendered precarious, when the tides of disastrous change have overwhelmed them, when they have lost their moorings, then they are trapped between the opposing bids of ruthless prophets of power, who promise them deliverance at the price of liberty. The worse the conditions or the more violent the crisis, the smaller chance is there that the ways of democracy can survive.[36]

The governments of societies threatened by severe economic crises are unlikely in the future to sit idly by while the crisis deepens. They will almost certainly attempt some sort of national economic planning. It is, of course, possible that the cure will be worse than the disease. It remains, then, to consider the implications for liberal democracy of national economic planning on a scale more extensive than the controls considered in this chapter. This will be the task of the following chapter.

[36] R. M. MacIver, *The Web of Government* (New York: The Macmillan Company, 1947), pp. 191–192.

CHAPTER XIV

PLANNING AND
LIBERAL DEMOCRACY

In discussing the prospects for liberty, in the preceding
chapter, we have dealt with the impact of the enlargement of the sphere of governmental functions; but many modern
ideas about "national economic planning" go so far beyond anything that has yet been attempted in a democratic state as to
constitute a qualitative rather than merely a quantitative difference in the problems raised. It is, of course, only with the political implications of these proposals and not with their economic
feasibility that we shall deal. For reasons that will appear, this
will be largely a matter of considering the effects on liberty, using that term to cover political as well as civil and personal
liberty.[1] The subject is a vast one, and the literature devoted to
it is very extensive. In spite of the fact that the center of attention of most writers on the subject has been on the economic
problems, the range of political considerations to be assessed is
so great that the present treatment must be highly synoptic.[2]

[1] Personal liberty is here used to stand for all elements of liberty as
previously defined that are not included in political or civil liberty.

[2] The subject is so important that we shall enumerate a few of the
most useful references that give attention to the political problem. The following writers, in varying degrees, take an unfavorable view of the implications of planning for democracy: Friedrich A. von Hayek, in *The Road
to Serfdom* (Chicago: The University of Chicago Press, 1944), and in
Freedom and the Economic System (Chicago: The University of Chicago
Press, 1939); Walter Lippmann in *An Inquiry Into the Principles of the
Good Society* (Boston: Little, Brown & Company, 1935, 1943); Ludwig
von Mises in *Bureaucracy* (New Haven: Yale University Press, 1944), and
in *Omnipotent Government—The Rise of the Total State and the Total
War* (New Haven: Yale University Press, 1945); Joseph A. Schumpeter in
Capitalism, Socialism and Democracy (2d ed.; New York: Harper & Broth-
ers, 1947), Pt. IV; John M. Clark in "Forms of Economic Liberty and What

To begin with, a word must be said about the use of terms. When we use the word "planning" alone, unless the context indicates otherwise, we refer to planning and controlling the economy on a national scale, by the government. Almost all government involves planning in some measure, but a government that followed a pure laissez-faire policy would "plan" only to the extent that the decision to pursue such a policy was itself a plan. Barbara Wootton's definition is a useful one. She defines planning as "the conscious and deliberate choice of economic priorities by some public authority."[3] The key point is the degree to which the determination of prices, and all that follows, is settled by the operation of the market process, and, conversely the extent to which the government makes these determinations itself. Broadly speaking, governments must choose between the polar alternatives of laissez faire and complete planning, or else select some point between these extremes.

Among the various way stations between the extremes a few may be singled out for brief mention. First there is planning for competition. It stretches the concept of planning as defined above to call this planning at all, but in any case a policy of

---

Makes Them Important," in Ruth Nanda Anshen (ed.), *Freedom—Its Meaning* (New York: Harcourt, Brace and Company, 1940), pp. 305–328; David McCord Wright in *Democracy and Progress* (New York: Macmillan & Co., 1948); and John Jewkes in *Ordeal by Planning* (London: The Macmillan Company, 1948). On the favorable side are the following: Herman Finer, *Road to Reaction* (Boston: Little, Brown & Company, 1945); Barbara Wootton, *Freedom under Planning* (Chapel Hill: The University of North Carolina Press, 1945); Carl Landauer, *Theory of National Economic Planning* (Berkeley and Los Angeles: University of California Press, 1944); Karl Mannheim, *Man and Society in an Age of Reconstruction* (New York: Harcourt, Brace and Company, 1940), Pts. V, VI; E. F. M. Durbin, *The Politics of Democratic Socialism* (London: Routledge and Kegan Paul, Ltd., 1940); George Soule, *A Planned Society* (New York: The Macmillan Company, 1932). Among the numerous books that present in some detail a middle-of-the-road solution, with the emphasis on preserving market determinations, Frank D. Graham's *Social Goals and Economic Institutions* (Princeton: Princeton University Press, 1942) is notable for its combination of political philosophy and economic theory. See also John Maurice Clark, *Alternative to Serfdom* (New York: Alfred A. Knopf, Inc., 1948).

[3] Wootton, *op. cit.*, p. 6. There are, of course, other quite proper and less restrictive uses of the word "planning" than the one used here, but they are not relevant for the present purpose.

governmental enforcement of competition by preventing or eliminating monopolies and monopolistic practices is a distinct possibility and quite different from pure laissez faire. Then there is what Mr. Lippmann calls a "compensated economy"—one in which the government confines its activities in this field largely to the effort to even out the business cycle by such devices as the manipulation of monetary and credit controls, the expenditure of public funds, and the use of the taxing power. A third type of planning, one that just skirts the definition given above, involves social insurance and similar measures for providing economic security. Going beyond this is a vaguely defined area that may be called "regulated capitalism." There are, of course, all degrees of regulation, but we are concerned with those that go to the heart of the market process. Price, rate, and wage fixing are the examples par excellence, but regulations affecting the flow of capital, the conditions under which new enterprises may be undertaken, the transfer of labor, and in general the terms on which business may be conducted fall in the same category. Such regulations may be applied either to all industry or only in selected areas of the economy. As regulations progressively narrow the range for business judgment and contractual agreements, they approach the point where the state must assume full responsibility as owner. The end point, therefore, for any particular branch of industry is collectivism.

It is clear, of course, that these policies are by no means mutually exclusive. In fact, the great majority of students of the subject would recommend some combination of all five of the possibilities suggested. With the extreme point of laissez faire we need not concern ourselves. It is academic in the extreme—impossible of attainment and not considered desirable even by the staunchest advocates of a free economy. On the other hand, comprehensive planning, such as would be involved either in a fully socialized state or in one where the government had complete potential control of the economy through such devices as subsidies and guaranteed profits as well as through taxation and other regulatory measures, must command our attention.[4] This procedure is indicated not merely because many people do favor this complete type of planning but also because in considering its political implications we shall go over most of the ground that needs to be covered for the appraisal of any particular combination of partial planning devices. It would be entirely out of the question to attempt separate appraisals of each of the part-planning devices within the scope of the present chapter.

1. Comprehensive Planning

PLANNING AND LIBERTY OF ACTION. We may begin our analysis of the political effects of comprehensive planning with certain general considerations about its probable effects on liberty. The very idea of comprehensive planning involves governmental control of acts that have hitherto been unregulated. If the planning should be carried out by means of commands and prohibitions affecting the detailed operation of economic processes it necessarily would mean a great restriction of liberty of action. The existing freedom to choose one's vocation, one's employer, and the way one would manage his savings or spend his income would give way in greater or less degree to regimentation in all these areas by governmental fiat. It might provide greater security or more equality, but it could hardly fail to reduce liberty. This is not to overlook the fact that we are by no means free agents in these areas today. Our freedom of choice is subject to many limits. But there is a difference, a vast difference, between deciding to become an electrician rather than a truck driver because one prefers the former or judges his prospects better in that line and, on the other hand, being told by an agency of the government that he will not be permitted to become a truck driver. There is an absolute finality and a potential brutality about the sanction of the law not attained by eco-

---

[4] It will be noted that we are using the term "comprehensive planning" to include situations falling somewhat short of really complete, or totalitarian, planning.

nomic sanctions except in the direst of circumstances. Furthermore, the wielders of economic sanctions today are many rather than one, and at least in some measure they are in competition with one another. There is much talk about the powerlessness of the employee—much talk that is singularly remote from actuality. Under conditions that prevail today in Britain and America, of course, it is obvious that most workmen can readily find alternative employment if they choose to quit their present occupation. The point to be stressed here, however, is that even in considerably less prosperous times, when to give up one's job may mean that one must choose between prolonged unemployment or accepting work on less favorable terms, the possibility of taking the latter alternative has a profound psychological significance for the worker. As long as this freedom exists, the worker has some power to wield and a tremendous buttress to his dignity and self-respect.

The other aspect of this freedom of the worker is restriction of the employer. It is not correct to say, as often is said, that the substitution of government control for market control creates no new power but merely redistributes it. When power is concentrated in one spot, monopolized, it becomes far greater than the sum of the powers so concentrated. If every employer, for example, had a complete monopoly of the possible sources of livelihood for his employees, then the creation of one gigantic government monopoly of employment (or control of employment) might be said to create no new power. Obviously this is far from the situation in contemporary capitalistic economies. Employers are limited by the fact that their employees may find other employment or become self-employed. Competition for labor, which would not exist if government controlled all employment, makes the difference between a vital area of freedom and potential wage slavery.

What has been said above proceeds on the assumption that planning would be executed by means of the power of the state to compel obedience to its orders under penalty of the law. This need not be the case. The state may substitute inducement for command. The optimum allocation of the labor supply may be accomplished by variations in wages rather than by compulsion. There is no assignable limit to the extent to which this kind of control might be used in lieu of positive commands. There are, however, certain practical factors that would operate as continuous temptations to governments to rely on command rather than inducement. One of these is the mere fact of simplicity. To arrange inducements with the nicety required to obtain the desired results would demand great ingenuity, and would probably not operate so quickly as commands. Furthermore, a system of financial inducements might result in such substantial inequalities of reward even for similar work as would be hard to justify, especially in a society dedicated to the goal of increasing equality. For these reasons there is at least considerable risk that the method of compulsion would be widely used.

Developments in Britain under the postwar Labour government lend strong support to these theoretical arguments. The British people are certainly deeply attached to personal liberties, such as the freedom of occupation, and so are at least most of the members of the present government. In February, 1946, Sir Stafford Cripps declared, "Our objective is to carry through a planned economy without compulsion of labour." [5] In less than two years, however, his government did in fact provide for a limited form of labor conscription. The significant point is that, in spite of his predisposition to the contrary, Cripps permitted the problem of maldistribution of the labor supply to be dealt with by means of legal restraints and constraints rather than by means of financial inducements. It appears that it was not only the practical difficulties in the way of the operation of inducements that determined the result. Even more the strong opposition of the trade unions to any intrusion by the state into the sphere of wage fixing dictated the choice of means.[6]

SOCIALIST COMPETITION. In spite of such important prac-

---

[5] Quoted by Jewkes, *op. cit.*, p. 200.
[6] *Ibid.*, pp. 198–202. On the eve of the 1950 General Election the government's power of directing employment was revoked.

tical and political considerations as have just been discussed, we should be doing less than justice to the possibilities of planned economies if we failed to point out that the substitution of inducements for commands is only one of the means by which the elements of arbitrariness and regimentation may in some measure be avoided. A planning state may introduce competition within its over-all monopoly and may permit market processes rather than human judgment backed up by the police power to make and enforce the major economic decisions. Increasingly socialist economists are coming to the conclusion that a market system involving "socialistic competition" would provide the best means for achieving the optimum use of resources and the maximum satisfaction of wants. (It should be noted that the term "socialistic competition" is used here in an entirely different sense from that in which it is used by Communists in describing competition among workers in the U.S.S.R.) Capitalist accounting practices would be followed, enterprises would be relatively independent and in competition with each other, and the success or failure of managers would be judged by their balance sheets. We need not concern ourselves with the economic feasibility or desirability of this idea, nor with the question of whether or to what extent it would involve a reintroduction of many of the evils of a capitalistic economy. It is a possible arrangement, and from the political point of view it would certainly impose severe limitations upon the otherwise potentially arbitrary power of governmental officials. Once more, and presumably to a greater extent than under the highly imperfect competition of modern capitalistic societies, workers would have the opportunity to choose among employments and employers, and people generally could elect freely as to how to enjoy the proceeds of their labor—that is, how to spend their money. The individual would make his own choices, based on his own value system, within the price framework; and even this framework would be largely determined by the automatic and impartial operation of the market rather than by "political" means.

We say "largely" determined by the market because there is

also one important qualification concerning the operation of socialistic competition. Not everything could be left to the market. Certain basic decisions would have to be made by the planning authority, as, for example, the decision as to the pattern of distribution of incomes.[7] To be sure, experience would indicate that different decisions on this point would lead to different total production levels, so there would be some objective basis—at least after the plan had been in operation for some time—for making this decision. It would still involve room for choice on the basis of relative preferences for higher production or more equal distribution. The fact of making this basic adjustment, or "setting" of the competitive frame, might, of course, suggest to various special interests the possibility of further adjustments for their particular benefit. It should not be hard for Americans to imagine that the South, the Midwest grain farmers, the silver states, the coal miners, the steel workers, the railroad workers, the automobile workers, possibly white-collar workers, and schoolteachers might not be willing to accept market determinations of their lot even though they were assured on the best authority that in a socialized economy these determinations were the very epitome of justice.

Indeed, the key question we must ask ourselves with regard to socialist competition in general is not how it could operate but how far it would be permitted to operate. There would be powerful pressures tending to interfere with it. There is an obvious psychological incompatibility between one of the major ideals that underlies the demand for "planning"—the ideal of conscious control by the people of the conditions making for their well-being—and the use of an automatic market mechanism for the accomplishment of this purpose. To judge the effects of planning on liberty on the assumption that a market mechanism would be used to govern all price and wage determinations would be as

[7] See A. C. Pigou, *Socialism versus Capitalism* (London: Macmillan & Co., 1937), Chap. 7. The extent to which present consumption should be curtailed to increase the future production of consumers' goods would also have to be determined by political means. See Jewkes, *op. cit.*, p. 132, and authorities cited there.

unrealistic as to evaluate a capitalistic system on the assumption that perfect competition would always prevail. Both procedures are academic in the worst sense of the word.[8]

COLLECTIVE CONTROL AS COMPENSATION FOR LOSS OF INDIVIDUAL LIBERTY. It may be said, however, that no liberty is really lost in a democratically controlled planned society, for what is given up individually is regained collectively. What is lost in terms of individual choice and initiative comes back in a fuller sense of group control. Certain areas of personal or individual liberty may be circumscribed, but political liberty will be vastly increased. As Fulton and Morris write, "Every democratic citizen will take his human and moral dignity, not from the routine labour which he contributes to the daily service of the machine, but from his political activities, in the broadest sense of the word. It is," they continue, "upon his full and active membership of a free society controlling its own economic organization, and not upon his deadening and unsatisfactory behaviour as servant of that organization, that he will securely base his self-respect.[9] It is important to note, however, that the very terms of this statement presume that economic decisions will be subject to popular control rather than be made automatically by a market process. Apart from this, there is real merit in the argument. But it must not be carried too far. Up to a certain point almost any kind of order (control) will increase individual liberty. Beyond that point control can be kept compatible with retention of the values of liberty to a still further point if the controls

---

[8] If support is needed for the proposition that the government of a planned economy would not be willing to leave the important decisions to determination by experts on the basis of formulas and statistics, one may point not only to the obvious kinds of political pressure referred to in the preceding paragraph but also to the actual experience of Great Britain. In opposing the development of an economic general staff, in February, 1946, Mr. Morrison declared that ministerial committees must always make the policy issues, tell the experts what they are to investigate and report upon, and decide what is to be done with the reports.—Jewkes, *op. cit.*, pp. 134–135.

[9] J. S. Fulton and C. R. Morris, *In Defence of Democracy* (London: Methuen & Co., Ltd., 1935), p. 209.

are worked out by the group and imposed by the group organization.[10] This is the principle of Rousseau's theory of liberty under the social contract: ". . . each man, in giving himself to all," declared Rousseau, "gives himself to nobody; and as there is no associate over whom he does not acquire the same right as he yields others over himself, he gains an equivalent for everything he loses, and an increase of force for the preservation of what he has." [11] The limitations of this reasoning are obvious. In gaining a proportionate share in the determination of what you shall have for dinner I do not gain an equivalent for my own freedom to eat what I like. A great deal will depend upon the kind of decisions made collectively. More will depend upon whether or not the group is of such a size that all can actively participate in arriving at the decision and do so with a full knowledge of the needs and desires of the others (as was the case with Lewin's group of children). This is perhaps another way of saying that the whole analysis with which we are dealing leaves out of account two things. The first is the satisfaction one gets from making his own, individual, and unique decision. This point must not be overlooked in emphasizing the value of participating in a group decision. It is not the whole of liberty, but it is an important part. If a man is drafted to work in the mines, his liberty is vitally curtailed even though he may have voted for the government in

[10] This was demonstrated for a group of children by one of Kurt Lewin's experiments. Three play groups were organized in one of which the adult leader acted as an autocrat, in the second of which the leader allowed the children almost complete freedom, and in the third of which (denominated the "democratic" group) he organized the group to make cooperative decisions on all important questions. Without going into details, the results may be summarized by saying that the children in the democratic group were apparently happier, more constructive and cooperative, and less aggressive than those in either of the other groups. Members of the democratic group actually showed more freedom of movement than those in the laissez-faire group, the latter apparently being limited by their lack of a perspective of worth-while goals agreed upon by the group.— Kurt Lewin, "Experiments on Autocratic and Democratic Atmospheres," *Frontiers of Democracy*, IV (July, 1938), 316–319.

[11] Jean Jacques Rousseau, *The Social Contract*, "Everyman's Library," trans. G. D. H. Cole (New York: E. P. Dutton & Co., 1923), p. 15.

power. The other omission is the problem of the dissenter or the minority group. And the larger and more heterogeneous is the whole group the greater does this problem become.

EFFECTS OF SUBSTITUTION OF DISCRETION FOR RULE. It is frequently charged that planning inevitably involves severe infringements of liberty from another quarter because it necessitates the substitution of discretion for rule, of judgment, not to say caprice, for law. Liberalism and the rule of law, it is said, are practically synonymous, while planning cannot abide the rigidity and the "mechanical" operation of constitutional government. The argument deals with both the legislative and the administrative levels. As long as the legislature merely establishes the rules of the game and does not attempt directly to fix the relative conditions of the various groups in society, it is argued, it can act impartially, for its members are not corrupted by taking into consideration their own or their constituents' special interests as opposed to the general interest. If they cannot anticipate what groups will benefit from their actions they can be moved only by the general good. It is interesting to note that here it is the anti-planners instead of the planners who are relying on the argument of Rousseau.[12]

The argument gains headway as it moves from the legislative to the administrative level. The principle of the rule of law involves legislative determination of a system of rights and duties. The application of this system can then be left to the initiative of private individuals who may have an interest in seeing that the law is enforced. Furthermore, the law will be interpreted and applied by the courts. Thus the functions of government are largely confined to judging disputes as to matters of facts and interpretations of law. For these there are generally agreed standards of judgment. But in a planned economy, so the argument runs, it is necessary to leave vastly more discretionary authority to government officials, who must constantly be making deter-

[12] Rousseau argued that the General Will must operate only on general questions to avoid the corrupting influence of self-interest.—*Social Contract*, pp. 27–29.

minations according to such vague standards as "reasonable," "in the public interest," "fair," and the like. Since these criteria are so vague and subject to such varying interpretations and applications, it follows that the average citizen cannot anticipate how the law will be applied to him and to his affairs. Yet the ability to know in advance what the law prescribes and proscribes is the very essence of a free society. In its absence, individuals do not know how to plan their own affairs, and certainty and security being lacking, business conditions tend to degenerate, and the state is forced to intervene more and more.

These in general are the charges. They do not go unanswered. It is quite properly pointed out that no legislature has ever been able to follow Rousseau's prescription. If liberty depended upon generality of legislative object, it would never have existed in any substantial degree in modern times. Modern legislatures are constantly enacting laws that affect different groups or classes of society differently and are intended to. One need mention only such obvious examples as tariff laws, minimum-wage and hours-of-labor legislation, price support for agricultural products, oleomargarine taxation, and "fair-trade practice" laws to make the point. Legislators do not have to operate blindfolded to give tolerable results. Experience indicates that in fact they do have sufficient regard for the general interest, or their special interests do sufficiently cancel one another out, or both, to discredit at least the worst fears of the critics.

The criticism has more bite in its application to administration. Planning does normally carry with it a great increase in the powers given to administrative officials. It does become increasingly difficult for the legislature to lay down specific standards. The idea of the rule of law must be modified if it is to find application to the administrative process. Professor Bodenheimer is not far wrong when he expresses the difference in the following terms: "Law is mainly concerned with rights; administration is mainly concerned with results. Law is conducive to liberty and security, while administration promotes efficiency and quick decision. The dangers of law are rigidity and stagnation; the dangers of administration are bureaucracy and autocracy."[13] This statement in itself suggests merely that a proper balance must be maintained between law and administration, not that the latter should be kept at the lowest possible level.

The important qualifications to be made regarding the dangers of administrative arbitrariness were discussed in the preceding chapter and need not be repeated here.[14] In addition to what was said there, we should add that neither at the legislative nor at the administrative level should we make the mistake of assuming a complete lack of good will on the part of those in power. Planners and others too frequently commit the error of overlooking the imperfections of governors and the fact that power tends to corrupt. But it is also easy, and not uncommon, to make the opposite error. Rousseau's insistence that the General Will must never be called upon to express itself with regard to particular objects came out of that half of Rousseau's ambivalent philosophy which was Benthamite in its assumption of psychological hedonism. He was more realistic when he recognized an element of altruism in everyone. All popular government depends on more than a coincidence of private interests and public interest; it rests on the solid foundation of a general concern for the popular welfare. No government that depended entirely on the good will of the governors would long escape tyranny—not even a popular government; but, on the other hand, no impartial observer of popular legislatures and administrations can fail to recognize the extent to which commitment to the welfare of other groups and to the public interest generally is an effective motive force. Public outrage in the United States against the tactics of John L. Lewis in recent years would undoubtedly have gone much further than it did had it not been for the widespread feeling that in the past the miners had received less than their due.

Nevertheless, it must be recognized that the reply to the at-

[13] Edgar Bodenheimer, *Jurisprudence* (New York: McGraw-Hill Book Company, Inc., 1940), p. 95.

[14] Above, pp. 318–320.

tacks upon administrative discretion that has been made here and in the previous chapter applies primarily to limited grants of authority such as characterize our own regulatory system. This reply is subject to a rapidly operating law of diminishing returns as central planning and control become more comprehensive. Anything approaching complete planning would involve a complexity of administrative procedure and regulations that would almost completely nullify the arguments presented above. Under such circumstances a new factor operates to prevent the persons affected from knowing what the law regulating their activities is. It is not that the administrative authorities have not announced their policy and promulgated their regulations; it is simply that the regulations, of necessity, are soon so complex that it becomes virtually impossible for the affected public to know them, understand them, and keep up with the changes. Nor is this situation confined to "complete" planning. We first became acquainted with it in the United States in the days of the NRA. Wholesale injustice was avoided only by the fact that no attempt was made to enforce most of the code provisions. The OPA brought similar problems. Even the very limited amount of central planning being attempted in England today involves a mass of regulations, so complex and ambiguous as to defy the efforts of the well intentioned to keep within the law.[15]

An incidental but important effect of the complexity of administrative regulations is that it gives the government a powerful club. Where businessmen, in the ordinary conduct of their business, violate the law through ignorance and commit perjury unwittingly in filling out endless forms, they are constantly fearful of doing anything that might offend the government, knowing they are certain to have been guilty of some offense for which they may be prosecuted.

Finally, in this connection, it should be observed that the defense of administrative discretion outlined above was based on the assumption that the authority would be exercised by independent boards. The argument would not be wholly inapplicable

---

[15] See Jewkes, *op. cit.*, pp. 217–221, for examples.

if the discretionary authority were to be exercised by ordinary departments, but it would be somewhat weakened inasmuch as independent boards tend to assure both continuity of policy and impartiality of administration. It seems too clear to need demonstration that a centrally planned economy could not rely on independent boards for its important regulatory or managerial functions. The very concept of central planning is incompatible with the notion of administration by agencies independent of each other and not subject to direction by a single authority.[16]

THREATS TO POLITICAL AND CIVIL LIBERTIES. Not only the rule of law but also civil liberties more generally and even political liberty itself are threatened by comprehensive planning. In large measure, this threat grows out of the problem of objectives. When the state confines its activities to setting the framework of rules for economic activity and policing the operation of these rules, it largely avoids the problem of selecting objectives. But a state committed to comprehensive planning must decide what it wants to plan for. "Welfare" is not enough. It means all things to all people, or nearly that. To one man it means the production of more material goods; to another it means greater leisure. All have convictions as to how the goods of the world should be distributed, but seldom are two alike. It is unlikely, as we saw above, that a planned society can dispose of this problem by submitting it entirely to the arbitrament of the market mechanism—or even that it can do so to the extent we do today. This means that political processes must be used to determine "who gets what," whether farmers should be better off than textile workers, whether teachers should be enabled to live as well as the parents of the children they teach (and if so what about

---

[16] It is interesting to observe that Barbara Wootton's in many ways very balanced discussion of planning makes a serious blunder on this point. After defining planning as "the conscious and deliberate choice of economic priorities by some public authority" (*op. cit.*, p. 6), and after devoting most of the book to a discussion of this kind of planning, she defends the compatibility of her program with democracy by proposing dependence upon independent boards (Chap. 9). Clearly this would involve giving up the kind of planning she had been discussing up to that point.

equality among teachers?), and whether housing or transportation or recreation facilities should have prior claim on the social dividend. These and scores of similar questions must be decided by means of the political process. Can agreement be obtained? Not unanimous agreement, but even majority agreement? The opportunity is certainly there for stultifying deadlock, for fascism-breeding deadlock.

We planned in war; surely we can plan in peace. This is a familiar argument, but a weak one. In war, the objective is clear: to defeat the enemy. There may be disagreements as to how best to accomplish that purpose, but the area of disagreement is sharply circumscribed; furthermore the people generally are willing to leave the decisions to the (military) experts. We have evidence enough from our own experience to indicate that it is far different when it is a matter of planning production and distribution in a peacetime economy—especially in an economy of abundance, where the absolute requirements for subsistence for all and for keeping the productive machine going do not serve to chart the course.

How serious a difficulty this is for comprehensive planning it is impossible to say, but it is clear at least that it spells a large negative for any notion of moving quickly to such a system. Once this is recognized, there are possibilities for gradual developments. Although there are no objective criteria by which we may judge whether it is better to use the water of Niagara River for the production of electric power or to enhance the rapture of honeymooners—or for a thousand and one similar choices—in fact, via the democratic process, areas of agreement do develop. It has not been so very long since there was no agreement in the United States on the need for social insurance. Today disagreement on this subject is largely narrowed down to the question of its extent; and even on this point it is significantly limited by general acceptance of existing standards as minimal. Even in the hotly contested field of labor-management relations, the area of disagreement is small in proportion to the area of agreement, which, incidentally, now includes the right of collective bargaining. This point about the growth of consensus and the closely related point that the standard of public morality may rise, rather than the contrary, during a period of expanding state functions needs to be emphasized.[17] But we must not gloss over the vast difference in degree between comprehensive planning and the sum total of agreed-upon areas of state control in any democratic, industrialized country of today.

Herein, incidentally, lies one of the great threats to civil and cultural freedoms implicit in planning. Those who are in power at any given time will be no more than human if they do not grow impatient when their plans are thwarted by lack of agreement. It would be only natural for them to turn for aid to the instrumentalities of the state, educational and other, and to the state's control over private agencies of opinion formation. This is particularly likely to happen if a given program has already secured majority support at the polls or in the legislature. The majority may, for example, enact a price control law the effective operation of which is being prevented by a large and active minority. (Or, for that matter, the law may be sabotaged by an actual majority. People may favor price control in general—that is for the other fellow—while seeking to evade it for themselves.) A variety of motives would then impel the government to use all available means to make the law effective. In the first place, it would believe the program was sound. Second, its own prestige would be intimately tied up with the law, for having initiated the law, the government would want it to succeed. Third, the government would have the moral support of knowing that a majority of the voters, or their representatives, had expressed themselves in favor of the law. Finally, it would have the sanctity of law behind it. The attempts made in the United States during the early New Deal days to whip up support for the Blue Eagle were not very strenuous—nor were they very successful. They do, however, serve to suggest not only the kind of device that such a program calls forth for its enforcement but the kind of atmosphere—charged with emotional and patriotic fervor—that

[17] Wootton, *op. cit.*, Chaps. 9, 10.

its backers must seek to develop. Under such conditions it is all too easy to equate dissent—even dissent on behalf of civil or cultural liberties—with disloyalty.

So closely related to the point just made as hardly to be separable from it is the fact that comprehensive planning brings to a single focus all the social discontents of the country. A government that assumes comprehensive powers must accept corresponding responsibility. Discontents are today dispersed. Some of our complaints and disappointments we blame on the government; others on our employers, or the unions; still others we are unable to trace to any definite source. In a fully planned society there would be but one recipient for the projection of all our discontents. And the result would be more than additive. A person against whom we bear two grudges engenders more feeling on our part than the sum of the feelings evoked by two different people who might be the recipients of the same grudges. Resentment feeds upon itself. The process is not unlike that of spontaneous combustion. The heat generated by the slow oxidation of drying hay well spread about will cause no damage, but the same process taking place in a closely packed mass provides the cumulative reinforcement that produces fire.[18] Liberal-democratic government, as we have said,[19] must have a strong foundation of constitutional morality. Individual liberties will never be secure in the face of apparent immediate needs for action or in the face of majority impatience with justified minority resistance if they rely for support solely upon a rational appreciation of their long-run value. They must be securely based on a strong emotional commitment to them and on a general spirit of tolerance and mutual forbearance. Liberal democracies generally, and the Anglo-American democracies in particular, have been remarkably successful in developing and maintaining this foundation. It is vital, however, that we should not test it too severely. In particular, a society in which the government accepts responsibility

[18] Perhaps the atomic pile is an example more familiar to the present generation.
[19] See above, pp. 213–214.

for the distribution of income invites the discharge of powerful aggressive forces against itself. Any system of distribution will result in feelings of injustice and frustration. If there is inequality, those who have less will think they should have more; and, as Aristotle pointed out, if there is equality, those with superior talents and those who work especially hard will feel aggrieved. It is not only that a planned society will concentrate these grievances upon a single center, although that is bad enough. Actually, in one respect at least, the total of grievances will be increased, because those who receive less in a planned society, where the smaller amount represents a public determination that they are worth less, will find this a greater blow to their dignity than they would where it can be blamed on the impersonal, perhaps accidental or arbitrary operations of the market.[20]

Another threat to liberty in a planned society arises out of the fact that comprehensive planning provides governments with the means of perpetuating themselves. It is the natural inclination of any government to want to stay in power. In a planned society two facts tend to make it easier for governments to satisfy that desire. In the first place, their means of controlling the electorate are greatly strengthened. The number of people who owe their livelihood to the government either through their own jobs or through those of members of their families is multiplied. Furthermore, and perhaps more important, administrators have discretionary power affecting the welfare of practically everybody. Even a few key controls, such as control of transportation and communication and the supply of credit, not to mention more specific commodity controls, such as a newsprint monopoly, carry with them almost unbounded possibilities of political influence.

It may be said that we have traditions of political integrity that protect us against this kind of abuse of power. It might even be thought that any government that sought to use its power in this way would thereby evoke such a strong reaction against itself as to ensure its defeat at the next election. Indeed, it seems

[20] See von Hayek, *The Road to Serfdom*, pp. 106–107.

clear that the growth in the size of the governmental bureaucracies in Britain and the United States has been accompanied by a rising standard of political morality. During the thirties in the United States it is notable that in spite of the great and unaccustomed increase of public expenditures for direct and indirect relief, relatively few and inconsequential evidences of abuse have been uncovered. Nevertheless, we should be ill-advised to place complete reliance on this tradition of integrity. We have seen it operate only in a society where a great many more people were relatively free from governmental control than were subject to it. It would be of no avail to seek to influence the votes of two or three million governmental employees if the effect would be to alienate millions of others. It is at least conceivable that the situation might be different if a majority of the electorate were subject to the edicts of the government. Even under such circumstances, however, the secrecy of the ballot is a great protection, and it is probable that this particular danger can easily be overrated. The curtailment of criticism of the government is just as serious as influencing the vote, and more easily accomplished. Moreover, control through fear (possibly unjustified) of discriminatory government purchasing policies, credit controls, and the like, would probably be more serious than the more easily exposed and proved use of the power over employment.

The tendency of governments to seek their own perpetuation may even find unsolicited support from large sections of the population, because of the great importance, under planning, of continuity and constancy of policy. Although many exaggerated claims have been made as to the alleged incompatibility of planning with shifting control of the government, the fact is that the greater the sweep of government control the stronger will be the pressure for constancy in their exercise. It cannot be expected that a neomercantilist state will be exempt from the pressures that, under mercantilism, favored a strong monarch as the best guarantee of stability of government.[21]

[21] See Philip W. Buck, *The Politics of Mercantilism* (New York: Henry Holt and Company, 1942), pp. 124–133.

The other fact referrred to above is hardly more than the opposite side of the shield. Not only would comprehensive planning increase the powers of government; by the same token it would deprive out-groups of the means of resistance. Traditionally in liberal-democratic countries, individuals and minorities have found their protection against the will of the majority in the philosophy of individual or natural rights and in the legally protected privileges that have reflected this philosophy. The right to own property and to do with it as one pleases, subject to certain well-defined restrictions in the public interest; the right to make contracts of sale, employment, and the like freely, again within a framework of limitations—these rights have given to the individual large areas of self-management that have been vital to his self-development and have served as defenses against the encroachments of even a popular government. But neither the attitudes that normally accompany a movement toward comprehensive planning nor indeed the exigencies of a planned economy are compatible with the retention of these large areas of individual autonomy.

This weakening of property rights increases the threat to civil liberties as well as that to the democratic process. It is widely assumed by those who advocate a state-managed economy (in greater or less degree) that the traditional rights pertaining to property, freedom of contract, choice of employment, and the like are quite separate and independent from the basic cultural and civil liberties, such as freedom of speech, press, association, and access to information, and freedom from arbitrary, oppressive, and inquisitorial methods of law enforcement. So also with political liberty. Separate indeed they are, and logically independent. But, as we have already seen, there will be powerful pressures and temptations operating to lead governments to use all the means at their disposal to ensure the success of their plans. Property rights have in the past been a very useful weapon not only to protect the economic interests of owners but also to protect more central areas of liberty. T. V. Smith has called attention to this fact in words hard to improve upon:

. . . property rights, I repeat, are human rights—in property. When these human rights are rendered insecure, other more intimate human rights are open to attack from the rear, from the flanks, and, in the event, brazenly in front. The privacy of homes is invaded, perhaps to search for *verboten* property, or to seek out the persons of those who, dispossessed of property, are by that fact deprived also of all personal security. Then freedom of speech is denied in the name of common safety. Disavowal of sanctity of person follows hard upon, for men who are not allowed to speak freely can be arrested on the charge of freely thinking what they are forbidden to say.

In the rapid revolution of arbitrariness, *habeas corpus* goes under. The right to bail upon arrest follows. The right to trial before peers passes into the wrong of being convicted by the simple device of being accused by a party member.[22]

These are extreme statements, and the author is referring to a situation in which democracy has ceased to operate. But what he says about the vulnerability of vital individual rights in the absence of property rights has applicability to any society in which there are differences of opinion.

Indeed, we may go further and say that the two greatest single sources of popular resistance to government today, in addition to the vote itself, are the bundle of rights designated by the term "property" and the right of all who work as employees of private employers to strike. The rights to withhold capital and labor give to their holders an independence that itself constitutes a powerful support for the independence of the voter, and of course a much-needed protection for minority interests. Political independence without a large measure of economic independence is a weak reed. But no society in which the government undertakes to make the major determinations of economic priorities can fail to make substantial curtailments of existing rights of property. Even less can it allow the rewards that are to go to the major factor of production—labor—to be determined by the irrational processes of economic warfare between giant monopolis-

[22] T. V. Smith, *Discipline for Democracy* (Chapel Hill: University of North Carolina Press, Inc., 1942), pp. 106–107. By permission of the University of North Carolina Press, Inc.

tic combinations of capital and labor.[23] That is to say, a fully planned society can hardly avoid doing away with its two most effective counterweights to the all-engulfing power of government.

SUMMARY. In summary, it is fairly clear that comprehensive planning of the economy by the state carries with it grave threats to liberty and democracy; the more complete the planning, the greater the threat. It seems almost certain that there would be severe limitation of individual liberty of action, especially in the economic realm. This might in some measure be offset by a gain in collective (political) control, but this avenue of compensation appears to operate subject to a rather steeply angled curve of diminishing returns. To a certain extent, also, losses in liberty of action might be accompanied by gains in security and prosperity. But we have seen above[24] that, while security and a measure of economic well-being are essential to the enjoyment of liberty, they are not substitutes for it. A still more serious threat arises out of the fact that powerful forces will operate in the direction of curtailing cultural and civil liberties. Finally, there will be a tendency to undermine that consensus without which democratic government must degenerate into anarchy or tyranny. If planning were to be carried to the extent of subjecting all social arrangements to centralized, political management, Professor Cole's prediction would not be too strong:

A vast army of public servants under centralized control will make a two-party system unworkable. The absence of organized opposition plus the expertness required of the administration will make the latter scornful of public opinion. The enforcement of a mass of minute regulations will entail the brutalization of punishment. The elimination of property rights will bring about the decay of personal rights, and some sort of dictatorship is not far in the offing.[25]

[23] Nor could a society long continue to allow these determinations to be made by the bargaining process where one side was permitted to form monopolistic combinations and the other was denied this privilege. This could end only in disaster.

[24] Pp. 58–63.

[25] Kenneth C. Cole, "Collectivism and Constitutional Liberty," *Washington Law Review and State Bar Journal*, XX (Apr., 1945), 74.

But planning need not go this far. Logically there are many stopping places short of totalitarianism. It is the task of statesmen and political scientists to discover politically feasible programs that will provide a maximum of economic security. economic justice, and prosperity, while minimizing the threats to liberal democracy inherent in complete planning.

2. Partial Planning

There is no reason to think that it is impossible to have some planning while avoiding complete planning. It is not within the scope of this book to attempt to outline an adequate program or institutions for the fulfillment of this objective. In any case, the program would not be the same for any two countries. Moreover, the proper combination for any given country will be discovered by the pragmatic method of trial and error rather than by detailed blueprinting. It is important that we should have in mind the broad objectives, together with some general principles to be followed and dangers to be avoided; but beyond this only a flexible approach can do justice to the complexity of the problem.

GENERAL CONSIDERATIONS. Perhaps the clearest lesson of history in this connection is the importance of maintaining a pluralistic society. Liberty, to paraphrase Holmes's famous remark, is secreted in the interstices of society. Any social group or organization tends to become absolute and tyrannical if it is the only outlet for the energies of its members. This is the same whether the group be a primitive tribe or sovereign state—or a relatively self-sufficient small town. The last example is particularly good for our purposes, for it suggests the truth that the greatest happiness and even the greatest liberty is to be found neither in the monolithic unity of the isolated and in-grown small town nor in the lonely freedom of an unintegrated metropolis. Human beings crave both the sense of belonging and the enhanced effectiveness that comes with membership in groups of at least a semipermanent nature; but the variety of human personalities, needs, and abilities is such that each of us demands for his fulfillment membership in a number of groups. Moreover, the domination of the group will become too strong unless there is some possibility for its members to abandon it and join another. We are indeed all familiar with the fact that either too much or too little social integration is a bad thing.[26] What we may overlook is that this proposition is directly applicable to the state. A state that does too little leaves a vacuum in social consciousness that will sooner or later demand fulfillment. This is especially true if, as is almost sure to happen under modern conditions, the result is to allow some of its constituent groups to become internally too integrated at the expense of the over-all community. But the converse is equally true. The state that absorbs into itself a preponderance of the functions of society cannot help stifle the centers of initiative and the wellsprings of energy. Individual purposes will be forced into a common mold, which is the very antithesis of freedom. Unity will give way to uniformity. No constitutional devices for decentralization and checks and balances will prevent this. Such devices at best are effective in a society where they merely provide avenues for expression or resistance by social groups possessing a large measure of relative independence. Lord Acton has been credited with the statement that freedom has never developed except on the basis of a balance of powers. Whether or not he said precisely this, the proposition would be hard to refute.[27]

Partly, then, what is needed is a balance between groups, between social forces, with the state playing both the role of ar-

[26] For an excellent discussion of this subject, see Georges Gurvitch, "Democracy as a Sociological Problem," *Journal of Legal and Political Sociology*, I (Oct., 1942), 46–71; see esp. p. 49.

[27] Lord Acton was a strong supporter of multinational states, on the ground that they were conducive to liberty. "Diversity," he declared, "preserves liberty by supplying the means of organisation."—John E. E. D. Acton, essay on "Nationality," in *The History of Freedom and Other Essays*, edited and with Introduction by John Neville Figgis and Reginald Vere Laurence (London: Macmillan & Co., 1922), p. 289. In support of the proposition stated in the text, see also Frank D. Graham, *Social Goals and Economic Institutions* (Princeton: Princeton University Press, 1942), Chap. 2, esp. pp. 14–15.

biter among groups and also the positive role of being itself a group for certain purposes other than that of holding the ring for the contestants.[28] Beyond this, there is need also for a balance between the principles of cooperation and competition. Human beings require both for their fullest satisfaction. Society requires both for its adequate regulation. Competition is the great check on abuse of power over the individual, as cooperation is the alternative to mutual frustration. During the nineteenth century, we allowed the virtues of freedom of contract and of competition to blind us to the fact that formal freedom often concealed a gross inequality of bargaining power, and that the dogma of freedom of contract often served to protect contracts contrary to sound public policy. Today, while some still mourn the passing of laissez faire, others are making the opposite mistake of forgetting the truths of liberalism. A major portion of the myriads of adjustments required in any great society must be made by free agreement among the individuals concerned, if they are to be effective in assuring either freedom or efficiency. The evils of laissez faire must not blind us to the crippling bonds of the mercantilist and feudal systems that preceded it. The fact that we plunged from one extreme to the other is no reason to repeat the process. Competition and the "cash nexus," which makes possible the free disposal of services and property on terms agreeable to the individual, is, as Professor Graham says, "the only means of securing social cohesion which offers any prospect of general freedom." [29]

NEED FOR PRIVATE PROPERTY. As is implied in the last statement, private property plays an important role in the maintenance of a sound social equilibrium. This does not mean that any

---

[28] This point is well made by Professor Hocking, who points out that nineteenth-century theorists too often overlooked the fact that there are certain functions that the state should perform because by performing them collectively people satisfy their "will-overflow," their desire for joint accomplishment in great endeavors, and also because common achievements help to create a common will.—William Ernest Hocking, *Man and the State* (New Haven: Yale University Press, 1926), pp. 161–165.

[29] Graham, *op. cit.*, p. 51.

particular concept of property is essential. It does not mean that property rights need not entail responsibilities, nor that their content can never be changed. It does mean, however, that they should carry with them real power, which within limits their possessors may use for good or for ill, and that their content should not be subject to arbitrary alteration. Property is a device for decentralizing power and responsibility. It is a means whereby government lays down rules by which individuals may make effective use of the products of their own labor—rules, too, that enable individuals to plan for the future, secure in the knowledge that presently secured rights can be translated into future realization. Nor is property an instrumentality of freedom only for its possessor. The fact of a multiplicity of owners gives to each one a number of potential purchasers of his product or his services. Competition for whatever we have to offer makes for us the difference between freedom and slavery. Abuses of property ownership need to be curbed, and limits must be placed on its (mal)-distribution; but this does not call for its abolition, even as it affects capital goods. We must beware of throwing out the baby with the bath.

THE ROLE OF FREE LABOR UNIONS. The pluralistic democracy of the future must retain private ownership of land and capital goods by individuals, corporations, and cooperative associations both to provide a market mechanism for controlling the allocation of resources and to supply the economic basis for independent social forces. It must also retain and perhaps even further develop the institution of free labor unions. In fact, it is the growth of unions that makes possible the retention of free contractualism. Not only Marxists but many liberals have grown so used to thinking in terms of the weakness of labor in relation to capital that they still insist that freedom of bargaining in this field is illusory and that economic power and ownership are synonymous. They overlook one of the greatest revolutions of our times. Today in large areas of the economy equality of bargaining power once more exists, where, indeed, the balance has not been tipped in the other direction. The economic power of organized labor, in fact, dwarfs that of capital because it is more unified. As these words are being written a typical example of this fact catches the headlines. Big Steel has given up the battle to hold the line against the third postwar round of wage and price increases, defeated by the concessions to labor made by other industries.

DANGERS. The goal of governmental planning, then, must be to maintain a balance of social forces, especially as between capital and labor, and to utilize this balance to allow a maximum of economic determinations and adjustments to be worked out by mutual agreement and by the market process rather than by governmental decision. This will involve also a balance between the principles of cooperation and competition. There are certain dangers, against which a government bent on the achievement of this goal must guard. One of these is the development of corporativism. Groups may be given powers that are too great. Capital and labor may be all too eager to cooperate if they are given the unrestricted right to combine to their mutual advantage at the expense of other groups. The danger along this line is not so much that groups given too much power will prey upon society as that the development of overpowerful enclaves within the state will compel the state itself to develop in the very totalitarian direction that it was seeking, by delegation, to avoid. Short of corporativism is the ever-present threat of restrictive planning. It is not only natural, it is almost inevitable, that the strongest forces working for governmental planning will be groups that stand to profit by it. They may be seeking protection against the inroads of competition, domestic or foreign, "stability" in the face of changing economic conditions, or positive group gains, possibly under the guise of recouping a lost status, American history is full of instances of this kind of activity, often successful, the grand example being the history of the tariff legislation. Agriculture provides numerous examples: crop restriction in pursuit of "parity prices"; protective taxation of oleomargarine;

health laws in excess of reasonable requirements, the effect of which is to limit competition. Trade unions are notorious for similarly restrictive practices, although for the most part they have obtained their objectives without direct resort to legislation.[30] This kind of piecemeal and restrictive planning by, or at the instance of, special groups runs counter to the general welfare in most instances. One of the first tasks of a state committed to control of the bottlenecks and sore points of the economy must be to put an end to this sort of thing. This means, however, that its legislative program cannot be merely the product of compromises among contending groups. It must have a positive plan of its own, drawn up on the basis of recommendations of disinterested experts. It must mobilize general consumer support for such a program and seek to expose to all the futility of restrictive measures. Fortunately there is considerable evidence that already the mutually defeating effect of such devices has made itself felt in some fields.[31]

Another danger of which the managers of a partially planned economy must beware is the pursuit of policies that will compel one step toward the limitation of the "private" economy to be followed by another and so on indefinitely until it has been wholly swallowed up. This danger is greatest, of course, when planning is strongly influenced by those who are convinced at the outset that nothing short of complete planning will work. Its most likely form is confidence-destroying threats, either expressed or implied. An industry which is told that it must modernize (or "rationalize") or else be nationalized is hardly in a good position to attract the capital without which it can do nothing. This is just one example of the many ways in which govern-

---

[30] For an instructive account of the successful attempts by the practitioners of all sorts of callings, from "beauticians" to lawyers, to get legislative assistance in their efforts to restrict entry to their fields, see J. A. C. Grant, "The Gild Returns to America," *Journal of Politics,* IV (Aug., 1942), 309–316 and IV (Nov., 1942), 458–463.

[31] The growth of interstate barriers to trade during the thirties was successfully checked. The more intelligent trade-union leadership is becoming aware of the fact that the introduction of laborsaving machinery must not be blindly resisted.

mental action may paralyze private enterprise and so necessitate, or seem to necessitate, further expansion of governmental control. The process mostly operates through fear on the part of businessmen as to what the government is going to do next. The answer is for the government to make abundantly clear well in advance what action it will take under certain specified circumstances. And of course those circumstances must represent reasonable conditions. All of this involves a clarity and constancy of governmental policy that is rather in advance of anything yet achieved in the United States. But it is a measure of what must be accomplished if even partial planning is to operate satisfactorily.

It is also imperative to avoid taxation policies that make it impossible for private industries to attract capital. The test of sound policy here is simple in principle, but with the great pressure for more funds for social services as well as for defense great vigilance will be required to see that it is applied.

SKETCH OF A PROGRAM. Subject to these warnings, we may sketch in half a dozen of the main headings of the program for a partially planned economy. First of all, the state must concern itself with the promotion of competition. This includes both vigorous prosecution of the perennial war against monopoly and also policing of the markets, seeing to it that buyer and seller are reasonably well informed of the facts relevant to their decisions. The latter involves not only the enforcement of elementary honesty, such as is provided for by regulation of the investment business and by pure-food laws and the like, but also the dissemination of information regarding market conditions and prospects. It is understood that no government will ever be completely successful in curbing monopoly, and it is easy to provide overdrawn pictures of the governmental bureaucracy that would be required even to approach this goal. Antitrust activity is only one avenue of attack upon the problem. The holding company is a creature of law that has done much to facilitate industrial combinations far beyond the point dictated by considerations of technological efficiency. It can be curbed by legislation, as has already been done in the public-utility field. Furthermore, monopolies are to a certain extent self-limiting. It is instructive to note, for example, that, even without benefit of effective legal action, the United States Steel Corporation today controls a smaller proportion of the market for steel in the United States than it did when it was founded. The same situation is even more striking in the aluminum field. New scientific developments are continually rendering old monopolies obsolete and, by the provision of substitute materials, broadening the area of competition. The recent victory of the Federal Trade Commission in its war against the practice of freight absorption shows that big business, even Big Steel, is by no means invulnerable to legal attack.

Perhaps the most serious question in this connection has to do with labor unions. The steelworkers' union exercises over the available supply of labor for the steel industry a control fully as monopolistic as that of any combination of steel manufacturers over the supply of steel. And in many other industries the only near monopolies existing are on the labor side. Can free competitive enterprise operate successfully under these conditions? If not, what are the possibilities? The result may be to promote a corresponding solid front on the part of capital.[32] Such an eventuality would set the stage either for destructive strife on an intolerable scale or for stultifying corporativism. The other possibilities would seem to be socialism, the institution of compulsory arbitration, or the application of antitrust laws or similar control to labor unions.

It is to be hoped for the sake of liberal democracy that a solution may be found other than socialism (which, incidentally, would not solve the problem, although it might be resorted to in the hope of solving it!) or general compulsory arbitration. In my opinion a solution can be found but it will not consist of any single formula. Some of the limitations imposed by the Taft-

[32] Such a development is already under way, not only within industries on a national scale, but also in the form of interindustry employers' organizations on a local basis.

Hartley Act are undoubtedly sound. Probably others should be added. Compulsory arbitration may have to be made the instrument of last resort in key industries. But not all advance, not all successful attacks upon the problem will come from governmental regulation. We are prone to forget this. Both the American and the British experiences suggest that some hope lies in the gradual education and maturing of labor leadership and of the point of view of the rank and file of union members. The development of a wider vision that would include an appreciation of the interests of other portions of the community may indeed be encouraged by the threat of unfavorable legislation; but also it may grow independently or outlive its occasion. Experience in the United States and in other countries is making it increasingly clear to all that the common welfare is directly dependent upon keeping the productive machine going. The idea that rising wage rates necessarily means more prosperity for the group immediately affected has been dealt some rude blows by experience with creeping inflation. The notion that labor, too, may price itself out of a market is not too subtle for the average union member to grasp. In abandoning their demand for a fourth-round wage increase, the textile workers in this country gave evidence of this fact.

Both the task of compulsory arbitration and the cause of obtaining reasonable voluntary agreements may be facilitated by the development of standards for the determination of wage rates as suggested in an earlier chapter.[33] These standards will be useful not only for the guidance of arbitrators and negotiators but also as the basis for formulas to be written directly into contracts. The General Motors contract, with its provision for relating wages to a price index, may be a straw in the wind. The desirability of tying wages to the cost of living rather than to productivity is open to serious question, but the use of some such formula is at least a move in the right direction.

Just as the story is not to be told entirely in terms of governmental regulation, so also it is not solely a matter of bargaining

[33] See above, pp. 287–288.

standards or contract arrangements. Management is just beginning to discover that the maintenance of healthy labor relations is not solely a matter of wages and hours. If government and management together are able to provide a much greater degree of job security in the future than they did in the past they will take a major step toward industrial peace. There are also other avenues. Large-scale industry, like the Leviathan state, has swallowed up its "citizens" to the extent that they have lost their sense of individuality and of participation. The need for a feeling of belonging, to which we have already referred, cannot be supplied entirely by membership in political and community organizations. Nor can trade unions completely fill the gap. Here, as on the governmental level, we are only beginning to discover what democratic living calls for. It means the development of manifold opportunities for each individual to voice his complaints, to express his judgments, and to participate in planning the activities of the groups to which he belongs. At first sight such a program would seem to involve a hopeless amount of time spent in endless meetings and discussions. But this is not only the price of democracy; it is a price that may well pay off in direct economic as well as indirect political returns. Time and again it is discovered that undreamed of reservoirs of both ideas and energy can be tapped in this fashion. There can be no doubt that the line between the "proper" spheres of labor and management will become increasingly fuzzy and flexible.[34]

Our discussion of the proper role of competition in a free economy and how to maintain it has taken us somewhat afield from our starting point, but not away from what is central to our problem. However, we must return to the subject of the role of government. Maintaining and policing the competitive sphere and doing its bit to keep industrial strife within tolerable limits is only the beginning. There will, of course, be areas of "natural monopoly" where competition is not feasible and where accord-

[34] Peter Drucker's series of articles on this subject are well worth anybody's time to read. Peter F. Drucker, "The Way to Industrial Peace," *Harper's Magazine*, CXCIII (Nov.–Dec., 1946), 385–395, 511–520, and CXCIV (Jan., 1947), 85–92.

ingly governments must choose between the devices of regulated monopolies and state enterprise. Moreover, there are numerous social values not included in the calculus of the market mechanism whose advancement will call for governmental intervention in the future as it has in the past. The conservation of natural resources is an obvious example. "Conservation," however, is not a broad enough term. Planning for the socially most desirable use of land and other resources will call for governmental guidance and even control in all sorts of areas and for numerous purposes from city planning through valley planning to planning for the use of the ether, which obviously must be organized on a national and even an international basis. The watchwords for such programs must always be decentralization and citizen participation —to the maximum the subject matter permits.

The provision of a minimum security against the hazard of unemployment and the needs of old age can today be taken for granted, and it is a testimony to the speed with which general agreement can develop that such is the case in the United States. The level of the security floor and the extent to which social security should embrace other hazards and groups not now included in the United States are important questions, but not ones with which we need concern ourselves here.

In general, the battleground today has moved on from the provision of compensation for unemployment to the provision of employment itself. And even here the main battle has been won. All sides are agreed that no industrialized state can again tolerate prolonged mass unemployment. There remain only the questions of just what the tolerance level is and what measures shall be taken when that level is crossed or threatened. These questions, to be sure, are large and momentous. Although few today dispute the fact that government spending must play an important role in this area, profound disagreements divide even the experts. Doubtless those disagreements will be resolved in the future, as similar differences have in the past, by the process of trial and error. From the political point of view, it is important to insist that controls operating by means of the manipulation of aggregates rather than by the detailed regulation of specific areas of the economy are vastly to be preferred. Controls that act through interest rates, tax levels, generalized spending programs, and the like, avoid the dangers inherent in large bureaucracies, in administrative power with discretion over individuals, and, to a large extent, in arousing pressure groups in search of favored treatment. One cannot be doctrinaire about these matters. The lines are not sharp. The money involved in spending programs has to be spent for something, and its spending is likely to involve the exercise of discretion and, quite possibly, direct benefits to certain groups. Even tax reduction plans inevitably benefit some more than others. Yet there is an obvious difference in degree between this type of generalized, compensatory control and programs of price fixing or investment direction.

Two more points, closely related to each other, remain to be made. Insofar as stabilizing and compensatory programs require differential treatment between classes of individuals, it is better that the basis for differentiation should be written into the governing statute than be left to administrative discretion. This practice will not always be desirable, but is a desideratum to be kept in view. Furthermore, wherever they admit of it, fiscal policies should provide incentives to private enterprise and especially to the kind of private economic activity most needed. We have learned to transcend the intellectual limitations of the fiscal year in planning the national budget and to think of balancing the budget over the period of the business cycle; it is time that we applied similar reasoning to our tax laws. For example, business profits set aside for maintenance of employment or plant expansion during bad times might be exempt from taxation, subject to an eventual accounting to see that they were so spent. This is only the beginning of a system of rewards and penalties that one could imagine for the purpose of stimulating private industry to take stabilizing and other socially desirable measures.[35]

[35] For a highly suggestive popular treatment of this subject, see Peter F. Drucker, *Concept of the Corporation* (New York: The John Day Company, 1946), pp. 264–290.

3. In Conclusion

What are the prospects that the leading democracies of the world will follow some such policy as the one we have outlined? The general trend in Britain for nearly a century has been toward collectivism. Of late, socialism nearly everywhere has adopted the policy of central economic planning. The immediate reaction following the conclusion of the war in 1945 was toward socialization and planning not only in Britain but almost everywhere else, except in the United States. Even here planning finds more support than does collectivism, and Americans have become security-conscious to the extent that any recurrence of hard times would undoubtedly call forth a great demand for national economic planning. The twentieth-century world has been beset by crises; and crises are not favorable to the liberal spirit. They induce fear; and fear, with societies as with individuals, is more likely to lead to paralysis or pointless activity than to stimulate constructive action. Furthermore, as society continues to grow larger and more complex, it would appear that the factors making for inadequacy of automatic control would grow and the need for conscious planning of the economy would increase.

There is, however, another side to the picture. The world has already seen numerous alterations of direction, cyclical swings, in the extent of centralized control of the economy. There is no reason to assume that each such movement must proceed to its logical conclusion (if by that is meant its most extreme form) before the tide is reversed. Particularly is this true if we are speaking of only one part of the world—for part of the world has already reached that extreme in the present movement. We may benefit by that example. Moreover, we may even hope that the swings of the cycle are shortening. A larger society and a more complicated economy will require proportionally more central planning, that is true; but as the sum of acts and relationships increases by geometrical proportion with such social development, the role of government need not necessarily increase relative to that of other spheres of activity.

In crisis periods there is much talk about freedom being a luxury. Probably this will always be the case. But there is at least reason to hope that we have learned something about the control of economic crises. Short of crisis-caused panic, there is a growing realization that freedom is not a luxury but the very foundation of our strength, our prosperity, and our happiness.[36] The postwar swing toward collectivism in Europe has already given way to a moderate trend in the other direction. Observation of the practical operation of totalitarianism as well as the current tension between East and West has contributed to this development. Partly, also, it arises out of growing realization from experience within the countries concerned that state operation and planning is no panacea and carries with it its own problems, both economic and political. There are encouraging signs of developing flexibility, pragmatism, and disenchantment with doctrinaire solutions from either the left or the right. This new trend may be reversed tomorrow. There is certainly no ground for complacency, but neither is there for defeatism. As long as people are aware of some of the dangers inherent in the extremes of either too much or too little government, as long as they cherish the value of freedom, and as long as they are willing to solve their problems in experimental fashion, there is no cause for despair. In Britian and America, in particular, different though their present policies are, those conditions appear to be presently fulfilled.

[36] See J. Frederic Dewhurst, and Others, *America's Needs and Resources* (New York: The Twentieth Century Fund, 1947), pp. 686–687.

For support for the belief that popular demands for security can be satisfied within the reasonable limits of what is compatible with security and progress, see Jerome S. Bruner, *Mandate from the People* (New York: Duell, Sloan and Pearce, 1944), p. 153.

CHAPTER XV

IN CONCLUSION

We have attempted in the course of this volume to appraise the desirability, practicability, and prospects of liberal democracy, in the light of philosophic doubts, changing climates of opinion, and revolutionized social and economic conditions. Our conclusion is that the essential elements of liberal democracy are still sound—sound as the human nature on which they are based; that its specific political institutions are practicable today and can be kept so with no more than the kind of continual modification that has been taking place to date, without departure from the fundamentals; and that there is a good prospect, at least as far as concerns Great Britain and the United States, that evolution will in fact continue in the liberal mold.

To be sure, the third proposition by no means follows from the first two. Many would agree with David McCord Wright, who declares that

the years since the eighteenth century Enlightenment have lived upon the moral capital of the ages which preceded them. Democracy requires a stiffening or framework of values, yet the philosophy of democracy carried to extremes and the effects of eighteenth century philosophy, and subsequent scientific influences, have very nearly destroyed values, including the basic values of democracy itself. We have almost exhausted our moral capital.[1]

[1] David McCord Wright, *Democracy and Progress* (New York: The Macmillan Company, 1948), pp. 66–67. As opposed to Wright we might set the following statement by Professor Clark: "Back of the shifting moral codes, normal man still seems incurably bent on living by some code that his fellows approve. There is discipline and leadership within groups; and between groups there is more recognition of the need of accommodation than often appears in public statements which take the form of political special pleading, with all the shortcomings to which that form of discourse is regularly subject."—John Maurice Clark, *Alternative to Serfdom* (New York: Alfred A. Knopf, Inc., 1948), p. 120.

We have found reason to think that what is easily made to appear as an exhaustion of moral capital is in reality only a realignment of moral principles to accord with the shift from a more to a less individualistic age, without losing sight of the individual as the center of value. We may, of course, be wrong about this. The growth of equalitarianism may go to extremes and lead to a completion of the classic cycle to tyranny. It might do this in spite of the continued desirability and feasibility of liberal-democratic institutions. The dialectic of history sometimes seems to move in long swings of the pendulum—reason-defying in their extent, even though rational in ultimate outcome. But this movement has not proved a useful basis for prediction in the past. It can be seen in retrospect because we pick the times when it applies. Furthermore, the progress of natural science does not follow the "law of the pendulum"; it does not reverse itself. The movement toward the increase of man's control over nature has continued, with varying pace, at least since the beginnings of the Renaissance.

We may take encouragement from the fact that past generations have also had their prophets of despair for the future of liberal institutions. Over sixty years ago, John Dewey observed that democracy's growth in practical extension was accompanied by increasing theoretical depreciation. "No observer can deny," he wrote, "that its defenders have never been so apologetic; its detractors so aggressive and pessimistic." [2] Since that time its practical extension has been expanded and then contracted. Many have been disillusioned by its failures. Perhaps these very facts have provided the challenge that will reverse the tide, if indeed they have not already done so. We can detect just such a change in the writings of certain leaders of opinion of our own day. Note, for instance, the works of the late Carl Becker. The deprecating tone toward liberalism of his *Heavenly City of the Eighteenth-Century Philosophers*[3] gave way to challenge and

---

[2] John Dewey, "The Ethics of Democracy," in *University of Michigan Philosophical Papers*, Ser. 2, No. 1 (Ann Arbor: 1888), p. 1.

[3] New Haven: Yale University Press, 1932.

moderate optimism in such volumes as *Modern Democracy*[4] and *Freedom and Responsibility in the American Way of Life*.[5]

Liberal democracy is part and parcel of a civilization committed to the fullest use of human reason. We have seen that if modern man's first discovery of the potentialities of a reason freed from tradition and dogmatism led to excessive optimism, just as surely the skeptical reaction ran to degrees of despair and cynicism that have no foundation in the facts and that have probably already passed their peak in popular acceptance. Our civilization continues to be based upon the products of reason at every turn—scientifically and socially. Science thrives on freedom of thought and free trade in ideas. It seems unlikely that the one will survive without the other.

The last sentence introduces a note that has been sounded at least twice before.[6] Suppose our whole civilization as we know it comes to an end. More particularly, suppose that wars and the fear of war turn the world into an armed camp, where all else is subordinated to the demands of self-preservation. Or suppose that, as the result of a struggle far greater than any the world has witnessed yet, something comparable to the breakup of the Roman Empire is repeated with the whole civilized world as the victim. This is not impossible, although it must be recalled that today there are no peoples devoid of all science and civilization who conceivably could challenge the civilized world. But there are undemocratic nations who could do so. These possibilities we mention not to appraise—that would be far beyond the scope of this volume—but merely to indicate their bearing on the problem at hand. Democracy, as we have said, requires the maintenance of a reasonable degree of international security.

[4] New Haven: Yale University Press, 1941.

[5] New York: Alfred A. Knopf, Inc., 1945. See esp. Professor Sabine's introductory essay.

[6] Directly, when we enumerated "a reasonable degree of international security" as one of the prerequisites of democracy, and by implication when, just above, we dated man's steadily growing control over nature back only to the beginning of the Renaissance. It was the prolonged "dim-out" of civilization following the fall of Rome that prevented us from tracing the steady progress of science much further back.

How much, no one can say. It is a tough and malleable way of life, not easily destroyed where it has once become firmly rooted. It can withstand temporary dictatorships of the Roman variety, such as it customarily resorts to, at least in modified degree, in times of war. It cannot be expected to endure for long if the chronic threat of war becomes so severe as to create virtual conditions of war in times of "peace"—nor can any other tolerable mode of existence. But if the communist-capitalist conflict, with its attendant "cold war," can be kept within manageable limits—even limits that from other points of view are very unsatisfactory—there is no reason to believe that the world situation will be fatal to liberal democracy.

In my opinion, if one reviews all the threats to liberal democracy that have been considered or even mentioned in the course of this book, one stands out as perhaps more fundamental than all the others. It is not fascism, nor is it communism. It is not the fact of growing class consciousness nor of conflicts of class or group interests; nor is it precisely the demands of equalitarianism. Neither is it the prospect that the demand for central economic planning will outrun our ability to conduct such planning within a liberal-democratic framework. Nor even is it war or the threat of war. But it is a condition that may give rise to any or all of these threats. It is excessive materialism. It is, that is to say, a scheme of values that places material goods and comforts at the top of the scale.[7] The prevalence of such a value system is dangerous to liberal democracy partly because it leads to a devaluation of liberty but chiefly because of its divisiveness. The possibilities of increasing total production are severely limited. A wealth of experience with industrial societies indicates that the rate of increase is fairly steady. On the other hand, the possibilities for increasing the material well-being of one group at the expense of others are almost without limit. This fact sets the stage for powerful disintegrative forces in a society where welfare is measured chiefly in material terms. The result may

[7] It will bear emphasis that we are not discussing materialism as an ontological doctrine but merely as a system of values, of demands.

be class strife or stultifying group conflict, eventuating in either communism or fascism. As between states, it may lead to wars between "haves" and "have-nots" or between representatives of the proletariat and of the *bourgeoisie*. In any event, it is destructive of unity and of the atmosphere of calm reasonability in which the liberal spirit flourishes.

Is our exaggerated materialism the incurable product of the vistas of ever-increasing quantities of material things opened up by the Industrial Revolution? If so, the future is dark indeed. Perhaps, however, materialism in what might be called its diseased form, that exaggerated materialism of which we have been speaking, is rather a product of spiritual emptiness, or psychological ill-health. It is on this latter assumption—for which there is considerable evidence—that the positive proposals set forth in Chapter XII were postulated. There is no need to repeat that analysis here. We need only remind the reader that if the various proposals for directly strengthening liberal-democratic valuations and for developing the healthy community life out of which those valuations grow are sound, and if they are acted upon, there is reason to believe that materialism may be kept in a benign rather than a malignant form. The future success of liberal democracy is by no means assured, but neither is its failure. The evidence suggests that if we act upon the knowledge at our disposal, its chances will be good.

BIBLIOGRAPHY

ACTON, LORD JOHN E. E. D. *The History of Freedom and Other Essays.* Edited and with Introduction by John Neville Figgis and Reginald Vere Laurence. London: Macmillan & Co., 1922.

ADDISON, CHRISTOPHER, C. R. ATTLEE, H. W. BRAILSFORD, and Others. *Problems of a Socialist Government.* Preface by Sir Stafford Cripps. London: Victor Gollancz, Ltd., 1933.

ALEXANDER, FRANZ. *Our Age of Unreason: A Study of the Irrational Forces in Social Life.* Philadelphia: J. B. Lippincott Company, 1942.

ALFANGE, DEAN. *The Supreme Court and the National Will.* New York: Doubleday & Company, 1937.

ALLEN, CARLETON KEMP. *Law and Orders: An Inquiry into the Nature and Scope of Delegated Legislation and Executive Powers in England.* London: Stevens & Sons, Ltd., 1945.

ALMOND, GABRIEL A. "Politics, Science and Ethics," *American Political Science Review,* XL (Apr., 1946), 283–293.

AMERICAN CIVIL LIBERTIES UNION. *The Bill of Rights in War.* New York: The Union, 1942.

———. *Freedom in Wartime.* New York: The Union, 1943.

———. *From War to Peace: American Liberties, 1945–46.* New York: The Union, 1946.

———. *In Defense of Our Liberties.* New York: The Union, 1943.

———. *In Times of Challenge. U. S. Liberties, 1946–47.* New York: The Union, 1947.

———. *Our Uncertain Liberties.* New York: The Union, 1948.

———. *In the Shadow of Fear.* New York: The Union, 1949.

ANDERSON, H. DEWEY, and PERCY E. DAVIDSON. *Ballots and the Democratic Class Struggle.* Stanford University, Calif.: Stanford University Press, 1943.

———. *Recent Occupational Trends in American Labor: A Supplement to Occupational Trends in the United States.* Stanford University, Calif.: Stanford University Press, 1945.

ANSHEN, RUTH NANDA (ed.). *Freedom—Its Meaning.* New York: Harcourt, Brace and Company, 1940.

ARNOLD, MATTHEW. *Culture and Anarchy.* New York: The Macmillan Company, 1883.

————. *Mixed Essays, Irish Essays and Others.* New York: The Macmillan Company, 1883.

ASCOLI, MAX. *Intelligence and Politics.* New York: W. W. Norton & Company, 1936.

————. "Realism versus the Constitution," *Social Research,* I (May, 1934), 169–184.

————, and ARTHUR FEILER. *Fascism for Whom?* New York: W. W. Norton & Company, 1938.

————, and FRITZ LEHMAN. *Political and Economic Democracy.* New York: W. W. Norton & Company, 1937.

AYER, ALFRED J. *Language, Truth and Logic.* New York: Oxford University Press, 1936.

BABBITT, IRVING. *Democracy and Leadership.* Boston: Houghton Mifflin Company, 1924.

BAIN, READ. "Freedom, Law and Social Control," *Journal of Social Philosophy,* IV (Apr., 1939), 220–236.

BARNETT, VINCENT M., JR. "Mr. Justice Murphy, Civil Liberties and the Holmes Tradition," *Cornell Law Quarterly,* XXXII (Nov., 1946), 177–221.

BARZUN, JACQUES. *Of Human Freedom.* Boston: Little, Brown & Company, 1939.

BEACH, WALDO. "The Basis of Tolerance in a Democratic Society," *Ethics,* LVII (Apr., 1947), 157–169.

BECKER, CARL L. *The Declaration of Independence: A Study in the History of Political Ideas.* New York: Alfred A. Knopf, Inc., 1942.

————. *Freedom and Responsibility in the American Way of Life.* New York: Alfred A. Knopf, Inc., 1945.

————. *The Heavenly City of the Eighteenth-Century Philosophers.* New Haven: Yale University Press, 1932.

————. *How New Will the Better World Be?* New York: Alfred A. Knopf, Inc., 1944.

————. *Modern Democracy.* New Haven: Yale University Press, 1941.

BECKERATH, HERBERT VON. "Economics and Politics," *Social Forces,* XIV (Oct., 1935), 42–53.

BERDYAEV, NICHOLAS. *The End of Our Time.* Trans. Donald Attwater. London: Sheed & Ward, 1933.

————. *The Fate of Man in the Modern World.* Trans. Donald A. Lowrie. London: Student Christian Movement Press, 1935.

———. *The Meaning of History,* Trans. George Reavey. London: Geoffrey Bles, 1936.

BINGHAM, ALFRED M. *Insurgent America.* New York: Harper & Brothers, 1935.

———. *The Practice of Idealism.* New York: Duell, Sloan and Pearce, 1944.

BODE, BOYD H. *Democracy as a Way of Life.* New York: The Macmillan Company, 1937.

BRECHT, ARNOLD. "Relative and Absolute Justice," *Social Research,* VI (Feb., 1939), 58–87.

———. "The Rise of Relativism in Political and Legal Philosophy," *Social Research,* VI (May, 1939), 392–414.

———. "The Search for Absolutes in Political and Legal Philosophy," *Social Research,* VII (May, 1940), 201–228.

BRETT, OLIVER. *A Defense of Liberty.* New York: G. P. Putnam's Sons, 1921.

BRIDGMAN, P. W. *The Intelligent Individual and Society.* New York: The Macmillan Company, 1938.

BROOKS, ROBERT CLARKSON. *Civic Training in Switzerland: A Study of Democratic Life.* Chicago: The University of Chicago Press, 1930.

BROWN, J. F. *Psychology and the Social Order.* New York: McGraw-Hill Book Company, 1936.

BROWNE, S. S. S. "How Can Ethical Principles Be Known?" *Ethics,* LVI (Apr., 1946), 186–192.

BRUNNER, EMIL. *Justice and the Social Order.* Trans. Mary Hottinger. New York: Harper & Brothers, 1945.

BRUNNER, JEROME S. *Mandate from the People.* New York: Duell, Sloan and Pearce, 1944.

BRYCE, JAMES, VISCOUNT. *Modern Democracies.* 2 vols. New York: The Macmillan Company, 1921.

BUCK, PHILIP W. *The Politics of Mercantilism.* New York: Henry Holt and Company, 1942.

BURNHAM, JAMES. *The Machiavellians: Defenders of Freedom.* New York: The John Day Company, 1943.

BURNS, C. DELISLE. *Modern Civilization on Trial.* New York: The Macmillan Company, 1931.

BURY, J. B. *A History of Freedom of Thought.* New York: Henry Holt and Company, 1913.

———. *The Idea of Progress.* London: Macmillan & Co., Ltd., 1924.

Bibliography

BUTLER, ROHAN D'O. *The Roots of National Socialism*. New York: E. P. Dutton & Co., 1942.

CARR, EDWARD HALLETT. "The Rights of Man," *United Nations Weekly Bulletin*, III (Oct. 21, 1947), 520–522.

————. *The Soviet Impact on the Western World*. New York: The Macmillan Company, 1947.

CASSIRER, ERNST. *The Myth of the State*. New Haven: Yale University Press, 1946.

CHEYNEY, EDWARD P. *Law in History and Other Essays*. New York: Alfred A. Knopf, Inc., 1927.

CLARK, JOHN MAURICE. *Alternative to Serfdom*. New York: Alfred A. Knopf, Inc., 1948.

COBB, HENRY V. "Hope, Fate and Freedom: A Soliloquy," *Ethics*, LII (Oct., 1941), 1–16.

COCHRANE, CHARLES NORRIS. *Christianity and Classical Culture: A Study of Thought and Action from Augustus to Augustine*. Oxford: The Clarendon Press, 1940.

COHEN, MORRIS R. *The Faith of a Liberal*. New York: Henry Holt and Company, 1946.

COKER, FRANCIS W. *Recent Political Thought*. New York: Appleton-Century-Crofts, Inc., 1934.

COLE, KENNETH C. "Collectivism and Constitutional Liberty," *Washington Law Review and State Bar Journal*, XX (Apr., 1945), 73–80.

COMMAGER, HENRY STEELE. *Majority Rule and Minority Rights*. New York: Oxford University Press, 1943.

COMMISSION ON FREEDOM OF THE PRESS. *A Free and Responsible Press*. Chicago: The University of Chicago Press, 1947.

THE CONGRESS ON EDUCATION FOR DEMOCRACY. *Education for Democracy*, proceedings of the Congress at Teachers College, Columbia University, 1939.

COREY, LEWIS. *The Crisis of the Middle Class*. New York: Covici, Friede, Inc., 1935.

CORWIN, EDWARD S. *The Commerce Power versus States Rights: "Back to the Constitution."* Princeton: Princeton University Press, 1936.

————. *Total War and the Constitution*. New York: Alfred A. Knopf, Inc., 1947.

COUDENHOVE-KALERGI, COUNT RICHARD N. *The Totalitarian State against Man*. Trans. Sir Andrew McFadyean. Glarus, Switzerland; Paneuropa Editions, Ltd., 1939.

Counts, George S. *Dare the School Build a New Social Order?* "The John Day Pamphlets," No. 11. New York: The John Day Company, 1932.

————. *The Prospects of American Democracy.* New York: The John Day Company, 1938.

Cousins, Norman (ed.). *A Treasury of Democracy.* New York: Coward-McCann, Inc., 1942.

Croce, Benedetto. *Politics and Morals.* New York: Philosophical Library, 1945.

Crouch, Winston W. "Trends in British Local Government," *Public Administration Review,* VII (Autumn, 1947), 254–262.

Cushman, Robert G. "'Clear and Present Danger' in Free Speech Cases: A Study in Judicial Semantics," in Milton R. Konvitz and Arthur G. Murphy (eds.), *Essays in Political Theory, Presented to George H. Sabine.* Ithaca: Cornell University Press, 1948.

Dawson, Christopher. *Enquiries into Religion and Culture.* London: Sheed & Ward, 1933.

————. *Religion and the Modern State.* London: Sheed & Ward, 1935.

Debs, J. T. "The Idea of Democracy," *Review of Politics,* V (Jan., 1943), 38–54.

Dennis, Lawrence. *The Coming American Fascism.* New York: Harper & Brothers, 1936.

Dewey, John. "The Ethics of Democracy," in *University of Michigan Philosophical Papers,* Ser. 2, No. 1 (Ann Arbor: 1888).

————. "The Future of Liberalism," *Journal of Philosophy,* XXXII (Apr., 1935), 225–230.

————. *The Public and Its Problems.* New York: Henry Holt and Company, 1927.

————. *The Quest for Certainty.* New York: Minton, Balch & Company, 1929.

————. "Theory of Valuation," in *International Encyclopedia of Unified Science,* Vol. II, No. 4. Chicago: The University of Chicago Press, 1939.

Dewhurst, J. Frederick, and Others. *America's Needs and Resources.* New York: The Twentieth Century Fund, 1947.

Dollard, John, Leonard W. Doob, Neal E. Miller, O. H. Mowrer, and Robert R. Sears. *Frustration and Aggression.* New Haven: Yale University Press, 1938.

DRUCKER, PETER F. *Concept of the Corporation.* New York: The John Day Company, 1946.

————. "The Way to Industrial Peace," *Harper's Magazine,* "I. Why Men Strike," CXCIII (Nov., 1946), 385–395; "II. Citizenship in the Plant," CXCIII (Dec., 1946), 511–520; "III. Can We Get around Roadblocks?" CXCIV (Jan., 1947), 85–92.

DUBS, HOMER H. "The Logical Derivation of Democracy," *Ethics,* LV (Apr., 1945), 196–208.

————. "*The Theory of Value,*" *The Monist,* XLII (Jan., 1932), 1–32.

DURBIN, E. F. M. *The Politics of Democratic Socialism: An Essay on Social Policy.* London: Routledge and Kegan Paul, Ltd., 1940.

EASTMAN, MAX. *Marxism, Is It Science?* New York: W. W. Norton & Company, 1940.

EDMAN, IRWIN (Herbert W. Schneider, collab.). *Fountainheads of Freedom: The Growth of the Democratic Idea.* New York: Harcourt, Brace and Company, 1941.

ELLIOTT, WILLIAM YANDELL. *The Need for Constitutional Reform: A Program for National Security.* New York: McGraw-Hill Book Company, 1935.

ERNST, MORRIS L. *The First Freedom.* New York: The Macmillan Company, 1946.

EWING, A. C. *The Definition of Good.* New York: The Macmillan Company, 1947.

————. *The Individual, the State and World Government.* New York: The Macmillan Company, 1947.

FAGUET, EMILE. *The Cult of Incompetence.* Trans. Beatrice Barstow. New York: E. P. Dutton & Co., 1911.

FEIBLEMAN, JAMES. *Positive Democracy.* Chapel Hill: The University of North Carolina Press, 1940.

FINDLAY, J. N. "Morality by Convention,"*Mind,* LIII (Apr., 1944), 142–169.

FINER, HERMAN. *Road to Reaction.* Boston: Little, Brown & Company, 1945.

FINLETTER, THOMAS K. *Can Representative Government Do the Job?* New York: Harcourt, Brace and Company, 1945.

FLUGEL, J. C. *Man, Morals and Society: A Psycho-analytical Study.* London: Gerald Duckworth, Ltd., 1945.

FOLLETT, MARY P. *Creative Experience.* New York: Longmans, Green and Company, 1924.

————. *The New State*. New York: Longmans, Green and Company, 1920.

Fosdick, Dorothy. *What Is Liberty? A Study in Political Theory*. New York: Harper & Brothers, 1939.

Frank, Jerome. *Law and the Modern Mind*. New York: Brentano's, Inc., 1930.

————. "Self-Guardianship and Democracy, an Editorial," *The American Scholar*, XVI (Summer, 1947), 265–267.

French, Thomas M. "The Psychodynamic Problem of Democracy," in Goodwin Watson (ed.), *Civilian Morale*. "Second Yearbook of the Society for the Psychological Study of Social Issues." Boston: Houghton Mifflin Company, 1942.

Freud, Sigmund. *Civilization and Its Discontents*. Trans. Joan Riviere. 3d ed. New York: Jonathan Cape & Harrison Smith, 1930.

————. *Group Psychology and the Analysis of the Ego*. Trans. James Strachey. London: The International Psycho-Analytical Press, 1922.

Friedrich, Carl Joachim. *Foreign Policy in the Making*. New York: W. W. Norton & Company, 1938.

————. *The New Belief in the Common Man*. Boston: Little, Brown & Company, 1942.

Fritts, Frank. *The Concept of Equality in Its Relation to a Principle of Political Obligation*. Princeton: Princeton University Press, 1915.

Fromm, Erich. *Escape from Freedom*. New York: Rinehart & Company, 1941.

————. *Man for Himself: An Inquiry into the Psychology of Ethics*. New York: Rinehart & Company, 1947.

Fuller, Lon L. *The Law in Quest of Itself*. Chicago: The Foundation Press, 1940.

Fulton, J. S. and C. R. Morris. *In Defence of Democracy*. London: Methuen & Co., 1935.

Galbraith, John Kenneth. "Germany Was Badly Run," *Fortune*, XXXII (Dec., 1945), 173–178, 196 ff.

Galloway, George B. *Congress at the Crossroads*. New York: Thomas Y. Crowell Company, 1947.

Gentile, Giovanni. "The Philosophic Basis of Fascism," *Foreign Affairs*, VI (Jan., 1928), 290–304.

Gini, Corrado. "The Scientific Basis of Fascism," *Political Science Quarterly*, XLII (Mar., 1927), 99–115.

GOLDEN, CLINTON S., and HAROLD J. RUTTENBERG. *The Dynamics of Industrial Democracy.* New York: Harper & Brothers, 1942.

GOMPERZ, H. "Cuius Regio, Illius Opinio: Considerations on the Present Crisis of the Tolerance Idea," trans. T. H. Nash, *Ethics,* XLVI (Apr., 1936), 292–307.

GOOCH, G. P. "Introductory: The Victorian Age, 1837–1901," in F. J. C. Hearnshaw, *The Social and Political Ideas of Some Representative Thinkers of the Victorian Age.* London: George G. Harrap & Company, 1933.

———, and HAROLD J. LASKI. *English Democratic Ideas in the Seventeenth Century.* 2d ed. Cambridge: Cambridge University Press, 1927.

GRAHAM, FRANK D. *Social Goals and Economic Institutions.* Princeton: Princeton University Press, 1942.

GRANT, J. A. C. "The Gild Returns to America," *Journal of Politics,* IV (Aug., 1942), 303–336; IV (Nov., 1942), 458–477.

GRIFFITH, ERNEST S. *The Impasse of Democracy: A Study of the Modern Government in Action.* New York: Harrison-Hilton Books, Inc., 1939.

GURVITCH, GEORGES. "Democracy as a Sociological Problem," *Journal of Legal and Political Sociology,* I (Oct., 1942), 46–71.

HAINES, CHARLES G. *The Revival of Natural Law Concepts.* Cambridge, Mass.: Harvard University Press, 1930.

HALLOWELL, JOHN H. "The Decline of Liberalism," *Ethics,* LII (Apr., 1942), 323–349.

———. *The Decline of Liberalism as an Ideology—with Particular Reference to German Politico-Legal Thought.* Berkeley and Los Angeles: University of California Press, 1943.

———. "Modern Liberalism: An Invitation to Suicide," *South Atlantic Quarterly,* XLVI (Oct., 1947), 453–466.

HAMILTON, ALEXANDER, JOHN JAY, AND JAMES MADISON. *The Federalist.* New York: The Modern Library, Inc., 1941.

HARRIS, JOSEPH P. "The Reorganization of Congress," *Public Administration Review,* VI (Summer, 1946), 267–282.

HARTMANN, GEORGE W. "A Field Experiment on the Comparative Effectiveness of 'Emotional' and 'Rational' Political Leaflets in Determining Election Results," *Journal of Abnormal and Social Psychology,* XXXI (Apr.–June, 1936), 99–114.

HATTERSLEY, ALAN F. *A Short History of Democracy.* Cambridge: Cambridge University Press, 1930.

HAYEK, FRIEDRICH A. VON. *Freedom and the Economic System.* Chicago: The University of Chicago Press, 1939.

————. *The Road to Serfdom.* Chicago: The University of Chicago Press, 1944.

HAYES, SAMUEL P. JR. "Voters' Attitudes toward Men and Issues," *The Journal of Social Psychology,* VII (May, 1936), 164–181.

————. "The Inter-Relations of Political Attitudes," *The Journal of Social Psychology,* "I. Attitudes toward Candidates and Specific Policies," VIII (Nov., 1937), 459–482; "II. Consistency in Voters' Attitudes," X (Aug., 1939), 359–378; "III. General Factors in Political Attitudes," X (Aug., 1939), 379–398; "IV. Political Attitudes and Party Regularity," X (Nov., 1939), 503–552.

HEARD, GERALD. *The Ascent of Humanity: An Essay on the Evolution of Civilization.* New York: Harcourt, Brace and Company, 1929.

HEIMANN, EDUARD. *Freedom and Order: Lessons from the War.* New York: Charles Scribner's Sons, 1947.

HERRING, E. PENDLETON. "The Politics of Fiscal Policy," *Yale Law Journal,* XLVII (Mar., 1938), 724–745.

————. *Presidential Leadership: The Political Relations of Congress and the Chief Executive.* New York: Rinehart & Company, 1940.

HITLER, ADOLF. *Mein Kampf.* Boston: Houghton Mifflin Company, 1939.

HOBSON, J. A. *Democracy and a Changing Civilization.* London: John Lane, Ltd., 1934.

HOCKING, WILLIAM ERNEST. *The Lasting Elements of Individualism.* New Haven: Yale University Press, 1937.

————. *Man and the State.* New Haven: Yale University Press, 1926.

————. *Present Status of the Philosophy of Law and of Rights.* New Haven: Yale University Press, 1926.

HOFFMAN, ROSS J. S. *The Organic State: An Historical View of Contemporary Politics.* London: Sheed & Ward, 1939.

————. *The Will to Freedom.* London: Sheed & Ward, 1935.

HOLMES, OLIVER WENDELL, JR. *Collected Legal Papers.* New York: Harcourt, Brace and Company, 1920.

————. *The Common Law.* Boston: Little, Brown & Company, 1938.

Bibliography

HOOK, SIDNEY. *The Hero in History.* New York: The John Day Company, 1943.

――――. "Naturalism and Democracy," in Yervant Kovhannes Krikorian (ed.), *Naturalism and the Human Spirit.* New York: Columbia University Press, 1944.

――――. "The Philosophical Presuppositions of Democracy," *Ethics,* LII (Apr., 1942), 275–296.

――――. *Reason, Social Myths and Democracy.* New York: The John Day Company, 1940.

――――. *Towards the Understanding of Karl Marx: A Revolutionary Interpretation.* New York: The John Day Company, 1933.

HORNEY, KAREN. *The Neurotic Personality of Our Time.* New York: W. W. Norton & Company, 1937.

――――. *New Ways of Psychoanalysis.* New York: W. W. Norton & Company, 1939.

HUDSON, JAY WILLIAM. *Why Democracy: A Study in the Philosophy of the State.* New York: Appleton-Century-Crofts, Inc., 1936.

HUME, DAVID. *Essays: Moral, Political and Literary.* Ed. T. H. Green and T. H. Grose. 2 vols. London: Longmans, Green and Co., 1875.

――――. *A Treatise of Human Nature.* "Everyman's Library." New York: E. P. Dutton & Co., 1911.

HUSZAR, GEORGE B. DE. *Practical Applications of Democracy.* New York: Harper & Brothers, 1945.

HUXLEY, ALDOUS. *Ends and Means.* New York: Harper & Brothers, 1937.

IRELAND, ALLEYNE. "Democracy and Heredity—A Reply," *Journal of Heredity,* X (Nov., 1919), 360–367.

JENKIN, THOMAS PAUL. *Reactions of Major Groups to Positive Government in the United States, 1930–1940.* Berkeley and Los Angeles: University of California Press, 1945.

JENNINGS, WILLIAM I. *Parliamentary Reform.* London: Victor Gollancz, Ltd., 1934.

JENSEN, HOWARD E. "William McDougall's Doctrine of Social Psychology," *Journal of Social Philosophy,* IV (Apr., 1939), 206–219.

JEWKES, JOHN. *Ordeal by Planning.* London: Macmillan & Co., 1948.

JORDAN, E. "The False Principle of Liberalism," *Ethics,* XLVI (Apr., 1936), 276–291.

JOSEY, CHARLES C. *The Psychological Battlefront of Democracy.* Indianapolis: The Butler University Press, 1944.

KALLEN, HORACE M. (ed). *Freedom in the Modern World.* New York: Coward-McCann, Inc., 1928.

KAPLAN, ABRAHAM. "Are Moral Judgments Assertions? *Philosophical Review,* LI (May, 1942), 280–303.

KARDINER, ABRAM. *The Individual and His Society: The Psychodynamics of Primitive Social Organization.* New York: Columbia University Press, 1939.

————. *The Psychological Frontiers of Society.* New York: Columbia University Press, 1945.

KAUFMANN, FELIX. *Methodology of the Social Sciences.* New York: Oxford University Press, 1944.

KELSEN, HANS. "Absolutism and Relativism in Politics," *American Political Science Review,* XLII (Oct., 1948), 906–914.

————. *Der Sociologische und der Juristische Staatsbegriff.* Tübingen: 1928.

————. *Vom Wesen und Wert der Demokratie.* Tübingen: J. C. B. Mohr, 1929.

KENDALL, WILLMOORE. *John Locke and the Doctrine of Majority-Rule.* Urbana: The University of Illinois Press, 1941.

————. "The Majority Principle and the Scientific Élite," *Southern Review,* IV (Summer, 1938—Spring, 1939), 463–473.

————. "On the Preservation of Democracy for America," *Southern Review,* V (Summer, 1939—Spring, 1940), 53–68.

KRIKORIAN, YERVANT KOVHANNES (ed.). *Naturalism and the Human Spirit.* New York: Columbia University Press, 1944.

KRUTCH, JOSEPH WOOD. *The Modern Temper.* New York: Harcourt, Brace and Company, 1929.

LA FOLLETTE, ROBERT M., JR. "A Senator Looks at Congress," *Atlantic Monthly,* CLXXII (July, 1943), 91–96.

LAMONT, W. D. *The Principles of Moral Judgment.* Oxford: The Clarendon Press, 1946.

LANDAUER, CARL. *Theory of National Economic Planning.* Berkeley and Los Angeles: University of California Press, 1944.

LASKI, HAROLD J. *Faith, Reason and Civilization: An Essay in Historical Analysis.* New York: The Viking Press, 1944.

————. *Parliamentary Government in England.* New York: The Viking Press, 1938.

————. *Reflections on the Revolution of Our Time.* New York: The Viking Press, 1943.

———. *The Rise of European Liberalism.* London: George Allen & Unwin, Ltd., 1936.

———. *The State in Theory and Practice.* New York: The Viking Press, 1935.

LASSWELL, HAROLD D. *Democracy through Public Opinion.* "Chi Omega Service Fund Studies," No. 4. Menasha, Wisc.: George Banta Publishing Company, 1941.

———. *World Politics and Personal Insecurity.* New York: McGraw-Hill Book Company, 1935.

LAZARSFELD, PAUL F., Bernard Berelson, and Hazel Gaudet. *The People's Choice.* New York: Duell, Sloan and Pearce, 1944.

LE BON, GUSTAVE. *The Crowd: A Study of the Popular Mind.* London: George Allen & Unwin, Ltd., 1896.

LECKY, W. E. H. *Democracy and Liberty.* New ed., 2 vols. New York: Longmans, Green and Co., 1896.

———. *History of the Rise and Influence of Rationalism in Europe.* Rev. ed., 2 vols. New York: Appleton-Century-Crofts, Inc., 1890.

LEDERER, EMIL. *State of the Masses.* New York: W. W. Norton & Company, 1940.

LENNES, N. J. *Whither Democracy? Does Equalizing Opportunity Create Hereditary Social Classes? A Speculative Study.* New York: Harper & Brothers, 1927.

LENTZ, THEODORE F. "Democraticness, Autocraticness, and the Majority Point of View," *Psychological Bulletin,* XXXIX (Oct., 1942), 594.

LERNER, MAX. *It is Later Than You Think.* New York: The Viking Press, 1939.

———. "Revolution in Ideas," *Nation,* CXLIX (Oct. 21, 1939), 435–437.

LEWIN, KURT. "Experiments on Autocratic and Democratic Atmospheres," *Frontiers of Democracy,* IV (July, 1938), 316–319.

———, Ronald Lippitt, and Ralph K. White. "Patterns of Aggressive Behavior in Experimentally Created 'Social Climates,'" *Journal of Social Psychology,* X (May, 1939), 271–299.

LEWIS, CLARENCE IRVING. *An Analysis of Knowledge and Valuation.* La Salle, Ill.: The Open Court Publishing Company, 1946.

LEWIS, JOHN D. "Democratic Planning in Agriculture," *American Political Science Review,* XXXV (April—June, 1941), 232–249, 454–469.

LEWIS, WYNDHAM. *The Art of Being Ruled.* New York: Harper & Brothers, 1926.

LIAO, WEN KWEI. *The Individual and the Community.* London: Routledge and Kegan Paul, Ltd., 1933.

LIKERT, RENSIS. "Democracy in Agriculture—Why and How?" in U. S. Department of Agriculture, *Farmers in a Changing World.* "Yearbook of Agriculture," 1940. Washington, D. C.: Government Printing Office, 1940.

LILIENTHAL, DAVID E. *TVA—Democracy on the March.* New York: Harper & Brothers, 1944.

LINDEMAN, EDUARD C. "Trouble at the Grass Roots," *Survey Graphic,* XXXIII (June, 1944), 280–282.

LINDSAY, A. D. *The Essentials of Democracy.* Philadelphia: University of Pennsylvania Press, 1929.

———. *I Believe in Democracy.* London: Oxford University Press, 1940.

———. *The Modern Democratic State,* Vol. I. London: Oxford University Press, 1943.

LIPPMANN, WALTER. *An Inquiry into the Principles of the Good Society.* Boston: Little, Brown & Company, 1935, 1943.

LIPSON, LESLIE. *The Politics of Equality: New Zealand's Adventures in Democracy.* Chicago: The University of Chicago Press, 1948.

LLEWELLYN, K. N. "American Common Law Tradition and American Democracy," *Journal of Legal and Political Sociology,* I (Oct., 1942), 14–45.

LOCKE, JOHN. *Of Civil Government.* "Everyman's Library." New York: E. P. Dutton & Co., 1936.

LOVEJOY, ARTHUR O. "Reflections on the History of Ideas," *Journal of the History of Ideas,* I (Jan., 1940), 3–23.

LÖWE, ADOLF. *The Price of Liberty: A German on Contemporary Britain.* Trans. Mrs. Elsa Sinclair. "Day to Day Pamphlets," No. 36. London: Hogarth Press, 1937.

McDOUGALL, WILLIAM. *The Group Mind: A Sketch of the Principles of Collective Psychology with Some Attempt to Apply Them to the Interpretation of National Life and Character.* 2d ed. New York: G. P. Putnam's Sons, 1920.

MACIVER, ROBERT M. *Community.* London: Macmillan & Co., 1917.

———. *The Web of Government.* New York: The Macmillan Company, 1947.

MACMAHON, ARTHUR. "Congressional Oversight of Administration: The Power of the Purse," *Political Science Quarterly*, LVIII (June–Sept., 1943), 161–190, 380–414.

MAGUIRE, JOSEPH P. "Some Greek Views of Democracy and Totalitarianism," *Ethics*, LVI (Jan., 1946), 136–143.

MALINOWSKI, BRONISLAW. *The Foundations of Faith and Morals*. University of Durham, Riddell Memorial Lectures, Ser. 7, 1934–1935. London: Oxford University Press, 1936.

――――. *Freedom and Civilization*. New York: Roy Publishers, 1944.

MANDELBAUM, MAURICE. *The Problem of Historical Knowledge: An Answer to Relativism*. New York: Liveright Publishing Corp., 1938.

MANDER, LINDEN A. "Civil Liberty after the War," *American Political Science Review*, XL (Feb., 1946), 70–79.

MANNHEIM, KARL. *Diagnosis of Our Time*. New York: Oxford University Press, 1944.

――――. *Man and Society in an Age of Reconstruction*. New York: Harcourt, Brace and Company, 1940.

MARTIN, EVERETT DEAN. *The Behavior of Crowds*. New York: Harper & Brothers, 1920.

MAXEY, CHESTER C. *Urban Democracy*. Boston: D. C. Heath and Company, 1929.

MAYO, ELTON. *The Human Problems of an Industrial Civilization*. New York: The Macmillan Company, 1933; Boston: Division of Research, Harvard Business School, 1946.

――――. *The Social Problems of an Industrial Civilization*. Cambridge, Mass.: Harvard University Press, 1945.

MELLEN, SYDNEY L. W. "The German People and the Postwar World," *American Political Science Review*, XXXVII (Aug., 1943), 601–625.

MENCKEN, H. L. *Notes on Democracy*. New York: Alfred A. Knopf, Inc., 1926.

MERRIAM, CHARLES EDWARD. *The Making of Citizens*. Chicago: The University of Chicago Press, 1931.

――――. *Systematic Politics*. Chicago: The University of Chicago Press, 1945.

――――. H. E. Barnes, and Others. *A History of Political Theories—Recent Times*. New York: The Macmillan Company, 1924.

METCALF, HENRY C., and L. URWICK. *Dynamic Administration: The Collected Papers of Mary Parker Follett*. New York: Harper & Brothers, 1942.

MICHELS, ROBERT. *Political Parties.* Trans. Eden and Cedar Paul. New York: Hearst's International Library Co., 1915.

MILL, JAMES. "Essay on Government," in Philip Wheelwright (ed.), *Essays on Government, Jurisprudence, Liberty of the Press, and Law of Nations.* New York: Doubleday & Company, 1935.

MILL, JOHN STUART. "Dissertations and Discussions: Political, Philosophical and Historical," in *The Works of John Stuart Mill.* 5 vols. New York: E. P. Dutton & Co., 1905.

————. *On Social Freedom.* Introduction by Dorothy Fosdick. New York: Columbia University Press, 1941.

————. *Utilitarianism, Liberty and Representative Government.* New York: E. P. Dutton & Co., 1910.

MILLSPAUGH, ARTHUR C. *Toward Efficient Democracy—the Question of Governmental Organization.* Washington, D. C.: The Brookings Institution, 1949.

MIMS, EDWIN, JR. *The Majority of the People.* New York: Modern Age Books, 1941.

MISES, LUDWIG VON. *Bureaucracy.* New Haven: Yale University Press, 1944.

————. *Omnipotent Government: The Rise of the Total State and the Total War.* New Haven: Yale University Press, 1945.

MONTAGUE, WILLIAM PEPPERELL. "Democracy at the Cross-Roads," *Ethics,* XLV (Jan., 1935), 138–169.

MORGAN, GEORGE, JR. "Human Equality," *Ethics,* LIII (Jan., 1943), 115–120.

MORGENTHAU, HANS J. *Scientific Man vs. Power Politics.* Chicago: The University of Chicago Press, 1946.

MORRIS, CHARLES W. *Pragmatism and the Crisis of Democracy.* "Public Policy Pamphlets," No. 12. Chicago: The University of Chicago Press, 1934.

MORROW, GLENN R. "The Philosophical Presuppositions of Democracy," *Ethics,* LII (Apr., 1942), 297–308.

MOSCA, GAETANO. *The Ruling Class.* Trans. Hannah D. Kahn, ed. Arthur Livingston. New York: McGraw-Hill Book Company, 1939.

MOWRER, O. H. "Authoritarianism vs. 'Self-Government' in the Management of Children's Aggressive (Anti-Social) Reactions as a Preparation for Citizenship in a Democracy," *Journal of Social Psychology,* X (Feb., 1939), 121–126.

MUELLER-DEHAM, ALBERT. "Freedom and the Basic Social Relations," *Ethics,* LVI (July, 1946), 309–316.

MUIRHEAD, J. H. *The Service of the State: Four Lectures on the Political Teaching of T. H. Green.* London: John Murray, Ltd., 1908.

MUMFORD, LEWIS. *The Condition of Man.* New York: Harcourt, Brace and Company, 1944.

————. *The Culture of Cities.* New York: Harcourt, Brace and Company, 1938.

————. *Faith for Living.* New York: Harcourt, Brace and Company, 1940.

MURPHY, ARTHUR E. *The Uses of Reason.* New York: The Macmillan Company, 1943.

MURRY, JOHN MIDDLETON. *The Defence of Democracy.* London: Jonathan Cape, Ltd., 1939.

MUSSOLINI, BENITO. "The Political and Social Doctrine of Fascism," Trans. Jane Soanies, *Political Quarterly,* IV (July–Sept., 1933), 341–356.

MYRDAL, GUNNAR. *An American Dilemma: The Negro Problem and Modern Democracy.* 2 vols. New York: Harper & Brothers, 1944.

NATHAN, PETER. *The Psychology of Fascism.* London: Faber and Faber, Ltd., 1943.

NATIONAL MUNICIPAL LEAGUE. *Democracy Must Think.* New York: Columbia University Press, 1939.

NIEBUHR, REINHOLD. *The Children of Light and the Children of Darkness: A Vindication of Democracy and a Critique of Its Traditional Defence.* New York: Charles Scribner's Sons, 1944.

————. *The Nature and Destiny of Man.* 2 vols. New York: Charles Scribner's Sons, 1941.

————. "The Pathos of Liberalism." *Nation,* CXLI (Sept. 11, 1935), 303–304.

NIETZSCHE, FRIEDRICH. *Thus Spake Zarathustra.* Trans. Thomas Common. New York: Boni and Liveright, Inc., 1917.

————. "Twilight of the Idols," in *Works.* Trans. Thomas Common, ed. Alexander Tille. New York: The Macmillan Company, 1896.

NORTHRUP, HERBERT R. "Proving Ground for Fair Employment: Some Lessons from New York State's Experience," *Commentary,* IV (Dec., 1947), 552–556.

OGBURN, WILLIAM F., and ABE J. JAFFE. "Independent Voting in Presidential Elections," *American Journal of Sociology,* XLII (Sept., 1936), 186–201.

ORTEGA Y GASSET, JOSÉ. *The Modern Theme.* Trans. James Cleugh. London: The C. W. Daniel Company, 1931.

ORTON, WILLIAM AYLOTT. *The Liberal Tradition: A Study of the Social Conditions of Freedom.* New Haven: Yale University Press, 1945.

PAINE, TOM. *Rights of Man.* "Everyman's Library." Introduction by George J. Holyoake. New York: E. P. Dutton & Co., 1915.

PALMER, PAUL A. "Benthamism in England and America," *American Political Science Review,* XXXV (Oct., 1941), 855–871.

PAP, ARTHUR. "The Verifiability of Value Judgments," *Ethics,* LVI (Apr., 1946), 178–185.

PARETO, VILFREDO. *The Mind and Society.* Trans. Andrew Bongiorno and Arthur Livingston, ed. Arthur Livingston. 4 vols. New York: Harcourt, Brace and Company, 1935.

PARKER, DE WITT H. "Reflections on the Crisis in Theory of Value. I. Mostly Critical," *Ethics,* LVI (Apr., 1946), 193–207.

PARSONS, TALCOTT. *The Structure of Social Action.* New York: McGraw-Hill Book Company, 1937.

PENNOCK, J. ROLAND. *Administration and the Rule of Law.* New York: Rinehart & Company, 1941.

———. "Reason, Value Theory, and the Theory of Democracy," *American Political Science Review,* XXXVIII (Oct., 1944), 855–875.

PERRY, CHARNER MARQUIS. "The Forms and the Substance of Liberalism," *Ethics,* XLVI (Apr., 1936), 308–329.

PERRY, RALPH BARTON. *General Theory of Value.* New York: Longmans, Green and Co., 1936.

———. *The Moral Economy.* New York: Charles Scribner's Sons, 1909.

———. *The Present Conflict of Ideals.* New York: Longmans, Green and Co., 1922.

———. *Puritanism and Democracy.* New York: The Vanguard Press, 1944.

———. "The Question of Moral Obligation," *Ethics,* XXI (Oct., 1910), 282–298.

———. *Shall Not Perish from the Earth.* New York: The Vanguard Press, 1940.

———. "What Do We Mean by Democracy?" *Ethics,* XXVIII (July, 1918), 449–464.

PIGOU, A. C. *Socialism versus Capitalism.* London: Macmillan & Co., 1937.

PINK, M. ALDERTON. *The Challenge to Democracy.* London: Faber and Faber, Ltd., 1946.

———. *A Realist Looks at Democracy.* London: Ernest Benn, Ltd., 1930.

PLAMENATZ, J. P. *Consent, Freedom and Political Obligation.* London: Oxford University Press, 1938.

POUND, ROSCOE. *Contemporary Juristic Theory.* Claremont, Calif.: Claremont Colleges Press, 1940.

———. "The Future of Law," *Yale Law Journal,* XLVII (Nov., 1937), 1–13.

———. *The Spirit of the Common Law.* Boston: The Marshall Jones Co., 1921.

President's Research Committe on Social Trends. *Recent Social Trends in the United States.* 2 vols. New York: McGraw-Hill Book Company, 1933.

PRIBRAM, KARL. *Conflicting Patterns of Thought.* Washington, D. C.: Public Affairs Press, 1949.

PRITCHETT, C. HERMAN. *The Tennessee Valley Authority.* Chapel Hill: The University of North Carolina Press, 1943.

QUEEN, STUART ALFRED, and LEWIS FRANCIS THOMAS. *The City.* 1st ed. New York: McGraw-Hill Book Company, Inc., 1939.

RADER, MELVIN. *No Compromise: The Conflict between Two Worlds.* New York: The Macmillan Company, 1939.

RANDALL, JOHN HERMAN, JR. "Liberalism as Faith in Intelligence," *Journal of Philosophy,* XXXII (May, 1935), 253–264.

———. *The Making of the Modern Mind.* Rev. ed. Boston: Houghton Mifflin Company, 1940.

RAUSCHNING, HERMANN. *Time of Delirium.* Trans. Richard and Clara Winston. New York: Appleton-Century-Crofts, Inc., 1946.

READ, HERBERT. *The Politics of the Unpolitical.* London: Routledge and Kegan Paul, Ltd., 1943.

RIESMAN, DAVID. "Civil Liberties in a Period of Transition," in Carl J. Friedrich and Edward S. Mason (eds.), *Public Policy.* "A Yearbook of the Graduate School of Public Administration," Harvard University (1942), III, 33–96.

ROCHE, PATRICK J. *Democracy in the Light of Four Current Educational Philosophies.* Washington, D. C.: The Catholic University of America Press, 1942.

SABINE, GEORGE H. "Democracy and Preconceived Ideas," a lecture delivered at The Ohio State University, May 18, 1945 (The Walter J. Shepard Foundation, The Ohio State University, Columbus, Ohio).

————. "The Historical Position of Liberalism," *The American Scholar,* X (Winter, 1940–1941), 49–58.

SAIT, EDWARD M. *Democracy* (New York: Appleton-Century-Crofts, Inc., 1929.

SCHUMPETER, JOSEPH A. *Capitalism, Socialism and Democracy.* 2d ed. New York: Harper & Brothers, 1947.

SHERIF, MUZAFER. *The Psychology of Social Norms.* New York: Harper & Brothers, 1936.

SIMON, HUGO FERDINAND. *Revolution: Whither Bound?* New York: Rinehart & Company, 1935.

SKINNER, CLARENCE R. *Liberalism Faces the Future.* New York: The Macmillan Company, 1937.

SMITH, T. V. *The American Philosophy of Equality.* Chicago: The University of Chicago Press, 1927.

————. *Discipline for Democracy.* Chapel Hill: The University of North Carolina Press, 1942.

SOREL, GEORGES. *Reflections on Violence.* Trans. T. E. Hulme. 3d ed. New York: The Viking Press, 1912.

SOROKIN, PITIRIM A. *The Crisis of Our Age.* New York: E. P. Dutton & Co., 1941.

————. *Social and Cultural Dynamics.* 4 vols. New York: American Book Company, 1937–1941.

SOULE, GEORGE. *A Planned Society.* New York: The Macmillan Company, 1932.

SPEARMAN, DIANA. *Modern Dictatorship.* New York: Columbia University Press, 1939.

SPENGLER, OSWALD. *The Decline of the West.* New York: Alfred A. Knopf, Inc., 1939.

SPIEGELBERG, HERBERT. "A Defense of Human Equality," *Philosophical Review,* LII (Mar., 1944), 101–124.

SPIGELMAN, JOSEPH H. "The Protection of Society," *Harper's Magazine,* CXCIII (July, 1946), 1–9.

STACE, W. T. *The Concept of Morals.* New York: The Macmillan Company, 1937.

———. *The Destiny of Western Man.* New York: Harcourt, Brace and Company, 1942.

STEPHEN, LESLIE. *The English Utilitarians.* 3 vols. New York: G. P. Putnam's Sons, 1900.

STEVENSON, CHARLES LESLIE. "The Emotive Meaning of Ethical Terms," *Mind,* XLVI (Jan., 1937), 14–31.

———. *Ethics and Language.* New Haven: Yale University Press, 1944.

STOCKS, J. L. *The Limits of Purpose and Other Essays.* London: Ernest Benn, Ltd., 1932.

———. *Reason and Intuition, and Other Essays.* Ed. and with Introduction by Dorothy M. Emmet. New York: Oxford University Press, 1939.

STRONG, DONALD S. "The Rise of Negro Voting in Texas," *American Political Science Review,* XLII (June, 1948), 510–522.

SUTTIE, IAN D. *The Origins of Love and Hate.* London: Routledge and Kegan Paul, Ltd., 1935.

SWABEY, MARIE COLLINS. *Theory of the Democratic State.* Cambridge, Mass.: Harvard University Press, 1937.

TANNENBAUM, FRANK. "On Certain Characteristics of American Democracy," *Political Science Quarterly,* LX (Sept., 1945), 343–350.

TARDE, GABRIEL. *The Laws of Imitation.* Trans. 2d French ed. by Elsie Clews Parsons. New York: Henry Holt and Company, 1903.

TAWNEY, R. H. *Equality.* New York: Harcourt, Brace and Company, 1929.

TOCQUEVILLE, ALEXIS DE, *Democracy in America.* Trans. Henry Reeve, ed. Phillips Bradley. 2 vols. New York: Alfred A. Knopf, Inc., 1945.

TOPKIS, JAY H. "How Bad Is Congress?" *Political Science Quarterly,* LXII (Dec., 1947), 531–551.

TOBEY, BARBARA SCHINNERER. "An Essay on the Ethical Basis of Equalitarianism" (Swarthmore College, 1945, typed).

TUFTS, JAMES H. "Liberal Movements in the United States: Their Methods and Aims," *Ethics,* XLVI (Apr., 1936), 253–275.

UNITED STATES CONGRESS, Joint Committee on the Organization of

Congress. "Organization of Congress," Hearings pursuant to H. R. 18, 79th Cong., 1st Sess.

——. "Fascism in Action," *House Document* No. 401. Washington, D. C.: Government Printing Office, 1947.

——. Subcommittee of the Senate Committee on Labor and Public Welfare. "Antidiscrimination in Employment," Hearings pursuant to S. 984, 80th Cong., 1st Sess.

VIERECK, PETER. *Metapolitics: From the Romantics to Hitler.* New York: Alfred A. Knopf, Inc., 1941.

VIVAS, ELISEO. "Animadversions on Naturalistic Ethics," *Ethics,* LVI (Apr., 1946), 157–177.

WALLAS, GRAHAM. *Human Nature in Politics.* 3d ed. New York: Alfred A. Knopf, Inc., 1921.

WEEKS, O. DOUGLAS. "The White Primary: 1944–1948," *American Political Science Review,* XLII (June, 1948), 500–510.

WEISS, PAUL. "Democracy and the Rights of Man," in the Conference on Science, Philosophy, and Religion in Their Relation to the Democratic Way of Life, *Science, Philosophy and Religion: Second Symposium.* New York: The Conference, 1942.

——. "The Universal Ethical Standard," *Ethics,* LVI (Oct., 1945), 39–48.

WELDON, T. D. *States and Morals.* London: John Murray, Ltd., 1946.

WEST, RANYARD. *Conscience and Society: A Study of the Psychological Prerequisites of Law and Order.* New York: Emerson Books, Inc., 1945.

WESTERMARCK, EDWARD. *Ethical Relativity.* New York: Harcourt, Brace and Company, 1932.

——. *The Origin and Development of the Moral Ideas.* 2 vols. New York: The Macmillan Company, 1906, 1908.

WHITEHEAD, ALFRED NORTH. *Adventures of Ideas.* New York: The Macmillan Company, 1933.

——. *Science and the Modern World.* New York: The Macmilan Company, 1925.

WILSON, FRANCIS G. "The Structure of Modern Ideology," *Review of Politics,* I (Oct., 1939), 382–399.

WILSON, M. L. *Democracy Has Roots.* New York: Carrick & Evans, Inc., 1939.

WOOLF, LEONARD. *After the Deluge.* 2 vols. New York: Harcourt, Brace and Company, 1931, 1939.

WOOTTON, BARBARA. *Freedom under Planning.* Chapel Hill: The University of North Carolina Press, 1945.

WRIGHT, BENJAMIN F. *American Interpretations of Natural Law: A Study in the History of Political Thought.* Cambridge, Mass.: Harvard University Press, 1931.

WRIGHT, DAVID McCORD. *Democracy and Progress.* New York: The Macmillan Company, 1948.

WRIGHT, H. W. "Intellect versus Emotion in Political Co-operation," *Ethics,* LVI (Oct., 1945), 19–29.

WRISTON, HENRY M. *Challenge to Freedom.* New York: Harper & Brothers, 1943.

INDEX

INDEX

Date Due